The Audience Effect

The Audience Effect
On the Collective Cinema Experience

Julian Hanich

EDINBURGH
University Press

Edinburgh University Press is one of the leading university presses in
the UK. We publish academic books and journals in our selected subject
areas across the humanities and social sciences, combining cutting-edge
scholarship with high editorial and production values to produce academic
works of lasting importance. For more information visit our website:
edinburghuniversitypress.com

© Julian Hanich, 2018

Edinburgh University Press Ltd
The Tun – Holyrood Road
12 (2f) Jackson's Entry
Edinburgh EH8 8PJ

Typeset in 11/13 Monotype Ehrhardt by
Servis Filmsetting Ltd, Stockport, Cheshire,

A CIP record for this book is available from the British Library

ISBN 978 1 4744 1495 1 (hardback)
ISBN 978 1 4744 1496 8 (webready PDF)
ISBN 978 1 4744 1497 5 (epub)

The right of Julian Hanich to be identified as author of this work has been
asserted in accordance with the Copyright, Designs and Patents Act 1988
and the Copyright and Related Rights Regulations 2003 (SI No. 2498).

Contents

List of Figures — vii
Acknowledgments — viii

Part I Establishing Shot: Definition and History

1 Introduction: What Is the Audience Effect? — 3
2 Excavating the Audience Effect: Precursors in the History of Film Theory — 34

Part II Long Shot: Types of Collective Viewing

Introductory Notes — 65
3 Quiet-attentive Viewing: Toward a Typology of Collective Spectatorship, Part I — 73
4 Expressive-diverted Viewing: Toward a Typology of Collective Spectatorship, Part II — 111

Part III Medium Shot: On the Cinema's Affective Audience Effects

5 I, You, and We: Investigating the Cinema's Affective Audience Interrelations — 143
6 Feeling Close: Conceptualizing the Cinema's Affective We-experiences — 168

Part IV Close-up: Case Studies of Affective Audience Effects

7 Chuckle, Chortle, Cackle: A Phenomenology of Cinematic Laughter — 189

8 When Viewers Silently Weep: A Phenomenology of Cinematic
   Tears   217
9 Trouble Every Day: A Phenomenology of Cinematic Anger   248

Part V Fade-out: Conclusion

10 The Audience Effect in the Cinema and Beyond   275

Glossary   284
Bibliography   293
Index of Names   313
Index of Subjects   320

Figures

2.1	Collective laughter about Chaplin in Louis Malle's *Au revoir les enfants*	52
4.1	Attention/Inattention in the cinema: Ferdinand Griffon in Jean-Luc Godard's *Pierrot le fou*	115
4.2	A dressed-up and play-acting cinema audience in Wes Craven's *Scream 2*	118
4.3	Individualizing himself within the audience: the aggressively laughing Max Cady in Martin Scorsese's *Cape Fear*	129
5.1	United in fear: Lolita, Humbert Humbert, and Lolita's mother Charlotte watching a monster movie in Stanley Kubrick's *Lolita*	147
5.2	A snobbish viewer on the balcony spitting down on the lower-class spectators in Giuseppe Tornatore's *Cinema Paradiso*	163
7.1	Laughing spectators in King Vidor's silent film classic *The Crowd*	209
8.1	Juliette Binoche as an individualized, silently weeping viewer in Abbas Kiarostami's *Shirin*	223
8.2	The two sisters Maisie and Eileen weep together in Terence Davies's *Distant Voices, Still Lives*	241
9.1	A French film critic annoys director Lars von Trier in his short film *Occupations*	249
10.1	Image of a virtual-reality cinema	278

Acknowledgments

It's never a good idea to start a book with a cliché. But what else can I do than to admit that this book would have been a very different and much worse one without the comments, suggestions and criticisms of colleagues, peers and friends? They have helped me from A to Z: Lisa Akervall, Marco Caracciolo, Francesco Casetti, Elizabeth Cowie, Philip Dreher, Jens Eder, Christian Ferencz-Flatz, Josef Früchtl, Philipp Hübl, Guido Kirsten, Miklós Kiss, Liesbeth Korthals Altes, Gertrud Koch, Kristina Köhler, Annette Kuhn, Leah LoSchiavo, Hans Maes, Winfried Menninghaus, Volker Pantenburg, Winfried Pauleit, Carl Plantinga, Ari Purnama, Martin Rossouw, Martin Seel, Murray Smith, Vivian Sobchack, Valentin Wagner, Eugen Wassiliwizky, and Rüdiger Zill.

I also want to thank my colleagues at the Arts, Culture and Media department of the University of Groningen, who have left enough space between teaching and administrative duties to work on this project. Further thanks go to Jelga van der Zee and Greet Bulthuis-Beens from the University of Groningen Library, who have ordered countless books and journals for me during the last years, not all of which have found entry into my bibliography. I am very much indebted to Gillian Leslie, the commissioning editor of Edinburgh University Press, who was so keenly interested in my material when we first met on a cold March day in Montréal. Kudos also to Richard Strachan and Rebecca Mackenzie at EUP for their help with the preparation of the manuscript. Moreover, I am deeply grateful to Emanuela and Giorgio Munari, who have hosted me in an extremely generous fashion in their home near the Lago di Garda: When I stayed there in summer 2015 and 2016 for writing retreats, not only my book grew thicker and thicker! Not least I wish to thank my parents Henriette and Hans-Peter, as well as my siblings Isabella, Philipp, and Theresa, for invaluable support over many years.

This book was a long time in the making. Some parts of it have been tried and tested as articles or chapters elsewhere, but these have now been thoroughly revised or are published here for the first time in English. In Chapter 2, the section on Bazin has appeared in an extended German version as "Kino, Theater, Fernsehen: André Bazins Publikumstheorie" (in Thomas Weber and Florian Mundhenke (eds), *Kinoerfahrungen. Theorien, Geschichte, Perspektiven*, Berlin: Avinus, 2017), and the section on Benjamin was part of the essay "Laughter and Public Awareness. The Cinema Auditorium as Public Space" (in *NECSUS – European Journal of Media Studies*, Vol. 6, Autumn 2014). My article "Watching a Film with Others. Toward a Theory of Collective Spectatorship" (in *Screen*, Vol. 55, No. 3, Autumn 2014) has become the foundation for Chapter 3. Some parts of Chapter 5 were published as "Collective Viewing. The Cinema and Affective Audience Interrelations" (in *Passions in Context. The Journal for the History and Theory of Emotions*, Vol. 1, No. 1, February 2010). Parts of Chapter 7 have appeared in German in an essay entitled "Laugh Is in the Air. Eine Typologie des Lachens im Kino" (in *Nach dem Film*, No. 12, October 2010). Very early ideas on the topic of Chapter 8 were articulated in "A Weep in the Dark. Tears and the Cinematic Experience" (in Ilka Saal and Ralph Poole (eds), *Passionate Politics. The Cultural Work of American Melodrama*, Newcastle: Cambridge Scholars Publishing, 2008). Finally, an earlier version of Chapter 9 was published – again in German – as "Wut im Kino. Anmerkungen zu einem vernachlässigten Alltagsphänomen" (in *Augenblick. Konstanzer Hefte zur Medienwissenschaft*, No. 56/57, Marburg: Schüren, 2013).

To
Maddalena

"Yet 'audience' is merely a word
which in no way denotes a uniform and constant entity."
Friedrich Nietzsche

"It is very curious to stand, for once, with one's back to the cinema screen
and to behold the auditorium."
Rudolf Arnheim

PART I

Establishing Shot: Definition and History

CHAPTER I

Introduction: What Is the Audience Effect?

Each individual audience member [. . .] is alone, by himself, looking at the world presented to him. Yet this isolation does not separate the individual from the group. He does not communicate with his fellows, but he sees and feels *with* them, if not like them. A kind of underlying connection is established between audience members shut up within their own contemplation. [. . .] Communication exists at the level of feelings and fascination.

Jean Mitry[1]

I. INTRODUCING THE AUDIENCE EFFECT

This is a book about the *collective cinema experience*. Unless we take the extremely rare case of an empty movie-theater, we never sit alone in the dark. In the cinema we usually watch a film with 2, 20, 200, or 2,000 others. But once we watch a movie with others, we become part of a collective constellation that has some kind of effect on our film experience, be it positive or negative. Or so goes the thesis of this book.

When we go to the cinema we always arrive with a bag filled with expectations. Not only do we expect to follow an uninterrupted projection of a film in a dark space; we also expect to cross a threshold into a public auditorium separated from the outside world, a space with specific behavioral rules in which we encounter other people.[2] A completely empty cinema is a weird and lonely place, precisely because its architecture presupposes a minimally social atmosphere.[3] When watching a film we, the cinemagoers, individually *and* collectively constitute and create an experience that does not precede us – it comes alive through us and continuously changes with us.[4] The collective cinema experience is thus not at all a static affair, but a constantly transforming outcome of our attention, intentions, actions, and emotions. Since the collective cinema experience is something else than the sum of the individual viewer experiences, watching a film with others is crucially different from watching a film alone.[5] In the jargon of social psychologists, various *facilitation* and *inhibition* effects play a role when watching a film. And this is all the more obvious once strong emotions and affective expressions come into play: fear, sadness, shame, guilt, laughter, screaming, tears …

The following chapters do not deal with criticizing, evaluating, analyzing, or interpreting *films*, then. Instead, they aim to enrich the existing descriptions of the cinema experience by giving more weight to the complexity and concreteness of what we feel *with* or *against* our co-viewers. My investigations therefore presuppose an audience that is *physically* co-present: The spectators share a place and a focus of attention – the film. But while the theatrical experience – the "projector-film-theater complex," in Francesco Casetti's words – will be paradigmatic, my discussions hopefully have value for non-theatrical collective film experiences as well.[6] In other words, even though the physically co-present audience of the cinema will serve as my prime example, studies of all kinds of screenings with others, be they public or private, may also profit from what this book tries to uncover.[7]

Note, however, that utopian visions of the cinema's collectivity and overt value judgments about the superiority of the movie-theater experience are not my goal – what's at stake is the mere charting of a phenomenon. That's why both positive *and* negative audience effects will figure prominently throughout this study. What I propose is no more and no less than a theory and phenomenology of the influence other spectators have on our film experience and the influence we have on theirs.

I call this *the audience effect*. This term has a long history in social psychology, where it refers to the positive or negative impact observers can have on one's performance and behavior.[8] I borrow the term and narrow it down to the more literal meaning of the effect an actual cinema audience can have on one's film experience.

To make this account tangible from the beginning, let me project three examples on the reader's mental screen. The first is based on a personal experience, a second one comes from an anthology of movie memories, and the third derives from a thought experiment.

In February 2013 I attended a screening of Claude Lanzmann's *Sobibor* (2001). The screening was part of an homage to the Jewish-French director at the Berlin Film Festival. As I was sitting in the packed auditorium with an international festival audience, something remarkable occurred. During this bleak documentary about a successful uprising in the eponymous concentration camp, parts of the audience broke out in laughter – not once, but twice. The first laughter occurred when Yehuda Lerner, the former camp inmate interviewed for the film and partially responsible for the success of the revolt, simply mentioned the *punctuality* of the German wards and soldiers. The second round of laughter rippled through the hall when Lerner explained what had enabled the inmates to carry out their plan according to a strict timetable and kill the German soldiers and wards – well, it was exactly the same German accuracy and punctuality.

But who laughed – and why? Since Yehuda Lerner talks about German punctuality and thus evokes an often-heard stereotype about Germans, it seems unlikely that Germans laughed themselves – less because Germans are incapable of laughing about themselves, but because Lanzmann's documentary is not a comedy, the pleasure of which can sometimes consist of expressing self-irony through laughter.[9] To me at least, it seemed a matter of decorum *not* to laugh about this film *as a German*, even if self-ironical laughter had been a possibility. Instead, it seems more plausible that the *non*-Germans in the audience used the occasion to express relief laughter during an otherwise harrowing film. But even relief laughter needs some cause that instigates it. Which one was it? Could the laughter have been sparked by the ingenuity of the Jewish victims who struck back at the perpetrators by taking advantage of German punctuality, and thus a characteristic that contributed to the obscene efficiency with which the Germans carried out the Holocaust? For the non-German viewers, it was 'allowed' to laugh about something the Germans in the audience felt better to remain politely quiet about.

Naturally these claims have to remain speculative. Let me therefore turn to how I recollect my own experience. Because I attributed this laughter to the non-Germans in the audience, I became *consciously* aware of a fact that I had implicitly expected all along: that there were a substantial number of non-German viewers in the audience. This fact had a strong influence on my emotional response: Had I been part of an audience consisting exclusively of Germans, I would have been able to remain in my position of *distance* from the Nazis, the heinous perpetrators wholly alien to my self-understanding. However, in the face of the non-German viewers, some of them quite likely Jewish, the situation changed drastically: Even though I abhorred the Germans that Lerner talked about and hence felt extremely distant from them, there was no denying the fact that the laughter about 'the' Germans and their characteristic punctuality somehow implicated me *as a German*. The public laughter thus reminded me of the historical weight of belonging to the nation responsible for the Holocaust. I experienced an upheaval of collective guilt.

But apart from collective guilt and a feeling of moral disgust toward the German Nazis, there was also a certain amount of surprise and relief. Even if I did not dare to laugh myself, I was surprised about and appreciated the laughter. It was astonishing and relieving to hear this reaction of what I took to be non-Germans, because it indicated that, for them, there seemed to be enough historical distance between 1943 and 2013 to laugh about the Nazis. Even more surprising and relieving was the possibility that these two scenes may have allowed some Jewish viewers in the audience to laugh *triumphantly* about the German perpetrators. Needless to say, had I watched the film alone these thoughts and emotions would have been highly attenuated, even inexistent. It was the collective constellation of the movie-theater that conjured up this complex mixture of cognitions and emotions.

My second and rather different example derives from a movie memory of lighting cameraman John Christie who was nine years old when his parents took him to the Fernandel movie *The Sheep Has Five Legs / Le Mouton à cinq pattes* (1954). This film contains a long scene with a beautiful Tahitian girl wearing a flower wreath barely covering her naked breasts. Here is how Christie remembers the event: "[The film was] giving the audience, every now and again, a fleeting glimpse of the girl. I was already sliding down in my seat trying to indicate to my parents without actually looking away from the screen that I wasn't at all interested, when suddenly there was a close shot [of her breast including her nipple]. What a sight! I sank down further until I could just see over the seat in front."[10] This is a strong audience effect: All of a sudden the boy seems to watch himself from the standpoint of his parents. He thinks that his mother and father follow his reaction reproachfully. Their look seems to burn on his shoulders, changing his attitude toward them. Before, the three of them were probably wrapped in a blanket of communality due to their deeply involved joint activity of movie-watching. The erotic scene tears this cloth apart and makes the boy feel singled out and opposed to his parents. Deeply ashamed, he actively wishes to vanish and to disappear from this situation of exposure, as his movement down the seat indicates. The boy's bodily comportment is supposed to communicate disinterest to his parents, even while he is so interested that he cannot avert his eyes. What is in fact only a short scene, presumably felt as if it went on forever, painfully stretching the boy's temporal experience. With a tongue-in-cheek nod to Sigmund Freud, I call cases like this the *primal scene of collective viewing*.

This type of primal scene is so widespread that we find evidence both in popular culture (the comedian John Oliver made fun of it in his *Last Week Tonight* show) and in empirical studies.[11] Psychologists Richard Jackson Harris and Lindsay Cook, for instance, looked at what can turn moviegoing into an emotionally uncomfortable experience.[12] Their results reveal that apart from the *content* of the film (especially explicit sex and violence), it is the *co-audience* that may become an important source of discomfort. Viewers can experience the co-presence of parents, spouses, first dates, but also lesser-known persons as unpleasant, particularly if it interacts with problematic content. As if the authors wanted to confirm John Christie's experience, it turned out that by far the most uncomfortable combination is watching a sexual movie with one's parents.¹³ As in my first example, we can assume that deeply embarrassed John Christie would have gone through a very different experience had he watched the film in solitude.

Finally, we can gauge the audience effect from a small thought experiment: What would happen to our collective experience in the cinema if all of us wore headphones? It is not hard to imagine that this would spark an entirely different experience, because we would be aurally encapsulated in our own 'sound bubble' and thus be acoustically isolated from each other, comparable to watching a film on a plane. We would not be able to hear the welcome responses of the other viewers, like laughter; and we would be protected from their unwelcome noises, like talking or popcorn-crunching. What is so interesting about this thought experiment is that it is not a thought experiment at all. Following the example of the silent disco phenomenon, where club-goers dance to music they only hear on their headphones, cultural entrepreneurs have been quick to establish silent theater, opera, and cinema events. The latter may have practical reasons. For one, they allow private rooftop screenings without bothering the neighbors. But watching a film with headphones also has an effect on the collective experience. As the website of a British Silent Cinema exhibitor describes it: "Silent Cinema is the perfect *private-public* cinema experience – immerse yourself in the soundtrack through individual digital wireless headsets. It's like enjoying a movie at home only you're in a big group. You can laugh, crunch and scream as loud as you like – in Silent Cinema no one can hear you!"¹⁴ Here, too, we can sense how the audience has an effect on experience, even though the co-present viewers experience themselves differently than in a regular movie-theater.

II. A BLIND SPOT: SCHOLARSHIP ON THE COLLECTIVE CINEMA EXPERIENCE

But if my claims about the importance of the audience effect ring true, shouldn't we find a long-standing debate in the history of film studies? Astonishingly, this is hardly the case. The fact that co-viewers influence our cinematic experience just as we can influence theirs has rarely figured in the equation, at least not in a systematically theorized way. When film scholars discuss the experience of the movies, they predominantly concentrate on the relationship between viewer and *film*.¹⁵ The subjective relationships between viewer and *viewer* in the dark space rarely come into view. But presupposing a *dyadic* relation between individual viewer and film is an artificial reduction – the collective constellation is always a *triadic* one between viewer, film, and the rest of the audience. The dyadic perspective loses from sight the fact that the shared space of the physically close audience in the movie-theater is unlike the unshared space of the solitary and dispersed audience in front of the TV or computer screen at home.

When film theorists in the past reflected on the relations between viewers, most of them assumed that the spectator, although part of an audience, is effectively unaware of other viewers. André Bazin, for one, claims in his two-part essay on "Theater and Cinema": "the audience in a movie house is made up of *solitary individuals*."[16] And a little later he continues: "*Alone*, hidden in a dark room, we watch through half-open blinds a spectacle that is unaware of our existence . . ."[17] Similarly, Christian Metz, in his famous essay "Story/Discourse (A Note on Two Kinds of Voyeurism)," maintains that the cinema "was born much later than the theater, in a period when social life was deeply marked by the notion of the individual [. . .]. The cinema is made for the *private individual* [. . .]."[18] Even more outspoken was Russian formalist Boris Eikhenbaum, who once maintained that "we do not, in essence, feel ourselves to be members of a mass at all, or participants in a mass spectacle, when we are sitting in a cinema; on the contrary – conditions at a film-show induce the spectator to feel as if he were in total isolation, and this feeling is one of the particular psychological delights of watching films." Eikhenbaum even goes so far as to claim that the spectator does not want any social experience at all: "his ideal is not to sense the presence of the other spectators, but to be alone with the film . . ."[19]

Not even at the height of the discussion about the cinematic dispositive did the collective experience become an important topic. Take Jean-Louis Baudry's seminal articles on the cinematic apparatus and dispositive.[20] For Baudry the cinematic dispositive consists of the darkness in the movie-theater, the relative passivity of the situation, its forced immobility, and the projection of moving images – but there is not a single word on the other anonymous viewers in the theater.[21] Even though Plato's allegory of the cave is a crucial reference point for him – an allegory that recurrently talks about the cave dwellers in the plural – Baudry relates every argument to the single viewing subject, as if the viewer sat in the cinema in utter solitude.[22] This fact alone should give us pause when it comes to the validity of Baudry's claims about the "anthropomorphic individualism" promoted by the cinematic dispositive.[23]

Or consider philosopher Stanley Cavell, who maintains, in a crucial passage of his reflections on film as a succession of automatic world projections, that when film reproduces the world magically, it allows us "to view it unseen." As such, cinema fulfills an age-old "wish for invisibility."[24] Sounding quite similar, Linda Williams claims that cinematic representation grants its viewers a "seemingly perfected form of invisibility" and allows them "to see and hear everything without being seen or heard themselves."[25] Cavell and Williams' observations strike me as both right and wrong. They are correct when we consider the *film* experience in splendid isolation. Sure, the characters beyond the boundary separating real world and filmic world can never reach out to us: Even when they look straight into the camera, they won't see the audience – the viewers always remain invisible. However, what might be correct from a film ontological perspective becomes questionable when we consider the actual phenomenological experience in a movie-theater. Only if we artificially separate *film* from *theatrical* experience can we overlook the fact that the viewer in the auditorium never feels completely unnoticed. While invisible for the characters, viewers sit within the immediate perceptual range of other spectators.[26]

The theatrical reception of films does not take place in some strange vacuum. In the cinema we are always part of a social situation in which the physical co-presence of other viewers is, at the very least, part of our background awareness. And sometimes it also becomes fully focused on. To be sure, the darkness of the auditorium, the unidirectional seating position, and the focus of attention aimed at the film allow viewers to partially hide from the presence of others (elsewhere I have called this the cinema's *hiding effect*).[27] But don't the countless dating couples in the history of cinema who took a seat in the very last row nicely and unwittingly illustrate that one can never feel completely unnoticed? Why would these couples head straight for the back row if not to avoid the looks of others? In a chapter of her ethno-historical study on 1930s cinema culture in Britain – tellingly entitled "This Loving Darkness" – Annette Kuhn has gathered a number of statements from filmgoers testifying to the titillating attraction of the back row.[28] The back row is not only the darkest place of the auditorium; with no one sitting behind you it is also the one least exposed. But even here, a complete escape from other viewers is impossible. Some informants even remember the back row itself as "the object of intense voyeuristic fascination," as Kuhn puts it.[29]

And while the cinema is a place that tends to hide us visually from others (in the modern multi- and megaplexes it also drowns our noises), the fact that we are not alone can be vividly *sensed* otherwise – for instance, through a positively attracting, negatively repelling, or simply neutral smell of others. We don't have to subscribe to an elaborate theory of olfactory transmission of affect, as Teresa Brennan did, to admit the importance of scenting in the cinema.[30]

Finally, an equally important indication for our awareness of the co-presence of others in the cinema comes from the tacit way we exert control over our bodies, even during strongly immersive scenes. In his wonderfully illuminating study *Behavior in Public Places*, Erving Goffman reminds us that being immersed in a social situation means that "an insufficient harnessing of the self" must not occur: "Half-aware that a certain aspect of his activity is available for all present to perceive, the individual tends to modify this activity, employing it with its public character in mind."[31] Imagine the unlikely case you end up in a cinema completely on your own: Should you 'unharness' your bodily controls during the film (no details necessary) and then suddenly realize that a latecomer must have sneaked in, and is now groaning disgustedly, you may well feel extremely embarrassed. This embarrassment is a vital and painful reminder of how you would have behaved had you known that this other viewer *was* present.

The lack of studies on the audience effect has not gone unnoticed, though. Writing in 1990, Ian Breakwell and Paul Hammond lamented in the introduction to their highly valuable but unsystematic collection of memories of cinemagoing: "We looked almost in vain at one hundred years of literature on cinema for evidence on how going to the pictures is experienced by audiences as a collective rite rich in surreal experience." Existing studies of cinema audiences, according to Breakwell and Hammond, have employed the methods of mass sociology and market research, but these "cannot fully capture the individual, subjective experience of filmgoing [. . .]."[32] Similarly, and more recently, Gabriele Pedullà has reproached film scholars for turning their heads away from the audience, noticing anything else but the collective experience: "Instead of watching the audience during the decisive moment – while watching the film – for the most part [in film scholars' accounts] we see it daydreaming just *before* the projection begins, or remembering the movie when the show is all *over* [. . .]."[33]

Obviously, it would be a wild overstatement to claim that there are no references at all to the audience effect in the vast literature on the film experience. In fact, I will draw on a variety of sources to support my theory and lend weight to my phenomenological descriptions: film criticism; movie memories; questionnaire-based interview studies; ethnographical fieldwork; films that thematize the audience effect; psychological studies; my own field notes, personal observations, and experiences . . . In Chapter 2, moreover, I will discuss at some length five precursors from the canon of film theory who made bigger or smaller steps toward theorizing the audience effect: Walter Benjamin, André Bazin, Edgar Morin, Roland Barthes, and Roger Odin. As valuable as they are, however, their remarks are too short, too unsystematic, too vague to account for the rich variety of the audience effect.

My study was furthermore informed by accounts of film as a collectively consumed form of art or a type of entertainment with a strong social dimension, among them theories of the cinematic public sphere, historical reception studies, interview-based empirical reception studies, and studies with a focus on the social dimension of moviegoing by proponents of New Cinema History.[34] More particular studies interested in the comedy, the cult film, the early cinema experience, or audiences in India also provided helpful insights.[35]

Finally, there are psychological studies that have, in their own way, shed light on the audience effect. Above, I have mentioned the article by Richard Jackson Harris and Lindsay Cook. Two other studies should also be mentioned here, if only to show that insights from psychology are a largely untapped resource when it comes to the social experience of the cinema. In 1986, Dolf Zillmann and his colleagues demonstrated that the *gender* of one's co-viewers and their *behavior* during a film can influence the experience of a horror movie.[36] The male participants of their study most enjoyed a scene from *Friday the 13th, Part III* (1982) when their female co-viewers displayed signs of distress and did not show any mastery over the scary content. The female participants, in turn, reported higher levels of enjoyment when their male co-viewers showed *no* signs of being scared. In fact, male participants with low *physical* appeal gained in *sexual* appeal and positive character traits when they appeared fearless.

In 2001, Esther Jakobs and her colleagues published a similarly notable study, for which their participants had to watch sad film scenes in five different viewing conditions: alone; with a stranger physically co-present; with a stranger watching the same scenes in another room; with a friend sitting next to them; and with a friend watching the same clips in another room.[37] The study yielded at least three noteworthy results. First, facial expressions of sadness were stronger when participants watched the scenes *alone*; second, the participants experienced *lower* levels of pleasantness when they watched the films with either friends or strangers in the room; third, the participants were more aware of their co-viewers and had a stronger motivation to communicate with them when these co-viewers were *friends* rather than strangers.

All of these contributions – whether from film studies or psychology – can be highly instructional in their own right. The study of movie audiences currently knows a plurality of methods: questionnaire studies, interviews, focus groups, ethnographic memory studies, talk out loud protocols, eye-tracking, fMRI studies, historical reception studies, and so on.[38] However, these various methods tend to deal with the viewer from a third-person perspective and thus do not provide what I aim at: to theorize and systematically describe the viewer relations of the cinema as a *subjectively lived experience* from a social *I–You* or *we* perspective. This is where phenomenology, as a method, has special merits.[39]

III. PHENOMENOLOGY: METHODOLOGICAL ADVANTAGES, MISCONCEPTIONS, AND LIMITATIONS

Phenomenology is a method that examines *structures of experience*, thus supplanting merely impressionistic, overly subjectivist accounts.[40] In his helpful introductory volume *Phenomenology of Practice*, Max van Manen notes that the difference between phenomenology and most other forms of research is that phenomenology studies the world as we ordinarily *experience* it – before we abstract or theorize it.[41] But if phenomenology is merely interested in giving voice to concrete experiences, one may ask why we need phenomenologists to describe them for us in the first place. Don't we all have these experiences ourselves?

1. Why phenomenological descriptions?

For phenomenologists the need for description has at least three reasons. First, most of the time we simply *live through* our experiences, but do not *reflect on* them. This seems to be particularly true when it comes to intensive experiences: When we are strongly affected by a film, whether positively or negatively, we usually do not assume a self-reflective stance.[42] Breaking out in passionate laughter about a funny movie, we usually don't think: 'Wow, it's astonishing how much I laugh at this moment.' Nor do we tend to reflect on what it is generally like to laugh in the cinema, and hence what the features of cinematic laughter are. Of course, this does not mean we are not conscious of our laughing experience: Consciousness always comes with some degree of self-awareness, but this self-awareness is *pre*-reflective and thus precisely not *self*-reflective.[43]

Second, we would not even be able to live in a constant state of self-reflection: A certain degree of *habituation* and *automatization* of our everyday activities is helpful, sometimes even necessary, because it allows us to devote consciousness to other things. If I were constantly reflecting on my laughter while laughing, I would neither enjoy it, nor would I be able to keep on following the film at the same time. Yet it is one thing to maintain that efficiently fulfilling a goal often depends on automatization and habituation, and quite another never to engage in reflecting on one's habituated experiences. Phenomenology is convinced that paying attention to experience can be a value in itself. Herein also lies one of its pleasures: to defamiliarize the overly familiar. "What makes phenomenology so fascinating is that any ordinary experience tends to become quite extraordinary when we lift it up from our daily existence and hold it with our phenomenological gaze," van Manen writes.[44]

Apart from the fact that we often live through our experiences and lead our lives with a necessary tendency toward automatization and habituation, some scholars add a third reason why it is important to give special attention to lived experience. They sense a problematic privilege of theory and criticism, analysis and meaning-making in academia and intellectual life, to the detriment of descriptions of experience, whether these experiences are aesthetic or otherwise. Using strong metaphors, phenomenologist Bernhard Waldenfels points out that an overly strong focus on criticism can forestall an exploratory openness: "The modern way to knowledge leads through the acid bath of criticism. As indispensable as criticism may be, one may ask whether a dominance of criticism does not cauterize a considerable amount of inquisitive and enlivening sensuousness."[45] Vivian Sobchack, preoccupied with the fleshless practices of today's humanities, goes in a similar direction. She worries about her graduate students' eagerness to professionalize and acquire a one-sided sophistication. This is why one of her pedagogical goals is to preclude a premature rush into formal analysis and interpretive readings.[46] Instead, she tries to help them to lose their suspicion of the subjective experience when watching a film: "They ignore, mistrust, and devalue it as trivial, mistaken, or irrelevantly singular – this last, a false, indeed arrogant, humility that unwittingly rejects intersubjectivity, sociality, and culture."[47] It is not surprising that Sobchack prescribes phenomenology as an antidote.

But the goal of film phenomenology is obviously not an encyclopedic enumeration of every kind of experience viewers have ever made in the cinema. Phenomenology does not remain satisfied with individual experiences of random viewers; it tries to shed the contingencies and idiosyncrasies of the *specific case* in order to arrive at a description of *common types* of experience. The goal of phenomenology – via the phenomenological reduction and description – is to move away from *subjective singulars* to arrive at *intersubjective invariants*.[48] Thus, in Chapter 9, the specific case of viewer A's anger about viewer B when watching film C in cinema D will only interest me as an illustrative anecdote from which some aspects can be generalized and which has something to say about *what it is like to be* going through an anger episode. Moreover, in Chapter 8, I will have very little to say on *why* viewer X has to weep about a scene in film Y, but rather *how* we subjectively experience it when we are in fact moved to tears by a film and in what relation this puts us to our co-viewers. The description focuses only on those aspects that cannot be seriously denied when we deal with a certain type of experience. To give a simple example, getting angry about a co-viewer *always*, if to varying degrees, implies an antagonistic I–you relation; one cannot seriously claim that anger implies a warm welcoming of the deeply annoying person.

Arriving at intersubjective invariants is not that simple, of course, otherwise there would be no need for a special methodology. For one, to describe an activity as habituated as moviegoing in a *phenomenological* way requires an effort to look at it as if for the first time, to assume a novice attitude, to treat the cinema with "the original amazement of a naïve observer" (Gaston Bachelard).[49] Doing film phenomenology – and being interested in it as a reader – presupposes openness to, curiosity in, even wonder about this most wonderful and wonder-full of objects we call the cinema – a "willingness to meet what is utterly strange in what is most familiar," in van Manen's words.[50]

Not least, there is a special linguistic burden on the phenomenologist: Since the descriptive power of language has such a special weight, words need to be chosen accurately and the text needs to be crafted with special care. "[P]henomenology, not unlike poetry, is a vocative project; it tries an incantative, evocative speaking," van Manen writes.[51] This invariably puts non-native speakers in a precarious position. Translating my own German texts into English always makes me painfully aware of my limited expressive horizon. Obviously, I am not pleading for extenuating circumstances – I simply don't always share the self-assurance of a native speaker like Laura Marks, who once expressed: "I am confident in the ability of language to condense experience and re-explode it in another form."[52] At the same time we must not underestimate the dangers of relying exclusively on suggestive writing. While the descriptions should be accessible and have a high degree of plasticity, suggestion cannot replace the basic work of searching for invariant structures of experience.

2. Criteria for a successful phenomenology

How, then, do we judge a convincing phenomenological description? The first litmus test for a successful phenomenology is the question as to whether it elicits a *pre-reflectively felt understanding*.[53] The text has to resonate with the reader's own experience, and this resonance can take two forms: Either the text appeals to the reader's *memory*, sparking recognition of what generally was the case during a given experience; or it strikes the reader's *understanding of the plausibility* of an experience he or she has never personally had.[54] This distinction also has to do with how general a description purports to be. While some experiences are presumably shared by everyone, others depend on cultural or historical contingencies: female or male, Western or Non-Western, hetero- or homosexual, old or young, and so on. If a phenomenological description tries to capture a feminine experience – for instance, how it is like to "throw like a girl" – a male reader will merely be able to judge the plausibility of the description.[55] One could therefore distinguish between a response like "Yes, exactly, that's precisely how I also experience it" and a response such as "Yes, indeed, it's very much possible that one would experience it like that." Following van Manen, we could say that a phenomenological description has to have a *revocative* quality for the reader in the first case and an *evocative* quality in the second.[56]

As in other domains of scholarship, a further criterion for success is *originality*. However, the originality of a good phenomenology does not only refer to its *newness*, that is, something that hasn't been shown by someone else and thereby strikes us as a contribution to scholarship. It also has to be original in the sense that it bears a certain *unexpectedness*. If the description is so commonsensical or superficial that the reader might as well exclaim "So what?" or "I knew this all along!", no felt understanding can save it.

A third criterion for a convincing phenomenological description is the reader's *sense of completeness*. The text may spark a sudden felt understanding and surprise you with its newness and unexpectedness, but still leaves you dissatisfied because something important seems missing. Unless this omission feels blatant, however, a feeling of incompleteness must not be lethal. Some phenomenologists have even claimed that this is unavoidable, because we can never expect to exhaust all aspects of a phenomenon, particularly if it is a complex one. A given description of experience thus always remains open to amendment and further detailing by other phenomenologists. As Hilge Landweer points out, phenomenology may be more dependent than other scholarly methods on those processes of *exchange* and *criticism* that ideally characterize science: Phenomenology is safe from being mere introspection, she says, when the assessment of descriptions of phenomena from various scholars and perspectives succeeds.[57] A particularly welcome form of critique of my project would therefore be a critique that engages with my suggestions and points out disagreements *publicly in writing*.

3. Some misconceptions about phenomenology

And still, for some scholars there might be a lingering feeling that all this is too subjective. It is therefore helpful to follow John Searle and distinguish between two easily conflated senses of the word "subjective": an *epistemic* and an *ontological* sense. With regard to the epistemic sense, Searle writes: "Epistemically speaking, 'objective' and 'subjective' are primarily predicates of *judgments*."[58] A judgment is considered as "subjective" when its truth or falsity cannot be settled "objectively," because the truth or falsity of the judgment does not depend on *facts* but rather on attitudes or feelings. So while it is *epistemically subjective* to claim that Martin Scorsese is a better director than Steven Spielberg, it is *epistemically objective* that Scorsese (born 17 November 1942) is more than four years older than Spielberg (born 18 December 1946). The former statement is based on opinions, the latter on facts.

The case is different with the *ontological* distinction between objective and subjective. Here we are dealing not with predicates of judgments but with predicates of entities and types of entities, which ascribe modes of existence. They depend either on subjects (hence they are ontologically subjective) or not (which makes them ontologically objective): "In the ontological sense, pains are subjective entities, because their mode of existence depends on being felt by subjects. But mountains, for example, in contrast to pains, are ontologically objective because their mode of existence is independent of any perceiver or any mental state," Searle notes.[59]

People worried about the alleged "subjectivism" of phenomenology often conflate epistemically subjective judgments and ontologically subjective entities. Just because something might be an ontologically subjective entity does not turn it into an epistemically subjective judgment. Or to put it differently, while a certain experience might be ontologically subjective because it depends on a subject who makes this experience, it can still be an epistemically objective fact. To claim that joy elates and elevates and opens the joyful person to other persons and the world is not a subjective judgment – it is an objective fact even though it is ontologically subjective. And it remains an objective fact until someone can falsify the claim and show that joy in fact constricts and shuts you off from the world.

Another misconception about phenomenology is that it is ego-centered, that its account of intentionality is monological, and that it has a quasi-solipsistic understanding of the subject. While this has always been wrong, it is all the more misguided in light of recent rediscoveries of early phenomenological writings on sociality and community that my study has much profited from (both directly and indirectly via its influence on current debates in social ontology). As Thomas Szanto and Dermot Moran write in their anthology on the phenomenology of sociality: "Arguably [. . .] when looking back over the last century of thinking about sociality, there seems to be no other single intellectual tradition within philosophy, or even in neighboring disciplines in the humanities and social sciences, including sociology, other than phenomenology, that has endeavored to address the issue of interpersonal understanding, collectivity and togetherness with such rigor and detail."[60] However, it is true that *film* phenomenology, both during its classical period in the decades after 1945 and during its ongoing resurge after 1990, was interested almost exclusively in individual viewers. This study is, not least, an attempt to change that one-sidedness of film phenomenology.

4. Limits of phenomenology

Despite my profound passion for phenomenology, there is no need to be ignorant about its limits. Only epistemological hubris or intellectual naiveté can make one believe in the complete infallibility of one's method. Let me therefore add some pitfalls.

First, there may be domains of our phenomenological experience that transcend the limits of our subjective capacity to recognize. Here intuition reaches its limits because it is too coarse-grained. David Roden therefore speaks of an unintuitable or "dark" phenomenology.[61] As potential candidates for a phenomenology that transcends our "subjective recognitional powers" he lists color, time, or pitch.[62]

Second, there is a danger of overestimating one's ability to describe an experience in its entirety via language. When we describe an experience, we *analytically* and *ex post* isolate and individuate a part from a larger whole that precedes it.[63] The phenomenologist will find it next to impossible to capture the holistic flow of an experience in its fullness and all its subtleties.[64] Hence a certain curtailment will most likely be the case. Apart from the dark areas of our intuition, there are also dark areas that lie beyond language. This modesty is not a cheap, window-dressing, in-advance excuse for potential shortcomings, but an admission of the necessary limits of one's descriptions, even if the goal remains depth, breadth, and completeness. But even if one were to call the phenomenological description "at best a useful approximation" of experience (as Roden says of Husserl's phenomenology of time), I would still defend it on the very grounds of this usefulness.[65] For in order to determine whether a phenomenological description is merely an approximation, we first must have a phenomenological description to see its limits.

A third important admission is that we cannot completely get rid of normative assumptions, despite phenomenology's ideal of a description free of presuppositions and biases. This also goes for the current study: One of my central claims is that the cinema is more social or collective than we tend to be aware of. This is what my theoretical distinctions and phenomenological descriptions try to raise attention to: We often simply live through and are too habituated to the social and collective dimension of the cinema, not becoming consciously aware of it. Since I cannot meaningfully describe what is at stake here with a completely different terminology, I have to rely on notions like "sociality," "collectivity," and "community." The problem is that these terms are always already fraught with expectations and normative assumptions: To be social, for most people, simply means something other and *better* than to be a-social. Thus, by pointing out the social and collective dimensions of the cinema, I have, in the eyes of some, unwittingly given it a positive value.

The normativity problem becomes even more pronounced once we admit that phenomenology works most effectively when an experience like watching a film in a cinema is compared with a different but related one. Taking this comparative standpoint, it is hard to avoid that readers may draw normative conclusions: The cinema could come across as more social than the experience it is likened to (in Chapter 2 we will see that for Bazin the cinema is less social than the theater and more social than television). As a consequence, and unsurprisingly, some people may feel that their own viewing preferences or research areas are denigrated.[66]

5. Focus on emotions and affective expressions

Throughout this book I will place special emphasis on emotions and affective expressions, because it is often in moments of strong emotions that we become vigorously aware of our fellow viewers, in positive and negative ways. Peak affective moments – we tend to call them emotions – influence the way we experience the film, the auditorium, and our co-viewers. While oftentimes it is the film that initiates the emotion, at other times it is the audience that initiates an emotional effect on our movie-theater experience. A film may scare us and thus turn the whole cinema into a fearful place, but it can also be the laughter of other viewers that alerts us to how funny a film is.

Here it is important to bear in mind that emotions can have a spatial effect on our subjectively experienced *lived*-body (as opposed to our mere *physical* living body): They can both *open* us to the world or *isolate* us from it. The important work of phenomenologist Hermann Schmitz reminds us that once we are overcome by an emotion, we often experience a phenomenological change in our lived-body's spatial sense of direction to the world. We might centrifugally expand into the world, with a strong openness to contact or even embrace others (in the case of joy, for example); or our emotional space might narrow down and we centripetally and a-socially feel withdrawn from the world (as with sadness).[67] This has undeniable ramifications for the relations between viewers watching comedies and melodramas.

Or take this movie memory by Martin Scorsese who reminisces about watching films with his parents: "I realize now that the warmth of that connection with my family and with the images on the screen gave me something very precious. We were experiencing something fundamental together."[68] Scorsese's quote illustrates a case of phenomenological *closeness*, even intimacy, between a boy and his parents, derived from watching a movie together in what I will call an experiential *we-connection*. In the primal scene of collective viewing, on the other hand, we encountered the polar opposite: In terms of its spatial experience, shame isolates and exposes the individual in front of a group, be it actual or imagined. The ashamed and enticed boy feels phenomenologically distanced and experiences an antagonistic *I-versus-you* relation with his parents.

This book will also allow me to revisit and refine some of the questions that occupied me in my previous monograph, *Cinematic Emotion in Horror Films and Thrillers: The Aesthetic Paradox of Pleasurable Fear*. In that book I argued that part of the pleasure of experiencing fear in the cinema can result from a particular form of collectivity.[69] However, considering the different focus of that book, my investigation of the collective experience had to remain limited to the emotion of fear in its varieties. Moreover, relying in no small part on the work of phenomenologists Max Scheler and Hermann Schmitz, I lacked the insights of recent debates in sociology and social ontology about collective emotions and collective intentionality. The latter, partly motivated by the rediscovery of important early phenomenologists, deals with the question of whether we can share actions, intentions, or emotions – and how these actions, intentions, and emotions are sometimes more than just individual but collective and joint.[70] *The Audience Effect* is thus an opportunity to expand and deepen my previous arguments.

My perspective will be purposefully one-sided, though, focusing strongly on the experiential side of the audience and remaining, mostly, silent about what is shown on the screen. This is not at all meant to decrease films to interchangeable stimuli – it obviously makes a tremendous difference if we watch a Wes Craven horror film or a Kenneth Anger avant-garde film, a Hollywood comedy or a Bollywood musical. But apart from the fact that I have to restrict my research objectives if the results are to reach a warranted depth, I also follow a rhetorical goal: My willful one-sidedness is supposed to counterbalance the previous lopsidedness of film studies, thereby revealing the necessity to extend current reception theories by incorporating responses that emerge from the lived experience of collective viewing. I do not consider this a *simplification*, but a *clarification*; my rhetorical exaggeration serves to highlight what might otherwise go unnoticed.

Along the way the book will gradually become more phenomenological in spirit, zooming in on ever-more concrete descriptions of affective audience effects. To round off the "establishing shot" of the current first part I will discuss, as mentioned, a series of precursors in the history of film theory who had similar intuitions about the audience effect (Chapter 2). I will then initiate a long and extended zoom that starts from a "long shot" in Part 2, in which I distinguish the two main *types of collective viewing*: quiet-attentive and expressive-diverted viewing (Chapters 3 and 4). Next follows the "medium shot" of Part 3 in which I first focus on *affective audience interrelations*, that is, the entire range of social relations that are based on emotions and affects as well as their concomitant expressive responses and that emerge between viewers while watching a film collectively (Chapter 5), before taking a detailed look at one specific affective audience interrelation: the mutually close *affective we-connections* we can have with others in the cinema hall (Chapter 6). Part 4 will consist of three "close-ups": case studies of the audience effects of breaking out in *laughter* (Chapter 7), being moved to *tears* (Chapter 8), and feeling *anger* about other viewers (Chapter 9). The "fade-out" in Part 5 eventually takes a brief prospective look at audience effects *beyond the movie-theater*, for instance when watching a film on one's laptop on a train, when at home connected via second screens with friends who watch the same film elsewhere, or when 'sitting' with others in a Virtual Reality cinema (Chapter 10).

IV. PRECONDITIONS FOR STUDYING THE COLLECTIVE CINEMA EXPERIENCE

In their sociological study on media audiences, Nicholas Abercrombie and Brian Longhurst claim that research questions are often regulated and constrained by a network of assumptions that predominates at a certain historical moment. Referring to Thomas Kuhn's classical term, they call this network of assumptions a *paradigm*. Since some questions have high priority within a paradigm, other equally important issues are not researchable: "Within the paradigm, what goes on most of the time is the ordinary solving of problems, Kuhn's 'normal science.' But, eventually, problems arise which cannot be solved within the paradigm boundary and the paradigm breaks up to be replaced by another one. These 'destructive' problems may be partly generated by the paradigm itself but will also arise out of changes in the world."[71] Yet are there shifts and currents in the world that propel my study? I think so, and I will single out two such developments.

1. Shifts in film viewing: individualization and privatization of the audience

It comes close to a cliché to claim that we often need historical shifts to realize what was too habitual to grasp at an earlier point: the overly familiar becomes de-familiarized once it is no longer the norm.[72] For our current question the most important transformations are the processes of relocation and remediation of the film experience: the decentering of the theatrical film experience and the possibility to watch films through various digital technologies.[73] In the twenty-first century, screens are neither found exclusively in movie-theaters, nor are films necessarily watched collectively. Of course, we still watch films in the multiplex, the arthouse theater, the IMAX. But, as we all know so well from our daily lives, the new digital technologies have multiplied the possibilities for film consumption. We increasingly watch films alone, with friends, or as members of dispersed audiences: via cable, satellite, DVD, or Blu-Ray on television screens at home; as digital projections in museums and art galleries; on seatback screens in the airplane; via video-on-demand or illegal downloads on computer monitors in buses, trains, or the doctor's waiting room.[74] Laptops, tablets, or smartphones have made it possible to watch films potentially everywhere; film viewing has become increasingly mobile.

What does this shift imply for the *social* aspect of the film experience? One can observe a double tendency toward *individualization* and *privatization*.[75] A 2011 study published by the British Film Institute showed that people in the United Kingdom watched only a small fraction of films in the cinema: they saw 57 per cent on television, 23 per cent on DVD and Blu-Ray, 8 per cent via downloads and streams, 4 per cent on a mobile device, 2 per cent on planes – and 6 per cent in the cinema.[76] This means that more than 90 per cent of all films were either watched alone or in the company of known and even well-known others like partners, family, and friends. Obviously, viewers are also surrounded by *anonymous others* when they watch a film in (semi-)public spaces such as trains, buses, or airplanes. These co-present others have effects on the film experience as well. What is lacking, however, is their joint attention to the film. This is an aspect that I will come back to in Chapter 10, my conclusion.

Precisely because the collective cinema experience is no longer the gold standard, we can begin to judge more precisely what it's worth. The multiple forms of individualized and privatized reception enable us to grasp with greater clarity the cinema's peculiar collectivity.[77] If it is true that *solitary* viewing takes place on a much more regular basis and on a larger scale, it seems opportune to ask what changes when the triadic viewer–film–audience relationship turns into the dyadic structure of viewer–film (including potential connections to others via second screens). And if it is true that there are fewer and fewer *non-anonymous others* co-present and jointly attending the film, we may also wonder what change this implies for the collective experience of film.[78]

2. Still, the cinema: the persistence of collective viewing

Isn't it a perilously retrograde endeavor, then, to focus exclusively on the cinema at the very moment when, according to some pundits, the cinema's death seems to be imminent and new media buzzwords like "connectivity," "second screen," or "participation" indicate a collective experience also *beyond* the cinema?[79] Apart from the fact that this logic of topicality would turn studies on opera audiences of the eighteenth century or theater audiences of the nineteenth century into outdated endeavors, collective viewing in the cinema persists against all odds (while we can at the same time observe the development of new forms of collective viewing, for instance of television series in bars or opera broadcasts in movie-theaters). Considering the still high number of cinema admissions, it might be premature to sound the death knell. Over the last two decades the overall box-office numbers have been astoundingly robust. In fact, in many countries the number of overall cinema admissions has increased, in the case of the United Kingdom and the Netherlands even quite substantially (see Table 1.1).[80]

The following statistics for admissions per person – numbers that are more significant, since they are not inflected by population growth – also show that viewers do not give up cinemagoing.[81] While Table 1.2 indicates decreasing

Table 1.1: Overall admissions per year (in millions of visitors).

	1990	1995	2000	2005	2010	2015
US/Canada	1190	1211	1383	1376	1339	1320
Germany	102.5	124.5	152.5	127.3	126.6	139.2
UK	88.7	114.6	142.5	164.7	169.3	171.9
Netherlands	14.6	17.2	21.6	20.6	28.2	30.8

Table 1.2: Annual cinema attendances per person.

	1996	2001	2005	2009	2013	2015
US/Canada	5.0	5.2	4.4	4.3	4.0	4.2
Germany	1.6	2.2	1.5	1.8	1.6	1.7
UK	1.5	2.7	2.7	2.8	2.6	2.7
Netherlands	1.0	1.5	1.3	1.7	1.8	1.9

attendances per capita in North America, the numbers remain largely similar in Germany and even increase in the UK and the Netherlands.

Even if we can observe a trend toward more individualized and privatized forms of spectatorship, the cinema is still around. How can we explain these seemingly contradictory tendencies? It appears that people simply watch more films than twenty years ago. The individualized and privatized reception of films on television screens, computer monitors, smartphone displays, and tablet screens does not *replace* but *complements* the theatrical experience.[82] While people in the UK and in the Netherlands today go to the cinema almost twice as often as in 1990, it is also true that the share of cinema attendance in all film viewings has dropped and that watching movies mostly takes place elsewhere than in the cinema.

Obviously I do not claim that every viewer *enjoys* being part of a cinema audience. There are innumerable reasons why people go to the movies: Some of them have to do with the film, some with the social experience of the cinema, and some with more mundane motivations.[83] At times films are even watched involuntarily, as when they are a compulsory requirement within an institution like schools or prisons.[84] For convenience's sake we can therefore roughly divide the audience attitudes toward collective viewing into three categories. First, there are those who go to the cinema exclusively because of the film and would in fact prefer to watch it alone. We may call them the *cinema atheists*. As an example one could quote Roland Barthes who once said: "I would prefer of course to go to the movies alone, because to me, the cinema is a completely projective activity."[85]

Second, there are those who go to the cinema because they want to see the film, but find it acceptable that others are around. Call them the *cinema agnostics*. An example could be an anonymous fan interviewed by Martin Barker and Kate Brooks for an empirical audience study on the movie *Judge Dredd* from 1995: He wants to concentrate on the film and not explain himself to others, but he can also see the attractive sides of going to the cinema in a big group, which is "more of a [. . .] laugh sort of thing."[86]

Finally, there are those who go to the cinema first and foremost because it enables a social experience. For these viewers the collective experience means a "willing suspension of our self-isolation" (Bert O. States).[87] Call them the *cinema believers*. Not least in the first two decades of the cinema, consciousness of other viewers seemed to be an important (if not the central) aspect of the entertainment films provided. As Emilie Altenloh pointed out in her sociological audience study from 1914: "many find it far more entertaining to watch other cinemagoers – especially female cinemagoers – than to watch the films."[88] This may remind us of the seeing-and-being-seen characteristic of going to the stage theater in the nineteenth century. In Chapter 4, which deals with what I call "expressive-diverted viewing," we shall have ample opportunity to encounter various types of film experience in which the focus on the other viewers is of extraordinary importance. In fact, Richard Maltby and Melvyn Stokes even claim that "for most audiences for most of the history of cinema, their primary relationship with 'the cinema' has not been with individual movies-as-artefacts or as texts, but with the social experience of cinemagoing."[89]

But these different preferences regarding the social experience of the movie-theater ultimately do not challenge a study of the audience effect: While cinematic "atheists," "agnostics" and "believers" may well differ substantially in how much they *value* the collective experience of the cinema, they are all subject to various audience effects, whether they want them or not. At the same time, we can also expect strong personality differences. Some viewers are simply more sensitive to their social surroundings: people who are averse to being close to others or are very susceptible to noise, for instance. Hence the audience effects described in this book will not affect everyone equally.

IV. UPSHOTS OF THIS BOOK

1. Enriching the viewing experience

Yet even if filling a research gap is one of the major motivations for this book, there are further aspirations that drive my investigation. An important goal is to make viewers more centrally aware of aspects of their film experience that usually remain at the fringe of consciousness: Most of what I describe in the following takes place on a *pre-reflective* level. As we have seen above, as viewers we rarely focus on the social aspect of the cinematic experience. Putting these experiences into words can bring them to the fore, making us more explicitly conscious of what we are usually only implicitly aware of.

An important assumption that grounds my study is that experiences – in the cinema and elsewhere – can be richer than we tend to be aware of. Distinguishing experiences conceptually, labeling them, and describing them with rigor helps to deepen and enrich our experiences. This is a bit like wine-tasting: The case of experiencing and appreciating wine shows that it is important to have a sophisticated vocabulary to enjoy rich experiences.[90] The same goes for our emotional life. Emotions are not "constructed" through conceptualization and labeling: We don't have to give an emotional experience a name to undergo it, as we couldn't understand the meaning of the label if we weren't able to correlate it with a prior type of experience.[91] But with Kevin Mulligan and Klaus Scherer I want to claim that "many of the aspects and features of emotions [...] cannot be conceptualized by their subjects simply because these subjects lack sufficiently fine-grained concepts."[92] In other words, viewers might simply be unable to conceptualize and describe what they have felt, despite the fact that they have clearly felt it. This is part of the reason why this study will offer a number of conceptual distinctions and describe experiences in some detail. (A glossary at the end of the book collects some of the main terms I introduce in this study.)

On the one hand, phenomenological descriptions can shed light on *prior* cinematic experiences. Readers may recognize what they experienced themselves in the past and had never really thought about. Reading a good phenomenological description often evokes a sense of astonishment and surprise, precisely because readers realize what they had experienced only on a pre-reflective level, at the fringe of consciousness. In addition, putting pre-reflective feelings into words can add a sense of fulfillment or completion.[93] What was experienced pre-reflectively – and hence remained 'foggy' or 'fuzzy' – turns into a 'graspable' form through verbalization. Reading a good phenomenological description evokes precisely this pleasurable sense of completion and a eureka-like "I see!"

On the other hand, the descriptions of the following chapters can also have an effect on *future* experiences. They may make it easier for readers – and here I think of both film scholars and lay cinemagoers – to recognize and reflect on experiences they encounter in the movie-theater. Clearly, differences exist in how much viewers are consciously aware of their *affective experiences*. Lisa Feldman Barrett therefore talks about various levels of "emotional granularity," that is, the precision with which people can describe their emotions.[94] As we have heard, viewers also vary in their individual dispositions to notice their *surroundings*: while some people are highly attentive to co-present viewers, others may be easily immersed in the film, thus becoming much less privy to the social aspect of the cinema. By putting pre-reflective states into words and making them explicit, my phenomenological descriptions hopefully enable the discovery of new aspects of the cinematic experience.[95] Reading a phenomenological description may be the first step for an interested viewer to perform the phenomenological skill of *epoché*, a skill that rests on a simultaneous *suspension* of one's inattentive immersion in experience and a turning of *attention* to the way in which something is experienced.[96]

One may object that enriching one's experience – feeling more and feeling better – is a mere hedonistic goal. During a research meeting, film scholar Gertrud Koch once described my phenomenological approach to bodily experiences in cinema in her typical dry-as-a-bone manner as "sophisticated wellness." How to respond to it? In recent years various scholars have called for films that enable new and more fine-grained affective experiences. Elena del Río, for one, claims that "the cinema has, in no small measure, contributed to the rigidification of the language and experience of emotion by relying on repeatable formulas."[97] And Sean Cubitt argues: "The scream, the laugh, the tear, the white knuckles, the racing pulse: the stimuli are clichés because the emotions they elicit and that audiences seek are clichés. Market research ensures, as far as anything can, that expectations will be met. Of course, such expectations derive from the past, never from the future, and so the hectic overproduction of affects is only ever repetitive of old emotions."[98] The two quotes express a considerable frustration with worn-out formulas and clichéd experiences. However, once we ask for greater differentiation on the side of the *film*, does it not make sense to also ask for more differentiation on the side of the *viewer*?

We should not relegate the responsibility to the filmmakers alone: we can train our own sensorium and actively increase awareness. The more people know about clichéd experiences, the more they will be able to appreciate what is fine-grained, subtle, and sophisticated. Precisely by increasing our sensitivity to what is so stereotypical about many cinema experiences we can open up to the new and unusual. Of course, we are *not unconscious* of our affective experiences. But by describing them, it will become easier to realize nuances. Consider this an *éducation sentimentale*, then, an emotional education.

2. Raising media competency

Connected to the *awareness* claim is my *media competency* hypothesis. Since today screens are ubiquitous and media reception can take place everywhere, we can hardly avoid becoming part of an audience. Some scholars have therefore questioned the analytical usefulness of the concept of the audience altogether: "As audiences are everywhere, they become increasingly indistinguishable and ultimately invisible – being an audience member has become synonymous with being an individual or social subject," Cornel Sandvoss notes.[99] But here he is throwing out a poor baby with the bath water. Precisely because of their ubiquity, it is necessary to reflect more profoundly on audiences, to distinguish various types and to describe experiential differences.

Moreover, in today's convergent media culture, storytelling takes place not only transmedially, where comparable narratives are told in a film, a comic book, a novelization, a computer game, and so on.[100] Viewers also encounter the same film through various media technologies and in diverse viewing surroundings, as when they watch a film like *The Dark Knight Rises* (2012) in an IMAX cinema as part of an anonymous crowd, on a television screen at home with their partner, a computer monitor in the library, or on a smartphone on the bus. Unless we want to claim rather absurdly that these media and viewing surroundings make no experiential difference, and thus subscribe to a strong causal model according to which only texts determine viewing effects, we should take a comparative position. Tom Gunning, not known as a dyed-in-the-wool phenomenologist, therefore insists that we "need to offer thick descriptions of how media work that is, phenomenological approaches that avoid defining media logically before examining the experience of their power."[101] Raising a sort of "awareness about awareness" may not only enrich the viewing experience, but might also raise media competency: our ability to consciously reflect on how being part of various media audiences may affect us. Of course, I do not suggest that being more conscious about the collective experience alone is sufficient for becoming a competent media user. But it can contribute to it.

Yet wouldn't this imply a fundamental change of what many viewers cherish most: the flow-like immersion in the film? I do not think so. Just as someone trained in hermeneutics does not always *interpret* a film, so a phenomenologist does not automatically start *describing* the cinematic experience. What it enables is the sheer *possibility* of becoming more aware. Put in existential terms, phenomenology enables a greater freedom from the film, because we can experience it in a more reflective mode: "The ultimate aim is not to break the flow of experience, but to reinhabit it in a fresh way," Evan Thompson claims.[102] This is not to say that increased media competency is easily achieved – it implies a pedagogical effort to which this book wants to contribute.

3. Laying a groundwork for empirical research

The philosopher Susanne K. Langer once wrote, in the introduction to her classic *Feeling and Form*, that nothing in her book was exhaustively treated and that every subject demanded further analysis, research, and invention: "That is because it is essentially an exploratory work, which – as Whitehead once said of William James's pragmatism – 'chiefly starts a lot of hares for people to chase.'"[103] I, too, consider my book an exploratory beginning. It sketches broadly what ultimately needs more fine-grained descriptions. But being modest is only a small step from sounding coquettish. Let me therefore claim as another upshot of this study its usefulness to start a lot of hares for other people to chase.[104]

This certainly goes for further phenomenological descriptions. But it also goes for more empirically driven research. No empirical study can do without basic assumptions and theoretical groundings – no matter how implicit they are and no matter how averse a given scholar may be to this fact. Here we find another reason why the following chapters will make a fair amount of conceptual distinctions and introduce categories that are new to film studies. As Étienne Souriau once put it in his famous article on the vocabulary of filmology: "if a science is not just 'a well-made language', to borrow Condillac's famous phrase, it does at least call for and presuppose such a language. To refuse the effort needed to establish, adopt, persist with, and correctly and normally handle such a language is to condemn oneself in advance to asking the wrong questions, as well as to vague research without hard and fast results, badly compiled observations, and provisional and confusedly speculative studies."[105]

Before film scholars can usefully interview cinemagoers and use questionnaires, for instance, they need guiding concepts and hypotheses to formulate their questions. Here phenomenology can be helpful, precisely because the various shades of collective viewing remain largely pre-reflective and are not always easily accessible. At the very least, then, my conceptual tools may serve as inspiration, corrective, or framework for interpreting data; and my phenomenological descriptions could provide hypotheses that other scholars take up and pursue with their own expertise and methodology: historians, ethnographers, psychologists, neuroscientists, sociologists.

I believe that even a moderate success in this endeavor would allow me to disprove Gilbert Seldes who once purported, tongue-deeply-in-cheek, to have discovered "a man of no practical capacity whatever: a theorist."[106]

NOTES

1. Mitry (2000 [1963]), p. 321.
2. This minimal definition of the cinema dispositive serves as an a-historical prototype from which historically and culturally specific instances deviate.
3. As John Ellis once wrote: "The experience of watching a film in an empty cinema is curiously desolate" (Ellis, 2002, p. 88). And in the words of Walter Benjamin: "In a painting salon, emptiness can be pleasant; in a Kaiserpanorama, this is no longer the case, and in the cinema not for all money in the world" (Benjamin, 2010 [1936], p. 27). In Nanni Moretti's early film *Sogni d'oro* (1981) the young film director Michele Apicella (Nanni Moretti) visits the cinema with his colleague Gaetano (Alessandro Haber). While purchasing the tickets at the box office, the two filmmakers run into the cinema-owner who had screened Apicella's last movie for months. The cinema-owner asks them to follow him into the cinema, where he shows them the newest idea for his audience: Since he considers the big auditoria too sad when they are empty, he has placed mannequins resembling nineteenth-century aristocratic theatergoers on all the unsold seats: "this way the audience no longer feels alone," the cinema-owner tells them. "People are starting to get out the house again and the cinema once again becomes a place where you meet people."
4. For a similar position with regard to the theater, see chapter 9 in Roselt (2008).
5. For a similar view, see Pedullà (2012). Pedullà argues that the introduction of television (and other personalized media like computers, smartphones, tablets) divided "the crowd of strangers that once sat in the dark side by side into a multitude of audiences of one";

"watching a film began to resemble a traditionally individual experience such as silent reading"; "Knowing that someone else is probably watching the same show is not enough to cancel out the enormous difference between these two experiences" (p. 66). Unfortunately, Pedullà touches upon the topic of the collective experience only in passing.
6. Casetti (2015), p. 7.
7. As such, my study focuses on a viewing constellation that is halfway between various kinds of *solitary* viewings and the *mass* viewings of television. The latter are epitomized by what Daniel Dayan and Elihu Katz have dubbed "media events," events that combine mass collective attention to a live event on a national or even worldwide scale, but lack the physical proximity of a co-present audience (Dayan/Katz, 1992). Other forms of watching films with others would comprise, for instance, university film clubs, screenings in libraries, home viewings with friends, or what Miriam Ross calls "community exhibition" (see Ross, 2013).
8. See, for instance, Mike Cardwell, *Dictionary of Psychology* (London: Routledge, 2013), pp. 20–1.
9. A good example would be the German comedy *Good Bye Lenin!* (2003) that demands self-irony from both West and East Germans.
10. Quoted from Breakwell/Hammond (1990), pp. 88–9.
11. Oliver's joke is available at https://www.youtube.com/watch?v=LojQz6jqQSo&feature =youtu.be (last accessed 19 March 2016).
12. Harris/Cook (2010): http://onlinelibrary.wiley.com/doi/10.1002/acp.1758/pdf (last accessed 16 April 2015). See also Costa et al. (2001). This study does not feature moving images, but slides of nude males, nude females, and erotic couples. However, the effect is very similar.
13. Harris/Cook (2010), p. 7.
14. http://www.silent-cinema.co.uk/how (last accessed 19 March 2016, emphasis added). Interestingly, the history of film exhibition knows a silent cinema precursor to the Silent Cinema: In 1898 the Cinemacrophonograph or Phonorama had viewers watch a projected film with earphones (other sources claim that it was a telephone receiver). See Abel (2005), p. 620; Boillat (2015), p. 239.
15. Film studies thus merely replicates what Beata Stawarska claims for the *egocentric tradition* in philosophy since Descartes, which "divorced the first- from the second-person experience" and committed itself to a "conception of humanity as a collective of lone individuals" (Stawarska, 2009, p. 4).
16. Bazin (1967b [1951]), p. 99 (emphasis added).
17. Bazin (1967b [1951]), p. 102 (emphasis added).
18. Metz (1982), pp. 95–6 (emphasis added).
19. Eikhenbaum (1982 [1927]), n.p.
20. Baudry (1986a [1970]) and Baudry (1986b [1975]).
21. For a definition of the term "dispositive" (or *dispositif* in French), see Frank Kessler's "Notes on *dispositif*": available at http://www.hum.uu.nl/medewerkers/f.e.kessler/ Dispositif%20Notes11-2007.pdf (last accessed 22 December 2016).
22. Acknowledging the co-presence of other anonymous spectators might have undermined Baudry's thesis about the cinema as a state of artificial regression. After all, only twins and triplets have experienced the warmth of the mother's womb with co-present others. My project can also be read, then, as an extension of Vivian Sobchack's elaborate critique of some theses of 1970s film theory, like the disembodied subject-eye of Christian Metz or Jean-Louis Baudry. While Sobchack made perfectly clear that the viewer always has

and is a body lived in a concrete cinematic surrounding, she did not stress the *collective* aspect of the cinematic dispositive. See Sobchack (1992).
23. The term "anthropomorphic individualism" comes from Cubitt (2005), p. 140.
24. Cavell (1979), p. 40.
25. Williams (1989), p. 32.
26. Richard Butsch underscores that even the famous Payne Fund Studies, the huge effort to study the effects of movies on audiences, were blind to collective experience: "Ironically, although Blumer and the other sociologists working on the Payne studies were part of the University of Chicago department renowned for its ethnographic approach that emphasized community and group subcultures, all of their studies, as well as those of the psychologists, methodologically treated the movie audience as individually affected by the movies with almost no investigation into the influence from their friends or the rest of the audience watching with them. Thus, from the initial conception of their research the Payne studies excluded from consideration the concept of the audience as a crowd or community, and concentrated almost exclusively on the audience as isolated individuals focused on the movie. They retained the mechanism of suggestibility but discarded the idea of the crowd, producing a picture of weak individuals vulnerable to the spellbinding influence of movies" (Butsch, 2007, p. 301).
27. Hanich (2010), pp. 63–4.
28. "When you were courting [ ] your best place, it's a cliché this, I know, and everybody laughs, but your main courting area was the back row of the cinema." Or as another informant recalls: "[One cinema] had double seats on the back row and we used to go and queue early to procure one of these back row 'seats for two' where we could cuddle up together to watch the program." Quoted from Kuhn (2002), pp. 164 and 145.
29. "Sometimes the goings-on in the back row proved more interesting than what was happening on the screen, as Brigadier J.B. Ryall recalls: 'When a youngster could sneak into the back row of the cinema he sometimes got more pleasure out of the corner of his eye at the "fumbling" and "squeaks" that sometimes went on.'" Quoted from Kuhn (2002), pp. 145 and 146.
30. See Brennan (2004). For the strong olfactory presence of other viewers, see the quotes by German politician Carlo Mierendorff in 1920 and philosopher/playwright Albert Camus reprinted in Paech/Paech (2000), pp. 37 and 62. And lest we forget it, there was a time when smoking was allowed in the cinema. See the complaint of art historian Élie Faure in Faure (1959 [1920]), p. 6.
31. Goffman (1963), pp. 27 and 33. Goffman once commented sarcastically: "At home with his family, a lower-middle class American may lounge in a chair, polish his eye-glasses with his shirt-tail, treat his children as if in many ways they were not really present, pick his nose, and be flatulent – the last, perhaps, only if his wife is not present. The same man in the same setting, but with his employer present, might be the very model of tight middle-class decorum" (p. 228).
32. Breakwell/Hammond (1990), pp. 7–8.
33. Pedullà (2012), p. 15 (emphasis added).
34. See Hansen (1991); Staiger (2000); Barker/Brooks (1998); Barker (2008); Kuhn (2002); Hill (1997); Maltby/Stokes/Allen (2007); Biltereyst/Maltby/Meers (2012).
35. See Paul (1994); Mathijs/Mendik (2008a); Elsaesser (2002); Srinivas (2002).
36. Zillmann et al. (1986).
37. Jakobs/Manstead/Fischer (2001).
38. For overviews of various methodologies, see for instance Shimamura (2013); Aveyard/Moran (2013); Reinhard/Olson (2016).

39. In neighboring art forms like theater and music, scholars have made first steps toward a similar theorization and phenomenology of the collective experience of these art forms. For the theater, see particularly chapter 9 in Roselt (2008); for music, see Cochrane (2009) and Krueger (2011).
40. See Sobchack (1992) and Sobchack (2004). For a methodological overview, see Ferencz-Flatz/Hanich (2016). For a more detailed formulation of my methodological position, see chapter 1 ("How to Describe Cinematic Fear, or Why Phenomenology?") in Hanich (2010).
41. Van Manen (2014), p. 65.
42. See, for instance, Landweer (1999), p. 25.
43. For Hans Bernhard Schmid this basic self-awareness is the *subjective* character of consciousness, which he usefully distinguishes from the *qualitative* character, which comprises the "feel," the "experiential dimension," the "what it is like" involved in consciousness (Schmid, 2014a, p. 6).
44. Van Manen, p. 38.
45. Waldenfels (2010), p. 279 (my translation).
46. Sobchack (2011), p. 192.
47. Sobchack (2011), p. 193.
48. Depraz (2012) p. 118.
49. Quoted from States (1985) p. 29.
50. Van Manen (2014), p. 223.
51. Van Manen (2014), p. 241.
52. Marks (2002), p. x.
53. Van Manen (2014), p. 289.
54. Van Manen (2014), p. 240.
55. My point of reference is, of course, Iris Marion Young's famous essay "Throwing Like a Girl. A Phenomenology of Feminine Body Comportment Motility and Spatiality" (Young, 1980). For some implications for feminist or queer film phenomenology, see Ferencz-Flatz/Hanich (2016), pp. 47–50.
56. Van Manen (2014), pp. 285 and 287.
57. Landweer (1999), p. 14.
58. Searle (1995), p. 8 (emphasis added).
59. Searle (1995), p. 8.
60. Szanto/Moran (2015), p. 2. See also Emanuele Caminada's comment: "Far from being restrained by a monological account of intentionality, the tradition of phenomenology has provided a dynamic account of it by from the very beginning facing up to the challenge of social embedment" (Caminada, 2014, p. 210).
61. Available at http://enemyindustry.net/blog/wp-content/uploads/2011/08/PhenNatFF1.pdf (last accessed 19 August 2016).
62. As Roden writes with regard to pitch, "the human capacity to discriminate musical pitch differences is more fine-grained than the human ability to identify or label pitch intervals" (Roden, n.d., p. 4).
63. See, for instance, Walther (1923), p. 12.
64. Van Manen (2014), pp. 42 and 54.
65. Roden (n.d.), p. 9.
66. In guest lectures and at conference talks, scholars have occasionally pointed out to me that by comparing the social experience of the cinema with watching a film alone on a television screen or computer monitor, I tend to ignore the variegated social facets of the latter (alone at home I can have an experience of imagined community; via a second

screen I may be texting with someone else; I may be aware of other persons sitting in the room next door; and so on). Yet ignoring the social facets of watching a film alone is not my intention. In fact, I consider them an important desideratum of my study.

67. Schmitz (1969). See also the first English translation of a Schmitz text, in which the German philosopher notes: "[Joy] is marked by a levitating inclination against the backdrop of which one is no longer impressed by the unchanged force of gravity ('to jump for joy', 'to float on air'). This may also be due to a heightened feeling of strength induced by joy. But there is also a more passive kind of joy in which one can let oneself go, for instance, in the case of being relieved of serious worries. Nonetheless, in such cases, too, joy is uplifting and this can only be due to the directed atmosphere of the moving emotion" (Schmitz, 2011, p. 258). Compare also Jan Slaby's description of the feeling of satisfaction after one's work is done: "Here, we might feel a kind of inner widening, an extension of our body volume, which is felt as something thoroughly positive and lets us feel quite 'at home' in our current surroundings" (Slaby, 2008, p. 436).
68. Available at http://www.nybooks.com/articles/archives/2013/aug/15/persisting-vision-reading-language-cinema/ (last accessed 19 March 2016).
69. Hanich (2010). On the collective experience, see especially pp. 72–7, 150–4, 195–201 and 241–51.
70. For an overview in German, see Schmid/Schweikard (2009).
71. Abercrombie/Longhurst (1998), pp. 3–4.
72. See, for instance, Mulvey (2006), p. 12. See also Ji-hoon Kim (2009).
73. Rodowick (2007), pp. 27–8.
74. See the numerous illuminating discussions in Casetti (2015). See also Atkinson (2014) and Tryon (2009).
75. Casetti (2009), p. 63.
76. Christie (2012b), p. 229.
77. In Gabriele Pedullà's words: "Only now that the frame has shed its false naturalness, thanks to the competition of new media, are we able to see it as an artificial construction that was perfected over the course of decades" (Pedullà, 2012, pp. 5–6).
78. An aspect I won't be able to talk about are the effects on the films themselves. Back in 1942 Margaret Kennedy noted: "Films intended for a small audience, a family, possibly only one person, in a dwelling room, would have to be different from those intended for a crowd in a hall. Anyone who has seen a popular film run through a small room, for one or two spectators, must have noticed how wrong the pitch seems to be. It is directed at something in him which he should share with several hundred people who are not there" (Kennedy (1959 [1942]), p. 108).
79. For studies that focus on watching films outside of the cinema, see among others Mundloch (2010); Balsom (2013); Atkinson (2014).
80. The statistics for US/Canada come from the National Association of Theater Owners, available at http://natoonline.org/data/admissions (last accessed 19 March 2016). The figures for Germany, the UK and the Netherlands come from Media Salles, available at www.mediasalles.it (last accessed 19 March 2016).
81. The statistics for US/Canada come from the Motion Picture Association of America (MPAA), available at www.mpaa.org (last accessed 23 April 2014), and Wayne Schmidt's Box Office Data Page, available at http://www.waynesthisandthat.com/moviedata.html (last accessed 19 March 2016). The figures for Germany, the UK, and the Netherlands come from Compendium: Cultural Policies and Trends in Europe, available at www.culturalpolicies.net/web/statistics-participation.php?aid=86&cid=74&lid=en (last

accessed 23 April 2014), Filmförderungsanstalt (FFA), available at www.ffa.de (last accessed 19 March 2016), the British Film Institute (BFI), available at http://www.bfi.org.uk (last accessed 6 December 2016), Union Internationale des Cinémas (UNIC), available at http://www.unic-cinemas.org/ (last accessed 6 December 2016), and Judith Thissen: "Understanding Dutch Film Culture: A Comparative Approach," in *Alphaville: Journal of Film and Screen Media*, Vol. 6, Winter 2013. Web (last accessed 23 April 2014).

82. Christie (2012b), p. 229. See also Evans/McDonald (2014), p. 160.
83. As Ian Christie reminds us, "the easily-ignored fact that film shows were the first popular entertainment to take place in darkness, with a proportion of those attending almost certainly not there for the movies, or easily distracted from the screen. Warmth, comfort, somewhere to sleep or pass the time; a chance to meet friends, and to make new ones; and a place for a 'date' – all of these were, and have remained, important reasons for cinemagoing, even if they are rarely acknowledged in film scholarship" (Christie, 2012a, p. 13).
84. Gregory Waller uses the term "captive audiences" for patients in asylums, prisoners in penitentiaries, or children in orphan homes (Waller, 2012, p. 90). Eric Smoodin speaks of "coercive viewings" when dealing with soldiers and prisoners who have to watch movies (Smoodin, 2004). See particularly chapter 5.
85. Quoted from Jay (1993), p. 481. Likewise, David Bordwell claims that for some people the communal experience may be valuable, but not for him: www.davidbordwell.net/blog/2012/02/28/pandoras-digital-box-from-films-to-files/ (last accessed 16 April 2015).
86. Quoted from Barker (2012), p. 191.
87. States (1985), p. 113.
88. Altenloh (2001 [1914]), p. 287. In the German original the observational mode is even more pregnant, since Altenloh writes that many viewers find doing "psychological studies" (*psychologische Studien*) on the other viewers far more entertaining than the films themselves (Altenhoh, 1914, p. 94).
89. Maltby/Stokes (2007), p. 2.
90. As Giovanna Colombetti notes: "Wine talk has several functions, and one of them is precisely to refine perceptual discrimination by making the taster attend to features of the wine that would otherwise go unnoticed, and that it would be difficult to bring into reflective attention. Whereas, arguably, a more sophisticated discriminatory capacity does not necessarily lead to a heightened enjoyment, there is little doubt that learning how to describe a wine brings about a change in one's experience and makes it more 'granular'" (Colombetti, 2009, pp. 21–2).
91. Mulligan/Scherer (2012), p. 355.
92. Mulligan/Scherer (2012), p. 355.
93. Colombetti (2009), p. 10.
94. See Feldman Barrett (2004).
95. See Colombetti (2009), p. 11.
96. It is no coincidence that many scholars interested in the body show an explicit interest in techniques that help to heighten bodily awareness. Think of philosopher Richard Shusterman who has embraced the Alexander technique or phenomenologist Evan Thompson's interest in mindfulness meditation. Evan Thompson even notes that there are similarities between the basic mental skills practiced in Buddhist mindfulness meditation and the phenomenological *epoché* (Thompson, 2007, p. 19).
97. Del Río (2008), p. 179.

98. Cubitt (2005), p. 238.
99. Sandvoss (2011), p. 230.
100. On convergence culture, see Jenkins (2006).
101. Gunning (2012), p. 49. See also Metz (1982), p. 53.
102. Thompson (2007), p. 19.
103. S. Langer (1953), p. viii.
104. A few scholars have already begun to incorporate my earlier studies on the audience effect in their research. See, for instance, Hughes (2016) and De Luca (2016).
105. Souriau (forthcoming [1951]).
106. Seldes (2001 [1924]), p. 324.

CHAPTER 2

Excavating the Audience Effect: Precursors in the History of Film Theory

> The familiar clatter of the film's motion stops, and tasteful lamps stream brightness over excited faces, ruthlessly exposing yet more damp eyes. Then, accompanied by music, everyone streams towards the exits, and what was once a whole disintegrates into atoms, for today. Perhaps tomorrow the individual will once again form a vital part of the whole [. . .].
>
> Resi Langer[1]

I. LOOKING FOR PRECURSORS

In this chapter I search for hidden traces the audience effect has left in the history of film theory. Moving backward in time, my discussion pays tribute to Roger Odin, Roland Barthes, Edgar Morin, André Bazin, and Walter Benjamin, five film theoretical precursors who had useful intuitions, but stopped short of systematizing the audience effect. Their ideas are thought-provoking and merit detailed discussions, but extracting their insights also involves pointing out important shortcomings.[2]

By focusing on these canonical scholars I also aim to demonstrate that the history of film theory is, in some ways, a story of missed encounters. No one has rigorously followed the traces of the audience effect, now largely covered by historical layers, left by these authors. Take, for instance, the strong influence of Barthes on film studies (when David Bordwell polemically rejected Grand Theory he specifically attacked the so-called SLAB theorists Saussure, Lacan, Althusser, and *Barthes*): It is a pity that his ideas on the "cinematic situation" and its focus on the viewer's bodily experience did not figure more prominently in 1970s apparatus or dispositive theory.[3] In light of the tremendous attention devoted to Benjamin's essay on the work of art in the age of its technological reproducibility, it is equally regrettable that his remarks on laughter and the "simultaneous collective experience" have not been used as a springboard for delving into investigations of the audience effect. What this chapter also tries to achieve, then, is to steer the history of film theory, somewhat belatedly, in the direction of the audience effect. And if the prestige of these canonical scholars lent additional authority and persuasive weight to the topic at stake, this would be a side effect I would not mind at all.

II. THE IMPORTANCE OF CONTEXT: ODIN AND THE SEMIO-PRAGMATICS OF FILM

Developed in the 1980s and 1990s, Roger Odin's semio-pragmatic approach to film spectatorship is a promising starting point for this chapter, since the *context* of viewing seems crucial to Odin. Trying to overcome purely text-centered semiotic approaches, he argues that a viewer's engagement with a film changes with context: "Meaning is not everything: affect and the interactions during production and reception must be analyzed."[4] What is more, Odin underscores explicitly that his approach attempts to understand "how audio-visual productions function in a *given social space*."[5] Now, taking into account context, social space, affect and interaction is precisely needed for an investigation of the audience effect. However, Odin rarely shows interest in actual audiences. Although he often comes close, he shies away from taking the final step toward looking at the influence of other viewers. I will therefore try to awaken what lies dormant in his account.

To begin with, Odin distinguishes between *mode* and *institution*. A mode is characterized by the type of *effects* it seeks to produce, either from the production or the reception side.[6] The fiction film, the home movie, or the documentary film can therefore be seen as modes that propel the viewer into a specific state of mind. For example, the director can try to put the *private* home-movie mode into play and thus attempt to make the spectator revisit his or her past; inversely, the spectator can watch a film in the private mode in order to relive a past experience. Or the director can use the *documentary* mode to inform the viewer about reality just as the spectator can watch a given film in the documentary mode to acquire information about reality.

The social aspect comes into play in Odin's model via the notion of *institution*. According to Odin, institutions are social structures that guide, constrain, and sanction the viewer's response to a film.[7] They function somewhat like instructions to produce meaning and affect – and hence meaning and affect change with the institution one is part of. Here is an example: the viewer's response to the documentary film changes depending on whether one watches it in a school or in a public library.[8] The institution of school (via the teacher) forces the documentary on the students, who may respond with disinterest, daydreaming, making noises, talking to their neighbors, or rebelling against the teacher. Chances are high that the situation is different in the public library, to which the viewer comes as someone wanting to see a documentary.

In light of his explicit interest in context and social space, it is astonishing that Odin looks at institutions merely with regard to how they change the viewer's pragmatic attitude toward the *film*, thus narrowing the breadth of context and social space. Very specific *spatial* cinematic contexts such as the multiplex cinema, the drive-in theater, or the IMAX hardly interest Odin. And apart from an important exception, to which I will return, concrete *social* viewing contexts do not play a significant role for him either. Hence, despite his alleged emphasis on context, his account relies predominantly on the dyadic relation between film and viewer.[9] What is more, Odin is not interested in the viewer as a flesh-and-blood person and experiencing individual: "For us, the *spectator* is a constructed entity, an actant; more precisely, he can be defined as the point of passage of a bundle of determinations."[10] Considering the spectator as an abstract "point of passage" may be a theoretically necessary move, but it eliminates almost everything that is crucial when we talk about the viewer's experience – among other things, the effect of co-present others.

His exclusion of the actual audience becomes even more pointed when he discusses the term "sanction." Doesn't the term "sanction" almost beg for being understood as a *social* concept? And, indeed, Odin quotes Alain Berrendonner, who defines the institution as a "normative power, subjecting the individuals to certain *mutual* practices of pain of sanctions."[11] Quietly glossing over Berrendonner's emphasis on mutuality, however, Odin again stops short of taking into account the social effects other viewers can have. He remains strictly within the bounds of the dyadic film–viewer relation – for instance, when he argues that displeasure would be the sanction pronounced on a fiction film that does not live up to the viewer's emotional expectations; or when he claims that a viewer, who had expected to see a fiction film and instead ends up watching a documentary, sanctions the latter by being bored. But why not admit that other viewers can also sanction us (just as we can sanction them)? Just think of a viewer who refuses to sing out loud in a sing-along like *The Sound of Music* (1965) or *The Rocky Horror Picture Show* (1975) and is called a spoilsport by others (see Chapter 4). Or think of a viewer talking during an intense scene in a psychological thriller who gets shushed by others (see Chapter 9).

Despite Odin's insistence on the importance of context and social space, his account may not look so promising for a description of the audience effect after all. In fact, Odin himself quotes critics like Christian Metz or Pierre Sorlin who have faulted the semio-pragmatic approach for being too abstract, saying nothing about how films are actually watched in concrete social spaces.[12]

A way out is offered by Frank Kessler, who presents us with a concrete example of how the change of social context and mode of presentation can alter the producers' intended meaning and viewing experience.[13] Take the case of a documentary shot in a small town or village: It can acquire the feel of a private home movie, because the viewers recognize not only the locations, but also the persons on the screen. Recognizing themselves is, after all, one of the reasons they want to see the film in the first place. Kessler illustrates his point with an illuminating quote from a daily newspaper that appeared in the German city of Trier on 14 July 1909. In this article the journalist reports how the audience cheered when images from Trier were shown: for instance, the exit of the cathedral or an exercise of the firemen, but especially when well-known faces at the cattle-market appeared. The children screamed the names of the people they recognized, while the grown-ups whispered the names of their acquaintances. The journalist concludes: "The cinema thus loses its character as a proper theater. The viewers feel more like at home and can unabashedly utter their critiques of acquaintances, friends and foes."[14] Had the same film been shown in Berlin, the reaction and experience of the Berliners would have been extremely different. And even if a lone Trierian had been among the Berlin viewers, she would have responded very differently: Among anonymous others it would not make sense for her to whisper (or even scream) the names of the persons she has recognized. Kessler's Historical Pragmatics thus points to a more concrete version of Odin's approach.

However – and here I would like to return to the aforementioned exception – Odin himself can be refreshingly specific when he discusses the institution of the home movie. For Odin the home movie follows a social ritual in the concrete but ordinary surroundings of the home: screen and projector have to be positioned; the room needs to be darkened; the members of the family have to be seated . . .[15] Since the home movie is first and foremost addressed at family members who have lived through the depicted events and are reminded by the film of a common experience, it summons a *private* mode of viewing: "Home movie images function less as representations than as *index* inviting the family to *return to a past already lived*."[16] It thus evokes a collective memory of the family members that often depends on an alternative way of film-watching: "Unlike fictional film screenings, interaction infuses the projection of a family film. Each family member reconstitutes a common past. A viewer might intervene to stop the screening (behavior prohibited while watching a fictional film) to develop the memory of an important scene."[17] Interaction and interruption aim at constituting an affective community – a *belonging-together* based on collective remembering that is often expressed *verbally*.[18] For Odin the viewers' affective inclination is celebratory, resulting in a "generally euphoric collective experience."[19] The members of the family feel united in front of the screen *as a family*.

No doubt, this is an accurate description of *some* home movie screenings and acknowledges their audience effects. However, Odin's assertions about the home movie seem overly general and fixed, thus standardizing and stabilizing what is in fact in constant flux and change. I would like to raise three objections to his account. First, the emotional experience can often involve *less-than-positive emotions*, changing from positive to negative emotions throughout various moments of the film. Think of nostalgia, a mixed emotion of positive and negative valence, which can easily be evoked by home movie images of a beautiful day spent together in a park or at a birthday party: the memory of the lovely event is suffused with an awareness that one watches the remnants of a bygone time forever lost.[20] Or think of the solemn emotion of sadness, elicited by a home movie showing a dearly loved pet now dead. To be sure, these emotions may still be experienced collectively and thus *unite* the family in nostalgia or sadness. But they are far from euphoric. Hence family films are not only about establishing a "euphoric consensus," as Odin implies, but possibly also about a nostalgic or sad collective.[21] In more recent texts Odin has nuanced his position. He now argues that in newer forms of the home movie, which came up with technological changes and transformations of family structures, the sanitized view of the family has made way for a more accurate representation of family life: with happy moments, but also instances of rivalry and conflict.[22] Although he does not spell it out, we may assume that the conflicts represented in the home movie can equally result in a variety of not-so-euphoric emotions of the family gathered in front of the screen.

My second critique refers to differences in how individual family members evaluate the images and how they emotionally experience them. Hence uniform responses are not always the case. Odin occasionally acknowledges these divergences when he distinguishes between collective and individual remembering as well as collective and individual emotions: the former are happy and shared, whereas the latter can be less euphoric and even outright negative.[23] While sometimes minimal and hardly worth mentioning, these divergences can at other moments constitute oppositional groups within a family, pitching parents against siblings or male members of the family against female ones.[24] Moreover, Odin talks about the widespread apprehension of seeing oneself on a screen in a family context: Who has not experienced the uneasiness of exposing oneself, more or less coercively, in front of one's family on the screen?[25] Here Odin hints at emotions like embarrassment and shame as well as the subtle ways emotions have to be worked on and regulated (a point that I will discuss in more detail in Chapters 5 and 8).

Third, the private home movie necessarily excludes persons who do not belong to the family or, at least, have not participated in the past events shown on the screen. Those who cannot *re*-member also cannot become a member. In fact, the further the person is from the family and the events depicted, the more distanced he or she may feel from those who belong to the family and/

or were part of the events. Watching a home movie with a family one does not belong to can create a strange feeling of exclusion. A sure sign for this phenomenological gap is the verbal bridge that members of the family try to build in order to reduce the distance: "Here you see how Tom learned to skate." or "Look, this is in the summer of 1988, when we took Kate to the zoo for the first time." If, instead, the family wallows in collective remembering and no one feels inclined to erect a bridge for the outsider, the phenomenological distance may be experienced as painfully big. In fact, the non-insider may tend to watch the film in a non-private mode, for instance with a documentary frame of mind.[26] The non-family member may look at the home movie as a document depicting a certain style of clothing or haircut; as an index of what a certain neighborhood looked like; as a trace of how the persons in the film behaved when they were younger . . .

But these different modes of viewing also necessitate different degrees of involvement and consequently different degrees of phenomenological distance to the film. This is a point underscored by Vivian Sobchack in her important phenomenology of the non-fictional film experience. Drawing on Jean-Pierre Meunier, Sobchack describes the viewer's relation to the home movie (or, quite fittingly in French, the *film-souvenir*) as one of evocation: through the film the viewers evoke absent persons or events they know; the film thus functions as a memory catalyst. As a consequence, Sobchack notes, "it is often boring to watch other people's home movies insofar as we are unfamiliar with their cinematic objects and have never experienced their evoked events. For us, the image fragments are neither catalytic nor mnemonic; we neither engage in the constitutive activity of re-membering nor feel the irrevocable loss of an 'original' experience that, through its cinematic evocation, creates in us the 'empty sympathy' that is nostalgic pleasure."[27]

Odin points out, however, that it is not always easy to switch into a documentary mode of viewing. Think of overly stereotypical motifs like ritual ceremonies (wedding, birth, family meals), daily scenes (mother with baby in her arms, the baby in the bathtub) or events on vacation (playing on the beach).[28] These stereotypes may limit the documentary value of the images and thus the viewer's epistemophilia. As a consequence, we can conclude that the person who does not belong to the inner circle of the family can experience the home movie in a state of *double distance*: the viewer might be distanced from a *film* considered as boring and from the *co-viewers* whose memories and familial bonding he or she does not share.

What makes Odin's discussion of the home movie valuable is that it takes co-present viewers into account and thus goes far beyond his own abstract semio-pragmatic model. However, it can only be a first step, since Odin has a tendency to sound (a) *too reductive* with regard to the variety of emotions home movies may evoke and the flux of affective experiences that come with it, (b) *too schematic* in how uniform he portrays the family response, and (c) *too one-sided* as he pays little attention to the experience of co-present non-family members. Moreover, the concrete spatial context of the screening, the specific viewing constellations, the place in which the viewing takes place – all this does not play a role either, which renders his discussion (d) *too abstract*.

III. NUMEROUS, POPULATED DARKNESS: BARTHES ON THE CINEMATIC SITUATION

At least for the last aspect, and possibly for some others, we can turn to a small essay by Roland Barthes, written in 1975. In "Leaving the Movie-theater" Barthes shows himself highly aware of the cinematic situation: the cinema, for Barthes, is "a dim, anonymous, indifferent cube where that festival of affects known as a film will be presented."[29] But it is not exactly what is shown on the screen that is of central importance to Barthes. Instead, going to the cinema implies a particularly strong awareness of the concrete place of the auditorium: "Whenever I hear the word *cinema*, I can't help thinking *hall*, rather than *film*."[30] What characterizes the experience of the cinema auditorium above all else is the darkness that encloses the viewer like a "veritable cinematographic cocoon" and which allows desire to grow and a diffuse eroticism to spread among the condensed anonymous individuals.[31] Here, in the dark, the viewers do not have to put on a show for others – the cultural appearance and the social play of seeing-and-being-seen typical of highbrow theaters does not exist. Instead, the viewers often relax: "how many members of the cinema audience slide down into their seats as if into a bed, coats or feet thrown over the row in front!"[32] Their bodies in such an idle posture, the viewers open up to the erotic solicitations of the cinema.

Critics like Dana Polan have expressed embarrassment about the later Barthes's focus on pleasure and erotics.[33] But I think it is precisely one of the merits of Barthes's text to draw attention to the erotics of the cinema and thus the bodily experience so strongly neglected in film theory at the time. The problem with Barthes's claim is rather that it sounds like a structural feature of the cinema, which is by no means the rule.

Let me therefore draw attention to a more important argument of his essay. Barthes asks himself: How can we avoid the hypnotizing spell of the movie, our strong immersion, the ideologically dubious fascination with the image? He first discusses the Brechtian aesthetics of epic theater and its alienation effect, and also considers a heightened ideological vigilance on the viewer's part. But then he goes on to suggest an alternative: rather than going to the cinema "armed by the discourse of counter-ideology," the viewer may just as well resist the ideological lure of the film by "letting oneself be fascinated *twice over*: by the image and by its surroundings – as if I had two bodies at the same time: a narcissistic body which gazes, lost, into the engulfing mirror, and a perverse body, ready to fetishize not the image but precisely what exceeds it: the texture of the sound, the theater itself, the darkness, the obscure mass of other bodies, the rays of light, the entrance, the exit: in short, in order to distance myself [. . .] I complicate a 'relation' by a 'situation.'"[34]

This is a remarkable suggestion at a time when the annihilation of pleasure was a widespread goal in film theory ("Leaving the Movie-theater" appeared three years after Peter Wollen's "Godard and Counter-Cinema" and in the same year as Laura Mulvey's "Visual Pleasure and Narrative Cinema" and Jean-Louis Baudry's "The Apparatus"). Ignoring the psychoanalytic jargon of the 1970s, we can conclude that Barthes's ideal viewers should be *simultaneously* aware of the film *and* the theatrical surroundings. Splitting attention, they should not only relate to the film, but also add an awareness of the *situation* in order to distance themselves from the ideological entanglement of the movie: "I must be in the story [. . .], but I must also be *elsewhere* [. . .]."[35] Taking into account the cinematic situation is not just a phenomenological given that the viewer, to a certain degree, can never avoid (as Vivian Sobchack, for instance, would argue in the 1990s).[36] Being *fascinated* by the cinematic situation becomes an alternative way of watching a film in the cinema, acquiring an almost ethical or political function.[37] Fascinated twice, the Barthesian viewer thus could have the cake and eat it: being lost in the film and being distanced from it at the same time. What counts for Barthes is the right balance between the two.

But where does this leave us in terms of the audience effect? For Barthes the audience merely consists of an "obscure mass of other bodies," an illuminated "head of hair, a face," a "human condensation." The situation of the cinema thus equals social anonymity. Anne Friedberg has pointed out that for Barthes the cinema is the endpoint of an urban itinerary, the final destination of a *flâneur*.[38] After having wandered through the city alone, the Barthesian *flâneur* ends up in the anonymous and indifferent dark cube of the movie-theater, alone, without accompaniment. But here, again, Barthes's text unnecessarily generalizes what is only one of many social constellations of the cinema. Certainly people visit the movies in company; and certainly neighborhood theaters, in which the viewer might know various other viewers, are an important factor in the history of moviegoing.

Of course, Barthes is highly aware that he does *not* watch a film alone in the "anonymous, populated, numerous" darkness of the movie-theater.[39] What he appreciates about the cinema's social anonymity becomes particularly obvious when he compares it to "the boredom, the frustration of so-called private showings!" and especially the familial social situation in front of the television screen: "here darkness is erased, anonymity repressed; space is familiar, articulated (by furniture, known objects), tamed."[40] Even though he does not spell out the various effects the co-presence of well-known others in private screenings can have, we sense that they must be detrimental not only to his eroticization, but also to other experiences. The other well-known individuals at home are, in a manner of speaking, *too close* to him. Possibly they absorb too much attention and thus destroy the balance of the viewer's devotion to the screen and the focus on the cinematic situation.

This may bring us back to the political dimension inherent in Barthes's suggestion to follow the film with "two bodies," one fascinated by the film, one fascinated by the cinematic situation. Presuming that immersion ("being lost in the story") is a matter of *degree*, Barthes's split-attention proposal may indeed be a viable suggestion for a "viewing position" less prone to ideological manipulation. However, there are two things Barthes overlooks. First, since he describes the cinematic dispositive *as such* without an eye on the films and the viewer responses they might elicit, he does not take into account that some films and genres do not need a viewer deliberately splitting his or her attention: sometimes the cinematic situation itself *demands* attention or even *forces* itself upon the viewer. Take the comedy and the main response it elicits: "[L]aughter allows the audience to become aware of itself," André Bazin once said, a point I will return to in this and later chapters. Second, Barthes lumps together the theater, the darkness, the obscure mass of other bodies, the entrance, the exit. *Each* of these elements may help to partially distract him from the hypnotic spell of the film. His essay therefore leaves out what makes the co-viewers special and particularly important.

IV. ISOLATED AND IN A GROUP: MORIN ON COLLECTIVE PARTICIPATION

In contrast, co-viewers *do* play a role in Edgar Morin's *The Cinema, or the Imaginary Man* from 1956, a book that might have had a strong influence on Barthes but is not footnoted in "Leaving the Movie-theater." Like Barthes, but almost two decades before him, Morin describes a viewing experience both intensely immersive and anchored in the here and now of the movie-theater. But unlike Barthes, Morin is well aware that this does not require a special effort on the viewer's part: it is simply a phenomenological *fact* that we never forget our place in the cinema. In the preface to a 1978 edition of his book, Morin underscores this point: "you, us, me, while intensely bewitched, possessed, eroticized, excited, terrified, loving, suffering, playing, hating – we do not stop knowing that we are in a seat contemplating an imaginary spectacle: *we experience the cinema in a state of double consciousness.*"[41]

Morin's remark can be read as a rebuttal of the politically susceptible but phenomenologically insensitive apparatus/dispositive theorists of the time. The history of film theory is full of analogies that imply a viewer fully lost in the film, and the 1970s were one of the heydays. When theorists like Barthes, Christian Metz, or Raymond Bellour compared the viewing experience to dreams, hallucinations, or hypnoses, they implicitly presupposed that the movie-theater and its audience do not enter our field of consciousness. As we have seen, this is the reason why Barthes suggests the viewer has to *actively* become aware of the cinematic situation. While *increasing* one's awareness is both possible and sometimes politically called for, this does not mean that we otherwise lose track of the cinematic situation. Morin's account is phenomenologically more accurate and his reference to the viewer's *double consciousness* is more precise and less metaphorical than Barthes's talk of the viewer's *two bodies*: "What we must precisely examine is the astonishing phenomenon *where the illusion of reality is inseparable from the awareness that it is really an illusion*, without, however, this awareness killing the feeling of reality."[42]

More than in Barthes's case, the awareness of the theater also entails the viewer's awareness of the presence of others: "So there he is, isolated, but at the heart of a human environment, of a great gelatin of common soul, of a collective participation, which accordingly amplifies his individual participation. To be isolated and in a group at the same time: two contradictory and complementary conditions [. . .]."[43] This passage clearly reveals Morin's sensitivity to the audience effect. The viewers may be isolated in one sense, but they are simultaneously enmeshed in a *common* soul (a little later he writes that the viewer is "enveloped in the double placenta of an anonymous community and obscurity").[44] His use of strange organic metaphors like "gelatin" and "placenta" (how can one be *enveloped* by a placenta? did he mean *uterus*?) may have inspired Barthes's notion of the "cinematographic cocoon." But while Barthes uses the metaphor predominantly to refer to the darkness in the theater, Morin sees the viewer enwrapped by both darkness *and* an anonymous community.

Morin is also phenomenologically more to the point than Barthes when he notices that the individual's participation *changes* in the presence of others; or, rather, the presence of anonymous others *increases* the participation of the individual. What in Barthes remains implicit in his discussion of private screenings is particularly explicit in Morin's coinage "collective participation." However, Morin remains rather one-sided here: the co-presence of others neither necessarily leads to a *collective* participation, nor does it always entail *amplification*. Other viewers can also spark social inhibition. Just imagine a viewer watching Sacha Baron-Cohen's *Borat* (2006) with a group of violent-looking, dyed-in-the-wool patriots from the "US and A" or Kazakhstan. While he might have otherwise found *Borat* a hilarious exposure of nationalistic pride, sitting next to the group of no-nonsense Americans or Kazakhs will most likely *attenuate* his amusement and laughter. What is more, the viewer's tight spot might elicit what in Chapter 5 I will call an *antagonistic I–you mode of social distance*: due to his clandestine judgment that this is a hilarious film, he feels distanced from the others who seem deeply annoyed. There are numerous cases when the audience is not a great gelatin of *common* soul.

Astonishingly, writing in 1956 and thus nineteen years prior to Barthes, Morin makes very similar remarks about television: "Television in the home does not get the benefit of this enormous resonance chamber [of the movie-theater]; it presents itself in the light, among practical objects, to individuals whose number has difficulty making up a group (that is why in the United States people invite each other to TV parties)."[45] Although Barthes lists practically an identical inventory, this passage marks an occasion when his account is more perceptive than Morin's. Since the movie-theater is merely a "resonance chamber" for Morin in which the responses of a group amplify the individual's reaction, people in front of the television feel the need to invite co-viewers in order to benefit from the collective participation.

What Morin overlooks is the inhibiting, diverting, annoying, embarrassing, or disgusting air that may arrive with co-present viewers, particularly when they know each other well. As we have seen, Barthes is quite aware of these potentially damaging effects when it comes to television. However, what transpires from both accounts is the problematic presupposition that the audience consists of an *anonymous* human environment, when in fact we often go to the movies with well-known others. What remains unclear in Morin's short passages is what *causes* the individual viewer's awareness of collectivity. Nor is Morin entirely consistent: He seems to contradict himself just a page later when he writes that the spectator in the cinema is "deep in his cell, a monad closed off to everything except the screen . . ."[46]

V. FILM, THEATER, TELEVISION: BAZIN'S COMPARATIVE AUDIENCE PHENOMENOLOGY

What significance did the collective cinema experience have for André Bazin, the French theorist who was, after all, the one who raised the famous question *What Is Cinema?*[47] To be sure, Bazin is hardly known as a prime theorist of the (individual) viewer and even less so as a theorist of the (collective) audience. Nevertheless, we find numerous references to the cinema experience in the roughly 2,600 articles he wrote in his short but productive life.[48] Among our five theorists, Bazin may be the one most strongly opposed to the idea of an audience effect – at least at first sight. But at various points he undercuts his own position, almost against his own will, especially when comparing the cinema to television. This makes Bazin's writings valuable for our goals, as he allows us glimpses into the difficulties in coming to terms with the audience effect.[49]

An inevitable starting point must be Bazin's famous essay "Theater and Cinema," in which he compares theater audiences with cinema spectators. Here Bazin largely follows arguments from an article that appeared in 1934 in the journal *Esprit*, written by an unknown author Bazin misspells as "Rosenkrantz," that he found "profoundly original for its period."[50] Due to their actual presence on the stage – and hence their objective reality in the theater – the actors are "objects of mental opposition" that call for an intellectual process of abstraction: the viewer's active willingness to turn the physically present actor into characters of an imaginary world. The cinema spectator, on the other hand, is absorbed in a rather primitive psychological identification with the characters of the film, thereby losing him- or herself in the filmic world, leading to a "depersonalization."[51] Thus the fact that the characters of the film are separated by the screen and belong to a different ontological order makes them more readily adaptable as fictional beings (which connects the film to the novel, according to Bazin). While the theater demands an active individual consciousness, the cinema merely calls for a passive accordance. Bazin's account thus presumes a largely inactive viewer, which also becomes apparent when he describes the darkness of the cinema as "the night of our waking dream."[52]

What consequences do the differences between the two art forms have for the collective cinema experience? Precisely because the passive cinema spectators are lost in the same identification process with the protagonists, differences in emotional experience are eliminated: "the result of which is to turn the audience into a 'mass' and to render emotion uniform."[53] Quoting again from Rosenkranz, Bazin notes: "Just as in algebra if two numbers equal a third, then they are equal to one another, so here we can say, if two individuals identify themselves with a third, they identify themselves with one another."[54] But even though the cinema audience becomes a mass with identical emotions, "the cinema cannot offer the spectator the community feeling of theater."[55] For Bazin, the cinema spectator is as lonely *psychologically* as the reader of the novel is *physically*.[56] As quoted in the introduction, Bazin's viewer is "[a]lone, hidden in a dark room."[57]

In these passages it sounds negligible as to whether the viewer watches a film alone or in a crowded cinema. Comparable to reading a novel, the pleasure of the film is one of "self-satisfaction."[58] What may sound like a contradiction is perfectly compatible for Bazin: "Crowd and solitude are not antinomies: the audience in a movie house is made up of solitary individuals. Crowd should be taken here to mean the opposite of an organic community freely assembled."[59] In comparison to the emphatic community feeling of the theater, the cinema only knows equalizing mass emotions that psychologically isolate the viewer. This immediately raises the question of what difference Bazin makes between "community feelings" and "mass emotions." Bazin seems to take for granted that the cinema spectators all feel the same, but everyone for him- or herself and without being aware of the emotions of others. But isn't it also possible that mass emotions lead to community feelings?

Imagine a captivated auditorium following the suspense-laden finale of Hitchcock's *Strangers on a Train* (1951), to pick a film from the year in which Bazin's essay appeared and from a director whose self-declared goal it was to elicit mass emotions: Is it not plausible that at least some viewers derive a pleasurable *individual* thrill from their immersion in the film, but at the same time draw an additional pleasure from the fact that *all of them* experience this thrill simultaneously and collectively (without necessarily having to reflect on this additional pleasure)? Rosenkranz's formula "if two individuals identify themselves with a third, they identify themselves with one another" does not rule out that the viewers know about each other and even share their emotions (for more on the concept of sharing an emotion, see Chapter 6). There is no doubt that Rosenkranz was critical of mass emotions and the collective mentality of the cinema audience, which shouldn't surprise us considering that he was a German-speaking author writing for a French magazine in 1934. But in his essay we do not find Bazin's reductive idea that viewers are isolated in their mass emotions.

In contrast, the community feeling of the theater, in Bazin's account, is first and foremost connected to the viewers' heightened awareness of being part of an audience and their place in the auditorium. This heightened awareness results partly, as mentioned, from the distance to the imaginary world caused by the presence of the actor onstage and partly from the more illuminated auditorium.[60] If we follow his biographer Dudley Andrew, Bazin often went to the theater, rarely because he was interested in a particular stage performance, but mostly because he liked its social aspect.[61] In the theater, Bazin apparently experienced the community feeling he missed in the alleged lonely crowd of the cinema. Again, Bazin diverts strongly here from Rosenkranz, who does not mention the community feeling of the theater at all. Quite the contrary: Rosenkranz refers to a phenomenological isolation of the theatergoer. Although Bazin quotes an important passage from Rosenkranz almost verbatim (without referencing him, by the way), he leaves out precisely the part on the isolating effect of the theater: "Even when it appeals to the lowest instincts, the theater up to a certain point stands in the way of the creation of a mass mentality. It stands in the way of any collective representation in the psychological sense, since theater calls for an active individual consciousness while the film requires only a passive adhesion."[62]

Here we see the boon and bane of Bazin's comparisons: Contrasting the audience experience of both art forms can be illuminating, but at the same time there is a danger of overexposure. (What do we do, for instance, with the broad apodictic claim, "The cinema calms the spectator, the theater excites him"?)[63]

It may be correct that *grosso modo* we are more aware of other viewers in the theater. But this does not imply that, in the cinema, we cannot experience what Bazin calls "community feelings." His strategy to play off the collectivity of the theater against the individuality and homogeneity of the cinema does not even work for Bazin himself, as many remarks in other essays testify in which he shows himself very sensitive to the audience effect.

Bazin was a regular attendant of the film festivals in Cannes and Venice, where he sat next to other critics and directors. For sure their co-presence did not slip his attention: "I was sitting next to Jean Cocteau at the last Festival de Cannes, when, for the first time, he saw a film screened in CinemaScope. The film in question was *Beneath the 12-Mile Reef* (1953). It was sheer pleasure to sense his enthusiasm."[64] In an early essay from 1944, published under the title "To Create a Public," Bazin also and quite outspokenly recognized what influence the flesh-and-blood presence of filmmakers can have on an audience: The audience rediscovers something of the human presence of the actors in the theater.[65] In 1944 he had invited the filmmakers Jean Grémillon and Louis Daquin to present their films to a crowded auditorium. As a result of the "human ambiance" they exuded, Bazin experienced "a community of spectators, a homogeneous public that felt itself at one with the work."[66] Naturally and without embarrassment, the viewers had used a form of collective expression known from the theater: applause. In this audience applause Bazin quite likely saw a breach of passivity, a moment of audience self-awareness, a collective emotional response and act of appreciation.

Bazin's awareness of the co-presence of other viewers and the potential "community feeling" in the cinema is even more explicit in an enthusiastic article about Charlie Chaplin's *Limelight* (1952): "I write on the basis of the remarkable gathering at Biarritz at which the whole French cinema world wept at the sight of the death of [. . .] Calvero, alias Chaplin. When I say wept, I am not exaggerating. As the lights went up, they revealed four hundred directors, screenwriters, and critics choked with emotion, their eyes red as tomatoes."[67] Trying to defend Bazin's "Theater and Cinema" position, one could claim that these viewers have wept for themselves without becoming aware of each other (they had a mass emotion, in Bazin's terms). But Bazin himself admits that the film was only one part of a larger, complex experience. The presence of Chaplin in the audience, but also the highly selective choice of directors, screenwriters, and critics, directed attention toward the auditorium: "The audience was at once the most alert and the most receptive ever assembled. [. . .] Half of the performance we attended was in the hall."[68] Here we hear no word on isolation and being lost in identification with the hero. Instead, Bazin seems to have felt that he was weeping *collectively* with the other viewers about the death of the protagonist; this is at least how I interpret his emphatic use of the first-person plural: "an extraordinary drama was enacted, with three characters: the audience, the film, and Chaplin. [. . .] Thus we were in Chaplin's presence at the spectacle of his death. And we wept with all the more emotion because we knew he was present and alive. Our tears were multiplied by the gratitude we felt, by the joy that we anticipated when the lights went up of seeing once more his silvery hair, his smile touched with emotion, his blue eyes."[69]

These examples might be exceptional cases. However, in Bazin's writings we also find more ordinary traces of the audience effect, especially when he deals with laughter, which, as we have seen above, allows the audience to become aware of itself.[70] Let us look at a passage from his essay "Charlie Chaplin" (1948), in which he describes vividly how the audience responds to a scene from *The Adventurer* (1917): "You laugh and your neighbor laughs too. At first it is all the same laughter. But I have 'listened in' to this gag twenty times in different theaters. When the audience, or at least part of it, was made up of intellectuals, students for example, there was a second wave of laughter of a different kind. At that moment the hall was no longer filled with the original laughter but with a series of echoes, a second wave of laughter, reflected off the minds of the spectators as if from the invisible walls of an abyss."[71] As we will see below, Walter Benjamin had already underlined the importance of laughter about Chaplin in his writings from the 1930s. With Bazin's discussion of the 1940s and '50s, laughter receives yet another facet. Bazin, for one, makes clear that there are various forms of laughter in the cinema (see Chapter 7). As his reference to diverse levels of education shows, Chaplin's comedies are suited for different kinds of humor: the more basic, unifying form of laughter based on shared humor, and the more sophisticated laughter that separates the audience into those who have not understood the gag and remain silent and those who have got it and send out a second round of laughter as an echo of the first.

Admittedly, Bazin's phrase "You laugh and your neighbor laughs too" might also insinuate that each viewer laughs for him- or herself and no one laughs together. It would fit his more general assumption about the individualizing effect of the cinema. But at the same time it would contradict his description of collective *weeping* about the death of Chaplin's character in *Limelight*. Even more importantly, it would contrast strongly with his thesis that "laughter allows the audience to become aware of itself" (even if he came up with this point only three years after the Chaplin article). Let us presume, then, that Bazin appreciated laughter, just like applause, as a collective response to the film, which makes the audience aware of itself and which introduces an aesthetic distance between auditorium and film. Instead of a strong intertwinement with the filmic world and its characters, there is a momentary awareness of a "we": not a "private zone of consciousness," as he had put it in the "Theater and Cinema" essay, but a collective awareness – a collective awareness which, to be sure, can easily splinter in the next instance, as Bazin's description about the second wave of laughter indicates.[72]

In our search for Bazinian remarks on the audience effect we finally have to turn to his texts on television, a medium which he began writing about in fall 1952. Bazin was well aware that the new medium, which so easily enters the private sphere, is likewise watched in company: "Due to its technological and economic basis, television is fundamentally condemned to being watched by families. The size of the image limits optimal viewing to the normal number of family members, that is, from two to five or six spectators."[73] However, in contrast to Barthes, for whom the television viewer was doomed to the family constellation, Bazin also knew solitary encounters with the small screen. In fact, he admitted that when watched alone the intimacy of the living room allows for emotional experiences and expressions that one might not have in the cinema. Bazin draws attention to this fact in an appositely titled article "Some Films Are Better on the Small Screen than the Large": "Some feelings do not resonate well with the *vague publicity of the darkened theater*, nor with the superhuman dimensions of the movie screen."[74] One of those emotional expressions is weeping. Bazin describes how he was watching Jean Renoir's Hans Christian Andersen adaptation *La Petite Marchande d'allumettes* (1927) one night on television, after three or four times in the cinema. When the heroine died, he had to weep.[75] Although he does not say so explicitly, we might speculate that Bazin finds his weeping noteworthy this time because he had *not* wept when seeing the film in the cinema. Even though this is not necessarily always the case – see the collective tears at the *Limelight* premiere – tears can imply embarrassment and even shame in front of other viewers (see Chapter 8). In front of the television screen Bazin could shed tears because he followed the movie in the intimate surroundings of his living room.

Elsewhere Bazin draws another interesting comparison between television viewers and cinema audiences. In his 1954 essay "A Contribution to an *Erotologie* of Television" he ironically discusses the charm and the erotic effects of television *speakerines* (which puts him in opposition to Barthes who, as we have seen, lamented the *lack* of erotics when it comes to television). In a footnote he even describes the extreme desire of a British viewer who found it necessary to send death threats to a female presenter should she not retire from television: "With the young woman's physique alone being enough to arouse the desire of the consumer in question, we can easily imagine that the latter might reach an intolerable state of exacerbation. [...] this specific reaction to live television is not conceivable in cinema," Bazin comments.[76] But why should this state of erotic arousal not be imaginable in the cinema?

Here it gets interesting: "Perhaps we must deduce from this that cinema is in fact much more social than we normally admit or, better, that its individualism is dialectically linked to its mass character. In the darkened cinema, I have the feeling that the starlet incarnates my dreams because she incarnates the identical dreams of the several hundred people who surround me. But with the *speakerine*, who talks to me every day and looks me in the eyes, even if I know that her image is repeated on hundreds of thousands of little screens resembling the facets of an enormous fly's eye, I am conscious that it is I who am looking at her."[77] Here we can clearly sense how Bazin begins to revise his earlier position. Against the background of his television experience he acknowledges the social aspect of the cinema, something he entirely underestimated when comparing the cinema with the theater. Alone at home in front of the television it is a singular, individual 'I' that looks at the TV presenter, even though this 'I' knows that hundreds of thousands of other viewers may also look at her simultaneously. In the cinema, on the other hand, this 'I' may be hidden in the dark and feel more individualized than in the more strongly illuminated theater. But the cinema spectator nevertheless has the impression that the starlet is the incarnation of his dream *and* the dreams of all the other co-present viewers as well. The individualism of the cinema seems to be compatible with a collective experience after all.

At the end, however, Bazin may not have trusted his new position. In an interview that appeared three weeks after his death, he returned to his older view. In comparison to television the cinema is anything but intimate, Bazin says, "since it addresses a group of spectators, even if this group remains individualized and doesn't create a community as happens in the theater."[78] He had come full circle to his "Theater and Cinema" essay.

VI. VIEWERS CONTROLLING ONE ANOTHER: BENJAMIN ON COLLECTIVE EXPERIENCE

In contrast to Bazin, Walter Benjamin was an outspoken proponent of the cinema's "simultaneous collective experience," as he called it. In fact, his famous essay on the work of art in the age of its technological reproducibility belongs to the few places in canonical film theory where it assumes a significant role: precisely because it is collective, the viewer's film experience enables public reactions whose very publicness turns out to be politically significant for Benjamin. In the following paragraphs I aim less at adding to the vast field of Benjamin exegesis than to reading some of his suggestive (albeit sometimes cryptic) comments in light of the audience effect.[79]

In section XII of the essay Benjamin maintains that the technological reproducibility of the artwork changes the relation between the masses and art. Confronted with a traditional art form like painting, the response of the audience (*Publikum*) is *split* between critique and enjoyment, and thus remains retrograde. With regard to a new form of art like film, the response becomes progressive, because the critical attitude, on the one hand, and the pleasure of watching and experiencing emotionally, on the other hand, *coincide*. This is particularly true for Chaplin comedies and slapstick films. But why is watching *The Circus* (1928) progressive, and the reaction to paintings by Picasso retrograde? In order to explain this point, I need to go into somewhat greater detail. For the moment let me hasten to say that for Benjamin it is key that film viewing is a *simultaneous collective* experience, whereas looking at a painting often implies an *individual* encounter. And even in those cases when large amounts of beholders look at paintings in galleries and salons, they do not do so simultaneously and collectively. Benjamin points out that, unlike the cinema, galleries and salons do not allow the masses to *organize* and *control* themselves in their response.[80] Although he remains vague at this point, we might surmise that this lack of organization and mutual control derives from structural differences between the two dispositives: in the cinema a co-present group of people watches the uninterrupted unfolding of a 90-minute film collectively, whereas in the gallery and salon everyone decides individually how long to remain in front of the painting. Consequently there can be a lack of *synchronization* of responses, and as a result the beholders cannot mutually *control* their reactions.

But why do critique and pleasure coincide at the movies? Benjamin answers: "The decisive reason is that nowhere more than in the cinema are the reactions of individuals, which add up to the massive reaction of the audience, from the onset determined by their imminent concentration and aggregation. By becoming public they control one another."[81] Since this passage is just as convoluted as it is complex, I will try to disentangle it step by step. First of all, it is important that the reactions of the individuals can, in sum, create a *massive* audience reaction. Of course, this cannot be true for each and every response: it is hard to fathom how collective feelings of beauty or boredom should add up to a *massive* reaction. But the argument certainly goes for *expressive* responses like screaming or laughter. What is more, from the very beginning these individual reactions are *shaped* by the fact that they will agglomerate and become part of an overarching response of the audience as a whole. However consciously, the viewers anticipate the fact that others will presumably respond in a similarly expressive way. Somehow knowing that their reactions will add up to a mass response, the spectators, probably rather intuitively, calibrate their reactions to this expected collective response. Remaining with Benjamin's example of Chaplin: precisely because viewers *expect* that others will also respond with laughter they express their amusement by laughing out loud. Would they watch the film alone (as under today's solitary viewing conditions), they would not anticipate a collective response and therefore refrain from attuning their response to this immediate concentration and agglomeration. They may be highly amused by and smile about Chaplin, but ultimately they would remain mostly silent. This is at least what Benjamin seems to claim, and it sounds

Figure 2.1: Collective laughter about Chaplin in Louis Malle's *Au revoir les enfants*.

convincing for those people for whom laughing *alone* is an awkward thing to do (for a nice filmic representation of laughter about Chaplin, see Louis Malle's *Au revoir les enfants* [1987]).

Hence in this passage Benjamin shows himself astutely aware of the audience effect. This becomes all the more evident when we take into account a sentence Miriam Hansen refers to in which Benjamin claims: "words, gestures, events perceived by the masses are different from those perceived by individuals."[82] As part of a group of people, individuals register things differently than when they are alone.

But let us return to the dense passage from section XII of the artwork essay, because Benjamin also touches upon political implications of the audience effect when he writes: "By becoming public [the individual reactions] control one another."[83] What does he mean to say here? I doubt that he refers to a control of affects in the sense of a *suppression* of emotional reactions. For one, the German verb "kundgeben" implies "to make something known" or, even more to the point, "to make something public" (the noun "Kundgebung" is a synonym for demonstration or rally). Hence Benjamin claims that if audience responses become public in the movie-theater, others can control them and judge them as misguided or even politically problematic: viewers reveal and make publicly available what they find funny and deem worthy of laughter.[84] The reactions of the others, once they are out there, are in turn themselves subject to scrutiny. We could even argue that there may be instances when people become critical of their *own* responses precisely because of their collective character: for instance, viewers could despise the fact that they have laughed about something *with* the others, something they shouldn't have laughed about.

The word "control," in academic discourse today often used in conjunction with the "disciplinary societies" (Foucault) or the "societies of control" (Deleuze) and thus connoted negatively, has a much more positive ring in Benjamin's text.[85] It is at this point that we can understand why Benjamin considered the cinema more progressive than a traditional art form like painting. In the movie-theater the viewer can enjoy the film and *at the same time* remain critical, because he or she monitors the potentially questionable or politically dangerous responses of other viewers (and also his or her own reaction).[86] For Benjamin this is not possible in front of a painting, since the reception of the painting does not take place collectively and simultaneously, but most often in an individualized and non-synchronized fashion (even if there can certainly be moments of overlapping attention, a point I will touch upon in Chapter 10).

But how do these audience reactions become public in the first place? What Benjamin does not mention explicitly is the fact that his idea of publicly available (and thus controllable) responses depends on *expressive reactions* and *conspicuous behavior*. After all, the darkness, unidirectional seating position, backrest, etc. make it difficult to judge the responses of other viewers. Even in Benjamin's time, if a viewer was deeply moved or embarrassed by a film, these emotions were not readily accessible to others – unless, of course, Benjamin would have thought of an audience that communicated during the film and commented verbally on what happened on the screen. In other words, he may have modeled his preferred mode of reception not on the cinema of his own time, but on the early cinema of the turn from the nineteenth to the twentieth century. This is at least what Miriam Hansen suggests: "the difference from traditional art that Benjamin ascribes to cinema's relations of *reception* is more characteristic of early cinema than of the classical paradigm that became hegemonic after World War I."[87] As Hansen points out: "the artwork essay's valorization of distraction (as opposed to the contemplative reception of traditional works of art) presupposes a type of cinema experience still patterned on the variety format, that is, the programming of shorter films (interspersed with or framed by live performances) on the principle of maximum stylistic or thematic diversity." But I don't think this is necessarily the case.

To me, the answer is simpler. What Benjamin had in mind is first and foremost an audience that laughs and by laughing makes its response publicly controllable. Benjamin's many references to Charlie Chaplin and slapstick films (*Groteskfilme*) in the artwork essay and elsewhere strongly support a reading along these lines. For instance, we can glean the significance Benjamin ascribes to laughter from his 1929 essay "Chaplin in Retrospect." Benjamin ends this essay with a remarkable quote: "In his films, Chaplin appeals both to the most international and the most revolutionary emotion of the masses:

their laughter. 'Admittedly,' [Philippe] Soupault says, 'Chaplin merely makes people laugh. But aside from the fact that this is the hardest thing to do, it is socially also the most important.'"[88] The weight of laughter can also be felt in the artwork essay, albeit more implicitly. While the Soviet montage cinema may be the other important filmic reference point in this essay, the films of Eisenstein or Vertov are conspicuously absent in Benjamin's discussion of the collective experience in section XII. Here references to Chaplin and slapstick films abound. Above I have mentioned the passage in which Benjamin opposes the progressive response to Chaplin with the retrograde reaction to Picasso. At the end of section XII he repeats this opposition by likening the progressive response to slapstick films with the regressive response to Surrealism.[89]

Moreover, in a footnote Benjamin claims: "Before the rise of the movie the Dadaists' performances tried to create an audience reaction [*eine Bewegung ins Publikum zu bringen*] which Chaplin later evoked in a more natural way."[90] Unfortunately, the English translation glosses over a crucial element: Benjamin does not refer to just any kind of audience reaction, but to one that implies movement (*Bewegung*). Undoubtedly, this movement comes from laughter shaking and stirring the audience.[91] Bodies put into motion through amused laughter, so memorably captured at the end of King Vidor's *The Crowd* (1928), make *visibly* manifest that the viewers find a scene funny. Hence the audience response can not only be *heard* but also *seen* via laughter. In an unpublished fragment entitled "Hitler's Diminished Masculinity" from 1934, written shortly before the artwork essay, Benjamin had already gestured in a similar direction. In this short fragment he contrasts the masses *moved* to laughter by a Chaplin comedy with the rigid masses of Nazi Germany: "Chaplin – the ploughshare that cuts through the masses; laughter loosens up the mass/the ground of the Third Reich is stamped down hard and firm, and no more grass grows there."[92] While Hitler's dictatorship (and presumably the huge rallies that became a hallmark of it) leads to dry, barren, and suppressed uniformity, laughing about a Chaplin comedy creates a fertile ground by temporarily shaking the viewers' rigid postures.[93]

For Benjamin, laughing about – and thus responding in a vocal and motor fashion to – a slapstick film or a contemporaneous Chaplin comedy like *City Lights* (1931) and *Modern Times* (1936) implies a progressive reaction. Sitting in the movie-theater gives the audience not only a way to synchronize their reception, but also to control one another. The public space created through laughter allows for a positive kind of surveillance, since inappropriate or even ethically questionable laughter may be exposed and thus can become publicly available knowledge. Alluding to a famous proverb, we might summarize Benjamin's position as both "Tell me *what* you laugh *about* and I'll tell you who you are" and "Tell me *who* you laugh *with* and I'll tell you who you are." Some films – think of *Borat* (2006), *Brüno* (2009) and other films by Sacha

Baron Cohen – use the public character of laughter in the cinema precisely for such revelatory purposes.

VII. EXPANDING THE EXCAVATION: FAURE, FREEBURG, FELDMANN

Have the preceding discussions covered all film theoretical precursors of the audience effect? Certainly not. The five scholars are merely the best-known ones. Moving further back in time, we can find scattered traces also in early film theory. In 1920 the French art historian Élie Faure, for instance, called the cinema a "collective spectacle" and compared watching a film to a ritual that would take over the place of the religious dance, the philosophical tragedy, the mystery play, and "all the great dead things around which the multitude once assembled in order to commune together."[94] Enthusiastically, Faure discovered an important social function: the cinema of the future would become "the spiritual ornament sought for in this period – the play that this new society will find most useful in developing in the crowd the sense of confidence, of harmony, of cohesion."[95]

Even more pertinent are some of the arguments American scholar Victor Oscar Freeburg put forth in his book *The Art of Photoplay Making* (1918). In a chapter entitled "The Psychology of the Cinema Audience" he claims perceptively: "It must never be forgotten that the theater audience is a crowd. A crowd is a compact mass of people held together by *a single purpose* during any period of time whether long or short. The various units are in close contact with each other, the crowd existing as such only while this *close contact* is maintained. In the theater a particular crowd exists as such only during the time of the performance and can never exist again once it has been broken up after the particular performance for which it came together."[96] Although Freeburg uses the notion of the "crowd" somewhat pejoratively, the passage raises important points: Freeburg not only underscores the weight of the audience's *co-presence* (its close contact), but also refers to what in the following chapter I will call *we-intention* (the single purpose).

He even points to what psychologists dub *emotional contagion*, a phenomenon I will discuss in Chapter 6: "The close contact is spiritual as well as physical. You not only touch elbows with your neighbor and live in his atmosphere but you are infected by his emotions and share his desires, purposes, reactions."[97] Moreover, Freeburg spells out explicitly one of the central tenets of the audience effect: "The individual in the crowd is *not the same* as when alone. He is *subconsciously* influenced by his companions or neighbors until his emotions are *heightened* and his desire or ability to think is lowered. He laughs more easily and at less comic things in a crowd than when he is alone.

In the crowd he is more responsive, more demonstrative, more kind, more cruel, more sentimental, more religious, more patriotic, more unreasoning, more gullible than when alone."[98] Here Freeburg, like Morin, clearly underestimates the attenuating effects of social *inhibition* (and thus too one-sidedly emphasizes social *facilitation*). Still, his observations are remarkably sensitive to issues that will occupy me in more detail throughout this book.[99]

The single most focused examination of the audience effect and the collective cinema experience may well be a little-known article by German philosopher and communication scholar Erich Feldmann, for whom I have reserved the prominent spot at the end of this chapter. Under the title "Considération sur la situation du spectateur au cinéma" (1956), it was first published in the *Revue internationale de filmologie* and later reprinted in Feldmann's *Theorie der Massenmedien* (1962).[100] Feldmann starts off with reproaching researchers who studied the film spectator as a mere solitary individual, detached from the specific theatrical situation of the audience. Urging film scholars – and filmologists specifically – to account for the experience of a viewer embedded in an audience is one of Feldmann's great merits. But credit also has to go to his broad distinction between two types of aggregates in the cinema. On the one hand, he identifies the *audience*, which consists of both individuals and groups who encounter each other with reserved neutrality or even disinterest. On the other hand, there are specific *groups* of viewers who either know each other from before or have formed contingently in the cinema. While the former is an "amorphous crowd," the latter is a self-contained formation that has a tendency to detach itself within the audience.[101] Let us briefly look at both aggregates.

In the anonymous *audience* Feldmann does not discover any we-consciousness and hence no community feeling. In contrast to the stage theater, which invites an exchange of ideas between theatergoers, the individual viewer in the cinema remains uncommunicative, isolated and distanced from others. Nevertheless, the audience is kept together as a kind of cooperative (*Genossenschaft*) by individual viewers, who voluntarily accept the conventions of the cinema and who share, without necessarily spelling this out, the same expectations.[102] There may even be a certain connection: Since everyone experiences the same film, there is a commonality of impressions, sensations, feelings, and opinions through which the individuals in the audience are subtly associated with each other. This is particularly true when the audience spontaneously breaks out in affirmative applause or dismissive responses. In instances like these, "the crowd can turn into a spontaneously acting mass that gains a collective dynamic."[103] Moreover, Feldmann notes specifically that a crowded auditorium full of interested and tense viewers can influence the mood (*Gefühlslage*) of the individual.[104] Just like Freeburg before him, he astutely anticipates the phenomenon of emotional contagion here.

Among specific, pre-established *groups*, on the other hand, Feldmann observes a feeling of togetherness (*Gefühl des Beisammenseins*) that lasts throughout the film and can be stronger at times and less consciously felt in other instances.[105] This feeling of togetherness is particularly pronounced if the group shares a separate box in the auditorium that invites talking. Especially younger couples visit the cinema in order to share an experience: "People go to the cinema as couples not only to fill out time, but also in order to experience the mutuality of sensations, concomitant feelings and effective responses, trying to stay close and exchange feelings directly with each other."[106] Written some sixty years ago, this claim still rings true today, as the following chapters will demonstrate.

VIII. ALONE IN THE DARK? REASONS FOR THE NEGLECT OF THE AUDIENCE EFFECT

But why did the audience effect not raise more systematic interest before? Why did the majority of film theorists treat viewers as if they somehow sat alone in the dark?

An important reason certainly was the historical importance to establish film as a form of art and object worthy of intellectual attention in its own right. Early and classical film theory aimed at medium specificity, focusing on what is unique to film and what distinguishes it from other objects of academic study. Since the cinema shares the collective experience with the orchestral concert, the opera, and, most dangerously, the theater, film theorists shied away from dealing with it. However, the logic behind this putative motive is questionable. Just because concerts, operas, and theaters have co-present viewers as well does not mean that the collective experience of the movie-theater is sufficiently similar (let alone identical) to neglect it. Quite the contrary: One would expect theorists and scholars to look more closely at what distinguishes the various collective experiences. After all, there might be something specific about the collective experience of the movie-theater, and in Chapter 3 I will discuss a number of these differences.

This medium-specificity argument is primarily valid for early and classical film theory, but not for so-called "contemporary" film theory which roughly coincides with the beginning of film studies as an academic discipline in the late 1960s and 1970s. At that time questions of medium specificity did not play a crucial role anymore, which can be judged, for instance, from the collaborative attempt to define film as a type of language. Why, then, have most proponents of contemporary theory overlooked the audience effect? Film studies developed as an academic field in the politicized late 1960s and early 1970s with ideology critique as one of its predominant goals. After the devastating historical precedents of Fascist and Communist regimes misusing film for means of propaganda and "fusing" viewers into a unified *Volkskörper* (as the German National Socialist Party would call it), thematizing the cinematic audience as a collective might have been inopportune.[107] But, again, this logic is not fully convincing: dealing with actual audiences and their experiences might have told film theorists that the cinematic apparatus does not create a monolithic block, but often causes divergences and distances within the audience – a point I shall have ample opportunity to demonstrate.

The disregard of the audience effect quite likely also derives from the fact that co-present spectators were simply taken for granted. For decades the movie-theater was almost the only place to watch films and other viewers were always around.[108] Just as hardly anyone paid attention to the aesthetic effect of the cinema's *architecture* – give or take some notable exceptions like Kracauer and his article on the movie palaces – so the audience may have been too obvious.[109] What was new to film theorists was not the collective reception of an artwork or medium: what astonished them was the new medium of film itself. But if this argument was convincing in the first fifty to sixty years of film history, it has gradually lost its power. Today, the seismic shifts in film viewing habits have made us particularly sensitive to the audience effect, as we have seen in Chapter 1.

Finally, a more recent reason for the insensitivity to the audience effect may be located in a specific theoretical limitation of cognitive film studies, whose important contributions have influenced the discussion of filmic emotions for more than twenty years. Traditionally, cognitivist approaches to filmic emotions have relied on psychological appraisal or philosophical judgment theories of emotion. This seems self-evident, because it is precisely the appraisal part that merits the term "cognitive" in the first place. However, with their reliance on appraisal theories, film cognitivists have inherited their neglect of social context. Affective relationships between *viewers and viewers* have therefore hardly played a role, the occasional reference to emotional contagion being the exception to the rule. However, as social psychologists Agneta Fischer, Antony Manstead, and Ruud Zaalberg inform us, emotions do not unfold in a micro-world consisting of the stimulus and the individual: "It is not only that emotions influence the social context; the social context also has an important impact on emotions."[110] Fischer and her colleagues therefore propose the notion of *social appraisal* – "the appraisal of behaviors, thoughts, or feelings of one or more other persons in the emotional situation, in addition to the emotional event per se" – which could serve as an ideal entry point for film cognitivists to join the research on the audience effect.[111]

In the following two chapters I cut from the "establishing shot" of Chapters 1 and 2 to a "long shot" that introduces two types of collective viewing I distinguish analytically in order to specify the "more or less collective experience of a film projected in a cinema" (Raymond Bellour).[112] I call them *quiet-attentive viewing* and *expressive-diverted viewing*.

NOTES

1. Langer (2015 [1919]), p. 164.
2. Here, the considerable differences in scope and proliferation of their contributions do not matter to me: While Odin's semio-pragmatic approach is a fully worked-out model of spectatorship put forth in numerous articles since the 1980s, Barthes's impressionistic notes on the movie-theater are condensed in a small essay (1975). In Morin and Benjamin's case the situation is even more extreme: I will predominantly draw on single sections from the French theorist's book *The Cinema, or the Imaginary Man* (1956), and the German critic's essay on the artwork in the age of technological reproducibility (1936).
3. Bordwell (1989).
4. Odin (2007), p. 261.
5. Odin (1995a), p. 227 (emphasis added).
6. Odin (1994), pp. 34–9.
7. Odin (1994), pp. 39–42.
8. Odin (1995a), pp. 231–3.
9. Odin (1995b), p. 216.
10. Odin (1995b), p. 215.
11. Quoted from Odin (1995b), p. 220 (emphasis added).
12. Odin (1994), p. 43. Francesco Casetti underscores that it is not by chance that Odin calls his approach *semio*-pragmatics: "if it is true that Odin makes the context responsible for determining the application of one or another mode of production of meaning, it is also true that Odin does not study these modes of production as social practices, but as preconditions of the text's intelligibility. [. . .] Odin's attention is, thus, devoted more to the linguistic than to the social dimension" (Casetti, 1999, p. 258).
13. Kessler (1996).
14. Quoted from Kessler (1996), p. 108 (my translation).
15. See Odin (2005), p. 115.
16. Odin (2007), p. 259 (original emphasis).
17. Odin (2007), p. 259.
18. Odin (2002), p. 54.
19. Odin (2007), p. 260.
20. For an influential psychological study on nostalgia, see Wildshut et al. (2006).
21. Claims that the family film aims at establishing a euphoric consensus can be found in Odin (2005), p. 12.
22. Odin (2014), p. 19.
23. Odin (2005), p. 112. See also Odin (2002), p. 54.
24. This oppositional stance also flashes up when Odin briefly mentions students' "uproar [and] dissension with the teacher" when forced to watch a documentary in school (Odin, 1995a, p. 232).
25. Odin (2005), p. 113. See also Odin (2014), p. 17.
26. Referencing Erving Goffman, Odin also calls this a "shifting of frame" (Odin, 2007, p. 262).

27. Sobchack (1999), pp. 248–9.
28. Odin (2007), p. 261.
29. Barthes (1989 [1975]), p. 346.
30. Barthes (1989 [1975]), p. 346.
31. Barthes (1989 [1975]), p. 346.
32. Barthes (1989 [1975]), p. 346.
33. Polan (1981), p. 42.
34. Barthes (1989 [1975]), p. 349 (original emphasis, translation slightly modified).
35. Barthes (1989 [1975]), p. 347 (original emphasis).
36. Sobchack (1992), p. 179.
37. Victor Burgin speaks of a "culturally dissident" way of watching movies (Burgin, 1997, p. 21).
38. Friedberg (2002), pp. 188–9.
39. Barthes (1989 [1975]), p. 346.
40. Barthes (1989 [1975]), p. 346.
41. Morin (2005 [1956]), p. 225 (original emphasis).
42. Morin (2005 [1956]), p. 225 (original emphasis).
43. Morin (2005 [1956]), p. 96.
44. Morin (2005 [1956]), p. 97.
45. Morin (2005 [1956]), p. 97.
46. Morin (2005 [1956]), p. 97.
47. We should not forget, however, that in French – just as in English – the word "cinema" can refer both to the film and the movie-theater.
48. The number comes from Andrew (2013), p. xx.
49. For a more detailed argument in German, see Hanich (2017).
50. Bazin (1967b [1951]), p. 99. As Timothy Barnard has shown, the author was actually called Rosenkranz and had probably written his article in German. Under the title "Film and Theater: The Situation of Theater Today", Rosenkranz's text is available in Barnard's English translation at: https://www.caboosebooks.net/sites/default/files/caboose_Rozenkranz_Film%20and%20Theater_second%20version_Jan%202016.pdf (last accessed 29 June 2016). The original was published in the journal *Esprit* in Raoul Adouin's French translation from the German original.
51. Bazin (1967b [1951]), p. 99.
52. Bazin (1967b [1951]), p. 107. A similar tendency can be found in his later essay "Marginal Notes on *Eroticism in the Cinema*" (1957), in which he considers the psychology of the viewer as basically "identical with that of the sleeper dreaming" (Bazin, 1971b [1957], p. 171). Dudley Andrew interprets in a similar way (Andrew, 2013, p. 54, emphasis added).
53. Bazin (1967b [1951]), p. 99.
54. Bazin (1967b [1951]), p. 99.
55. Bazin (1967b [1951]), p. 112.
56. Bazin (1967b [1951]), p. 100.
57. Bazin (1967b [1951]), p. 102.
58. Bazin (1967b [1951]), p. 100.
59. Bazin (1967b [1951]), p. 99.
60. Bazin (1981 [1944]), p. 69.
61. Andrew (2013), p. 42.
62. Bazin (1967b [1951]), p. 99.
63. Bazin (1967b [1951]), p. 99.

64. Bazin (2014e [1954]), p. 295.
65. Bazin (1981 [1944]), p. 69.
66. Bazin (1981 [1944]), p. 69.
67. Bazin (1971a [1952]), p. 124.
68. Bazin (1971a [1952]), p. 124.
69. Bazin (1971a [1952]), p. 127.
70. Bazin (1967b [1951]), p. 121.
71. Bazin (1967a [1948]), pp. 146–7.
72. Bazin seems to presuppose that a strong immersion in the filmic world precludes an awareness of the collective experience. This is a strong thesis one does not have to follow (see Chapter 3 below).
73. Bazin (2014b [1954]), p. 109.
74. Bazin (2014d [1954]), p. 160 (emphasis added).
75. Bazin (2014d [1954]), pp. 160–1.
76. Bazin (2014b [1954]), p. 113.
77. Bazin (2014b [1954]), p. 112.
78. Bazin (2014a [1958]), p. 209.
79. For an impressive recent attempt in Benjamin exegesis, see chapters 3–7 in Hansen (2012).
80. Benjamin: "Although paintings began to be publicly exhibited in galleries and salons, there was no way for the masses to organize and control themselves in their reception. Thus the same public which responds in a progressive manner toward a grotesque film is bound to respond in a reactionary manner to surrealism" (Benjamin, 1989 [1936], p. 583).
81. The German version reads: "Und zwar ist der entscheidende Umstand dabei: nirgends mehr als im Kino erweisen sich die Reaktionen der Einzelnen, deren Summe die massive Reaktion des Publikums ausmacht, von vornherein durch ihre unmittelbare Massierung bedingt. Und indem sie sich kundgeben, kontrollieren sie sich" (Benjamin, 1977a [1936], p. 33, the above translation is mine).
82. Benjamin (1977b [c. 1931]), p. 1193 (my translation). Mentioned also in Hansen (2012), p. 100.
83. Other translators have rendered the passage as "No sooner are these reactions manifest than they regulate one another" (Michael W. Jennings in Benjamin 2010 [1936], p. 29 and Benjamin 2008 [1936], p. 36) or "The moment these responses become manifest they control each other" (Harry Zohn in Benjamin 1989 [1936], p. 583).
84. For slightly different interpretations of section XII in Benjamin's artwork essay, see Hansen (2012), p. 100 and McBride (1998), p. 469.
85. See Foucault (1995 [1975]); Deleuze (1992).
86. Why this should be the case "nowhere more than in the cinema" – and not also, for instance, in stage comedies – remains open in Benjamin's text. Moreover, we have to add that while pleasure and critique coincide in Chaplin comedies, this does not presuppose that pleasure is a *prerequisite* for critique, which may well be possible in an Eisenstein film that we may watch without a pleasurable attitude (*genießende Haltung*).
87. Hansen (2012), p. 86.
88. Benjamin (2008 [1929]), p. 337.
89. Curiously, Hansen does not discuss these allusions. The fact that she overlooks Benjamin's references to comedies is symptomatic of the general problem that the genre poses for the neat divide between early cinema and classical cinema: basically existing ever since 1895, comedies transcend the boundaries between film historical periods.

Moreover, even if the mode of address of the comedy may have changed throughout the decades, its laughing audiences are hardly the absorbed, voyeuristic spectators often deemed typical for the classical paradigm.

90. Benjamin (1989 [1936]), p. 584.
91. In the German original Benjamin notes: "Ehe der Film zur Geltung kam, suchten die Dadaisten durch ihre Veranstaltungen *eine Bewegung ins Publikum zu bringen*, die ein Chaplin dann auf natürlichere Weise hervorrief" (Benjamin, 1977a [1936], p. 37, emphasis added).
92. Benjamin (1999 [1934]), p. 792.
93. Compare also this quote from Rudolf Arnheim: "Sometimes laughter moves through the darkness, then all the bodies sway to and fro, as if the wind went through the trees" (Arnheim, 2004 [1927], p. 83, my translation).
94. Faure (1959 [1920]), p. 13.
95. Faure (1959 [1920]), p. 14.
96. Freeburg (1918), pp. 7–8 (emphasis added).
97. Freeburg (1918), p. 8.
98. Freeburg (1918), p. 8 (emphasis added).
99. For a more detailed discussion on the audience effect in early film theory in German, see Hanich (2016). For further early sources on the audience effect, see the texts by Arthur Mellini and Resi Langer in Kaes/Baer/Cowan (2015) as well as the texts by Ricciotto Canudo, Louis Delluc, and Jules Romains in Abel (1988).
100. Feldmann (1956) and Feldmann (1962). My translations are based on the German version. I am grateful to Francesco Casetti for bringing this article to my attention.
101. Feldmann (1962), p. 118.
102. Feldmann (1962), pp. 120 and 122.
103. Feldmann (1962), p. 120.
104. Feldmann (1962), p. 122.
105. Feldmann (1962), p. 123.
106. Feldmann (1962), p. 124.
107. Now that we face more and more individualized and privatized forms of spectatorship, the value of collective viewing might come back into view for critical theory. Evidence can be found in the work of Jacques Rancière. Rancière has variously referred to Plato's concept of "the *choreographic* form of the community that sings and dances its own proper unity," in which no one remains a motionless spectator, everyone follows a communitarian rhythm, and which for Plato was a good form of art. See Rancière (2004), p. 9 and Rancière (2007), p. 272. Accordingly, Slavoj Žižek writes: "the lesson of Rancière is that one should be careful not to succumb to the liberal temptation of condemning all collective artistic performances [and I would add: collective spectatorships] as inherently 'totalitarian'" (Žižek, 2004, p. 73).
108. On early instances of non-theatrical viewing, see Waller (2012).
109. Kracauer (1987 [1926]). For a similar view, see Gabriele Pedullà: "The reflections of a small number of architects excepted, the movie-theater has remained the great lacuna in twentieth-century film theory" (Pedullà, 2012, p. 5). See also Paul (2016).
110. Fischer/Manstead/Zaalberg (2003), p. 176.
111. Fischer/Manstead/Zaalberg (2003), p. 175.
112. Bellour (2012), p. 206.

PART II

Long Shot:
Types of Collective Viewing

Introductory Notes

1. TWO TYPES OF COLLECTIVE VIEWING

Chapters 3 and 4 will deal with two kinds of collective viewing: the *quiet-attentive* and the *expressive-diverted*. The former describes viewers who silently and collectively focus their attention on the film, thus sharing an activity based on their intention to jointly attend to the single object of the film. The latter refers to expressive viewers whose collective responses become obvious to the other spectators and who divide their diverted attention between the film and the rest of the audience.

These distinctions are not supposed to create an either-or binary between two exclusive types. Holding such a position would be as unproductive as it would be inaccurate, both diachronically and synchronically. Historically, no single viewing type ruled completely, even if one may have predominated over the other at some point.[1] And even during a given screening the two types can rapidly succeed each other and easily blend, fuse, morph into one another. When theorists come up with clear categorical distinctions they do not believe that the world actually consists of such neatly differentiated phenomena – we always encounter overlaps and ambivalences in the world. But in order to point out and describe *hybrid* forms we need categorical distinctions.[2] To put it differently, what we gain from categorical distinctions is the ability to perceive what is mixed and ambivalent.

However, it is also true that theorizing means to come up with productive categories *at some distance from the particular*, which implies a certain degree of abstraction.[3] As the late Umberto Eco once remarked, those who write scholarly essays "must impoverish the wealth of the real in order to permit definitions."[4] For a theory to be productive it has to ignore vast areas that it does not want to incorporate or considers irrelevant.[5] But claiming that my distinctions imply abstraction does not imply that they are not grounded in reality. The ultimate 'quality check' for my categories will be a pragmatic, not a dogmatic one: Are they useful? Can they improve our understanding of audiences and the effects this book is devoted to? Do they allow distinctions with reference to related concepts?[6]

Of course, I am not the first to suggest an audience typology. What is key for my distinction is the question of what these viewing types imply for the collective experience of the cinema and the audience effect. And this has not been at the heart of earlier typologies. Take Francesco Casetti's distinction between *attendance* and *performance*. Casetti focuses on a historical shift in spectatorship. On the one hand, there is the more traditional type of viewer who openly, but passively witnesses the singular event the film projection constitutes in the cinema (attendance); on the other hand, there is the type of viewer more widespread today who actively controls technological devices such as DVD players or smartphones on which films are watched in everyday surroundings and who is often involved in various choice-making processes (performance).[7]

In cases where social aspects of the audience became a defining feature of the typology, the distinction was not focused on the cinema. For instance, in their otherwise illuminating sociological analysis of contemporary audiences, Nicholas Abercrombie and Brian Longhurst suggest three broad types: the simple audience, the mass audience, and the diffused audience.[8] The *simple* audience rests on a performance that is restricted to a local space, takes place in public, and involves a high degree of attention. It also implies a substantial ceremonial quality such as following the rules of etiquette (for instance, remaining silent or cheering enthusiastically). Prime examples would be stage plays and football matches, watched in a theater or a stadium. Even though Abercrombie and Longhurst presuppose a fairly direct, rather unmediated communication between the performers and the receiver, they also consider cinemagoers as members of a simple audience. In contrast, people who watch television represent prototypical *mass* audiences: While the performance can be followed worldwide, the audiences confront it in private surroundings. The ritual aspect of it is less pronounced and the attention is fluctuating, moving in and out of involvement, with the medium often constituting the background of everyday life. Finally, the concept of the *diffuse* audience tries to capture the fact that being a member of an audience is nothing exceptional any longer: "in contemporary society, everyone becomes an audience all the time."[9] In a society of the spectacle and a culture of narcissism, people constantly feel as members of an audience following a spectacle, while simultaneously they are narcissistically assuming themselves to be watched by others.[10]

Needless to say, this distinction is too broad for our purposes. We would need to introduce further subtypes of the *simple* audience to make it productive for studying the collective cinema experience – and, in a way, this is what my concepts of quiet-attentive and expressive-diverted viewing try to achieve. However, as the following chapters will show, describing these collective viewing types as "simple" does not capture the complexity of their respective experiences. Hence I will refrain from using the term "simple audience."

II. TWO HISTORICAL IDEALS ABOUT COLLECTIVE SPECTATORSHIP

To illustrate the two types of collective spectatorship one could loosely tie them to two historical ideals about the cinema: Peter Kubelka's Invisible Cinema, on the one hand, and Vachel Lindsay's Conversational Theater as well as Jonathan Rosenbaum's cinema-cum-public-forum, on the other hand.

In Kubelka's Invisible Cinema, designed for the Anthology Film Archive in New York, the quiet-attentive type would find an ideal sanctuary. Its alleged sole function was to bring "the filmed message from the author to the beholder with a minimum of loss;" here "the film can completely dictate the sensation of space," as Kubelka, the Austrian inventor of the Invisible Cinema, put it.[11] No latecomers were admitted. Apart from some exit signs installed for safety reasons, everything was kept in black. The elevated seats with their shell-like structure shielded the viewer's upper body, thus making it impossible to see the neighbors to the sides, in the front and in the back. While this constellation might sound like the *antithesis* of collective experience, Kubelka did not favor a *solitary* confrontation with the film. In fact, the "aspect of community" was central to him. In 1974, shortly after the Invisible Cinema had to be closed, he described its collective dimension: "You knew that there were many people in the room, *you could feel their presence*, and you also would hear them a little bit, but in a very subdued way, so they would not disturb your contact with the film. A sympathetic community was created, a community in which people liked each other." This put the Invisible Cinema in opposition to "the average cinema where the heads of other people are in the screen, where I hear them crunching their popcorn, where the latecomers force themselves through the rows and where I have to hear their talk, which takes me out of the cinematic reality which I have come to participate in." Kubelka wanted to prevent viewers starting to dislike each other: "Architecture has to provide a structure in which one is in *a community that is not disturbing to others*."[12]

Expressive-diverted viewing, on the other hand, can be tied to Vachel Lindsay's Conversational Theater. The American poet's model of a movie-theater with no sound except the critically conversing, intellectually active audience murmuring "like a pleasant brook" is the prototype of a public sphere of communicative exchange.[13] In 1915 Lindsay proposed this way of film exhibition and reception to local exhibitors, encouraging them to make viewers discuss and aesthetically judge the picture with their friends in a kind of running commentary.

Extending Lindsay's ideas, the film critic Jonathan Rosenbaum equally embraced a cinema with ongoing communication, but also non-verbal interaction and performative elements. This is why he repeatedly comes back to the ritualistic, performative screenings of *The Rocky Horror Picture Show* with their scattered and divergent audience attentions and expressively voiced commentaries: "What is it about these shows that is so energetic and exciting? Above all, I think it is the experience of a film's being used by people as a means of communicating with one another – not after the film has ended, but while it is still in progress."[14] According to Rosenbaum, the film must not be able to *impose* the filmmaker's meanings, but the audience should learn to use a film as "a means of communicating with itself."[15] Sometimes Rosenbaum even sounds as if he preferred a cinema in which communicative communal events *around* movies were more important than the film itself.[16] With acerbic distaste he asks: "Are commercial movies today public forums and community meeting-places, or private sites of narcissistic pleasure, figurative or literal porn images to masturbate to?"[17]

While for Rosenbaum the liveliness and expressivity of a conversing cinema audience exemplifies a truly social experience, in Kubelka's opinion a sympathetic community establishes itself once a concentrated audience watches a film together in respectful quietude. These are two opposed views on collective spectatorship and social life, but both can be accommodated in the cinema, as I will show in the following chapters. The Conversational Theater and the Invisible Cinema may involve very different types of collectivity – *both* are collective nonetheless.

III. EMPIRICAL VARIABLES

Let me repeat that the two types of collective spectatorship I suggest in Chapters 3 and 4 do not exist in an artificial vacuum. In reality they are influenced by a variety of empirical variables, ranging from the design of the movie-theater to its technological equipment, from the projected films to various social and psychological factors. I suggest that the predominance of the collective experience and the strength of the audience effect in an actual cinematic situation depend on at least fifteen variables:

1) Intimacy of the social connections: Do I attend the film alone or with one or more companions? Do I know all of the other viewers or are we a completely anonymous group of people?
2) Number of spectators: Do I watch the film with five or eight hundred other viewers?

3) Density of seating: Do I sit very close to my co-viewers or are we scattered around the audience, sitting far apart?
4) Size of the cinema: Do we sit in a small, rather intimate shoebox theater or in a large modern-day megaplex?
5) Place in the audience: Do I choose a seat in the front, the center, or the back of the theater? (It makes a difference if I have the other viewers in front of me or surrounding me.)
6) Architecture of the movie-theater: Does stadium seating hide me from others and my co-spectators from me?
7) Interior design: Does reflection from the walls or lights from exit signs illuminate the audience or are we mostly hidden from each other in a dark 'invisible' cinema?
8) Air conditioning: Does the smell of other viewers become noticeable because we sit in a hot auditorium or is our olfactory awareness of other spectators reduced through regulated temperature?
9) Sound system: Does the loudness drown the presence of the other viewers and turn my attention predominantly toward the film or am I conscious of their silent attention?
10) Size of the screen: Are we placed in front of a small screen or an IMAX screen that dominates attention?
11) Type of image: Are we watching a regular 2D film or a 3D movie?
12) Immersive affordance of the film: Do we watch a suspenseful thriller or an anti-immersive gross-out comedy, a deeply moving melodrama or an avant-garde film full of Benjaminian shocks and Eisensteinian attractions?
13) Institutional context: Are we attending the film at a premiere, a press screening, a film festival, or in an educational context such as a seminar screening? (The discussions of Odin and Bazin in Chapter 2 have already pointed in this direction.)
14) Degree of social and cultural connectedness: Do I feel closely connected to the other viewers or distanced from them because of social and cultural differences?
15) Personality variables and health conditions: Am I averse to being close to other people (asociality, misanthropy, social anxiety) or very sensitive to noise (sensory-processing sensitivity, hyperacusis) or smell (hyperosmia)?

Some empirical evidence exists that emphasizes these variables. Consider how the difference between 2D and 3D projections, including the infamous 3D glasses which "isolate you from your neighbors," as Dudley Andrew has observed, can influence the collective experience (point 11).[18] In an empirical study, Brendan Rooney and Eilis Hennessy compared viewers who watched the 2D and the 3D version of the film *Thor* (2011) respectively. They found out that "participants in the 3D condition were less distracted."[19] Given that the researchers measured audience attention with questions like, "Please indicate how often you found yourself distracted by [. . .] other people in the cinema talking, laughing, using their mobile phone," it is fair to conclude that during the 3D projection the viewers paid *less attention* to their co-viewers – and hence had a different social experience.[20]

Another empirical study sheds light on how the number of spectators influenced the audience effect (point 2). Sheldon G. Levy and William F. Fenley jr. were able to establish a correlation between audience size and the audience's laughter about Robert Altman's anti-war comedy *M*A*S*H* (1970).[21] For this study, between three and six researchers attended fifteen different screenings in a cinema in Houston (Texas) and tried to unobtrusively observe the audience reactions and count the number of laughs. The study revealed that viewers responded more often and more intensely with laughter the bigger the group size was. Based on their evidence, the researchers believed that a social facilitation effect was responsible for the increase in laughter, that is, viewers laughed more often because others were doing the same thing. The two psychologists thus lent empirical evidence to an observation Roberto Rossellini once articulated in an interview with André Bazin: "Something that you see in a projection room with an audience of fifteen people has an entirely different meaning than when you see it in a movie-theater with two thousand people."[22]

Finally, a recent empirical study on trash films revealed how important the various types of social connection are for the enjoyment of this genre (point 1). Keyvan Sarkhosh and Winfried Menninghaus showed that regular trash film viewers clearly prefer to watch these films alone or with friends instead of family members or strangers. As a consequence, they watch trash films most often at home, followed with great distance by viewings in cinemas, film festivals and, least of all, on mobile devices.[23]

Unfortunately, the empirical evidence for most other variables is scarce. This should hardly surprise us, given the limited attention devoted to the collective cinema experience. It would therefore be worthwhile to gather more empirical data about these variables in the future: via third-person quantitative research, via second-person qualitative interviews, via first-person phenomenological descriptions, or some productive combination thereof.[24] Matthew Reason has recently emphasized the value of empirical audience research: "it both reminds us and requires us to avoid overly generalizable statements and to recognize the fundamental diversity of audience responses."[25] This is a valid point, as no one can be interested in overly lofty generalizations. However, as we have seen in Chapter 1, empirical audience researchers cannot do without generalizations. It is naïve to assume that scholars can simply accrue data – what the data needs is a theoretical framework.[26] The two collective viewing types I explore in the following chapters are intended precisely as such a framework.

NOTES

1. For a similar position, see Gabriele Pedullà's remark: "the movie-theater has always been a hybrid and extremely permeable space, despite efforts to rigorously discipline the audience's reactions. Pure cinema, like pure art, was always only an aspiration [. . .]. In the Teatro Olimpico in Vicenza or the Opéra Garnier in Paris, in [Louis] Delluc's picture palaces or at [Frederick] Kiesler's Film Guild Theater, order and disorder, attention and inattention, were always part of the spectator's experience" (Pedullà, 2012, p. 131; see also p. 80).
2. Wiesing (2015), p. 77.
3. Branston (2000), p. 19.
4. Rosso (1983), p. 8.
5. Branston (2000), pp. 26–7.
6. Echterhoff/Higgins/Levine (2009), p. 501.
7. Casetti (2015), pp. 185–6 and 199/200. See also Casetti (2010).
8. Abercrombie/Longhurst (1998). See particularly chapter 2, pp. 39–76.
9. Abercrombie/Longhurst (1998), p. 68.
10. Abercrombie/Longhurst (1998), p. 75.
11. Kubelka (1974), p. 32.
12. Kubelka (1974), p. 34 (emphasis added). Ken Kelman, a founding member of the Anthology Film Archives, also stresses the efficiency of their movie-theater in preventing verbal disturbance: "it discouraged people from talking to the person next to them, and in those terms of counteracting certain disturbances the theater largely succeeded" (quoted from Sitney, 2005, p. 106).
13. Lindsay (1915), p. 196.
14. Rosenbaum (1995), p. 151. Revolted by the cinema culture of the late 1970s, Rosenbaum hopes for the "potential return of the *active* audience, in contrast to the passive, refrigerated, cut-off, narcissistic sensibilities that so many recent movies and movie-theaters take (or ask) us to be" (p. 149, original emphasis). Rosenbaum longs for "a community of common interests inside a theater, rather than a set of separate, elegantly upholstered masturbation stalls" (p. 149).
15. Rosenbaum (1995), p. 177.
16. Rosenbaum (1995), p. 130.
17. Rosenbaum (1995), p. 175.
18. Andrew (2014), p. 25.
19. Rooney/Hennessy (2013), p. 452.
20. Rooney/Hennessy (2013), p. 448. The findings seem intuitively plausible. However, we have to be cautious with interpreting the specific results of this study, because its design has a serious drawback: while the 2D group comprised 86 viewers in an auditorium that could host 157 viewers, the two 3D groups consisted of 72 and 67 viewers in auditoria that could host 375 and 230 viewers respectively. In other words, the 2D group watched the film with *more* viewers in a *smaller* cinema, which makes it hardly surprising that the 3D groups were not as distracted as the 2D group.
21. Levy/Fenley jr. (1979).
22. Bazin (2014c [1958]), p. 193.
23. Sarkhosh/Menninghaus (2016).
24. For a recent attempt to scan the field of empirical audience research, see Reinhard/Olson (2016). Comparing and reproducing audience studies results from related fields like theater studies would also be a valuable endeavor. In her interview-based study,

Dominique Pasquier writes with regard to the intimacy of the social connections in stage theaters (point 1 in my list of variables): "people tend to be highly attentive to the reactions of the other people in the audience, especially those who accompanied them on the outing. The emotional charge of this contagion of negative and positive emotions differs, depending on whom the person is with. For instance, we identified differences between reactions in couples, on the one hand, where one partner (most often the woman) shows anxiety if their companion (generally the man) seems to be disinterested in the play; and on the other hand, between groups of friends, where, on the contrary, there seems more likely to be a sense of complicity that enables them to laugh together afterwards about their flopped theatrical experience" (Pasquier, 2015, pp. 226–7).
25. Reason (2015), p. 280.
26. This is a point forcefully emphasized by D. N. Rodowick: "The danger of empiricism is to believe that direct knowledge of the real is accessible without the mediation of concepts or theoretical practices, or that knowledge resides in objects and needs only to be extracted by direct and unmediated observation" (Rodowick, 2014, p. 236).

CHAPTER 3

Quiet-attentive Viewing: Toward a Typology of Collective Spectatorship, Part I

[T]he complicity of the crowd in the experience of a film is very necessary. It is not only the film itself that licenses the activity of the spectator, silently watching, but also the presence of others who are engaged in a similar activity without disturbing each other.

John Ellis[1]

Embedded in the silence of great masses the field of attention changes also for the individual.

Walter Benjamin[2]

I. QUIET-ATTENTIVE VIEWING AS JOINT ACTION

This chapter discusses the first type of collective viewing, the *quiet-attentive* one. A major argument will be that collectively watching a film with quiet attention can often be regarded as a *joint action*. To make this – potentially provocative – claim sound convincing I will introduce and discuss a number of philosophical terms like we-intention, joint attention and joint action. Furthermore, I list consequences of this argument for film theory and historiography: among other things I will mount a critique of an influential film historical thesis. Another goal will be to explore the *benefits* and *pleasures* connected to the collective experience of watching a film together with quiet attention. Last but not least, I investigate the differences between the collective experience of the cinema and other art forms that also involve quiet-attentive viewing, such as the theater. As I have argued in Chapter 2, eager to demonstrate what is specific about the cinema, film theorists in the past largely downplayed what cinema *shares* with other arts. It still remains an open question, however, what distinguishes various types of collective viewing. Since I don't want to argue that theater, opera, and cinema involve an identical form of collective experience, I will engage in an act of comparative phenomenology.

As an important prerequisite I take it for granted that the viewers in the cinema are actively involved with the film, a position I share with diverse film theoretical approaches. Proponents of cultural studies, cognitive film theory, film phenomenology, or reception aesthetics assume that the viewers decode and give meaning to the film, consciously build hypotheses and draw inferences, fill blanks and omissions, visually imagine what is suggested but not shown, and so on.[3] "The viewer must process the rapid sequence of audio-visual information; perceive what is represented on the screen; comprehend the characters, spaces, and actions depicted; and engage in the construction of the narrative throughout the film," film cognitivist Tim Smith writes. "A film viewer will move his or her eyes to different points on the screen about two to five times a second. During a typical 90-minute feature film, this amounts to around 21,600 eye movements."[4] This is not to deny that watching a film is simultaneously characterized by a certain passivity, particularly when compared to other more prototypical actions. Granting a passive as well as an active *doing* makes it possible to ignore the much discussed but overly broad and fuzzy distinction between an active and a passive viewer: while passive in some senses, the viewer is simultaneously active in others.[5]

Moreover, when silently watching a film together in a cinema, viewers are by no means always engaged in *individual* actions that run parallel to each other: quietly watching a film with others often implies a joint activity based on a collective intention in which the viewers jointly attend to a single object – the film. To be sure, this type of joint action is not in every respect comparable to more emphatic and skillful collective activities such as ballet dancing, singing in a choir, or marching in a peace parade. Compared to playing a piece of orchestral music or playing badminton, watching a film with quiet attention is a somewhat special case. For one thing, it is also *possible* that we do it alone; for another, the common goal of watching the film is rather easily achieved. These deceptively simple facts should not make us oblivious to the social experience of the theatrical situation and the joint action it may involve.

Now it is, of course, a notoriously thorny issue to define actions.[6] Nevertheless, I believe that "quietly watching a film" consists of various characteristics that should allow us to treat it as an action proper. "Watching a film" can be considered a *mental* action once we devote our ongoing attention and interest to the film in order to follow it to its end. This act is voluntary, not only in the broad sense of "under my control", but also in the sense that it is specific to human action: it is motivated by my own desire as well as my intention to find out how the film progresses. I seem to have a free choice and nothing stands in the way of me performing it. Moreover, once we agree that some doings are actions even if our effort is limited and happens with no great strain, "watching a film" should be regarded as a *sustained* action. Inversely, we would have trouble with defining "watching a film" as an action only if we, firstly, restricted the definition of action to overt bodily actions like paying for admission, but did not allow mental actions like paying attention to a film; and, secondly, if we only included events like walking to the cinema, but not purposely watching moving images for ninety minutes with the intention of following the progress of the film to its end, and of enjoying it. Let us briefly draw a comparison to meditation: We would most likely have no problem in granting that meditation is an instance of a sustained action. Silently watching a film is a bit like meditating: It is a sustained mental act that lasts some ninety minutes or so.[7]

But if you as spectator and I as spectator and the others in the audience as spectators are all active, sitting in the same cinema watching the same film in a quiet, attentive way, does it sound totally weird to argue that in some important sense you, I, and the others are acting jointly? Just compare the qualitative difference between quiet-attentive viewing and, say, a crowd of people sitting in a train compartment or sleeping next to each other in a hospital ward: while this chapter will hopefully be able to convince readers that the former act jointly, it is much more difficult to do the same for the latter groups. Moreover, it can hardly be denied that there is a substantial phenomenological difference between watching a film in a cinema *alone* and following the film as part of a quiet and attentive audience. I will therefore propose that quietly watching a film as part of an audience is a joint action based on a *we-intention* and a *joint attention* focused on a collective intentional object.

There is no doubt: The quiet collectivity of the movie-theater experience rarely becomes thematic in a fully fledged sense. The audience predominantly experiences jointly *without reflectively* experiencing each other. But this is not necessary. As philosopher Hans Bernhard Schmid puts it: "There is a difference between people being pre-reflectively aware of themselves, collectively, as a group, and people having an explicit reflective self-understanding of themselves, collectively, as a group. People can intend, believe, and act jointly, as a group, without explicitly and reflexively thinking of themselves as a group [. . .]."[8] I therefore need to emphasize that the viewer's *conscious* experience of others is predominantly a phenomenon at the *margins of consciousness* that can become explicit, but it certainly does not have to be reflected upon. This implies, in turn, that even when an audience pays full attention to the film, the individual viewer has not forgotten the other co-present spectators – they have simply receded to the fringe of consciousness, a fact I have already alluded to in the introduction. What is more, throughout the film this *basso continuo* of pre-reflective or reflective joint *action* may be supplemented by at least three forms of *affectively* experiencing jointly to be discussed in Chapter 6. During specific moments of high emotionality the collectivity can reach a higher level:

joint action *plus* shared emotions, emotional contagion, or feeling together. Again, this is not to say that these affective collective experiences are necessarily fully reflected upon, but they may be more likely to become part of the audience's focal consciousness (a point I will elaborate on in Chapter 5). In special cases the collective experience can thus become thematic (that is, reflective) in the strong sense of the word.

Suggesting that collectively watching a film with quiet attention should be considered a kind of *joint action* also raises the question of how I define "watching a film with others". Arguing that the joint action of quiet-attentive viewing is based on joint attention presupposes that there is attention to the film in the first place. People who sleep, who kiss, who send text messages on their cell phones, or talk about something else other than the film do *not* attend (let alone attend jointly) in the emphatic sense of the word, and hence do not watch the film in the way I define it here. This is, of course, not to deny that people may temporarily drift away. By granting that not all viewers in the audience watch the film together all of the time, my definition is not blind to the widespread phenomenon of inattention. However, those who focus their attention on the film – most viewers most of the time – contribute their individual share to the joint action in the quiet-attentive type.[9] Theorizing quiet-attentive viewing as a category of its own implies that I have to downplay the fact that in reality the silence might be interrupted by instances of commenting, laughing, screaming, or gasping. These and other forms of expressive response bring the collective aspect to the fore in different ways and will be discussed in the next chapter.

Still, my strong claim about the jointly acting audience needs to be qualified in one important respect. I obviously do not imply that spectators necessarily act jointly *in every respect* when they pay attention to the film in a quiet-attentive way: the joint action of quiet-attentive viewing I describe in this chapter will often serve as the *background* against which various episodes of acting individually can stand out throughout the film. Just think of a viewer who comes up with her own hypothesis about how a whodunit might end or a spectator who discovers a unique camera movement and wants to communicate this to his partner sitting next to him: In these cases the viewers clearly have a pronounced sense of hypothesizing and discovering *individually* rather than collectively, and hence these *specific* mental acts are not part of the overall joint action. But the joint action of watching the film together still continues in the background with the individual action playing out on top of it: While acting jointly in one respect, these viewers simultaneously act individually in another. We may loosely compare it to a team sport like football: When the center forward aims to score a goal with a brilliant piece of individual dribbling, he does not stop jointly acting with his teammates – he tries to score himself, but also for the team. And the teammates at the same time position themselves so that a potential counter-attack might be prevented. Similarly, the viewer who develops a hypothesis about the ending or detects a remarkable stylistic feature engages with a specific part of the film individually (the plot or the camera movement respectively), but at the same time continues to watch the film, as the joint intentional object, with the others.

II. UPSHOTS FOR FILM THEORY AND HISTORIOGRAPHY

This chapter draws heavy inspiration from recent debates in analytic philosophy and phenomenology about collective intentionality and affective collective experiences. Following the lead of Raimo Tuomela and John Searle, philosophers like Hans Bernhard Schmid, Margaret Gilbert, and others have refined this complex discussion about social ontology. I will rephrase some of their arguments with the cinematic constellation in mind to show that this import of social philosophy can have productive ramifications for film theory and historiography. It serves at least three goals.

Firstly, it may help to re-evaluate quiet-attentive viewing, which in recent years has been (either implicitly or explicitly) compared unfavorably with the more expressive type of collective spectatorship discussed in Chapter 4. However, there is much to be said in favor of the "active silence" of quiet-attentive viewing.[10]

Secondly, my argument may have consequences for film historiography. Later in this chapter I test my proposal by using it as the backbone of a critical rereading of an influential film-historical thesis. For scholars like Miriam Hansen and Thomas Elsaesser, the transition from early cinema to classical Hollywood cinema implies a profound change in terms of the social relations of the cinema: a loss of collectivity and an individualization of the audience. This "individualization thesis", as I call it, has gained the status of received wisdom and is repeated unquestioningly in articles and encyclopedias.[11] However, it seems overstated to me, precisely because the quiet-attentive reception of classical cinema more easily allowed for joint attention, joint action, and even shared emotions. Hence it is far from clear why classical reception should automatically result in individualization. What happens is a shift in types of collectivity. Audience interrelations may no longer be dialogic. Yet they are not merely imaginary (as are, for instance, the "imagined communities" of dispersed television audiences). This chapter may therefore also be seen as a critique of normative conceptions of collectivity based on communicative discourse and face-to-face interaction.

Thirdly, this proposition will be my first step toward a comprehensive theorization and phenomenology of collective spectatorship and the audience effect in the cinema. What we have been missing thus far in film studies is not only a comprehensive phenomenology of the cinema's collectivity as such – the lived experience of being part of an audience – but also, and more specifically, a discussion of the collective experience of quiet-attentive viewing.

III. THE EQUALIZING EFFECT OF THE CINEMA DISPOSITIVE

Before I delve into my detailed argumentation about joint action, however, I would like to devote a few paragraphs to how two characteristics of the cinema dispositive support its specific collectivity: I claim that due to its darkness and behavioral rules the movie-theater flattens hierarchies and tends to lessen differences among its viewers.

The darkness – "possibly the least acknowledged aspect of the cinema" (Heide Schlüpmann) – not only has an important perceptual function, increasing the viewers' concentration, reducing visual sources of distraction, and focusing the audience's attention on the screen;[12] it also has a transformative effect: by 'engulfing' *all* viewers, it backgrounds their individuality, it diminishes differences by literally dimming awareness of differences.[13] Umberto Barbaro captures this aspect nicely in his 1936 essay "Natura del cinema": "enveloped by darkness, [the cinematic spectator] cannot show himself and his clothing off."[14] If the saying rings true that all cats are grey in the dark, then the cinema's collectivity – composed of various anonymous individuals and small groups – is supported by this equalizing effect.[15]

The situation is quite different when the lights are up, a fact astutely captured in John Ellis's description of an illuminated auditorium where the individual viewers can clearly see each other: "It is no longer a crowd, but a gathering of individuals, mutually suspicious rather than mutually affirming."[16] We do not need to endorse Ellis's antagonistic notion of "suspicion" to agree that seeing others and being seen by them brings with it a much stronger awareness of difference. And here we may find a first discrepancy between the cinema's collectivity and the collectivity of other art forms: in contrast to the auditoria in the theater, the opera, or the orchestral concert (not to speak of the museum), the cinema auditorium is *grosso modo* less illuminated and thus tends to blend out the individuality of the co-present others to a stronger degree.

Just consider the experience of arriving late at a film: Entering an auditorium while the film is fully underway, you initially do not feel part of the audience, but you may sense a vague psychological distance to those who are present because of your overt visibility as a moving object. Perhaps you even feel being-looked-at and therefore have the impression that you embarrassingly stand out as an intruder, thinking, "These other viewers consider me as a 'you' – *you*, the intruder – and not as part of their 'we' yet." This may lead to a wish for a quick integration into the amorphous grayness of spectators to which you do not yet belong. Only when you have taken your seat and have merged into the 'we' of the audience do you feel more relaxed. Your individuality has been 'swallowed up' by the cinema's darkness.

A second factor that contributes to the cinema's equalizing effect are the behavioral rules that, in most cases, apply to each and everyone. Gabriele Pedullà, for one, has emphasized that those early film theorists who celebrated the cinema as the promise of an egalitarian society were probably mistaken in highlighting its *political* implications. Instead, for Pedullà the "fraternity of the auditorium" is to be found "in the system of constraints and prohibitions that required everyone – rich and poor, educated and illiterate – to submit to the same imperatives."[17] Because everyone has to follow the same rules, no one can claim superiority. Each viewer, by and large, has the same obligations and entitlements, a point I will return to. (Exceptions to the rule exist, of course, and I will mention some of them in section VII of Chapter 5. Just think of racially segregated cinemas or movie-theaters where viewers are separated according to class or caste.)

IV. WE-INTENTION, JOINT ATTENTION, JOINT ACTION

To lay the groundwork for my argument on the joint action in quiet-attentive viewing, I will now address three terms that so far have only been mentioned in passing: we-intention, joint attention, and joint action.

1. We-intention

In what way can we say that each individual member of the audience has a *we*-intention to watch the film *jointly* rather than an *I*-intention to simply watch the film? I believe there are various reasons why we can assume that watching a film with others implies an intention and commitment to watching the film *jointly*. Of course, we-intentions come in various degrees. Consequently, we can expect a continuum from weak to strong forms of collective intention.

On the *strong* end of the spectrum, there is a straightforward we-intention to watch the film together – an intention often expressed verbally. Think of the family, the couple, or the group of friends who go to the cinema *as* a family, a couple, or a group of friends. Provided they have collectively decided to watch the film, their decision expresses a *we*-intention to go to and attend the film rather than a mere *I*-intention. Or think of the film night in my home to which I invite various friends; we must all have a strong intention to watch the film *together*, since my friends would easily be able to rent the DVD on their own. Another example is *Star Wars* fans who, having camped in front of the cinema for hours or even days, eagerly watch the first screening of the newest installment of George Lucas's saga in a midnight opening. In an illuminating study on the phenomenon of midnight movie premieres, Carter Moulton has claimed that these "midnight blockbusters are for committed, knowledgeable fans only": "fans become insiders merely by accessing a more inaccessible form of cinemagoing and by enduring the spatial and temporal elongations that accompany the midnight event (advance-ticket sales, long lines in the parking lot, the consequences of staying up late on a work night, and, in some cases, the nine-hour marathon screenings). In other words, *you should only attend midnight blockbusters if you are a serious fan, but to attend a midnight blockbuster is to be a serious fan.* To be there is to fit in."[18] Moulton has collected a number of fan responses that explicitly voice a strong we-intention. Here is one: "The first screening is filled with *like minded* fans that are there because *they want to be there.*"[19] Another viewer said: "The crowds are much better. No young children, generally you're with people who REALLY, REALLY want to see the movie. In the case of the hobbit [*sic*], enough to order tickets more than a month in advance. *These are my people!*"[20] I label these examples instances of *strong we-intention*.

In the case of *medium we-intention* we may think of a group of people going to the cinema largely anonymously, but still as part of a specific collective or community. The Danish Embassy in Berlin invites fellow Danes to watch the opening film of a small festival devoted to Danish cinema. Fans of Manchester United, and of Eric Cantona in particular, go to see Ken Loach's *Looking for Eric* (2009), in which the former football star plays a major role. Devotees to the work of Apichatpong Weerasethakul go to the Vienna Filmmuseum to attend a retrospective of the celebrated Thai filmmaker. These groups share a certain identity as Danes, Manchester United fans, or Apichatpong admirers. Here the we-intention is not as strong as in the first examples. But as long as the individual members of the audience consider themselves part of these larger collectives, we may assume there will be a *medium* we-intention to watch the film together.

Yet even in the majority of cases in which we simply drive to the neighborhood cinema in order to watch the newest film, we can speak of a *weak we-intention* once we slightly change the perspective. Most of the time we may not have an explicitly formulated intention to watch a film *together* with other anonymous viewers. However, sitting at this time of the day in this cinema in this neighborhood with this audience for this film, the experience stands out from the normal flow of life. It implies a concrete decision *in favor* of the movie-theater (including, *nolens volens*, its collective experience) and *against* watching the film alone at home.[21] This is a particularly significant decision as nowadays it would be so much easier to avoid going elsewhere and let the film come to us: "when I download a film from the Internet [. . .] the word *access* no longer implies that I must pass over a threshold and enter into a particular place; rather, it indicates that something arrives before my eyes at my command. We now need to have everything 'here,' as opposed to being obliged to move 'elsewhere'," Francesco Casetti claims.[22]

Simply by choosing a certain film, deciding upon a specific screening time, driving to the cinema, standing in line, buying a ticket, and taking a seat in the audience, we signal that we have the *common goal* of watching this particular film. As such, we perform a minimal practical we-intention for each other: by attending the film we *share a goal* and therefore *form a voluntary association* for a certain amount of time.[23] This *practical* collective intentionality (we have a common goal right now) can be distinguished from *cognitive* collective intentionality (we share a *common opinion* or *conviction* at this moment) or *affective* collective intentionality (we have a common *emotion* or *mood* right now).[24] The former does not have to presuppose a shared cognition and affect, but often it includes both. Firstly, by attending the show we also signal a *common interest* in this particular film: the cognitive collective intentionality refers to sharing the opinion or conviction that this film is worth watching and that we might all have a *common taste*. Secondly, from the outset our co-presence might also indicate a minimal affective collective intentionality as we presumably share the *common hope* for a good film and the *common anticipation* of an experience that is worthwhile – otherwise we would not be here. Of course, stronger forms of shared emotions and moods – being afraid together, say, or enjoying the film together – can later supplement this minimal affective collective intentionality throughout the ninety minutes or so.

Moreover, once we adhere to the social norms of behavior, we implicitly acknowledge that we have a common we-intention: to watch the film. Here we might also remind ourselves of the relatively high price we pay in terms of personal freedom. Thomas Elsaesser once characterized the theatrical experience as a "fixed term of imprisonment." The viewer is "pinned to his seat" and "enclosed in a darkened room, cut off visually from the surroundings."[25] Comparing the filmic atmospheres of three *dispositives* – the living room, the museum, and the cinema – Margrit Tröhler points out the freedom to come and go when looking at a moving-image installation or projection in a museum.[26] In a museum we are much more dependent on our decision to stay or go than we are in the cinema. Since in the cinema the common intention of watching the film requires such a comparatively strong *adherence to social norms*, we can infer that accepting these social norms and rules implies that we tacitly signal our (albeit weak) we-intention. We *all* want to see this film. And we all accept to see it *together*. This is not to deny that there might be many reasons why we go to the cinema rather than watching the film at home: the film comes out earlier, the screen is bigger, the quality of the image is better, the sound-system is more impressive, and so on. At the same time, and this is crucial for my argument, we do not behave as we would in our private surroundings: the fact that we sacrifice many of our short-term self-interests like answering the phone or talking to our partner underscores our joint – not just private – intention to watch the film (I will return to the cinema's normative agreement below).

Lest this might sound too schematic or homogenizing, let me point out that various levels of we-intention can exist simultaneously within a single auditorium and even within a single spectator. A viewer from Copenhagen visiting a festival of Danish films in Berlin can at one and the same time have a strong we-intention to watch the film with her husband, a medium we-intention to view it with the other co-present Danes, and a weak we-intention to see it with the whole audience.

2. Joint attention

A critic might object that my description of weak we-intention could be applied to all kinds of social situations. However, coming back to an earlier example, we can easily see that the weak we-intention of anonymous co-viewers is qualitatively different from the people sitting in the same train compartment. To begin with, the latter do not have a common goal, as each traveler will assume that other passengers will get off at different stops (their only common goal may be to go in the same direction). Moreover, their cognitive collective intentionality will be extremely weak, because unlike the film the train is not an end in itself, but rather a means to an end: It would sound overblown to claim that passengers who take this train signal each other that they share a conviction that this is a train worth taking and that they have a common interest in this particular train *as a train*. The same goes for the affective collective intentionality: We would have a hard time describing the passengers' presence as a statement of their common hope for a good train ride and their common anticipation of an experience that is worthwhile. Without even taking into consideration the much looser social norms in the train compartment that allow people to chat on their cell phones, play a guitar, and give children the license to run up and down the aisle, the we-intention to take the train *together* will be miniscule. (But here, too, we might consider degrees of we-intention: Even the group of individuals who take this train together at this time of the day may be described as sharing a we-intention, even though their collective intention pales in comparison to stronger forms of we-intention.)

What crucially distinguishes the train ride from the movie-theater, however, is the fact that the viewers in the cinema also jointly attend a single intentional object. Joint attention refers to the fact that you, I, and other individuals have a common understanding of what we are doing and that we are not focusing on the same thing by accident.[27] We must have a minimal mutual awareness that we are perceiving the same thing. But, again, this awareness need *not* be reflective: I do not have to focus on the others jointly attending; it can also be relegated to the fringe of consciousness. Tom Cochrane, in an essay on joint attention to music, points out that "joint attention can vary in intensity [. . .] as a product of how much we monitor each other."[28] Given that in quiet-attentive viewing there is little or no verbal communication and little or no face-to-face interaction, how can we *explicitly* infer or *implicitly* presuppose that we, as an audience, follow the film in joint attention?

First, there are the preconditions of the cinematic dispositive, which rule out that we have the same intentional object by accident. Our seats are all facing the illuminated screen which stands out from the surrounding darkness. The unidirectional seating position prevents us from looking at each other; our vectors of perception and attention are directed toward the film. How smoothly the cinema grants us access to this single intentional object of joint attention (and how taken-for-granted this easy access seems to be) becomes more graspable when we look at situations in which this is not a given. Consider, for instance, the funny account of a rainy drive-in theater experience that film critic Jonathan Rosenbaum went through with his family: "After a while, we are running the windshield wiper. We alternately keep the windows open and shut. When they are shut all the windows steam up rapidly and we can't see a thing. I would be disposed to accept this state of things quite cheerfully, but the kids object. So we open the windows. The glass clears, and also Jonny is enabled to stick his head out of one of the back windows, which he claims is the only way he can see. But the rain drives in on all of us, it is cold and windy and James, who has a cold, starts sneezing. So we close them. Then we open them again. Etc., etc."[29] Or take, again, the museum experience where there are so many more objects to focus on. When moving through the museum the visitor is constantly confronted with questions about the time and attention he or she should pay to various objects. Citing an observation by Serge Daney, Volker Pantenburg argues that in fact the museum visitor's aimless stroll past video installations resembles (window-)shopping behavior.[30] Film viewers, on the other hand, do not have to face the same series of choices, because they are usually devoted to the single object on display.

Secondly, there is an absence of motor activity. The structure of most cinemas is not conducive to bodily activity; viewers rarely wander around, but remain seated throughout the film. Consider, once more, the case of watching a film in a museum: the black box projection room or the space in front of the monitor is a place of transition.[31] The dispositive of the museum is much more mobile and individualistic and thus allows for joint attention only briefly, if at all. In contrast, sitting in their seats, viewers in the cinema deactivate specific parts of their body, rob themselves of their motor freedom, in order to pay full attention to the film.[32] As Pantenburg points out, the early 1970s were not only the age of apparatus theory, which characterized the cinematic situation as a captivity, but also a time of utopian ideas about the cinema as a place of focused, concentrated perception. Filmmakers like Hollis Frampton, Peter Kubelka, or Robert Smithson regarded immobility and stillness as preconditions for (joint) attention.[33] (Here one might spot the seeds of an ethical argument in favor of quiet-attentive viewing. As in recent discussions about *slow* or *contemplative* cinema and its merits in terms of the "dedicated attention" and "emotionally rich experience" in minimalist film, the joint attention of quiet-attentive viewing may potentially imply more meaningful ways of watching films in our contemporary "attention economy".[34])

Thirdly, and most importantly, we can explicitly infer or implicitly presuppose that we follow the film in joint attention once there is silence and an absence of verbal interaction prevails. As the *perception of silence* is rather important for my argument, I will demonstrate in a somewhat lengthy excursus that silence in the cinema is an *audible* phenomenon just like talking, laughing, or screaming. As phenomenologist Bernhard Waldenfels puts it: "Silence does not mean that *nothing* is heard, but rather that *not something* is heard."[35] Similarly, philosopher Roy Sorensen argues: "Hearing silence is successful perception of an absence of sound. It is not a failure to hear sound."[36] Since Sorensen does not give detailed support for his claim, I draw on a famous phenomenological description from Jean-Paul Sartre's *Being and Nothingness* to illustrate that in the cinema and elsewhere we perceive *absences* – such as the absence of sound.

In his example, Sartre describes how he comes fifteen minutes late to a meeting in a café with his friend Pierre, who is usually very punctual, but upon looking around cannot be glimpsed. Sartre argues that popular wisdom gets it right when someone exclaims something like: "I suddenly saw that he was not there." Why? When looking around in the café all the objects are synthetically organized to form the *ground* on which the *figure* of Pierre should appear. The café as the ground is only marginally attended to – what is focused on is the figure of Pierre. But Pierre is not present. He is not absent from a specific *part* of the café, according to Sartre, but he is absent from the *whole* café. The café "carries the figure everywhere in front of it, presents the figure everywhere to me," Sartre writes. "This figure which slips constantly between my look and the solid, real objects of the cafe is precisely a perpetual disappearance [. . .]." While the ground demands the *appearance* of the figure of Pierre, it only "slips as a *nothing* to the surface of the ground. It serves as foundation for the judgment – 'Pierre is not here.'"[37] Hence Sartre shows that Pierre's absence is given *in* perceptual experience: Sartre genuinely *perceives* the absence of Pierre and does not simply *infer* or *imagine* it. Note that a phenomenological description is interested only in what is given in experience. The ontological status of Pierre's absence is irrelevant here.

In the cinema something comparable takes place when we perceive the absence of sound *as silence*. To be sure, we only perceive silence where we expect sound, just as in Sartre's example the perception of Pierre's absence derives from the expectation of Pierre's presence. Had Sartre gone to the café without expecting Pierre, he would not have perceived his absence (just as, when perceiving Pierre's absence, he does not perceive the absence of billions of other people that potentially could be present). Hence our perception of silence in the cinema always hinges on our expectation of sound: "We are primed to hear sounds and so hear the absence of sounds. Absences are relative. They draw their identity from their relata," Roy Sorensen points out.[38] But why should we expect sound in the cinema? Because the cinema is filled with 2, 20, 200, or 2,000 other viewers from whose presence we would expect sound, as humans are bound to make noises: sound is the natural state and silence the convention that holds it in check.[39] Inversely, this implies that when we watch a film alone, we do *not* perceive silence, because we do not expect sound in the first place (and hence we do not infer the *attention* and *concentration* of an audience 'signaled' by silence).

Obviously, the cinema is not devoid of sound: there is always the sound of the film. But silence does not have to be absolute and complete in order for us to become aware of it. We can easily perceive silence in one place, while *simultaneously* hearing sound in another. Sorensen gives the following example: "a teacher can hear the silence of her classroom while also hearing a lawnmower outside. She thinks 'It is silent in here but noisy out there.'"[40] The same goes for the silence in the movie-theater: we can hear the sound of the film – and still, however peripherally, perceive the silence of the audience. Nor do we have to *focus* on the silence of the audience to perceive it: "Hearing silence does not depend on reflective awareness of the silence. Sometimes we become aware of a lengthy silence only after it has been broken. A marginal kind of sensitivity suffices for hearing silence," according to Sorensen.[41]

Recall that in my definition of quiet attention I presuppose attention. My definition therefore rules out an auditorium of sleeping viewers. The quiet attention's silence is the outcome of a concentrated audiovisual attention. Of course, this definition presumes a third-person perspective that simply *postulates* attentive viewing. But what about the first-person perspective? As long as I do not actively assume that the other co-present viewers are sleeping or absent-minded (which for various reasons I usually do not), I will always tacitly presuppose that their silence indicates attention. Seen from this perspective, we can describe silence as a specific type of communication: it signals that the film *and* its collective reception prevail over individual reactions. Hence silence does not mean an absence of collectivity. Once other viewers start to talk, send text messages, or move around the auditorium, we realize that during these moments their attention and our attention are *not* joint. Here the background assumption we have kept all along becomes negatively foregrounded.

The fact that quiet-attentive viewers are united in joint attention during the film may become even more obvious when we compare it to the moments before the film begins. People walk through the auditorium looking for seats; they chat with their neighbors; they talk on their mobile phones; they read magazines. Once the lights go out, a transitional period begins that consists of commercials and trailers and may involve the film's opening titles. During this phase one can sense a shift: the scattered foci are gradually united and directed toward the film. A "phenomenal change" takes place, as Hans Bernhard Schmid would put it, from the dispersed attention of individuals to a we-intention and joint attention of the audience.[42]

3. Joint action

The final term that I need to clarify is joint action itself. Joint action is sometimes mentioned in the same breath as joint attention. For instance, Anika Fiebich and Shaun Gallagher argue that intentional joint attention – that is, joint attention in which individuals "*intend* to be mutually attentive towards the same entity (where the shared intention may just be to maintain joint attention)" – already qualifies as a *basic* joint action.[43] Here I discuss joint attention and joint action separately, partly because I wish to emphasize the stronger – and perhaps more controversial – claim that the joint action of quiet-attentive viewers goes beyond the "basic" joint action of joint attention. In the literature on collective intentionality, at least three aspects recur with regard to joint action: attuned behavior, we-intentions, and normative agreements.

I begin with attuned behavior, which philosopher Angelika Krebs defines as follows: "In joint action the participants continuously attune their inputs to the inputs of the others and to the action to be actualized [. . .] taking the others to be doing the same kind of attuning."[44] If in an orchestra one person plays a different tune, it becomes blatantly obvious. If one dance partner stops moving, there can no longer be a joint action. On the face of it this seems different in the cinema. Here, behavior that is not in tune with the common goal of watching the film together *can* become conspicuous (think of talking on the mobile phone), but it can also go unnoticed (someone falling asleep). However, the fact that someone can stop acting jointly without becoming noticeable does not disqualify watching a film together with quiet attention as a case of joint action. While in many paradigmatic cases of joint action the whole cannot be thought without the individual parts, this does not apply to every case: the viewer who falls asleep simply does not partake any longer, but the rest of the audience is still acting jointly in attuned behavior. Due to the darkness of the cinema and the viewers' restricted vocal and bodily expressivity, quiet-attentive viewing makes it easy to withdraw into activities like sleeping or daydreaming without being sanctioned, only to reconnect rather easily to the joint action of watching the movie together a moment later.

Furthermore, prototypical joint action seems to be characterized either by identical motor movements (walking in a parade) or attuned motor movements (playing in an orchestra). Again, *prima facie*, this seems to be different in the cinema, since the cinema audience is characterized by its *lack* of motor movements. How can we speak of action, then, let alone joint action? We can use the term precisely because of what I have indicated above: Actions must not be reduced to motor movements. Even if prototypical examples of action rely on motor movements, paying attention to a film – watching and listening to its unfolding – is a *mental action* based on perception. Secondly, we may talk about *joint* action as long as the collective audience fulfills a necessary condition of joint action: attuned behavior. When spectators watch a film quietly and attentively, the synchronization and coordination of behavior depends on three prerequisites: stillness, silence, and attention. Viewers show restraint in motor activity by not going in and out or walking around; viewers do not talk on their mobile phones, whistle, scream, burp, moan, and so on; viewers refrain from other quiet activities like reading, fondling or playing with their mobile phone, devoting their attention to the film. Taken together, sitting and watching in silence do not imply an absence of motor movements, but are a form of *synchronization* of activity: silence and motor stillness *coordinate* what might otherwise result in highly diverse motor movements, comportments, and expressions, and thus they signal a joint attention. Of course, there are the more obvious examples of cinematic joint action that I discuss in the next chapter, such as laughing together, screaming together, singing along together, or speaking the dialogue together. However, this would not only reduce action to expressive behavior and ignore the active attention in quiet-attentive viewing, but would also give too much weight to less predominant kinds of behavior.

However, the synchronized and coordinated behavior of joint attention is merely a necessary condition from which one might infer the joint action of the quiet-attentive type, but it is not sufficient.[45] As a consequence, the joint action of the cinema is not something that can be observed from a third-person perspective, for instance via infrared cameras. In an extreme case the camera might show four hundred people silently following the film, when in fact they are all daydreaming about very different things. Following Hans Bernhard Schmid, we may assume that *we-intentions* are another necessary condition for joint action and group membership.[46] Importantly, and this point requires re-emphasis, a *reflective* awareness of being part of a group is not a necessary condition for the existence of a group: we do not have to reflect on the fact that we belong to a certain collective in order to be part of it.[47] As long as there are we-intentions and the attuned behavior of joint attention, we do not need to be centrally aware of our collective activity; it can remain on the fringe of consciousness.

It is crucial, however, that the three types of we-intention do not contradict each other: *practical* collective intentionality (sharing a goal); *cognitive* collective intentionality (sharing an opinion or conviction); *affective* collective intentionality (sharing an emotion or mood). Even in the case of a practical we-intention to watch a particular film as well as an active joint attention of the whole audience, one would not be able to decide from a third-person perspective that every single viewer following the film with quiet attention is part of an audience that acts jointly. Joint attention and the common goal of watching the film are not enough when the practical collective intentionality is disrupted or contradicted by the fact that there are differences in cognitive or affective collective intentionality. Think of a female viewer who watches a misogynist action film with male spectators and interprets their silent attention as a sign of a pleasurable viewing experience that she cannot share. Here the quiet attention of the other viewers signals to the individual viewer her difference in terms of cognitive collective intentionality (she finds the film politically retrograde, whereas the others do not care) as well as affective collective intentionality (she is angry at the filmmakers, whereas the others enjoy the film). This particular viewer would hardly say that she and the other viewers watch the film jointly. It seems important, however, that in this case the audience situation becomes *reflective*: the viewer is fully *conscious* of her difference. As long as it does not become foregrounded in a negative way, the we-intentions and joint attention of quiet-attentive viewing are simply presupposed. The assumed commonalities often prevail until differences become foregrounded, another point I will come back to.

Perhaps the most obvious objection to my argument that quiet-attentive viewers act jointly is the fact that every single viewer would also be able to watch the film in identical fashion alone. However, the similarity between a viewer who watches a film alone and someone who watches it as part of a group exists only from the outside. As John Searle has put it in a slightly different case: "Externally observed, the two cases are indistinguishable, but they are clearly different internally."[48] The objection not only ignores the necessary we-intentions mentioned above – it also overlooks the important point that once I watch the film as a group I immediately have to take into account the *normative agreement* this entails, including its social obligations and entitlements. However, once I follow the social norms of the cinema and rely on all the others to do so as well (absence of talking, motor activity, and other pursuits), the perspective changes from *I* watch the film to *we* watch the film.

Let us first discuss the social *obligations* that come with the we-intentions to watch a movie jointly. Erving Goffman has variously raised attention to the "mutual commitments" of social gatherings and the "committed 'presence'" one has to show in a social situation.[49] Just as it would be odd (and potentially offensive) if someone was reading a book during a rock concert or in a football stadium while the others follow an important match, it is equally strange (and even impolite) to the joint action of the movie-theater if someone plays a video game on his smartphone or sends text messages throughout.[50] In this case Goffman would speak of "engagement disloyalty": "To engage in situational impropriety [. . .] is to draw improperly on *what one owes* the social occasion."[51] My colleague Christian Ferencz-Flatz has raised the objection that libraries, for instance, are places with strong social rules of silence and restrained motor movements as well. However, while it might be true that we are all involved in the same activity of reading books, he claims, we wouldn't call our activity "reading together". My objection that in contrast to the library there is joint attention to a single intentional object in the cinema – we are all focused on the screen, whereas in the library there are as many books as readers – does not save the case for him.[52] Yet I believe that he overlooks a crucial difference between the specific social experiences of the cinema and the library: While in the library we would not be offended if someone played a computer game on his or her smartphone as long as this activity does not interfere with each individual's *personal* goals (the *I*-intention to read the book), this is different in the cinema where we (implicitly) presume a *we*-intention, a joint attention, and a joint action.

Let me give further support to this claim by discussing the following illuminating quote by Goffman: "two persons in a movie-theater, quietly talking together about something entirely unconnected with the evening's entertainment, may thereby exhibit an unoccasioned mutual-involvement, and by doing so cause more resentment than those who make much more physical sound but do so in expressing their approbation or disapprobation of what is being seen."[53] Why does Goffman's observation sound plausible? Persons who make a loud comment on an onscreen event merely switch from quiet-attentive viewing to expressive-diverted viewing (discussed in the following chapter), whereas the persons who talk about something else entirely assume a mode of *inattention*. The former viewers become annoying for disrupting the tacit we-intention to watch the film jointly in a quiet-attentive way. But they remain committed to the we-intention to jointly watch the movie, even if momentarily in an expressive-diverted way not implicitly agreed on at the beginning of the film.[54] The persons who discuss a wholly unconnected matter, on the other hand, breach the we-intention and joint action completely.

Importantly, going to the cinema not only implies that we follow social *obligations*, it also grants the *entitlements* that come with the commitments of we-intentions. This is a point that Margaret Gilbert has drawn attention to.[55]

Discussing the example of walking together, she notes: "As long as people are out on a walk together, they will understand that each has an *obligation* to do what he or she can to achieve the relevant goal. Moreover, each one is *entitled* to rebuke the other for failure to fulfill this obligation. It is doubtful whether the core obligations and entitlements in question are moral obligations and entitlements. At the same time, they are not merely a matter of prudence or self-interest. Importantly, they seem to be a direct function of the fact of going for a walk together."[56] Let me rephrase Gilbert's talk about obligations and entitlements in terms of the film experience. As a backdrop I return to the not-so-hypothetical case of watching a video-film individually on a monitor in a museum or art gallery. There are people standing in the surrounding area whose talk about a different exhibit distracts me from concentrating fully on the film. In contrast to the cinema, where the same kind of talk with the same kind of loudness would annoy me a great deal more, I do not feel entitled to reproach them, just as they do not feel an obligation to remain silent. This is the case because in the museum space we often do *not* have a we-intention to watch the film together in a quiet-attentive way, while in the cinema we do.[57] Reproached cinemagoers often acknowledge other viewers' entitlement to rebuke them for being disruptive: reminded of their obligation, they usually do not argue back.

Now, this is important: The more we expect the cinematic situation to be an activity we do *together*, the more significant the normative agreement, the stronger the obligation to act accordingly, and the bigger the entitlement to be angry about its disruption. Take the case of noticing someone falling asleep next to you. If you only have a very weak we-intention to watch the film with this person because the co-viewer is an anonymous other, you might find it strange that he sleeps, but you will hardly wake him up to remind him of his obligation to attend to the film together.[58] However, if you see a film with your husband or wife and presuppose a strong form of we-intention because this is a film that you were both looking forward to watching together, you might feel disappointed or even angry if your partner falls asleep. The differences between what viewers are entitled to expect, and what they can remind others of, are thus dependent on the strength of the expectation of a we-intention. In turn, persons going to the cinema predominantly for other reasons – let's assume a teenage couple who intends to use the darkness for kissing and fondling – may not be at all angry at someone who does not participate in the joint action of watching the movie. In fact, they may not even notice the disruption, because there was never an expectation of a joint action in the first place.

Further evidence for considering collective viewing as a joint action derives from the built-in teleology of joint actions and the obligations and entitlements that come with it: Once we start a joint activity, it usually implies the expectation that we *finish* it together.[59] We can see the pertinence of this point if we switch to the example of watching a film together on television at home. If I watch a film jointly with a couple of friends, there is an implicit commitment to watch it until the end. Even if I am bored with the film, I commit myself to not changing the channel, to not reading a newspaper, and to not setting off for a walk with my dog. These diversions would be considered impolite. Of course, it is always possible to negotiate verbally about doing something else, but this would involve changing the joint action. In the cinema my commitment to finishing the film as well as the other viewers' entitlement to expect me to watch the film through to the end may not be so obvious (and probably not as strong), but it certainly exists as well. One indication is that in the cinema viewers tend to feel reluctant about leaving prematurely: if there were no implicit commitments to watching the film jointly, why should these anonymous viewers feel a disinclination toward, or even embarrassment about, leaving the cinema?[60] No such commitment exists, of course, when I watch a film without others: watching a film alone on television, I am far more likely to channel-surf or turn off the DVD, and thus not finish the film.

Here we can find an argument, by the way, for the crucial difference between a collective experience based on physical co-presence and a collective experience based on an audience that I imagine watching the same film in another cinema at the same time.[61] Apart from the fact that in the latter case we cannot be influenced by the affective atmosphere in the cinema and the emotional contagion it may imply, there are no real obligations and entitlements *vis-à-vis* those other imagined viewers.

Finally, my case for considering quiet-attentive viewing as a form of acting together can be strengthened by another common characteristic of joint actions: "In many cases, acting jointly allows us to *bring about outcomes that a single agent could not* – or could not easily – bring about on his or her own," Elisabeth Pacherie notes.[62] Watching a film jointly *with others* can also have positive effects. This is true not only for the increased enjoyment of a comedy in joint laughter (see Chapters 5, 6, and 7), but also for the heightened attention and concentration when watching a film together quietly. Just compare watching a 5.5-hour Lav Diaz film like *From What Is Before/Mula sa kung ano ang noon* (2014) or a 7-hour Béla Tarr film like *Sátántangó* (1994) alone on your computer at home or in a cinema with other quiet-attentive viewers: chances are high that the latter will afford a beneficial concentration effect because one does not divert oneself with other activities.

V. THE CINEMATIC JOINT ACTION AS COLLECTIVE EXPERIENCE

So far my argument has been couched largely in negative terms. Let me now formulate my case for joint action more positively: the *absence* of verbal communication, expressive non-verbal comments, motor activity, and diverse foci of attention is at the same time the prerequisite for the perceived *presence* of silence, stillness, and a shared intentional object.

Consider silence: Michal Pagis suggests that in sociological research a negative view predominates, taking silence exclusively as a forced, oppressive situation. As a result of power relations that deny the self-expressive voice, destroy the communication-based affinity between people, and therefore create social distance, silence allegedly implies the opposite of freedom and community.[63] This also seems to be the view that underlies much of the film-scholarly work discussed in Chapter 4, which celebrates the cinematic practices of talking, call-and-response, singing along, and suchlike as liberating and creative of social bonds. In contrast, I believe that we have to understand silence not as a forced absence of talk, sociality, or conviviality, but as a productive *enabling condition*.

First, it allows us to accept that the film fills the cinema with its presence. As early film theorist Louis Delluc once put it: "The popular public hears because it listens. It listens because it is silent. Silence genuinely helps in looking and seeing."[64] The silence of the audience allows the film to be the only, or at least main, source of sound inside the auditorium: the film can become the figure on the (back)ground of silence.[65]

Second, silence is an enabling condition also for joint attention and joint action. Or, to be more precise, joint attention and joint action are manifested in silence, whose *meaning* could be summarized as "We are all paying attention right now!" This is a point we should not overlook: silence does not imply a complete absence of meaning, but can be filled with its own signification. As Don Ihde points out: "In conversation when the other is silent there is also a 'speaking': we see the face which 'speaks' in its silence. We feel the flesh which 'speaks' in its silence."[66] Obviously silence does not have a *default* meaning; its signification always relates to the context in which we encounter it. Depending on the circumstances it can mean assent, dissent, uncertainty, respect, etc.[67] In the cinema the silent viewers 'speak' first and foremost about their attention to watch the film and the willingness to accept the rules of conduct: by remaining silent we indicate that we, together, watch the film and do not act individually by, for instance, speaking out loud. Just as for Ihde the concentrated attention-direction of listening is a gesture toward silence, silence signifies concentrated attention.[68]

The fact that silence does not necessarily imply a negative absence of communication could mean that at least some types of silence and stillness should be cherished rather than condemned (although I do not deny that other types of silence can be either regulatory and oppressive or negatively disruptive, as some examples in the next chapter will make clear). Further arguments along these lines come from ethnographic work on silent meditation. As Pagis shows, there are chosen and shared silences that function as constitutive mechanisms allowing for certain experiences to surface in the first place. In the cinema the fact that the audience remains quiet often functions as a precondition for a synchronized collective experience, because it allows for the tacit supposition that the others not only *act* as I do, but also *experience* similarly to me and hence that we act jointly and experience something collectively. Social psychologist Gerald Echterhoff and his colleagues call this type of synchronized collective experience *shared reality*.[69]

As the notion of "tacit supposition" indicates, this is not something we have to consciously focus on. Collective aesthetic experience often relies on silence as an important precondition, because expressive reactions – and verbal comments in particular – often bring experiential *differences* to the fore. Just think of derisive laughter or comments like "Wow, look at this!", "Come on, that's unbelievable!", or "He's so cute!" While these expressive reactions might include some viewers, they simultaneously exclude others who think or feel differently. And even those who feel included in terms of the aesthetic judgment might feel a rupture with regard to joint action, because commenting verbally on the film involves *not* attending to it in silence. What was synchronized joint action a moment earlier now temporarily veers in a different direction. Silence, on the other hand, can allow for a more inclusive, albeit tacit, intersubjective experience. As Pagis puts it, "Silent intersubjectivity is [. . .] qualitatively different from the type articulated by speech. It allows for a more general and inclusive form of intersubjectivity, a form that is not obsessed with content, with exact comparisons of one mind to another. Silent intersubjectivity can actually prevent such processes of 'othering' by allowing for difference under a general rubric of sameness. It offers a wide canopy that connects people based on embodied involvement in the same event."[70]

Quiet-attentive viewing is particularly conducive to this kind of intersubjectivity. This is, of course, not to say that the other viewers do indeed experience just as I do. As Pagis points out, "since miscommunication and misinterpretation are quite common, intersubjectivity is more an experience than an actual truth claim about the world."[71] One might be totally wrong about the experience of one's co-viewers and still experience collectively a shared reality with them.[72] Even if in actuality we often do *not* think and feel the same – a point that reception studies have made quite clear – the viewer tacitly takes it for granted as long as not proved otherwise. Empirical studies lend evidence to this, if you want, narcissistic projection of one's own thoughts and feelings onto others. As Echterhoff and his colleagues point out: "Research on egocentric projections of knowledge and false consensus demonstrates that people tend to presume inner states in others that match their own inner state. Indeed, the motivation to establish a subjective experience of reality by social sharing is so strong that people often assume that most others agree with them even when this is not the case."[73]

In aesthetic contexts we often subconsciously 'project' our individual experience onto others and thus make it unintentionally and pre-reflectively a temporary norm. Cinematic joint action and experience appear in the likeness of our own experience, as long as no one disproves it by doing and feeling something else or until my focus shifts on the singularity of my own experience (and I even make this singularity public, for instance through connoisseur laughter or verbal comment). If this sounds too much like Freudian narcissism, it might become less controversial when put the other way round. In aesthetic experience, individual viewers do not presuppose that everyone feels differently all the time: the likeness of the experience is tacitly taken as a default.

To be sure, there are instances when we do not take the likeness of the collective experience as the norm from the beginning: when we feel excluded or put ourselves deliberately outside the group. If I watch a film in a cinema known for its ethnically diverse audience, I might not presume to share a lot with the other viewers. Here a *difference in response* may be the default expectation.[74] A yardstick for the assumption that we share a reality, and hence our thoughts and feelings, could therefore be the surprise (or even anger) about the difference in experience once it occurs: When I do not presume a big communality from the outset, I won't be surprised or angry if someone else responds very differently. Here it might be in fact all the more positively surprising and enjoyable to find out that we do share the same response, for instance when we all laugh about the same joke. However, in cases where no explicit (sociological or cultural) differences exist from the outset, the shared reality default holds – and quiet-attentive viewing proves particularly advantageous in this respect.

VI. THE BENEFITS AND PLEASURES OF WATCHING WITH QUIET ATTENTION

This raises the question: Why do we engage in the joint action of quiet-attentive viewing in the first place? Can we find good reasons that support the joint action argument also when we look at the *purpose* it may fulfill for cinemagoers? In the following I discuss some of the benefits of *joint action*, somewhat brutally separating it from the question of affective collective experience and the debate about collective emotions. I am aware that in reality these *two* levels of collectivity – the joint action level and the affective collective experience level – are often mutually intertwined, but for analytic reasons it seems useful and tolerable to keep them apart for the moment.

Philosopher Marion Godman takes issue with the one-sidedness of the debate about joint action which, in her opinion, is too strongly focused on the shared intentions of problem-solving and achieving concrete target goals. Godman seems to reject the implicit instrumental rationality that takes jointly acting with others merely as a means to an end. As an example we might think again of the positive concentration effect that watching slow Béla Tarr or Lav Diaz films *with others* can have on one's attention: If I go to the cinema with colleagues to mutually boost my concentration, I try to achieve a common goal through our joint action.

Godman, instead, claims that many joint actions are driven by shared motivations that are *intrinsically* social in character. She distinguishes two such social motivations. First, there are *long-term benefits* of establishing or strengthening social bonds, effects that lie beyond the joint action itself but are based on and derive from it.[75] For example, I may eventually fall in love with a girl who I had invited to several 'movie dates'. Or I can bond with my old buddies through rewatching the favorite comedy of our high school days.[76] Second, and even more relevant for our discussion of the cinema experience, there is the *short-term benefit* of taking pleasure in doing things with others: "we are socially motivated to engage in joint action simply because we find the social experience rewarding in its own right."[77] Doing things with others is often more pleasurable than doing the same things alone, no matter if we do these things with close friends or anonymous others.[78] Hence watching a film jointly with quiet attention enables a collective experience *per se* that we, as viewers, do not have to reflect upon in order to enjoy. Just as I can prefer taking a walk with someone to walking alone without thinking about the fact that we are doing this together, I can enjoy watching a film collectively without being fully aware of it.

However, over and above the pleasure of doing things jointly, I want to postulate another type of pleasure which is connected to the concepts of "pleasure in functioning" (Karl Bühler) and "(social) flow" (Mihály Csíkszentmihályi). Broadly speaking, the former emphasizes the pleasure we can take in the uninhibited and smooth functioning of activities that do not aim at purposeful results but show our skills; the latter describes the psychological state of being deeply absorbed by an activity and enjoying it. Quiet-attentive viewing can provide the sheer pleasure in functioning as a group of people who are immersed in doing the same thing together smoothly, unimpeded, and skillfully. If in watching a film we lose ourselves collectively in immersed viewing, pleasure can derive from the fact that we are dedicated to and lost in a quiet activity together. In contrast to the other main type of collective spectatorship, quiet-attentive viewing is particularly conducive to this kind of pleasure because the smooth synchronization and unimpeded coordination of our joint action is rather easily achieved: we simply have to focus on the film and watch it with quiet, motionless attention. Alternative kinds of joint action in the cinema – singing along, speaking the dialogue, screaming, even laughing together – are not as easily synchronized and coordinated, as we shall see in Chapter 4. Once again, the pleasure does not need to be *reflected upon* during the experience. But it can become reflective *ex negativo*, as when the pleasure in functioning collectively is interrupted by people who do not act jointly and thus disturb the social flow.

In fact, quiet-attentive viewing has a serious drawback because its preconditions are so easily undermined. The fragility of silence derives from a feature of our sense of hearing: In contrast to vision, which we can more actively *seek* out due to our ability to *block* it, sound turns us into comparatively passive receivers.[79] The fragility of silence increases in direct proportion to the importance we grant it. The more we perceive the absence of sound, the easier fringe noises will intrude into our awareness.[80] In other words, the sounds of people whispering to each other, crunching popcorn, or receiving text messages do not intrude because we focus on them, but precisely because of the opposite: "In the auditory realm our focusing, which should effect an *exclusion*, negates itself and produces the contrary effect of *increased vulnerability* in an increased openness to the environment's presence," Don Ihde writes.[81] However, once the silence is destroyed and our expectations for a quiet-attentive joint action remain unfulfilled, we react with appropriate emotional responses: disappointment or even anger, a fact I return to in Chapter 9. I would therefore warn of a simplifying critique of discipline that treats it as overly oppressive and negative *per se*: "Not every act of discipline is a form of education, but all educative processes (even of an aesthetic nature) require an irrefutable dose of constraint and violence," Gabriele Pedullà reminds us.[82]

VII. DIFFERENCES TO THE COLLECTIVE EXPERIENCE IN THE THEATER

Now, even if the account given above were accurate, wouldn't it also apply to other collectively experienced art forms, particularly those that take place on stage like theater, opera, or ballet? No doubt there are many similarities between the collectivity in the cinema and those in the theater, opera, and ballet. In the following section I will therefore take a look at three differences in terms of collective experience. For the sake of brevity I restrict myself to theater, but most of what I say also goes for opera and ballet. Phenomenology often works best when experiences are compared: what is central about an experience becomes more palpable when put against the background of a related but different experience.

1. The actor's presence: differences in emotion

Despite our suspension of disbelief in the theater, we cannot forget the conspicuous live presence of the actor onstage: "The human being is all-important *in the theater*. The drama *on the screen* can exist without actors," Bazin claims in his essay on theater and cinema that we have encountered in Chapter 2.[83] The concept of *photogénie* even has it that inanimate objects can come to life via camera and projector. As Jean Epstein maintains in a much-quoted passage, the cinema possesses an *animistic* power: "Through the cinema, a revolver in a drawer, a broken bottle on the ground, an eye isolated by an iris are elevated to the status of characters in the drama."[84] In his excellent phenomenology of the theater Bert O. States discusses the exceptional cases of child actors and animals onstage that easily break the "spell" and introduce a sense of the real. In the theater one can hardly watch children and animals without a "double vision", as diegetic characters *and* as real children and animals on a stage: "Who has ever seen a child on stage without thinking, 'How well he acts, for a child!' or [. . .] 'Do they *understand* the play?'"[85] With regard to animals like dogs, States mentions the feelings of nervousness and delight that come with our realization that animals cannot be depended upon (will they bark, run off the stage, or urinate?), but also our feeling of surprise that they indeed act as if they knew that they were in a play.

To a lesser degree this 'double vision' is also at play when we watch professional theater actors. Unlike in a film, we can never know what will happen to them onstage. While in film we rely on the implicit assumption that what we see is intentional, controlled, and non-accidental, the stage actor introduces the specter of contingency that can haunt the theater experience: Will the leading actor forget his lines? Will the main actress stumble and break her ankle? Will the extras bump into each other when doing a complicated choreography?[86] States claims: "One of the reasons that it may be easier to become lost in a film than in an enacted play is that the film removes the *actual* aspect of performance and leaves us with the record of an actuality into which we can safely sink. But in the theater our sympathetic involvement with the characters is attended by a secondary, and largely subliminal, line of empathy born of the possibility that the illusion may at any moment be shattered by a mistake or an accident."[87] While veteran theatergoers will have actually *encountered* these cases, for all the other patrons it is at least a constant *possibility*.[88]

Inversely, we know that the actors know that we are their witnesses, and we know that they know that they have to carry "the weight of everyone's eyes," in Sören Kierkegaard's words.[89] We are aware that the actors onstage are open *and* vulnerable to our response: our rapt attention, our laughter, our boredom, our booing . . . We are also aware of the fact that the actors may react to our response by adjusting the way they play. And, finally, we know that at the end

– as convention has it – the actor will stand in front of us hoping for applause. States calls the curtain call "a decompression chamber", a metaphor congenial to the theater because it evokes the pressure built up in the auditorium with respect to the actors onstage: by applauding we can perform a motor movement that serves to 'let off' the very steam we have withheld during the play.

The knowledge that we are in the presence of real actors onstage has an important effect. Precisely because we are aware of the co-presence not only of the other *viewers*, but also of a number of *actors* on the stage, the collectivity of the experience, all things being equal, will not be the same as in the movie-theater. In the theater we are not only spectators, but also *witnesses* – witnesses to something that could potentially go wrong and that could even exert a call to act on our part, as when an actress hurts herself or an actor suffers from a heart-attack on stage. In the cinema, on the other hand, we are only *spectators* who are temporally, spatially and, in the case of fiction films, ontologically removed from what happens on the screen. In the theater we *share a space* not only with the other viewers, but also with the actors-cum-characters who always act and feel differently than the viewers they face. Hence the collective experience must be a different one to that in the cinema, where we do *not* share the space with the actors. Above I have claimed that in quiet-attentive viewing individual viewers do not presuppose that everyone feels differently all the time: the likeness of the experience is tacitly taken as a default. This cannot be the case in the theater, as we always have to presume that at least the actors experience differently and thus disrupt the unanimity of what we 'project' onto others.

Of course, I am not making the absurd claim that filmic characters and actors have no influence on us, nor am I stipulating that the theater audience does not have its own form of collective spectatorship. What I am arguing is that the form of collectivity in the theater must be differently structured, because as theatergoers we always tacitly have to assume that unanimity with *all* the persons present in the room is foreclosed precisely because of the actors' presence. As we have seen in Chapter 2, Bazin even maintains that actors are "objects of *mental opposition* because their real presence gives them an objective reality."[90] If this sounds too intangible, one may gauge what I am aiming at when we think of an instance of increased unanimity that *unites* actors and spectators: the collective joy after the premiere of a tense and complicated drama. The relieved and joyful applause of the audience coincides with the relieved and joyful bowing of the actors. While audience and actors do not feel identical – their relief and joy rests on different experiences after all – the viewers may still sense a remarkable change in comparison to the two hours before in which their experiences strongly differed. What can be felt in moments of relieved applause, I submit, is an *increased* unanimity of experience.

2. The varying sightlines: differences in perceptual access

A second important difference is the discrepancy in sightlines. David Bordwell has repeatedly pointed out that in the cinema we encounter the *monocular* projection of the *Cyclops-like* vision of the camera: "thanks to the laws of optics, the film camera captures a pyramidal chunk of space, with the tip of the pyramid at the lens and the playing space radiating out from there."[91] In contrast to the theater, the camera thus yields a uniform view on the action that takes place in the filmic world. Importantly, changing one's viewing position in the cinema does not reveal more of what the camera shows us – a fact satirically commented on in Jean-Luc Godard's *Les Carabiniers* (1963), in which an inexperienced cinemagoer tries to get a glimpse of a naked woman lying in a bathtub: He moves toward the screen and jumps up in order to see what is hidden inside the bathtub, thereby clumsily tearing down the screen. Bordwell writes: "On a stage the performers are watched from all over the auditorium, so the action must be visible from a wide range of positions. In cinema, however, the action is relayed to every member of the audience from exactly the same point – the lens."[92] To be sure, while the projector gives us the single optical entry point of the *camera lens*, in the cinema the viewers do not share the same view on the *screen*. In big megaplex cinemas the viewers in the front row and the spectators in the back row may get to see what is shown in very different *proportions*.

However, these discrepancies pale in comparison to the theater, where viewers may face enormous differences in sightlines, especially if we think of the classical proscenium theater. A spectator in the first row to the very left, who can almost reach out to the actors and may even get a glimpse of the wings, has an entirely different sightline to a spectator sitting high up in the balcony, for whom the actors are tiny creatures acting from afar. Many theaters even have places where part of the action is blocked and from where some viewers cannot see the performance in its entirety. This certainly has ramifications for the way viewers engage with the drama onstage. For someone sitting close to the actors, empathy with the human face will play an important role, whereas someone in the balcony has to rely on kinesthetic or motor empathy. As a consequence, we can expect differences in experience between various viewers inside the auditorium.

Of course, this presupposes a third-person perspective of someone able to compare those differing experiences. It therefore does not necessarily preclude my first-person 'projection' of a unanimous collective experience. Yet the more my attention is drawn to the fact that I'm sitting far away in the balcony and have a very different sightline compared to the spectators in the first row, the more the difference in experience may become foregrounded. This can be the case when the viewers in the first row realize something I cannot (yet) see;

for instance, when they are leaning forward in order to see something happening close to the wings, an event my sightline does not grant me visual access to. In such cases there might be a rift in collective experience that cannot occur in the cinema.

3. The direct address: differences in individuation

Last but not least, in the theater it can happen that actors 'break the fourth wall' and address the audience. They look at particular viewers, point their finger at someone, or even speak to a person directly. What a second ago felt like a taken-for-granted invisible witness position changes abruptly from an experience of being-*there* on the stage and in the fictional world to an experience of being-*here* in the theater seat. Sartre describes the effect nicely with recourse to an example from everyday life: "when I observe a couple quarreling in some public place, if they suddenly pay attention to me when I turn my head their way, I abruptly feel myself observed, and I jump back into my skin, immediately shrink away, and suddenly have the sensation of being looked at."[93] In addition, the theatergoer is also part of an audience in front of which he or she feels *singled out*. Being looked at, gestured at, or addressed as an *individual* person means that this very person does not belong to the rest of the audience any longer but feels individualized: 'I' opposed to 'them.' While oftentimes this is only fleetingly the case, in some forms of participatory theater (but also in stand-up comedy performances or in the circus) this rupture of the collective experience can go on more extensively. Breaking the fourth wall thus can also imply a crack in the theater's collective experience – a crack which cannot occur in the cinema.

But don't we have the look into the camera in the cinema?[94] Yes, but a character looking into and talking toward the camera is different from the direct address of the stage actor. When a character looks into the camera, I usually do not feel observed and "jump back into my own skin." When the character addresses me as "you," I am not embarrassed or even ashamed: "Looking at the film audience is clearly never 'direct' in any material sense; it is also rare that its effect or meaning is as obvious as 'direct' implies," Tom Brown writes.[95] Note that I am far from arguing that looks into the camera may not have an effect on the viewer: for instance, a distanciation from the diegetic world, as proponents of Brechtian counter-cinema like Peter Wollen would argue. What I claim is that being "looked at" and "talked to" can never be *direct* in film. The spatial, temporal, and ontological gap that separates me from the actor/character in the diegetic world prevents a direct address including the phenomenological effects of actual cases of being-looked-at or being-talked-to.

But even if we grant that there is an attenuated, mediated form of being-looked-at-ness also in film, in the public space of the cinema it can never be *me* personally who is being looked at, gestured at, or talked to, because I, as an individual, *share* the same perspective toward the screen and into the diegesis with *all the other viewers in the auditorium* (see point 2). Leaving out those looks into the camera that are not meant for the audience but are addressed either to a diegetic *character* in a parametric shot/reverse shot structure (for instance, in Ozu's *Late Autumn/Akibiyori* [1960]) or to a diegetic *camera* (as in *The Blair Witch Project* [1999]), looks into the camera addressing *the movie-theater* must be directed at 'the collectivity of spectators interpellated as a collectivity,' as Pascal Bonitzer puts it.[96] The knowledge that all the other viewers have very similar perspectives toward the character facing the camera does not allow me to feel singled out by him or her. (This does *not* preclude, however, that I can feel addressed personally when I watch a film alone.) The film would have to address me by name in order to speak to me personally, something which would only be possible in a home movie. As a consequence, in the cinema it is rather a 'we' that feels addressed, whether we explicitly reflect on this 'we' or pre-reflectively take it for granted.

How can we reconcile this argument with Jean Châteauvert's claim that in early cinema we find both camera gazes directed at an imagined collective audience and gazes signaling a collusive union with an individual spectator?[97] Just think of the Peeping Tom genre: Does the film address a collective of voyeurs or rather an individual viewer within a group of other viewers? My answer would be that the *implied* (rather than the *actual*) viewer of the film can be addressed as an individual, but the dispositive of the cinema with its collective audience stands in opposition to this individual address for the reasons given above. To put it differently, while some films do indeed address an *implied individual viewer*, in the cinema auditorium the *actual collective viewer* cannot feel addressed individually. Even if the spectator realizes that the film tries to address him or her individually, in the cinema the film is always for 'us' not just for 'me.' (Elsewhere I have argued that this is one of the reasons why people prefer to watch some types of films – such as pornography – alone.[98])

VIII. CRITICIZING THE INDIVIDUALIZATION THESIS

By now it should be evident that I take quiet-attentive viewing in the cinema to result in *a specific kind of collectivity*. However, this is a far from common opinion. A widespread position, most forcefully articulated by Hansen and Elsaesser, sees individualization at work. In this section I will therefore put my argument to the test and mount a critique of their individualization thesis.

Both Hansen and Elsaesser argue that historical changes in film style and mode of address, exhibition practice, and behavioral norms have consequences for viewers' mode of reception as a collective. As proponents of New Film

History and steeped in the history of early film, both scholars paradigmatically contrast two important periods: early cinema versus classical cinema. Hansen and Elsaesser describe the difference between these periods in terms of an increasing regulation of the collective audience: a story of discipline and order. Hansen favorably cites the buzz and idle comment, the booing and applause, the howling of small boys in neighborhood cinemas.[99] Elsaesser regrets that the audience had to learn to remain seated and concentrate on the screen: the change from early nickelodeons without rows of seats to later cinemas implies a regulation of an audience forced into order.[100] In contrast, early cinema was characterized by a constant coming and going, with movement enabling or even favoring communication. People smoked in the theaters, drank beer, read dime novels, and ate sweets: "peripheral activities that provided potential for an alternative organization of public experience," as Hansen puts it.[101]

The transition from the small neighborhood nickelodeon to the elegant picture palace, from the exhibitionist cinema of attractions to the voyeuristic classical Hollywood cinema, thus led to an individualization of viewers. In Hansen's words, an "institutionalization of private voyeurism in a public space" took place in which an "invisible, private consumer" replaced the "social audience" (or "collective audience," in Elsaesser's phrase).[102] Hansen even talks about an "isolation endemic to the classical apparatus."[103] What once was a lively place – a communicative public sphere – turned into a lonely crowd of isolated recipients sitting obliviously next to each other. More recently, writing with considerable regret about the quiet audience, Jean Châteauvert and André Gaudreault note that "with silence, the regime of film consumption may have let the spectator move imperceptibly from a *solidary* to a *solitary* mode of consumption!"[104]

Both Hansen and Elsaesser come from a critical background, following specific goals in film-historical debates of the 1990s and early 2000s. However, their critical formation led these theorists to throw out the baby with the bathwater by neglecting important facets of the audience's collective phenomenology. Hansen and Elsaesser believe that once new modes of exhibition and new norms of behavior were established, the film would cast a spell on viewers, who would henceforth follow the flow of moving images in isolated absorption. This at once overestimates the impact of the film and underestimates the impact of the collective viewing situation. Or, perhaps more precisely, Hansen and Elsaesser seem to believe that a collective audience experience and absorbed viewing are mutually exclusive. But is it not possible that "addressed as individuals, we simultaneously feel embedded in the crowd," as Tröhler puts it?[105]

Hansen's concept of the public sphere and Elsaesser's notion of the collective audience depend on verbal communication and other kinds of communicative interaction, which they oppose to the still, quiet, and absorbed audience of classical Hollywood. The individualization thesis is therefore particularly convincing if we consider the social experience of the cinema in terms of face-to-face interaction and expressive participation. But this is a reductive perspective on social life. We can easily think of examples of strong collective experiences without face-to-face interaction and expressive participation. Just think of playing music together, meditating together, or silently mourning together during a funeral. The individualization thesis is one-sided, because it conceives of social life in a specific, highly normative way. This normativity becomes all too obvious when Hansen decries the rule of silence as a middle-class suppression of "working-class norms of conviviality and expressivity" and Elsaesser considers silent and concentrated reception as a contradictory behavior that is not natural but has had to be learned.[106] Here the authors come close to articulating a romanticized anti-bourgeois idealization of the communicativeness and liveliness of the lower classes. They overlook that we-intention, joint attention, and joint action can imply a different *type* of collectivity.

Furthermore, the assumption that the diverse boisterous audiences of the nickelodeon necessarily formed a collective sounds somewhat problematic. Hansen notes that the early-to-classical transformations "subdue the social and cultural distinctions among viewers and turn them into a homogenous group of spectators."[107] But if there were strong social and cultural distinctions with in-groups and out-groups in early cinema, how could there be a collective audience in an emphatic sense?

Moreover, the individualization thesis harbors another contradiction: the individualization of the viewer supposedly took place at the moment when, in the urban centers of North America and Europe, the audiences inside cinemas grew massively in size. At the end of the 1920s the famous Roxy theater in New York offered seats to more than 6,200 viewers. In Europe cinemas like the Ufa-Filmpalast in Hamburg existed with more than 2,700 seats. Did the viewers in these cinemas have no sense of watching the film jointly, but rather considered themselves as lonely individuals in a crowd? Compared to the dozens of viewers in small storefront theaters, the hundreds and even thousands of people following a film in the 1910s and 1920s meant a completely different collective experience.[108] We might ask, then, why viewers would accept all these negative transformations? Was the story of loss maybe even intertwined with a story of gain? Hansen and Elsaesser seem to remain oblivious to this compensatory reward.[109]

IX. RE-EVALUATING QUIET-ATTENTIVE VIEWING

Pointing out that even quiet-attentive viewing implies a type of collective experience, my argument may ultimately underscore what is at stake once the film experience increasingly becomes a *truly* individualized experience, when viewers watch films *alone* on television screens, computer monitors, smartphones, and the like. There has been no intention here of intoning a nostalgic aria about the disappearance of the cinema experience. But at the same time I want to go beyond simply noticing that something is, for better or worse, changing. I wish to present a strong argument as to why silently watching a film alone is not the same as silently watching a film jointly minus the other viewers. In an important way, it is a different experience. Quiet collective attention is an enabling condition for another type of collectivity – one very much in tune with societies that insist on remaining highly individualized, and yet simultaneously yearn for a collective experience.[110]

However, to some readers my re-evaluation of quiet-attentive viewing may seem retrograde or normatively constraining. My arguments may sound like an apologia for the culture industry and the *embourgeoisement* of the cinematic experience, especially when placed against the background of a Brechtian/Benjaminian/Frankfurt School critique of mass culture and the 'bourgeois' reception practices of uncritical absorbed contemplation (a critique that feeds the individualization thesis). This is definitely not my intention.

Firstly, my vindication of quiet-attentive viewing is valid also for the reception of many experimental, avant-garde, or modernist works. The suspenseful reception of a Hollywood thriller like *The Silence of the Lambs* (1991) may look like the prototype. But the focused attention paid to a modernist work like Ingmar Bergman's *Persona* (1966) in an arthouse cinema counts just as well as the silent concentration that audiences in a cinematheque devote to an avant-garde film like *Wavelength* (1967) by Michael Snow. I am not saying that these types of film are experienced identically. What I have tried to show is merely that where people watch a film with quiet attention, my argument about the cinema as joint action is applicable to all types of film.

Secondly, my argument for the quiet audience's collective dimension does not subscribe to a 'bourgeois' understanding of aesthetic experience, with its connotation of an *individual* devotion to and contemplation of the work of art. In this respect I agree with Walter Benjamin, who, as Chapter 2 has shown, contrasts the solitary experience of a painting with the experience of film as "an object of simultaneous collective reception."[111] However, unlike Benjamin, I have not celebrated distracted spectatorship as politically emancipating or morally significant here. Rather, my argument implies that watching a film with quiet attention can enable one of the rare instances in our culture in which we do not have a dissonance of intentions requiring coordination (since we *all* intend to do the same thing); we are not subject to a permanent imperative to decide (since we have *already* decided what to do); and we are not forced to create collectivity through verbal or written interaction (since our joint action is based on *collective* quiet attention). This neither implies that I want to discard Benjamin's intervention, nor does it mean that I intend to set quiet-attentive viewing as the norm. Although this chapter may be read as a forceful plea to reconsider the benefits of quiet-attentive viewing, I have tried to avoid sounding normative.

Thirdly, my argument does not depend on naive, uncritical absorption, but allows for critical distance and reflection. In fact, collective quiet attention may be particularly conducive to reflection. In this regard, Alexander Horwarth favorably compares the cinema with the museum: "in today's socio-economic and cultural climate the spatially and durationally *unflexible* space of cinema is potentially more inviting to a reflective or critical experience of the world via images than most museum spaces are."[112] Note that the type of joint action suggested in this chapter has its roots in analytic social philosophy and philosophical theories of action rather than in political science. One would expect too much from the notion of joint action if it were understood in terms of resistance or collective struggle: joint action, as I use the term, does not equate to political activism (even if it does not rule out more political forms of action in the long run).

Last but not least, in my previous book on the phenomenology of cinematic fear I have myself argued for the advantages that expressive reactions can have for the establishment of collectivity. Voluntarily screaming collectively in moments of shock, for instance, can precisely be a way of communicating with others, and thus enabling a collective experience.[113] In this chapter I have offered a heuristic that allows us to differentiate quiet-attentive viewing from the other collective viewing type in which expressivity, performance, and interaction prevail. While I have not celebrated audience communication here, this does not mean that I reject the other kind of collective spectatorship, as the following chapter will make abundantly clear.

NOTES

1. Ellis (2002), p. 88.
2. Benjamin (1977b [c. 1931]), pp. 1193–4 (my translation). The German original reads: "Die von Massen bemerkten Worte, Geberden, Geschehnisse sind anders als die von einzelnen bemerkten. In der Ruhe von großen Massen aber ändert sich auch für den einzelnen schon das Merkfeld."
3. Sounding quite similar, Jacques Rancière argues with regard to the *theatergoer* that his or her "looking is also an action": "The spectator is active [. . .]. He observes, he selects, he compares, he interprets. He connects what he observes with many other things he has observed on other stages [. . .]" (Rancière, 2007, p. 277). Rancière opposes his view to the way Guy Debord has treated viewers of the theater, a perspective that stands exemplary for a long tradition of criticizing looking as a form of passivity. Rancière notes: "The spectacle is the reign of vision. Vision means externality. Now externality means the dispossession of one's own being. 'The more man contemplates, the less he is,' Debord

says" (p. 274). With this position Rancière cannot agree. He wants to question a whole set of equivalences and oppositions that we have received from the tradition Debord stands for: "the equivalence of theater and community of seeing and passivity, of externality and separation, of mediation and simulacrum; the opposition of collective and individual, image and living reality, activity and passivity, self-possession and alienation" (p. 274).
4. Smith (2013), p. 167.
5. In recent years film spectatorship has even been described as a form of *labor*. See, for instance, Beller (2006) and Hillyer (2010).
6. For a good overview, see A. Mele (2007).
7. As philosopher of action Alfred Mele tells us, "Mental action [. . .] has received far less philosophical attention than overt action, and certainly less attention than it deserves" (Mele, 1997, p. 247). If my arguments sound convincing, we do not have to go as far as recent proponents of enactivism who claim that perception *in general* should be considered an action (see Noë, 2004).
8. Schmid (unpublished draft). Available at http://univie.academia.edu/HansBernhardSchmid (last accessed 12 December 2016).
9. For a similar point, see Kennedy (2009), p. 14.
10. I borrow the felicitous term "active silence" from Richard J. Gerrig and Deborah A. Prentice, who argue that film-viewing is comparable to the side-participation of a conversation: the silent attentive viewers are prepared to respond in an *as-if* mode that approximates the response they would have, were they actually part of the film's events (Gerrig/Prentice, 1996, p. 402).
11. See, for instance, Châteauvert/Gaudreault (2001), p. 190 and Dibbets (1997), p. 214.
12. Schlüpmann (2002), p. 113 (my translation). For an ideological critique of the cinema's darkness and its connection to an allegedly inactive viewer, see Comolli (1986 [1966]).
13. See also Barthes (1989 [1975]), p. 346.
14. Quoted from Pedullà (2012), p. 64.
15. See also Antonello Gerbi's 1926 essay "Initiation to the Delights of the Cinema": "The spectators – subdued by the darkness, dull, wan and weighty without light inside, lacking any space around them or a bright background behind them – sit there silent and well-behaved, one next to the other, one just like the other." Quoted from Casetti (2015), pp. 203–4.
16. Ellis (2002), p. 88.
17. Pedullà (2012), p. 127.
18. Moulton (2014), p. 371 (original emphasis).
19. Moulton (2014), p. 371 (original emphasis).
20. Moulton (2014), p. 371 (original emphasis).
21. As Sean Cubitt puts it: "the generic action of going out to see [a film], or even of checking it out from a video store, [is] an act that defines itself differentially, for example, as 'not watching television'" (Cubitt, 2015, p. 343).
22. Casetti (2015), p. 12.
23. There may be other reasons why some viewers are present, for instance as accompanying partners or professional critics, but initial individual preferences and motives are not decisive for joint action, even if they may play an important role for the duration and stability of acting jointly. What is crucial is the *actual doing*. See Schmid (2005), p. 19.
24. For this distinction between three types of collective intentionality, see Schmid (2005), p. 47.
25. Elsaesser (1981), p. 271.

26. Tröhler (2012), pp. 58–9.
27. Gilbert (2007). Available at http://www.fil.lu.se/hommageawlodek/site/papper/GilbertMargaret.pdf (last accessed 13 June 2014).
28. Cochrane (2009), p. 65.
29. Rosenbaum (1995), p. 122.
30. Pantenburg (2010), p. 70.
31. Tröhler (2012), p. 59.
32. Christian Metz speaks of a "socially imposed under-motricity (lessened motor activity) and overperception" (Metz, 1979, p. 20).
33. Pantenburg (2012), pp. 82–3; Pantenburg (2010), p. 71. The re-evaluation of alternative types of audience and dispositives not only deplores silence (favoring expressivity), but also stillness (favoring mobility). Pantenburg (2012) launches a convincing critique of the idea that spatial mobility implies more intellectual activity (p. 80).
34. Biró (2006). See also Flanagan (2012). Jonathan Crary speaks of an "annihilation of the singularity of place and event" through the adoption of wireless technologies: "since no moment, place, or situation now exists in which one can *not* shop, consume, or exploit networked resources, there is a relentless incursion of the non-time of 24/7 into every aspect of social and personal life" (Crary, 2013, pp. 31 and 30). Hence one could claim that there is an almost ethical imperative to keep the cinema a place where we can live the freedom from the permanent obligation to answer a call or respond to a message or go online for consumptive reasons.
35. Waldenfels (2010), p. 178 (my translation).
36. Sorensen (2008), p. 267.
37. Sartre (1992 [1943]), p. 42.
38. Sorensen (2008), p. 274.
39. The fact that concentrated silence is not something that goes unnoticed can be gleaned from a participant in an ethnohistorical study who several decades later recalls the audience response to the dance films with Fred Astaire and Ginger Rogers: "we all used to sit there and sigh. You know, when we see them come on. Well you'd hear a pin drop" (quoted from Kuhn, 2002, p. 178).
40. Sorensen (2008), p. 280.
41. Sorensen (2008), p. 268.
42. Schmid (2005), p. 18.
43. Fiebich/Gallagher (2013), p. 577.
44. Krebs (2010), p. 9. Available at www.ethics-etc.com/wp-content/uploads/2010/02/krebs.pdf (last accessed 13 June 2014).
45. Schmid (2005), p. 19.
46. Schmid (2005), p. 99.
47. Schmid (2005), p. 98.
48. Quoted from Schmid (2005), p. 53.
49. Goffman (1963), pp. 90 and 214.
50. See also Abercrombie/Longhurst (1998), p. 54.
51. Goffman (1963), pp. 181 and 194 (emphasis added).
52. In a personal email to the author.
53. Goffman (1963), p. 214.
54. However, as we shall see in the next chapter, the inverse case is also possible. Think of someone ostentatiously remaining silent when all others accompany the songs of *The Rocky Horror Picture Show*: other viewers might consider this person's stubborn refusal to act jointly in the expressive-diverted mode as negatively disruptive.

55. There is no consensus among proponents of collective intentionality whether or not it necessarily implies social norms. Gilbert thinks that collective intentions *always* imply commitments, obligations, and entitlements, whereas Searle believes that this is not the case. Hans Bernhard Schmid takes a moderating position (see Schmid, 2005, p. 205).
56. Gilbert (1990), p. 6.
57. This is not true for those cases in which one can watch the film collectively, as in a projection room or black box. In terms of silence, we encounter similar obligations and entitlements as in the cinema.
58. What might be the reason why a *sleeping* person seems to generate much less scorn about his non-participation in the joint action of movie-watching than someone, say, playing a video game during the movie? With Sartre's existentialist phenomenology we might arrive at a speculative answer. Sartre argues that the appearance of another person generally and necessarily introduces a perspective on the world that is not mine and that undermines my own: "there is a total space which is grouped around the Other, and this space is made *with my space*; there is a regrouping in which I take part but which escapes me, a regrouping of all the objects which people my universe" (Sartre,1992 [1943], p. 255, original emphasis). Against the background of the *joint attention* to the single intentional object of the screen, the entirely different perspective of the person who engages in a different activity must be all the more blatant: someone who sends text messages to friends beyond the cinema or plays a video game does not have the rest of the cinema auditorium's *shared perspective* on the world. The sleeping co-viewer, on the other hand, does not even have a perspective on the world and therefore implies much less of a rupture.
59. Fiebich/Gallagher (2013), p. 6. See also Katz (2012).
60. In an illuminating article on disgust and boredom in the cinema, Mattias Frey has pointed out why the "costs" for leaving the cinema are not identical throughout the history of film (Frey, 2012).
61. For the latter case, consider Louis Delluc who claims that the collectivity of the cinema can encompass the entire globe: "The most separated and most diverse human beings attend the same film at the same time throughout the hemispheres. Isn't that magnificent?" (Delluc, 1988a [1921], p. 257).
62. Pacherie (2014), p. 37 (emphasis added).
63. Pagis (2010), pp. 311–12.
64. Delluc (1988b [1918]), p. 163. Similarly, Roy Sorensen writes with regard to music: "The composer Leopold Stokowski once reprimanded a noisy audience: 'A painter paints his pictures on canvas. But musicians paint their pictures on silence. We provide the music, and you provide the silence.' The silence of the audience does not mean that the auditorium is silent. The whole point of refraining from making sounds is so that the musicians can fill the hall with music" (Sorensen, 2008, p. 285).
65. Also with regard to music, Don Ihde notes: "Ideally, if music is to reach its full presence, it must be 'surrounded' or 'secured' by a silence that allows the sound to sound forth musically" (Ihde, 2007, p. 111).
66. Ihde (2007), pp. 110–11.
67. See also Sorensen (2008), p. 278.
68. Ihde (2007), p. 222.
69. Echterhoff/Higgins/Levine (2009), p. 496.
70. Pagis (2010), p. 324.
71. Pagis (2010), p. 314.
72. As Echterhoff and colleagues point out: "For the achievement of shared reality, people

need to subjectively experience both the commonality of inner states and the referential aboutness of inner states. From this perspective, there can be a shared reality even if both assumptions of sharing are objectively wrong. That is, for Person A to experience a shared reality with Person B, it is not necessary for B to actually have the same inner state as A or for B's inner state to actually refer to the same referent that A has in mind. What is critical is that A believes that B's inner state and the referent of that inner state match A's inner state and referent" (Echterhoff/Higgins/Levine, 2009, p. 501).
73. Echterhoff/Higgins/Levine (2009), p. 501.
74. I thank the philosopher Hans Maes for this example.
75. Godman (2013), p. 593ff.
76. Godman also mentions the long-term effect of establishing or reinforcing social *hierarchies*, a point I will come back to in Chapter 4.
77. Godman (2013), p. 589.
78. Angelika Krebs usefully distinguishes between personal and impersonal forms of sharing an activity: "In *personal* shared practice you intrinsically value sharing with particular others (going to see a movie with a friend), in impersonal shared practice you do not mind who the others are as long as they make good partners (singing in a choir)" (Krebs, 2010, p. 12, original emphasis).
79. Similarly, Dominique Pasquier notes on the stage theater: "The arousal of collective emotion can be disturbed by tiny, seemingly harmless incidents. Coughing, squeaking seats, yawns, light snoring, sighing, or whispering have a real ability to undermine the audience's solidarity" (Pasquier,2015, p. 228). As Don Ihde points out: "sounds are *given*. When they are given they penetrate my awareness such that if I wish to escape them I must retreat 'into myself' by psychically attempting to 'close them out'" (Ihde, 2007, p. 108).
80. Ihde (2007), pp. 221–2.
81. Ihde (2007), p. 222 (emphasis added).
82. Pedullà (2012), p. 57. See also Žižek (2004), p. 74.
83. Bazin (1967b [1951]), p. 102 (emphasis added). Of course, there are forms of theater that do not present human actors on the stage (as in puppetry), but they do not concern us here.
84. Epstein (2012 [1924]), p. 295.
85. States (1985), p. 31.
86. For States the intimacy of the theater lies not in the intimacy of being *within* its world, but "of being present *at its world's origination* under all the constraints, visible and invisible, of immediate actuality" (States, 1985, p. 154, emphasis added).
87. States (1985), p. 119. See also Morin (2005 [1956]), p. 96. The inverse point-of-view of the film actor is famously described in Benjamin (2010 [1936]), pp. 22, 23 and 25.
88. States also mentions two extreme cases in the history of theater: Molière and Edmund Kean, who were stricken onstage and died shortly thereafter (States, 1985, pp. 154–6).
89. Quoted from States (1985), p. 127. Summarizing an early empirical study by Raymond Ravan and Paul Anrieu on how actors perceive the audience from the stage, Dominique Pasquier writes: "The actors [. . .] said that all the noises in the theater were messages from the audience: silence is an indicator of strong emotion – and thus of a very good public – while small noises of discomfort are interpreted as boredom, and isolated laughs without the rest of the audience joining in signify a misunderstanding of the script or the staging" (Pasquier, 2015, p. 227).
90. Bazin (1967b [1951]), p. 99 (emphasis added).
91. Bordwell (2005), p. 60.

92. Bordwell (1997), p. 182.
93. Sartre (1976 [1944]), p. 9.
94. For more detailed discussions of the look into the camera, see Bonitzer (1977); Vernet (1989); Brown (2012).
95. Brown (2012), p. x.
96. Quoted from Vernet (1989), p. 63.
97. Châteauvert (2004).
98. Hanich (2011).
99. Hansen (1991), p. 66.
100. Elsaesser (2002), p. 75.
101. Hansen (1991), p. 233.
102. Hansen (1990), p. 233; Hansen (1991), p. 34; Elsaesser (2002), p. 69. See also Elsaesser (2000), p. 194.
103. Hansen (1991), p. 94.
104. Châteauvert/Gaudreault (2001), p. 190 (original emphasis).
105. Tröhler (2012), p. 67 (my translation).
106. Hansen (1991), p. 95 and Elsaesser (2000), p. 36.
107. Hansen (1991), p. 66.
108. Recently, Petra Löffler has launched a slightly different critique of the individualization thesis, especially the version suggested by Thomas Elsaesser. According to Löffler, Elsaesser's claims about the standardization of film production and the consumption-like attitude of the audience does not hold. Löffler disagrees with the argument that film consumption, just like any other form of consumption, individualizes for two reasons: first, because, in contrast to shopping, the individual does not consume individually in the cinema, but precisely with a mass of like-minded other viewers; second, because in the cinema there is not just an exchange between viewer and screen, but also between viewers themselves, whose reactions may be contagious. Moreover, Löffler also takes issue with the individualization thesis against the backdrop of the cinema's program structure, particularly in the movie palaces of the 1920s. Given that their programs consisted of a changing, variety-like format of which the film was only the end point, the viewer cannot be conceived of as a consumer: Instead, this type of program, which according to Kracauer is typical for the cult of distraction, lends itself to forms of collectivizing as well as individual self-guidance (Löffler, 2014, pp. 282–3).
109. To be sure, Hansen mentions the effect but seems unwilling to draw the consequences when she notes that the changes "subdue the social and cultural distinctions among viewers and turn them into a homogenous group of spectators" (Hansen, 1991, p. 66).
110. Hansen notes: "the cinema rehearsed new, specifically modern forms of subjectivity and intersubjectivity" (Hansen, 1991, p. 105). If this is true for early cinema, one could claim that the classical cinema rehearsed specifically *advanced* modern forms of subjectivity and intersubjectivity. For an argument along these lines, see Hanich (2010), chapter 9.
111. Benjamin (2008 [1936]), p. 36
112. Quoted from Pantenburg (2012), p. 92 (original emphasis). In this respect we should not forget that today movie-theaters are often used for live broadcasts of operas or classical concerts (for instance, of the Met or the Berlin Philharmonic). One could argue that the movie-theater can become the space of a live screening of a musical event precisely because it offers the perfect structure for a deeply concentrated and yet collective experience.
113. Hanich (2010). On screaming and shock, see in particular chapter 5.

CHAPTER 4

Expressive-diverted Viewing: Toward a Typology of Collective Spectatorship, Part II

[T]hose film shows [...] where one can see the spectators, often young children, sometimes adults, rise from their seats, gesticulate, shout encouragements to the hero of the story, and insult the 'bad guy': manifestations, in general, *less disorderly* than they seem: it is the institution of cinema itself, in certain of its sociological variants (i.e. the audience of children, the rural audience, the audience with little schooling, the community audience where everybody in the cinema knows everybody etc.), that provides for, sanctions, and integrates them. If we want to understand them, we must take account of *the conscious game-playing and group demands*, the encouragement given to the spectacle by the play of motor activity.

Christian Metz[1]

One goes to the cinema to suspend the usual modes of communication for a while.

Félix Guattari[2]

I. DEFINING EXPRESSIVE-DIVERTED VIEWING

The last chapter has looked at quiet-attentive viewing and its effects on the cinema's collectivity. But this is neither the only way of collectively watching a film, nor should it be. In this chapter I will sketch the outline of a second type, which I call expressive-diverted viewing. It is *expressive* because emotional responses, thoughts, and judgments become explicit via facial, motor and, particularly, vocal expressions of both the verbal and non-verbal kind. (I prefer the term "expressive" to "communicative" because, as we have seen, the silence of the quiet-attentive type also communicates its viewers' attention to the film.) And it is *diverted* because viewers do not focus their attention primarily on the film, but also on the rest of the audience. (I use the term "diverted" instead of "distracted" because for many film scholars the term "distraction" is too strongly tied to a Benjaminian and Kracauerian understanding.) If in the previous chapter silence was seen as an enabling condition for the film's strong presence, diverting expressivity will foreground the liveness of the here-and-now in the cinema. Note that "diversion" is not a polemical term here – I want to reserve a positive connotation to it as a form of *divided* attention.

Importantly, spectators of both collective viewing types are actively paying attention, even if their attention is structured differently. The quiet-attentive type focuses primarily on the film *up there on the screen*, whereas the expressive-diverted type devotes attention also, sometimes even primarily, to the other viewers *down here in the auditorium*. While quiet-attentive viewing bears resemblance to audiences of the stage theater and the classical concert, commentators of expressive-diverted viewing have drawn very different analogies. Lakshmi Srinivas, for instance, claims that the atmosphere in Indian movie-theaters may take the tone of a festival, a carnival, or the folk performance of myth.[3] Robert E. Wood compares a cult film like *The Rocky Horror Picture Show* to a rock concert.[4]

In the past three decades high hopes have been put on non-quiet and diverted viewing.[5] Think of the praise for early cinema spectators, the boisterous consumers of gross-out movies, the Indian audience, or the vocal viewers of cult films. As we have seen, Miriam Hansen approvingly talks about the "casual, sociable if not boisterous, atmosphere" of the nickelodeon and contrasts it with the "merely passive experience" of the restrained middle-class viewer of classical Hollywood.[6] William Paul similarly honors the expressive activity of spectators of gross-out horror films and animal comedies.[7] Srinivas favorably compares the "overtly interactive and spontaneously expressive style of reception" of Indian audiences with mainstream audiences in Western societies: "Rather than the loss of community and face-to-face relations, which theorists such as Adorno and Horkheimer associated with the growth of mass culture in the West, the Indian case reveals the generation of community and face-to-face interaction through consumption of mass media."[8] Last but not least, writings about cult films are suffused with celebrations of a rebellious, anti-mainstream, non-bourgeois attitude, nicely exemplified by Ernest Mathijs and Xavier Mendik's introduction to their *Cult Film Reader*: "the consumption of cult cinema relies on continuous, intense participation and persistence, on the commitment of an active audience that celebrates films they see as standing out from the mainstream of 'normal and dull' cinema. That audience aligns itself fully with what they perceive to be an attitude of rebellion or a sense of shared belonging."[9]

Where does this tendency to praise "active" and "participatory" audiences come from? As the last chapter has shown, the rule of silence and immobility is often interpreted as a sign of oppression and discipline, especially when contrasted with earlier forms of reception. As theater scholar Dominique Pasquier has pointed out: "For centuries theater audiences were undisciplined; they used their right, as an audience, to tyrannize the actors, to challenge the dramatist's text, and to talk to the people around them."[10] Beginning in the late eighteenth century, however, theater, opera, and orchestra audiences gradually changed behavior: The audience was expelled from the stage, the members of the parterre had to sit rather than stand, the auditorium was darkened, and silence became the rule. To be sure, this was a slow process: Far into the nineteenth century, audience attention remained divided between the stage on the one hand, and conversation partners and interesting guests on the other.[11]

From a Foucaultian perspective, the growing silence and attention to the stage and the screen implies a relinquishing of power. Theater scholar Baz Kershaw, for one, argues that when audiences were gradually impoverished in terms of permissible responses, their participation was undermined and their cultural power taken away. As a consequence, a shift took place from the audience as patron, to client, to customer.[12] Seen from this angle, acts of resisting the oppressive forces through expressive articulations must come across as a form of self-empowerment. Additionally, in film studies a specifically strong fear of the medium dominated for a long time. Film theorists considered the film in general, and the classical Hollywood film specifically, as the Pied Piper who ideologically manipulated his submissively following audience rats. Against this background, unruly, boisterous, expressive audiences must have looked like a fortress of resistance.

It should be evident that I do not equate audience activity with being subversive or resistant in the cultural studies sense.[13] And for obvious reasons I avoid the highly normative terms "participatory" and "active" for expressive-diverted viewers: Using these qualifiers would disqualify quiet-attentive viewing as passive and not participating, while in the last chapter I have tried to show precisely that quiet-attentive viewing is not only active, but it can imply in fact acting jointly. Viewers who quietly attend the film participate in the audience's overall activity, even if in different ways than the proponents of the "active" or "participatory" audience would have it. Moreover, as we will see further on, being expressive and diverted is certainly not always an act of resistance against 'bourgeois' rules of conduct. Quite the opposite, it is often expected from viewers who are obliged to perform expressive acts.

II. DIVIDED ATTENTION: DIVERSION VS. INATTENTION

Diversion is not the opposite of attention but a specific type of it, a form of *divided* attention.[14] In the cinema this implies that viewers under certain conditions divide their attention between the film and the audience. As mentioned in the introduction, Emilie Altenloh pointed out as early as 1914 that many viewers found it far more entertaining to watch other cinemagoers than to watch the film.[15] Likewise, Srinivas has observed that, because in India the cinema is a place where one meets people from very different areas of life, "[p]art of the experience of watching the film is seeing others and being seen."[16] More recently, in an illuminating study on Tommy Wiseau's cult/trash film *The Room* (2003), Richard McCulloch has drawn attention to the fact that its ritualistic audience reception depends on a strong awareness of other viewers: "newcomers to the film are effectively in a position where they must rely upon more knowledgeable attendees to provide some of their entertainment. Interestingly, this is also the case for the more experienced attendees, who know the film so well that most of their pleasure comes from hearing new heckles or observing other people's reactions to certain scenes."[17] In John Ellis's well-known terminology, expressive-diverted viewers do not *gaze* but *glance* at the screen, reserving parts of their attention for their co-viewers. Following an equally famous distinction by Stanley Cavell, we could also say that these spectators do not *view* but merely *monitor* the film in order to keep an eye on what goes on in the auditorium.[18]

However, these formulations sound almost too deliberate, as if spectators were always able to neatly divide their attention. In analogy to the distinction between active and passive attention, I therefore distinguish between *active* and *passive diversion*.[19] While in the former case viewers *willfully* steer their attention to their co-viewers, in the latter case they are diverted by others, dividing their attention between film and auditorium *involuntarily*. In both cases they multiply their centers of attention, passing their focus from one source to another, as if multitasking in the cinema.[20] Now, this does not at all imply that a double-centered form of attention lessens the overall intensity of the experience. According to Abercrombie and Longhurst, it is commonsensical to assume that the stronger the audience attention on a given performance, the greater the intellectual and emotional impact.[21] However, the intensity of the experience does not necessarily depend on the attention toward the performance *on the screen* alone – it can receive boosts from the performance of *the audience itself*.

It is important to bear in mind, however, that – as a form of divided attention – diversion does not mean *inattention*. As mentioned in Chapter 3, by definition I rule out cinemagoers who are *inattentive* to the cinema experience.

Inattentive individuals neither follow the film nor pay attention to the other viewers *as viewers*: People who kiss and fondle in the back row, who send text messages, who chatter about topics unrelated to the movie, do not follow the film in one of the two types of collective spectatorship suggested here, even if they are physically present and surrounded by other viewers.[22] These cinemagoers fall into the category of *mere present others*. Yet saying that they are mere present others does not mean that they cannot swiftly change status. They may have drifted away temporarily, withdrawing for whatever reasons, but they can rapidly reintegrate themselves by paying attention to the film and the audience again. Just think of Ferdinand Griffon (Jean-Paul Belmondo) in Godard's *Pierrot le fou* (1966): Griffon sits in a cinema and switches attention between reading Élie Faure's *Histoire de l'Art* and looking at the images of Jean Seberg on the screen. Moreover, it would be wrong to claim that mere present others do not contribute to the audience effect. As we shall have ample opportunity to see in Chapter 9, mere present others can be a source of serious anger and hence severely alter the cinema experience.

Following Erving Goffman, the inattention of a viewer can be defined as an *overinvolvement* in a task unrelated to watching the film or the other viewers *as viewers*. Since the next section will be devoted to various forms of expressive behavior, let me briefly mobilize Goffman to illustrate inattention through undue noise: "The ruling against undue noise is sometimes seen as a rational response to the obligation to 'show consideration' for those in the vicinity, in this case those who might be disturbed by the sheer physical effect of the sound. Yet in actuality, large amounts of noise (from a purely physical point of view) are often tolerated," Goffman writes. "What is an affront to the gathering, however, is overinvolvement in some situated task. Noise, in short, becomes an offense only when it exhibits overinvolvement – not, in the last analysis, because it is noisy."[23] My neighbor's laughter and her funny

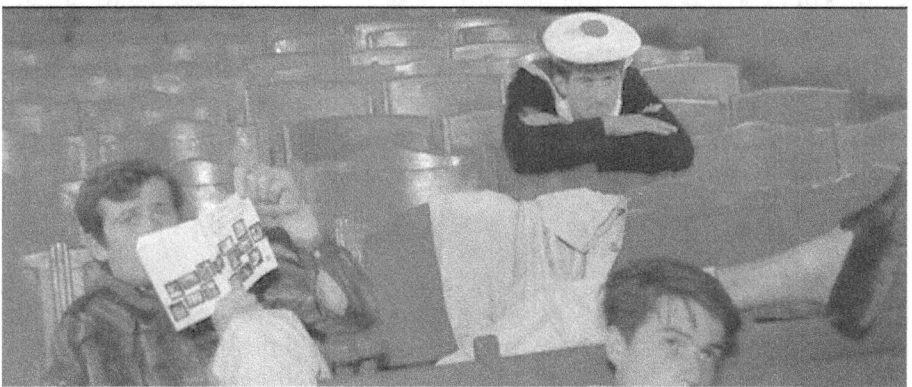

Figure 4.1: Attention/Inattention in the cinema: Ferdinand Griffon (Jean-Paul Belmondo) in Jean-Luc Godard's *Pierrot le fou*.

comments may objectively be louder than another person's cell phone conversation, but it is the latter that comes across as inattention because it reveals an overinvolvement in an unrelated task. Inattention is therefore the opposite of joint attention: While joint attention implies that viewers simultaneously focus on the film together, inattention means that viewers are engaged in something else entirely.

III. FORMS OF EXPRESSIVE BEHAVIOR IN THE CINEMA

Expressive behavior is a major source of both active and passive diversion: I can willfully divert myself by starting to talk, but the expressive behavior of others can also attract my attention. When we think of expressive behavior in the cinema, what often comes to mind first is talking. And, indeed, who would deny that talking is a frequent phenomenon in the movie-theater? Janet Staiger has shown that throughout the history of classical Hollywood viewers of all identities were talking during a wide variety of genres: horror, thriller, war film, male melodrama, romance.[24] This certainly goes for many other national cinemas, genres, and filmic modes as well. But the cinema knows a much wider variety of expressions, both verbal and non-verbal, than talking.

In fact, while in the presence of co-viewers, these others can always interpret my activities as communicating something: "Although an individual can stop talking, he cannot stop communicating through body idiom; he must say either the right thing or the wrong thing. He cannot say nothing," Gofffman writes.[25] As we have seen in the previous chapter, merely going to the cinema and watching in silence can be interpreted by my co-viewers as a communicative act that signals "I want to see the film in silence (with you)." With the *collective* dimension of the cinema in mind, I will broadly distinguish five categories of expressive behavior, because these forms of expression – to varying degrees and in ways to be explored below – make viewers aware of each other. When audiences become expressive they (1) *re-act* to the film, (2) *play-act* for other viewers, (3) *inter-act* with others, (4) *jointly re-act* to the film, or (5) *synchronically act* together. Again, these neat analytical distinctions should not imply that in reality we can always easily set these five categories apart.

1. Re-acting to the film

Let's begin with expressively re-acting to the film. As I define it here, re-acting is a largely involuntary response that can also occur in the private sphere when watching a film alone. Think of a startled scream, a disgusted shriek, an overwhelmed laugh, or restlessly moving in one's seat due to boredom. Here the body, as it were, takes over agency from the self: The involuntary responses at the fringes of consciousness remain predominantly on the non-verbal level, but we might also think of brief exclamations like "No!", "Oh!", "Ugh!" or "Oh my God!" Importantly, a re-action is addressed to no one: The viewer does not intend to convey a message, but in the social context of the cinema the co-viewers can always interpret the expressive response as communicating something to them. For instance, the non-intended message might tell us that the re-acting viewer has found something startling, disgusting, funny, or boring; at the very least it communicates that the film has caused a strong expressive response. When communication occurs *without* deliberate control, Michael Tomasello speaks of "communicative displays." He contrasts them to "communicative signals," which are strategically selected and intended for certain social motives.[26] Our next category counts precisely as a communication *signal*.

2. Play-acting for other viewers

With the term "play-acting" I refer to playful expressive responses to the *film* that are in fact addressed to the other *viewers*, at times in a tongue-in-cheek fashion, at other times to show off; sometimes to invite viewers to respond to the play-acting, sometimes to merely make a statement to stand out. Play-acting therefore comes close to what Dennis Kennedy calls "performed arousal": "the learned behavior of spectators that has been authorized by convention and is playful and ironic."[27] When play-acting, viewers crack jokes and make fun of characters.[28] Viewers whistle or boo.[29] Viewers anticipate what happens next in the film and verbally predict the plot.[30] Viewers warn characters or cheer them on.[31] These performative expressions are directed at other viewers, and the social element of the cinema is their "breeding ground."[32] Since these expressions are hardly ever synchronized, the result is a criss-crossing of individual expressions, rarely directed at a specific person but instead at the anonymous audience as a whole.

Horror movies and certain porn film screenings are fertile soil for play-acting audiences. As Britt Hayes has observed during a screening of the horror film *The Purge* (2013): "There was some understandable cheering when the protagonists overpowered the bad guys a couple of times [. . .]. And then things just became more confusing – people were cheering when the bad guys hurt the good guys, and a couple of audience members made sexy catcall whistles at the various guns and weaponry as they were introduced."[33] The dressed-up cinema audience at the beginning of Wes Craven's *Scream 2* (1997) can serve as a filmic example of such play-acting.

Thomas Morsch, similarly, describes how in horror films, gross-out movies, and animal comedies the viewers enjoy their disgust experience: They don't remain silently encapsulated within their bodily affect, but expressively

Figure 4.2: A dressed-up and play-acting cinema audience in Wes Craven's *Scream 2*.

act out their enjoyment through sounds of revulsion and imitating the retching reflex.³⁴ Likewise, Linda Williams, Gertrud Koch, and Janet Staiger have shown how pornography and stag film screenings can become a means for camaraderie, homosocial bonding, and male initiation: Joking, teasing, and showing off can strengthen male camaraderie and reduce the fears of the inexperienced, but also dissolve sexual tensions in the auditorium.³⁵

Note that it is not always easy to draw a clear line between re-acting and play-acting. Take the case of the startled scream. Building on the work of Robert Baird, I have elsewhere argued that screaming in shock is located at the juncture between nature and nurture, where involuntary and voluntary parts flow into each other, and, in our current terminology, a strong physiological re-action (a being-done-by) and a play-acting response (an active doing) often go hand in hand.³⁶

3. Inter-acting with other viewers

When viewer expressions take on the form of a *film-related* and *intended* communication between viewers who respond to another's response, I use the term "inter-acting". Following Antonella Carassa and Marco Colombetti, I consider the communicative acts of inter-acting structured by *offers* and *acceptances* (or *non-acceptances*, for that matter) that are not necessarily based on a linguistic sentence but can rely on other communicative signals as well.³⁷ Hence inter-acting often but not always depends on verbal expressions. Just consider your neighbor nudging you and pointing to something on the screen: With this deictic gesture he *offers* you the opportunity to inter-act silently and you *accept* it by quietly nodding and showing that you have understood him. In turn, when a person asks you something during the film and thus offers an invitation to talk – that is, expresses a communicative intention – your very short-spoken answer or utter silence implies a rebuttal and non-acceptance of the offer: "I don't want to talk (to you) right now." Since inter-acting implies a response to a response, it is directed at *concrete others* in the auditorium. These concrete others do not have to be familiar, but can also comprise anonymous viewers sitting five rows in front. Giving in to my proclivity for alliterations, I propose three subtypes of inter-acting: call-and-response, criticizing, and conversing.

a) Call-and-Response is the playful practice of talking back and commenting on the (often full-throated) response of another viewer.[38] Here the inter-acting frequently takes place between anonymous others in the dark, but this is not necessarily so. *Play*-acting is an offer to the other viewers, which they can accept by responding through *inter*-acting in a call-and-response way: Someone whistles, boos, cheers, or makes fun of a character, and another viewer takes up this invitation and responds in a vociferous manner. Already in 1913 German novelist and critic Kurt Tucholsky wrote vividly about the inter-acting audiences who attended the screening of erotic films, where viewers were screaming, guessing, grunting, cheering on, and comparing.[39] Be aware, however, that not only *play*-acting, but *re*-acting can also be a cause for the call-and-response practice: An unexpectedly loud scream, an embarrassingly disgusted shriek, funny or awkward laughter can invite an ironic comment from another spectator.[40] Call-and-response proper revolves around *film-related* comments and hence does not include, for instance, angry and humorless verbal complaints about some apparent misbehavior (more on this in Chapter 9).

b) Criticizing: The second subtype of inter-acting involves more serious aesthetic, political, and ethical discussions about the film. I therefore call it criticizing. This type of interaction mostly takes place between two viewers seated next to each other, but it can also involve small groups. Here it is likely that the viewers know each other. Above I have referred to Vachel Lindsay's Conversational Theater. Although it was never formally institutionalized, its idea of a critically commenting audience was revived informally at various points throughout cinema history. Sometimes the filmmakers actively encouraged it. Think of Fernando Solanas and Octavio Getino's four-hour Third Cinema classic *The Hour of the Furnaces/La Hora de los Hornos* (1968): the documentary contains intertitles that ask the audience to think about the film and discuss it. Reportedly, the film was sometimes interrupted during its second part so that the audience could deepen their discussion.[41] Sometimes, however, the viewers took responsibility into their own hands and started discussions during the screening. Despite her slightly ironic tone, Mary Heaton Vorse acknowledges the seriousness in her neighbors' discussion: "The young man next to me had an ethical point of view. He was a serious, dark-haired fellow, and took his moving pictures seriously. He and his companion argued the case of the cowboy who stole because of his sick wife. [. . .] Ethics were his strong point, evidently."[42] For Dudley Andrew, the drive-in theater was particularly conducive to this form of interaction: Inside the "private screening room" of their station wagon he and his fellow cinephiles "would freely criticize the film and discuss its effects."[43] That the aesthetic judgment of the film does not always come in the benign, controlled form Vachel Lindsay had envisioned can be gleaned from Janet Staiger's description of the New York Underground cinema audiences of the 1960s: "Accounts of these screenings describe them as quite rowdy, with people vocally expressing their judgments of the films."[44]

c) Conversing: The third subtype comprises all forms of inter-acting that fall neither into the playful call-and-response category nor among the more serious critical discussions. Here we might think of "bringing [companions] up to date on the events, explaining character motives, translating cultural ambiguities."[45] Yet we might also consider the various forms of connecting a film to one's own life and finding personal relevance in it. With a slightly mocking tone, Roger Wakeling describes what I have in mind here: "Try watching *Witness* [1985] in Dublin, where the inhabitants use films as an aid to conversation. Every appearance of the boy Samuel is greeted with, 'Ah, doesn't he just remind you of Kevin/Michael/little Christy? Sure, they're all coming up on the bus from Mullingar/Limerick/Cork on Friday for the whole weekend.' Even when Samuel is facing death by having his throat cut in the Gents the exchange goes like this, 'Mother of Mary, that reminds me of my poor Joseph going. Didn't he have the anemia, and the Hodgkiss, and a touch of leukemia too. How's your own then?'"[46] Thus when viewers are conversing, they are engaged neither in the joking call-and-response practice nor in serious criticizing, but they are sharing useful information or are connecting via small talk (even if the borders separating the three subtypes are certainly permeable).

4. Jointly re-acting to the film

When viewers *jointly* re-act to a film by laughing out loud, cheering, or applauding together, their response is more than a mere aggregation of re-acting individuals. *Jointly* re-acting implies simultaneously an individual *and* a collective response. Importantly, this expressive response is also addressed to the other viewers and hence includes a communicative signal: I *and* we find this scene worthy of laughter, cheering, and applause.[47]

Just think of viewers applauding together. Although by far not as common as in the opera or the theater, applause exists in the cinema as well. *Before* and *after* a screening we can hear viewers applaud, for instance, when the actors or the director appear in front of the audience at a premiere; when spectators pay tribute to the performance of a piano player or orchestra of a silent film screening; when the audience respectfully thanks a film critic or scholar who introduces the film or leads the Q&A. *During* the film rounds of applause occur, for example, when the projectionist takes care of an annoying interference (the image was out of focus or the sound too low); when the name of an actor, director, cinematographer, etc. appears during the credit sequence at a film festival or a retrospective that celebrates the work of this artist; when the audience honors a particularly exhilarating move in a fighting sequence, unbelievable acrobatics in a heist film, or an unexpected and graceful escape in an action film. In the latter cases the body seems to seek relief from the tension that comes with suspense and bursts out into the world with a liberating explosion of hand movements.[48]

Applause is a conventionalized gesture of appreciation and thankfulness, which sometimes is fed by and channels physiological energy. But sustained applause is not something we do on our own; applauding alone for more than a brief interval seems almost impossible.[49] When we applaud, we normally jointly re-act together, which also means that our individuality recedes somewhat into the background: "we lose something of ourselves in putting our hands together with others in public," Baz Kershaw notes.[50] Applause, which can be contagious like laughter, can swiftly 'fuse' us into a collective 'we'. (But, of course, there are also cases where my half-hearted applause distances me from my neighbor whose cheering and standing ovations seem exaggerated and alien to me. As we shall see in Chapter 5, this can result in an experience of "I–you antagonism".)

A particularly impressive example comes from a former student of mine. In summer 2009 Tamir Shoham watched Quentin Tarantino's *Inglorious Basterds* in a Tel Aviv cinema. Due to the film's counterfactual nature, an unexpected audience expression occurred at the film's climax, when Sergeant Donny Donowitz (Eli Roth) and Private Omar Ulmer (Omar Doom) manage to kill Hitler in a Parisian movie-theater: "At that point something that I have never thought I would see had happened: Unitedly, and without any further discussion, orchestration or choreographic organization, everybody in the crowd started cheering, applauding and shouting as a part of a massive standing-ovation," Shoham notes. This expressive outburst was not only repeated again during the final credits, but also about a week later, when Shoham watched the film in a different theater.[51]

But in what sense are joint applauding or cheering both an individual and a collective response? To answer this question I want to take a brief look at joint laughter from a linguistic point of view, focusing on the communicative side of the laughter utterance. As Beata Stawarska has pointed out, "one rarely hears an extemporaneous 'we' uttered simultaneously by a group of people without prior consultation with the others (how would you know that the others are going to join in?)."[52] With laughter this is different. When several viewers burst into laughter during a funny scene, they arguably make *two* statements at the same time – an I- and a we-statement. They simultaneously exclaim to the others "*I* find this funny" (individually) and "*We* find this funny" (collectively). This implies that they do not only use an equivalent of the term 'we', but also that they use the term 'we together', which is different from almost all instances of everyday speech (importantly, this integrative 'we together' can sometimes simultaneously also have the excluding meaning of 'we together, but not you.' Excluding others and creating hierarchies within the audience is a point I come back to below.)

How do I justify this strong claim? Here it might be helpful to draw a comparison to stand-up comedy performances or hip-hop concerts during which the comedian or the MC asks the audience a rhetorical question ("Hi everybody, have you all been looking forward to seeing my show?") or makes the audience repeat a phrase ("Everybody in the house say 'Yeah!'"). In both cases *each individual viewer can be sure* that a number of people will exclaim "Yeah!" Since we know that we will answer *with* the others, the exclamation will be both an individual *and* a collective one. Along similar lines, the funny scene in the movie-theater solicits a laughing response from the viewers, which a part of the audience (or maybe all spectators) will provide. Since we *expect* the others to laugh *with* us and thus respond to the film and its makers' solicitation, our laughter is not only an individual but also a joint communicative expression. Just as it would be wrong to claim that "everybody in the house" responds to the comedian and the MC merely individually, it would be wrong to maintain that each viewer sends out a solitary laugh that aggregates into a collective one.[53]

That part of the function – and the pleasure – of the warm-up moments during performances is to create a feeling of *we*-connection within the audience becomes immediately clear once we think of doing the same thing alone in front of the television screen: The thought of uttering the (entirely correct) individual I-statement "Yeah!" to the question "Have you been looking forward to my show?" seems absurd. It is, of course, true that some, maybe even many, people *laugh* alone in front of the television. However, this is not a lethal argument against my claim that *in the cinema* we deal with an I- *and* a we-statement. How else would we explain, for instance, the embarrassment of the cinemagoer who is *the only one* who bursts out in laughter in an otherwise dead-silent cinema? Contrary to individuating forms of laughter that serve to distinguish and hence to distance the laughing viewer from the rest (see Chapter 7), the embarrassed viewer in this case had presumed a we-response from her co-viewers. Since no one else responds *with* her, she is singled out and feels embarrassed.

5. Synchronically acting together

Finally, viewers also synchronize and coordinate their expressions and thus enter into a type of joint action that differs from the one we have seen in the previous chapter. Consider a feature of many cult film viewings: "the most common act of veneration for any cult film is the quoting of its dialogue, or, more precisely, the *performance* of its dialogue (i.e., being true to the precise inflection, accents, etc.)," Robert E. Wood tells us.[54] When viewers of *The Rocky Horror Picture Show* or *The Room* recite character conversations together, they not only lip-synch the dialogue onscreen but also lip-synch their verbal performance offscreen in the auditorium.

Another type of vocal synchronization occurs in case of the sing-along: Audiences who collectively sing the songs of *The Sound of Music*, *Dirty Dancing* (1987), or *Moulin Rouge* (2001) have to synchronically act together in the here-and-now of the cinema as well. As Mathijs and Mendik note: "The sense of communion and community to be experienced at such events might be described as pre-programmed, and sometimes even semi-automatic . . ."[55] The audience follows known behavioral scripts, guidelines of how to act in specific moments, sometimes literally instructed at the beginning of the screening. As a newspaper report about the New York City premiere of the *Sound of Music* sing-along noted in September 2000: "Revelers were instructed to cheer for Maria, hiss the Baroness, and boo Nazis. [. . .] The crowd was invited to march in place as each [von Trapp] child was introduced, and to rise as the bridal couple came down the aisle."[56] Synchronically acting together in this case implies both vocal and motor coordination. Here Adrian Martin's description of *The Rocky Horror Picture Show* as a "sing-along (and shout-along, dance-along, and dress-along)" seems rather apt.[57]

In his study on the *Origins of Human Communication*, Michael Tomasello distinguishes three "basic human communicative motives": requesting, informing, and sharing.[58] We can find all of them among the five types of expressive behavior distinguished above. *Requesting* means getting others to do what one wants them to do. It ranges from *individual* imperatives, which imply a direct ordering, to *cooperative* imperatives, which comprise polite hints of a desire that one expects others will fulfill. Demanding one's partner explain the meaning of a joke or an allusion would be an example for an *individual* imperative, whereas expressive play-acting behavior can be seen as a *cooperative* imperative, requesting the "response" to one's "call". With *informing*, Tomasello refers to the offering of information that one thinks another person or group will find helpful or interesting (which does not preclude that there are also non-altruistic motives involved). Here we can think of the pointing gesture that directs another viewer's attention to something noteworthy on the screen – an effect that is also achieved in a more expressive but less pointed form by what in Chapter 7 I will call "comprehension laughter" (laughing as signal of understanding). Or think of a play-acting form of what I dub "conversion laughter" (laughing as evaluative transformation) by which a viewer in, say, a trash film screening lets other inexperienced viewers know that this is actually not to be taken seriously, but should be laughed down upon. *Sharing*, finally, describes a communication motive based on people's mere wish to share feelings and attitudes. A whole range of examples given above falls into this category, from making fun of characters to booing to criticizing to collective applause. For the other viewers, even an unintentional re-acting scream can come across as a form of sharing, because the scream communicates that the viewer was deeply startled.

But not all categories of expressive behavior in the cinema qualify as a *joint action*, as we have encountered it in the previous chapter. Due to its largely involuntary, reflex-like nature (and contrary to the impression its name might give us), *re-acting* is not a form of action proper, if we consider control and voluntariness as characteristics of actions. But if it is not a full-blown action, it cannot be the basis for joint action either. Nor can the individual responses we encounter in play-acting: while its various varieties may imply an *offer* to others, this offer has yet to be *accepted* (if it will be accepted at all) and hence does not consist in any form of sharedness. In expressive-diverted viewing, a movie will become a form of joint action only in inter-acting, jointly re-acting, and synchronically acting together. Conversing with one another or singing along together would be prime examples of a joint activity in expressive-diverted viewing.

IV. COMMITTED BEHAVIOR: RESPONSIBILITIES, OBLIGATIONS, AND ENTITLEMENTS

Watching a film in an expressive-diverted way does not mean that we can do whatever we want. Here, as in every other social situation, certain norms and behavioral rules prevail which we have to accept (or deliberately breach), but which we can only ignore by an oversight or if we don't know them at all.[59] First and foremost comes the responsibility to show jointly committed behavior. We have to demonstrate, in one way or another, that we are aware of the other persons by being open to the social situation and respectful of it: "It is a demonstration of his committed 'presence' in the situation that the others may want of the individual, even more than the substantive value of the considerateness itself," Goffman writes.[60] "Readiness for interaction," "controlled alertness," and "interaction tonus" are other terms he uses to describe what we owe a social gathering.[61]

To a greater or lesser extent, expressive-diverted viewing implies that one owes what Margaret Gilbert calls a "public performance" to the other viewers. In turn, they have an *entitlement* to expect a certain kind of expressive behavior as well: They can *demand* this action and *rebuke* for not performing it.[62] Think of *play*-acting: If you go to a gross-out comedy, a stag movie screening, a trash film viewing, or a teenage horror film strongly expecting to watch it in an expressive-diverted way and no one comments on the plot or makes funny remarks about the characters, you might feel deprived of an experience you had looked forward to. Being the only one who shouts and whistles, you feel the entitlement to ask them to join in, or even reproach them for being spoilsports. As Goffman has pointed out, silence in situations where individuals are supposed to be loud can be a silent kind of noise that diverts attention just as the loud kind can.[63] Or consider cases of *inter*-acting: If you and your friend are generally very talkative during a movie, you might feel negatively surprised if she did not answer your question or even shushed you aggressively. This would be a prime example of what Goffman calls "engagement disloyalty."[64]

Finally, here is an example of *synchronically acting* together: A group of friends, verbally, decides to attend a sing-a-long of *The Sound of Music* and thus, implicitly, agrees on not only singing the songs of their beloved movie but also enjoying it in one way or another. They assume that enjoying the experience is part of their joint commitment, or else why would they go in the first place? In the cinema all the friends sing along and move their bodies in a way that clearly expresses their enjoyment. Only one of them, let's call him Hans, flagrantly refrains from singing, sends various text messages with his smartphone, and even yawns audibly at one point. Hans's stubborn refusal to act jointly comes across as negatively disruptive to the others. They feel entitled to demand a more active participation and hence rebuke him mildly by first looking at him in an encouraging way, then animating him verbally, and finally telling him angrily that he is a killjoy.

To repeat what I claimed in the last chapter: The more we expect a screening to be a shared activity, the more significant the normative agreement, the stronger the obligation to act accordingly, and the bigger the entitlement to be angry about its disruption. In turn, this implies that the lower the expectation of the collective viewing to be a joint action, the lower the obligation to follow the rules. Following Goffman's distinction between *tight* and *loose* social regulations, we can presume that the social regulations of quiet-attentive viewing are tight, whereas they remain loose in the expressive-diverted type.[65] But we shouldn't overlook that sometimes expressive-diverted viewing can also be regulated rather tightly.

Cult films and screenings in the presence of devoted fans are cases in point. The official fan website of *The Rocky Horror Picture Show*, for instance, provides a "Rocky Horror Etiquette" that literally tells you that the "difference between a true RHPS fan and someone just out for a rowdy time can be seen in their *manners and etiquette*." There are six guidelines, like "Never make fun of someone for 'dressing up' – especially if their costume or make-up is not exact," "If visitors from other theaters or areas come to visit, don't try to 'shout them down'. Respect the fact that they might yell different 'lines'," or "Calling Brad an 'asshole' and 'neck lines' to the criminologist are funny in their proper place, but should not be yelled every time you see these characters' faces. It does get boring and monotonous."[66] Although he fully rejects this assumption, Jonathan Rosenbaum finds it necessary to mention that some commentators have judged "the implications of this practice to be fascistic and mindless."[67] What these commentators must have had in mind are precisely the tight social regulations that make you "mindlessly" follow the rules.

Another example for tight social regulations comes from Richard McCulloch, who notes that the Prince Charles Cinema in London distributed a "Viewer's Guide" to every spectator in the months after the UK premiere of the cult film *The Room*. It contained necessary information for inexperienced viewers on how to mimic the expressive behavior known from the film's American audience: "even those attendees with a very limited knowledge of the film were aware, before they even entered the cinema, of the implicit pressure to fit in with the rest of the audience."[68] The audience might be free to laugh whenever they like; what will be sanctioned, however, is *not* participating: "the fervent participatory behavior of *The Room*'s audiences effectively positions anybody not taking part as an outsider. Natalie Haynes implicitly stresses the importance of fitting in at these screenings when she writes that, 'If you want to go along, don't forget to take plastic spoons with you. Then, when the audience shouts "Spooooon" and begins hurling cutlery at the screen, you won't feel left out'."[69]

To cite a final example of tight social regulations, I refer to the growing phenomenon of midnight premieres of blockbusters such *The Hobbit* (2012–14), *Harry Potter* (2001–11), or *Star Wars* (1999/2002/2005), which are often attended by devoted fans dressed up as their favorite characters. Carter Moulton has pointed out that in comparison to midnight movie screenings of cult films such as *The Rocky Horror Picture Show*, *El Topo* (1970), or *Eraserhead* (1977), the so-called "midnight blockbusters" allow expressive behavior only before and after the film – *during* the screening fans consider "non-communal or negative behavior" as a violation that can be sanctioned.[70]

As indicated, not all types of expressive-diverted viewing demand the same kind of commitment and obligations. Depending on the genre and the viewing context, the social regulations and behavioral rules may be more formal or informal. Even within a single film one can expect sudden metamorphoses of the social regulations.[71] Just think of moments of comic relief in a suspense-laden thriller: Their accompanying laughter not only breaks the 'armor' of the viewers' tense bodies; the laughter also loosens the obligation of quiet-attentiveness and briefly allows for a less tight engagement. Comic relief scenes momentarily invite a different type of behavior, and turn quiet-attentive viewers into expressive-diverted ones. (Here we can see that my two types of collective viewing are indeed theoretical categories. In reality, most expressive-diverted viewing is not expressive throughout the whole film – often the quiet-attentive type will be the background, from which the expressive-diverted type temporarily parts and stands out.)

Again taking up an idea by Carassa and Colombetti, let me draw attention to two levels of normativity that can be involved in the cinema.[72] On the one hand, there is the level of *general norms* that everybody understands who endorses them. Here we can think of the general rule of silence and motor inactivity in quiet-attentive viewing or the norm that talking in expressive-diverted viewing is allowed. On the other hand, there is the level of *specific norms* that are more situation-dependent. Here the normativity is, as it were, contractual: It will be negotiated between those persons who create these norms during specific interactions, as in concrete instances of inter-acting or synchronically acting together. Since the latter pertain only to expressive-diverted viewing, we can note a first significant difference between the two types. Since quiet-attentive viewing does not know any concrete interactions, it does not deal with *specific* norms and hence exclusively remains on the first, general, and already-agreed-upon level of normativity. In expressive-diverted viewing, instead, the concrete negotiations about specific norms often play an important role. What Richard McCulloch notes for the cult viewings of *The Room* seems to apply for expressive-diverted viewing more generally: "Far from being a homogenized, unified group of cinemagoers with established 'rituals', the participatory behavior that takes place at *The Room*'s theatrical screenings is always the result of negotiation and compromise."[73]

But if this is the case and even loosely regulated forms of expressive-diverted viewing know norms and rules of behavior, why not stay at home and watch the film alone? The answer has already loomed large in the last chapter and should be spelled out here again: We are often driven by social motivations and simply enjoy doing things with others, which can be rewarding in its own right. Moreover, these inherently rewarding joint actions might also lead to long-term outcomes like forming social bonds. But, as Marion Godman has shown, joint actions need not always be cooperative – they can also become *competitive*. "It is, however, important to remember that even in competitive or antagonistic joint actions, like having a debate or a fight with someone, there are likely to be social motivations involved (for instance, social emotions like resentment and shame)," she writes.[74] A consequence could be the establishment of social hierarchies.

V. INDIVIDUALIZATION: DIVISION, DISTINCTION, DISTANCE

In Chapter 3 we have seen that quiet-attentive viewing often seems to be formed in the likeness of my own experience, which I can tacitly 'project' onto the other viewers whose reactions do not become obvious due to their silence and stillness. Its effect is equalizing – some critics would say homogenizing – and largely remains on a pre-reflective level. The expressive-diverted type, in turn, veers in more extreme directions. On the one hand, its inter-acting, jointly re-acting, and synchronically acting expressivity can divert the viewer's attention from the screen and convert it into a *heightened awareness of audience collectivity*; on the other hand, notable viewer expressions can also bring about *divisions within the audience*: they may lay bare differences and social hierarchies and create conflict and social distance. At both ends of the continuum the viewer's awareness tends to be – *grosso modo* – more pronounced than in the quiet-attentive type.

This double tendency has not gone unnoticed. Staiger, for one, has pointed out that the call-and-response practice can be employed either to "*focus attention on the individual* producing the commentary or to *create a socially bonded audience* . . ."[75] Srinivas has observed that for Indian audiences films can "become a resource both for the *formation of community* and for the *generation of conflict*."[76] And in *Rocky Horror Picture Show* screenings Jonathan Rosenbaum has encountered "competitive divisions and hierarchies," but especially a communal spirit that is "markedly democratic and non-elitist."[77] In this section I will concentrate specifically on what undermines the collective experience of expressive-diverted viewing.

First, we have to distinguish those viewers who individualize themselves *within* the audience from those individuals who position themselves *outside of* the audience by withdrawing from the film completely (if often only temporarily). Among the first we can count viewers who comment loudly or laugh extravagantly at points when no one else does. Here we can think of a movie-theater scene in Scorsese's *Cape Fear* (1991), in which Max Cady (Robert De Niro) is the only one who laughs wildly and aggressively during some of the less-than-funny scenes in *Problem Child* (1990).

An example of the second group are people who talk on the phone or send text messages and thus connect to the outside world. In a manner of speaking, they cut the tie that binds them to the audience *in here* by reaching out and establishing a bond with someone else (or even a different audience) *out there*. As their inattentiveness and engagement disloyalty positions them outside the cinematic audience and thus turns them into mere present others, I will not consider them here.

In contrast, play-acting viewers who crack jokes, cheer characters on, or

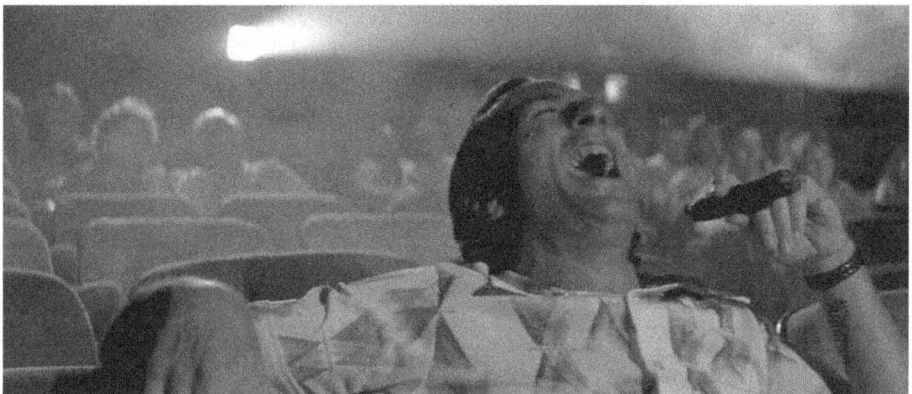

Figure 4.3: Individualizing himself within the audience: the aggressively laughing Max Cady (Robert De Niro) in Martin Scorsese's *Cape Fear*.

shout other comments individualize themselves *within* the audience. These expressive viewers momentarily stand out and thus posit themselves beyond the rest. But this is only half of the story, because we have to come back to a distinction hinted at above: between those whose expressions are an *offer* other viewers are invited to accept as the initiation of an inter-action (such as in call-and-response); and those expressions that are a mere *statement* that does not ask for a response (like someone who shouts out a short derogatory comment about the film). While the former aim to create a bond, the latter tend to stand aloof in order to reap cultural capital or bathe in what Freud famously called "the narcissism of minor differences."[78] Inter-acting and jointly re-acting *fractions* of the audience might equally stand out. This is hardly surprising: Most forms of inter-acting involve only two people or small groups, and in many cases of jointly re-acting not the whole audience is involved.

One consequence of expressive behavior can be a transformation of the intended emotions and meanings of a film – certainly an audience effect if ever there was one. As McCulloch writes, "*The Room* demonstrates the impact of audience participation on a film's reception, which in this case transforms an ostensible drama into a comedy experience."[79] Similarly, Srinivas has observed how viewers transform a low-brow melodrama into satire in an Indian cinema: "Two members of the audience who were seated together chose to comment on the melodramatic quality, overstatement of the tension and the lack of subtlety in the scene by chanting coquettishly 'yes', 'no', 'yes', 'no' in turns till the tension was broken by a shift in the scene. Other members of the audience laughed, although the scene itself was intended to be a serious and dramatic one."[80] When a viewer *actively* decides to expressively counter the emotional effect or meaning of the film, he or she assumes agency, either alone or with other members of the audience. However, this also implies that those who do not agree with the transformation have to *passively* accept that the film's intended emotions and meanings are modified *for* them. Due to the expressivity of the other viewers they can hardly do anything about it, unless they take action and retaliate by shushing or calling the others to order, which may foreground the divisions among spectators, as Srinivas illustrates: "Viewers who laughed at [a melodramatic] scene had to face disapproval: one viewer turned around in her seat and reprimanded them with 'Have you no pity?!'"[81]

Hence not everyone might be happy about how the expressivity of others can sway their experience. When the journal *Cineaste* asked the author Tim Lucas how the change in cult films dispositives – from cinemas to one's own electronic devices – has altered the cult experience, his response was ambivalent: "The loss of the shared experience has its positive and negative sides. It was a great feeling to be among the first people to have seen, for example, *Eraserhead* – you could make friends with a stranger simply by discovering that you happened to see it at the same time and place; it didn't even matter if you both liked the picture or not – only that it was an event you both survived. On the other hand, the way an audience feels about a film collectively can sway the individual viewer's opinion, so a cult film experience today is far more intimate and undiluted."[82]

To be sure, a modification of the film's meaning can occur in quiet-attentive viewing as well. Just imagine a comedy that you found extremely funny on previous viewings and that you attend in a cinematheque with a completely quiet group of devoted cinephiles who seem to focus exclusively on acting style, montage innovations, or the social meaning of the film. Watching *What's Up, Doc?* (1972) – one of my favorite comedies – with students forced me to question my own humor and the quality of the film one day: During a screening the students mostly remained dead silent, hardly ever laughed, thus disqualifying what to me was a hilarious film into a dumb and dull slapstick attempt. Again, the expressive-diverted type merely veers into more obvious territory and hence comes across as more pronounced.

On the other hand, scholars who consider silence and stillness as discipline and oppression seem to presuppose that expressive viewings are safe harbors of equality and conviviality. What they overlook is that expressivity and verbal commenting can easily establish hierarchies and inequalities, not least because the one who speaks is the one that others have to hear. Just take this statement from a participant in Adrian Mabbott Athique's study on Indian cinemas: "You basically have people who basically start hooting and howling at anything and everything that just comes up on screen. They can't sit quietly and appreciate the movie that's going on."[83] Moreover, the cultural capital that those cash in whose comments are particularly witty or erudite equally involves a form of power, as McCulloch has observed: "for some people at least, there is a definite sense that those most familiar with the film are to be admired, and knowledge as power."[84] A particularly unpleasant form of domination comes with bashing or attacking others along gender, race, class, or other lines. Again, Srinivas's observations about incidents in Indian theaters where the audience division became blatantly obvious are helpful here: "Viewers may want to drive home to others that they are not 'taken' or 'done' by a film as when male viewers pretended to cry in imitation of a woman who sobbed loudly during an 'emotional' scene, the interaction leading those witnessing it to laugh. Alternatively those who are taken by a film may experience anger and irritation with others who remain skeptically aloof."[85] These hierarchies on the micro-level can of course also reflect and entrench pre-existing inequalities on the macro-level (such as class distinctions or differences in gender).

Staiger has therefore voiced a critique of the optimistic political aspirations implicit in the idea of the cinema as a public sphere: "A lot of talk is not talk that promotes any democracy, intelligent dialogue, or progressive critique of the movie's plot."[86] For Staiger, talk – and by extension other forms of expression – can be "quite incendiary."[87] Here silence clearly reveals an advantage: With reference to the work of Michal Pagis, I have pointed out that it can allow for a more inclusive, albeit tacit, intersubjective experience as we do not compare, so to speak, one mind to another, allowing for difference under the rubric of sameness. Thus, the divisive tendency of expressive-diverted viewing curiously runs counter to the claims of the "individualization thesis" *à la* Elsaesser and Hansen. Rather than creating sociality and conviviality, we have encountered conflict and competition, division and distance. However, this is only one tendency, and it would be rather one-sided and distorting if we overlooked the heightened awareness of *collectivity* that can also come with expressivity.

Before I discuss this aspect, let me briefly emphasize that diverting expressions can become a source of pleasure in themselves, even if they don't invite me into a collective experience. An obvious example would be amusing ways of re-acting, play-acting, or inter-acting. Hence McCulloch has pointed out that subversive or embellishing jokes, mocking comments, or the use of props can provide "entertainment in its own right."[88] But we could also think of the aforementioned funny shrieks or screams of others. With a mix of class-based condescension and open fascination for the audience, Mary Heaton Vorse has noted in 1911 that she cannot go to the cinema in New York "without having a series of touching little adventures with the people who sit near you, without overhearing chance words of a *naiveté* and appreciation that make you bless the living picture book that has brought so much into the lives of the people who work."[89] The "ready to laugh, ready to applaud" audience was amused – and hence also amusing to her.[90]

VI. COLLECTIVIZATION: COORDINATION AND COMMONALITY

Talking about a heightened awareness of collectivity as a result of audience expressivity could imply that collective experiences are possible only in the physical co-presence of others. Let me again disperse this erroneous assumption, an assumption that could also be spurred by my self-restraint on the collective *cinema* experience. In her intriguing but largely unknown study *Zur Ontologie sozialer Gemeinschaften* (1923), phenomenologist Gerda Walther claimed, a long time before television and social media dominated daily life, that imagining real or even fictitious others having the same experience can lead to a collective experience – we can have a communal experience with a "fictitious we" as well.[91] Following the much-anticipated new season of *Game of Thrones* on my TV screen I can, however vaguely, *imagine* watching the first episode with a few million other viewers at the same time; or when alone on my couch, watching a deeply moving film about a sad relationship on my laptop, I can *feign* watching it with a potential partner that, in my miserable loneliness, I conjure up for myself.

Although undeniable phenomenological differences exist between experiences of what we could call *co-present*, *imagined*, and *fictitious* communities, they all count as collective experiences.[92] Still, Walther also postulates an ontological difference between putative communities "for oneself" (*für sich*), such as the imagined and fictitious communities, and full-blown communities "properly speaking" (*an und für sich*): the latter need *knowledge* of the other members of the community and cannot rest on assumptions or hypotheses about them.[93] An in-depth discussion of this claim would lead us too far astray at this point. Suffice it to say that it is preferable to speak of a *continuum between* the various types of community rather than *differences in kind*, as knowledge about other members of the community comes in degrees rather than in an either-or form. After all, I *know* that I am not the only one who watches the new episode of *Game of Thrones* when it is broadcast on HBO. In turn, I must have some implicit *assumptions* about other viewers in the quiet-attentive type as well, even though they are co-present. And while the degree of knowledge about my co-viewers is highest in expressive-diverted viewing, especially in my subgroup with a strong we-intention, I cannot be a hundred per cent sure about their experience either. While not all collective experiences depend on physically co-present others, in the cinema many of them do.

In this respect, Elisabeth Pacherie hints at a helpful distinction between *common* affordances, on the one hand, and *joint* affordances, on the other.[94] As an example of the former she refers to a kiosk in a park that, in case it suddenly starts raining, affords protection to individuals and groups alike. Since the kiosk can shelter not just one but many people, it constitutes a common affordance. She reserves the term "joint affordance" for cases where an object affords action to two or more people which it may not afford to each of them individually. The cases therefore depend on a physical co-presence. An example from the same park would be a seesaw, which provides fun for two kids, but remains boring for a child that arrives alone.

Along these lines, a film can be described as an object that offers both common and joint affordances. There are films that afford common responses to individual viewers just as much as to physically co-present viewers. The scariness of a horror movie might result in fearful responses no matter if I watch it alone or in a group (needless to say that I don't deny that there are experiential differences between the two constellations). However, there are also films for which co-present others are necessary to fully realize their affordances. Or to put it slightly differently, sometimes we can discover joint affordances only when we follow a film with others: Watching the film alone we would simply overlook or ignore the joint affordances or they would not exist for us individually in the first place. To mock a film that is meant seriously may not have occurred to me had the other viewers not started it; to sing along with Nicole Kidman or Ewan McGregor when watching *Moulin Rouge* I would find pointless alone; to laugh at a cheap joke in a Jerry Lewis comedy would not have crossed my mind in front of my laptop. "It's quite rare I think that someone would burst out laughing hysterically if they were sat in their flat on their own, so seeing the room en mass [sic] with fellow fans seemed the only way to enjoy it," says one participant of McCulloch's study on the cult film *The Room*.[95] Finally, we should not forget that films can also contain *individual* affordances – affordances which *don't* lead to a response in the co-presence of others or which will be strongly inhibited. A good example would be the masturbatory affordance of pornography.

Jointly re-acting and synchronically acting together are particularly obvious examples for joint affordances. In Chapter 3 I have noted that these joint actions are harder to synchronize than quietly paying attention together, a point underlined by a participant in Moulton's study on midnight blockbusters, who praises the advantages of fan audiences: "Being in a room full of true fans is far better than being in a room full of average theater goers. You'll get more informed reactions to the movie, so people will be less likely to laugh in the wrong places and such."[96] At the same time, it seems evident that the expressive type of synchronized responses – that is, an expressive form of joint action – foregrounds the collective experience to a *stronger degree* than its quiet equivalent. As audible responses, laughing or applauding together make viewers more centrally aware of the joint action (even if viewers don't have to reflect on their communal response and fully thematize it).

The satisfaction of having achieved it collectively might also be higher. Recall that in the previous chapter I emphasized two sources of pleasure connected to joint action. First, we can take pleasure in the uninhibited and smooth functioning of activities (Bühler's pleasure in functioning); second, we can enjoy being deeply absorbed by an activity together (Csíkszentmihályi's social flow). At least in some moments of acting jointly the expressive-diverted type can evoke the sheer pleasure in functioning as an anonymous group immersed in doing the same thing together smoothly, unimpeded, and skillfully. While more difficult to achieve than watching a film in silence together, the satisfaction can be all the more pronounced precisely because it is less easy to arrive at speaking the dialogue together.[97] We are dealing, then, with a pleasure in *doing* something together in a well-timed manner, but we must not confuse it with shared emotions, emotional contagion, or feeling together. A distinction of these three types of *affective we-experience* will be the goal of Chapter 6.

VII. QUIET-ATTENTIVE VS. EXPRESSIVE-DIVERTED VIEWING

Following Gerda Walther, one could distinguish communities according to their intentional directedness – what intentional objects a given community is about.[98] On the one hand, there are communities in which the individual is *directly* directed to other people with whom the individual creates the community. Walther calls them *person-directed* communities (*personale Gemeinschaften*). On the other hand, we find communities in which the individual is directed toward non-human objects (like a painting, a statue, a literary work) and becomes unified with other people because they are also directed toward that object. These indirect communities Walther dubs *object-oriented* communities (*gegenständliche Gemeinschaften*). Both types of collective spectatorship – quiet-attentive and expressive-diverted viewing – are mediated by the film; thus none can imply a person-directed community proper. But in contrast to quiet-attentive viewers, who don't address each other expressively at all, expressive-diverted viewers do engage each other, if to varying degrees. While play-acting and inter-acting can count as intentional attempts to communicate *directly* with one another, jointly re-acting and synchronically acting are mediated by the film. Here we might find a reason why theorists like Hansen deny quiet-attentive viewing the status of community: It is less built on direct communication, but rests on a mediation of the film.

However, as indicated above, the two collective viewing types are neither diachronically nor synchronically exclusive. Oftentimes they occur in a single screening, oscillating between the two types. Good examples for this intermingling are the fan-populated midnight blockbuster screenings described by Carter Moulton. Here the viewers – predominantly dedicated fans, sometimes dressed up in costumes – follow tight social regulations. They refrain from diverting themselves and others by sending text messages or making noises and remain quiet almost throughout: "When the title screen appears, the crowd goes wild and then falls to a dead silence," one viewer reports.[99] But the spectators are also expected to respond correctly at appropriate moments with laughing or cheering, thus jointly re-acting in a synchronized way.[100] Again, quiet-attentive viewing is the norm, from which expressive-diverted moments can stand out all the more prominently.

In the case of these fan-populated screenings the theater space itself becomes important and foregrounded even in the absence of an expressive response. In the here and now of the auditorium the spectators, who have often anticipated this special screening for months or even years, affirm their own fandom and create a camaraderie and feeling of togetherness. Moreover, a *thematic continuity* exists between the (dressed-up) fans and the diegetic world on the screen, permeating, as it were, the ontological boundary between the two worlds. Building on the work of Barbara Klinger and Will Brooker, Moulton calls this permeation "thematic immersion": "midnight blockbusters [. . .] allow fans to become immersed in a highly thematized world, one which has room for fellow fans, the cultified theater space, and the diegesis all at once."[101] What Moulton's description tells us, then, is that the viewer's attention in quiet-attentive viewing does not always have to be film-dominated and depend on immersion. Nor is diversion, in the sense of a divided attention, always dependent on expressivity: one can be focused on the "in-auditorium 'liveness'" also for other reasons.[102]

NOTES

1. Metz (1982), pp. 101–2 (emphasis added).
2. Guattari (2009), p. 258.
3. Srinivas (1998), p. 336.
4. Wood (1991), p. 164.
5. According to Pedullà, theorists such as the ones I quote in the following paragraph "see a promising sign of resistance to Hollywood in every form of 'perverse spectacularity' (out of tune with the rules of conduct traditionally imposed by movie customers)" (Pedullà, 2012, p. 126).
6. Hansen (1991), p. 61.
7. Paul (1994), pp. 17–18
8. Srinivas (2002), pp. 171–2.
9. Mathijs/Mendik (2008b), p. 4. Compare also Robert E. Wood's praise for the cult film experience: "In becoming a cult object [. . .] a film radically alters the normal experience of its exhibition. It intensifies the conditions of its showing and, in the process, solidifies its separation from ordinary life. In return, the viewing community enhances its own sense of communal identity and intensifies its synchronized action. In this respect, the cult film locates and reinvigorates something important that has largely been lost in the

moviegoing experience – the cultic nature of film itself. By reclaiming this experience, the cult film counters a contemporary tendency – encouraged and accelerated by the video industry – for filmgoing to become less communal, less festive, and in many ways less significant" (Wood, 1991, p. 157).
10. Pasquier (2015), p. 223.
11. Brandl-Risi (2012), p. 79.
12. Kershaw (2001), p. 135. I agree with Kershaw that the "communities that the theater customarily constructs through its rituals of silence and applause, through its disciplinary procedures, may not be as enlightened, nor as benevolent, as one might like to think" (p. 139). At the same time, it sounds highly exaggerated to me when he claims that through their "increasing capitulation to near-fascistic forces" (p. 141) Western theaters "more often than not have discouraged democracy" (p. 138).
13. Along these lines, Abercrombie and Longhurst comment: "Audiences can be active and give their own meanings to texts without any implication that the preferred meaning of the text is being subverted" (Abercrombie/Longhurst, 1998, p. 30).
14. Petra Löffler has revalidated the concept of "distraction" along similar lines. See Löffler (2014). Sounding similar, Francesco Casetti speaks about "multicentered watching, at once attentive and divided" (Casetti, 2015, p. 256).
15. Altenloh (2001 [1914]), p. 287. See also Löffler's discussion of a cinema experience described by Alfred Döblin (Löffler, 2014, p. 320).
16. Srinivas (1998), p. 330.
17. McCulloch (2011). p. 207.
18. Cavell (1982), p. 85.
19. For a distinction between paying passive and active attention to a film, see Hanich (2010), pp. 52–6.
20. Casetti (2015), p. 182.
21. Abercrombie/Longhurst (1998), p. 43.
22. Needless to say, they are inattentive only from the point of view of the collective cinema experience: Unless they are sleeping, inattentive cinemagoers do pay attention, namely to other objects and events.
23. Goffman (1963), p. 213.
24. Staiger (2000), p. 50.
25. Goffman (1963) p. 35.
26. Tomasello (2008), p. 14.
27. D. Kennedy (2009), p. 187.
28. See McCulloch (2011), p. 212.
29. When attending a 1913 adaptation of Emile Zola's *Germinal*, the famous linguist and diarist Victor Klemperer experienced whistling in the cinema. See Paech/Paech (2000), p. 39.
30. "Viewers often shout out comments or 'give advice' to characters on-screen. If the hero and heroine are fleeing from the villain, viewers shout out 'Run! Run faster!' [. . .] Particular scenes may draw a standing ovation" (Srinivas, 1998, pp. 327–8).
31. See Srinivas (1998), p. 336.
32. I don't deny that many viewers also engage in some form of *silent* "inner speech" – like silently predicting the plot or warning characters – as we could claim in loose reference to Boris Eikhenbaum's term. Some people even respond to the film in an expressive, perceptible form when they watch a film *alone*, but this would not count as play-acting as I define it here, as play-acting presupposes co-viewers to which these expressions are directed.

33. Hayes (2013). Available at http://badassdigest.com/2013/06/06/when-is-cheering-for-violence-in-movies-okay/ (last accessed 1 April 2016).
34. Morsch (2007), p. 297.
35. Williams (1989), p. 112; Koch (1989), p. 97; Staiger (2002), p. 48.
36. See chapter 5 in Hanich (2010).
37. Carassa/Colombetti (2014), pp. 156–8.
38. On call-and-response of African American audiences, see Staiger (2000), pp. 46–8 and Dunn (2008), pp. 19–22. On call-and-response of horror audiences, see Olney (2013), p. 63 and Clover (1992), p. 202.
39. See Paech/Paech (2000), pp. 54–5.
40. As Goffman puts it with regard to embarrassing physical actions, "when an individual finds himself in a momentarily peculiar physical position, as when he trips, slips, or in other ways acts in an awkward, unbecoming fashion, he lays himself open for light comment, for he will need a demonstration from others that they see this activity as one that does not prejudice his adult self, and it is in his own interest to allow them to initiate a joking contact with him for this purpose" (Goffman, 1963, pp. 126–7).
41. Barnard (1996), p. 47. Art historian Grant H. Kester (2004) makes a strong claim for works of art that generate dialogue – not with or about a finished object, but works of art that facilitate, solicit, and incorporate dialogical exchange as part of the *aesthetic experience*.
42. Vorse (1911), p. 446.
43. Andrew (1986), p. 14.
44. Staiger (2000), p. 46.
45. Staiger (2000), pp. 52–3.
46. Quoted from Breakwell/Hammond (1990), p. 30. In an interesting ethnographic study, Jennifer Deger describes a similar movie-watching habit of the Aboriginal Yolngu people in Northern Australia. When watching a film in family constellations in the private home or during a public screening at the basketball court, the Yolngu comment on the film and draw strong *connections to their own communities and kinships*, making overt links between the people on the screen and local characters and family stories: "The thing that people do talk about easily and avidly in front of the screen – often with much laughter – are the relationships between on-screen characters. [. . .] This sense of the importance of relationships as structuring story and motivation often extends beyond the frame of the film to include viewers who, in certain movies, 'adopt' characters as kin. 'That's me, that's you; they are our sisters,' I might be told by someone pointing at the screen or DVD cover as I settle down to watch a local favorite for the first time. In just this simple move, we all gain preassigned 'viewing positions.' These playful maneuvers mean that everyone present becomes related (the Yolngu, the anthropologist, and the characters on screen) so that the patterning of the social through kinship extends into the dynamics of the film itself" (Deger, 2011, pp. 463–4).
47. See also Roselt (2008), p. 330. Roselt points out that spontaneous applause in the theater cannot be reduced to the individual decisions of the 600 theatergoers who during the act of applauding are surprised that the others also had the same idea.
48. Lakshmi Srinivas has described the Indian audience as particularly prone to applauding. Srinivas (1998), p. 336. For an amusing example of applause in a British cinema, see Breakwell/Hammond (1990), p. 26.
49. Brandl-Risi (2012), p. 79. This goes for a whole range of expressive reactions. Referring to an empirical study that used video recordings of stage theater audiences, Pasquier notes that "audience members coordinate with one another to laugh at the same time. An

individual who laughs alone will stop laughing if others do not join in" (Pasquier, 2015, p. 227).
50. Kershaw (2001), p. 135. Note, however, that for Kershaw this applause is nothing to applaud: "applause unthinkingly aims to dismiss dissent, to suppress difference, to forge a particular kind of community" (p. 140).
51. Email to the author, 10 February 2016.
52. Stawarska (2009), p. 74.
53. This argument is clearly prefigured in the Benjamin quote discussed in Chapter 2: "nowhere more than in the cinema are the reactions of individuals, which add up to the massive reaction of the audience, from the onset determined by their imminent concentration and aggregation" (Benjamin, 1977a [1936], p. 33, my translation).
54. Wood (1991), p. 158 (original emphasis).
55. Mathijs/Mendik (2008b), p. 4. Richard McCulloch observes how audiences of *The Room* ironically mock a character by humming or singing the theme from *Mission: Impossible*. McCulloch (2011), p. 204.
56. Esch/Ehren (2000). Available at http://www.playbill.com/article/crowds-turn-out-for-opening-of-sing-a-long-sound-of-music-in-nyc-com-91701 (last accessed 1 April 2016). See also my comments on *The Rocky Horror Picture Show* etiquette below.
57. Martin (2008), pp. 39–42.
58. Tomasello (2008), pp. 84–8.
59. See also Sean Cubitt: "Acceptable behaviors in cinemas vary from place to place (and showtime to showtime: children's matinees, evening performances, midnight screenings) but they are always shaped by acceptability, a correct way to watch a film. To become audience, we have to submit to that discipline, or knowingly transgress it. To paraphrase Marx, people make themselves audiences, but not under conditions of their own choosing" (Cubitt, 2005, p. 334).
60. Goffman (1963), p. 214.
61. Goffman (1963), pp. 24–5.
62. Gilbert (2014).
63. Goffman (1963), p. 214.
64. Goffman (1963), p. 181.
65. Goffman (1963), p. 198ff.
66. Available at www.rockyhorror.com/participation/etiquette.php (last accessed 4 April 2016, emphasis added).
67. Rosenbaum (1995), pp. 151–2.
68. McCulloch (2011), pp. 202 and 200.
69. McCulloch (2011), p. 206.
70. Moulton (2014), p. 373.
71. See also Goffman (1963), p. 210.
72. Carassa/Colombetti (2013). Available at https://ssl.lu.usi.ch/entityws/Allegati/pdf_pub7127.pdf (last accessed 6 April 2016).
73. McCulloch (2011), p. 203.
74. Godman (2013), p. 8. Competitive joint actions, in turn, can also lead to the forming of social bonds: "Just think about how verbal sparring between two individuals becomes a form of flirtation, possibly resulting in a romantic relationship" (Godman, 2013, p. 10).
75. Staiger (2005) p. 159 (emphasis added).
76. Srinivas (1998), p. 323 (emphasis added).
77. Rosenbaum (1995), p. 151.
78. Freud (2010 [1930]), p. 72.

79. McCulloch (2011), p. 189.
80. Srinivas (1998), p. 340.
81. Srinivas (1998), p. 338.
82. Briggs et al. (2008), p. 46.
83. Athique (2013), p. 382.
84. McCulloch (2011), p. 195.
85. Srinivas (1998), p. 338.
86. Staiger (2000), p. 51.
87. Staiger (2000), p. 55. However, Staiger is aware that talk can also connect people and be supportive.
88. McCulloch (2011), p. 212.
89. Vorse (1911), p. 442.
90. Vorse (1911), p. 446.
91. Walther (1923), p. 80.
92. The parallel in imagined communities between viewers watching the same episode of a series and Benedict Anderson's newspaper readers who consume the news simultaneously in the morning is, of course, intentional. See Anderson (1983), p. 35.
93. Walther (1923), p. 81.
94. Pacherie (2014), p. 31.
95. McCulloch (2011), p. 207.
96. Moulton (2014), p. 374.
97. Not everyone is equally impressed, though. Theater scholar Baz Kershaw, for one, complains that "applause, like laughter, is the *unthinking component* of a system that creates oppressive and/or competing communities." The audience community that comes into being by collective expressions like applause or laughter is based "more on an *elimination of difference* than on a recognition of legitimate debate" (Kershaw, 2001, p. 140, emphasis added).
98. Walther (1923), pp. 48–9.
99. Moulton (2014), p. 375.
100. Moulton (2014), p. 374.
101. Moulton (2014), p. 374.
102. Moulton (2014), p. 370.

PART III

Medium Shot: On the Cinema's Affective Audience Effects

CHAPTER 5

I, You, and We: Investigating the Cinema's Affective Audience Interrelations

> Why has nobody ever wanted to study in all its specificity the lived experience of the audience, the emotional fluctuations and the changes to social patterns that are produced by the ritual of film-viewing? [...] How can systematic research be organized "from the point of view of the spectator"?
>
> Gian Piero Brunetta[1]

In Chapters 3 and 4 I have dealt with the collective cinema experience on a more general level of intentions, attention, commitment, expressions, and action. The *affective* dimension has not played a prominent role yet. But this is precisely what the remainder of this book will be about: I will take up film historian Gian Piero Brunetta's call to study the lived experience of the audience with its emotional ups and downs, and the numerous metamorphoses of its affective relations during a film. From the "long shot" in Part II, I am now zooming in on a "medium shot" in Part III: Chapter 5 will focus on *affective audience interrelations*, those social relations between viewers that are based on emotions and affects as well as their concomitant expressive behavior, and which emerge while watching a film collectively. My guiding question will be how can we usefully distinguish and investigate the various affective experiences viewers can have with and against their co-viewers.

Altogether I will present seven phenomenological axes of investigation: 1. The degree of awareness: How conscious am I of the other viewers? 2. The experiential mode: What kind of interrelation do I have with the other viewers? 3. The changeability of the collective experience: How fluctuating is the experiential mode? 4. The degree of volition: How much control do I have over the affective audience interrelations? 5. The strain of emotion work: What's the impact of the situational frame? 6. The question of intimacy, closeness and significance: How important is the type of relationship I have with other viewers? And finally, 7. The source of the audience effect: Where do the affective audience interrelations originate? At the risk of eliciting taxonomical fatigue, I will go through these axes step by step, promising invigorating examples along the way.

1. HOW CONSCIOUS AM I OF THE OTHER VIEWERS? THE DEGREE OF AWARENESS

Emotions like joy, shock, or sadness, and concomitant expressive reactions like laughing, screaming, or weeping, can change the *degree of awareness* of our relationship to other viewers. I have variously argued throughout this book that the collective cinema experience is not something we tend to actively focus upon. However, this can easily change: Via emotions and concomitant expressions, elements of the collective experience that might have lingered at the fringe of consciousness might move closer to the center; conversely, those that were in the foreground at first can be relegated to the background of awareness.

Since watching a film does not mean looking at an unchanging representation, but following a constantly shifting series of moving images, the degree of awareness of other viewers is far from static. It is in a continuous state of flux, where we become strongly aware of our co-viewers in one moment, while they are shoved to the fringe of consciousness in the next instance. We get a sense of this constant shifting and changing in a quote from film scholar Martin Barker who recollects watching the movie *Master and Commander* (2003): "In one scene, a moment of by-play produces a ripple of light laughter in the small audience – this increases my own response. There is a burial-at-sea scene during which I feel tears form. I notice my wife wiping her eyes, and realize I wasn't alone in my response."[2] While in moments of strong immersion the viewer might be primarily focused on what goes on in the fictional world, the field of consciousness can quickly be restructured when an awareness of others suddenly moves to the center.

This is often the case in anti-immersive and theatrical moments of aggressive humor, disgusting scenes, and cinematic shocks in slapstick films, slasher horror, thrillers, splatter films, and gross-out comedies. When I laugh, when I am shocked, or when I experience strong revulsion, I may be distanced – sometimes even extricated – from my engagement with the film itself. It is as though the film has shoved me away, decreasing my immersion in its world and increasing my awareness of the movie-theater. While this certainly does not automatically result in a focus on my fellow viewers, it can do so more easily when the highly affective, anti-immersive scenes are accompanied by my co-viewers' expressive responses such as laughing, roaring, screaming, or moaning. These audible responses cut through the darkness and force their way over the soundtrack, *signaling* not simply the presence of other viewers, but also *communicating* their current emotions: This is hilarious! This is shocking! This is gross!

But apart from audible expressive re-acting, play-acting, inter-acting, jointly re-acting, and synchronically acting together, which *physically* announce the presence of others, there are also *imaginary* phantoms that noiselessly and somewhat malevolently whisper in our ears, "You are not watching the film alone." This is the case, for instance, when social emotions like embarrassment, shame, or guilt come into play. Their effect does not necessarily depend on face-to-face interaction, but often relies on the imagined, phantom-like gaze of others. When the young teenage boy feels ashamed watching a sex scene with his parents, it is simply on the basis of him having *imagined* his parents' disapprobation at his arousal. Here the parents' actual presence has a strong bearing on the imagination. The situation would be different were the teenage boy watching the film with his friends or alone – situations in which the phantom menace of his parents' disapproval would have been weak or non-existent.

Another example might illustrate the way the emotion of guilt can make us aware of other viewers. Some years ago I was watching the documentary *One Day in September* (1999) in a San Francisco theater with my girlfriend at that time, a Jewish-American woman highly sensitive to instances of anti-Semitism. The film deals with the terrorist attack on the 1972 Summer Olympics in Munich in which eleven Israelis were killed. Moreover, the movie emphasizes the incompetence of the Bavarian police force: had they acted more professionally, many lives could have been saved. As a German from Munich – not only the capital of Bavaria, but also the capital of Hitler's National Socialist movement – I felt a strong sense of collective guilt, or, more accurately, "membership guilt."[3] During the film, I was imagining, distractedly, what my girlfriend might feel and think, constantly triangulating between the film, my own feelings, and hers. Again, it was her *actual* presence that made me take on an *imagined* version of her perspective. Without her, I might have responded with anger or regret or a vague feeling of collective guilt.[4] But I would not have been anchored as strongly in the theater.

To drive home my point about triangulating in imagination the reaction of other viewers, we may take those particularly strong moments of reflection that come into play when you urge others to watch a specific film – simply because you think the movie is worthwhile for instructive reasons or because you have a strong affectionate relationship to the film and want the other person to like it as well. (Here we might also remind ourselves again of the fact that the cinema was and is a prime venue for first dates.) The more important the invited person and the more affectionate value the film carries for you, the more you may feel as if your own self stood on trial variously throughout the film. Especially when the responses of the other persons are less-than-reassuring (was she yawning and moving in her seat impatiently? was his laughter meant appreciatively or derisively?), you may start thinking: Is the film too boring, too pretentious, too complicated, too risqué, too cheap, too vulgar, too disgusting, too violent, too melodramatic, too banal, too tear-jerking for him, for her, for them?

Thus other viewers may force themselves into awareness via our sense perception as well as imagination, but there is yet a third way how the collective situation of the movie-theater can become prominent. Coming back to the distinction between active and passive diversion, we could think of moments when we *actively* remind ourselves of the presence of others, for example when we need to soothe ourselves: At a certain point a terrifying horror film can create a strong urge to counter the phenomenological distance typical of fear by *deliberately* focusing on the collectivity of the situation: "I am not alone, hence there is less reason to be afraid." A number of psychological and neuroscientific studies have shown that fearful emotional experiences create a need for social connection and sharing of emotions. At the end of the 1950s Stanley Schachter provided evidence for this "stress and affiliation effect" in a classical experiment: people who were anxious at being exposed to an electric shock preferred to wait *in the company of others*, while others whose threat was low expressed a preference to wait alone.[5] Likewise, in an fMRI study James A. Coan, Hillary S. Schaefer, and Richard J. Davidson subjected married women to the threat of electric shock.[6] The women either held their husband's hand, the hand of an anonymous male experimenter, or no hand at all. The results clearly indicated that threat-related neural activation in the participant's brain *decreases* with spousal handholding – in fact, the better the marriage, the higher the attenuation effect. Even holding the hand of a *stranger* decreases the activation in brain regions related to being threatened, albeit to a lesser extent. Now, handholding is, of course, also a frequent strategy for dealing with fearful experiences in the cinema. To pick a random scene that illustrates this proclivity, think of Stanley Kubrick's *Lolita* (1962): Watching a scary movie in a drive-in theater, Humbert Humbert (James Mason), Lolita (Sue Lyon), and her mother Charlotte (Shelley Winters) are overcome by fear and therefore try to catch each other's hands to alleviate the need for social connection.[7]

An *active* shift of focus toward the other viewers might also have a mere *epistemic* motivation. Imagine yourself in a situation in which you don't understand a given film properly (a) because you find it too challenging intellectually, (b) because the film deals with, perhaps, a remote Indian village or comes from Uzbekistan, or (c) because the film is shot in a dialect of your own language that you hardly understand (say, Cockney or Bavarian or Sardinian). Or (d) imagine yourself sitting next to an important movie critic whose evaluations and interpretations you tend to admire. Variously throughout the movie

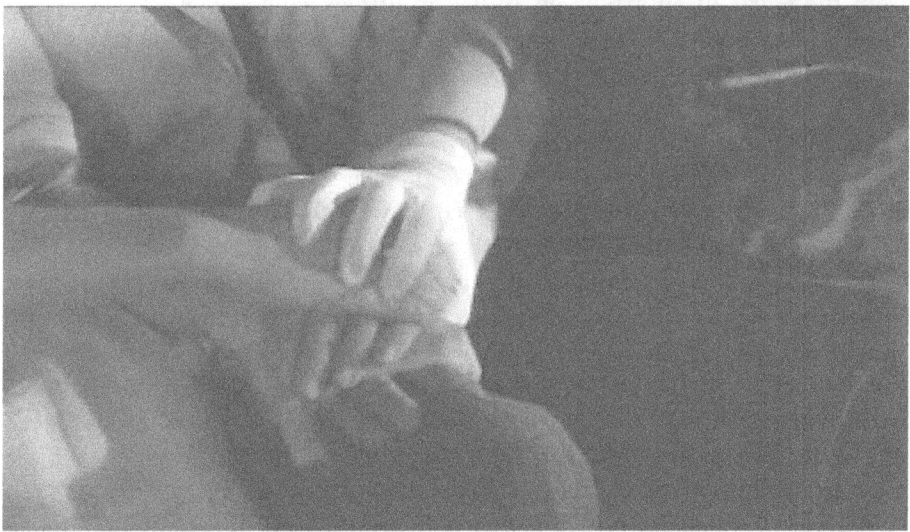

Figure 5.1: United in fear: Lolita (Sue Lyon), Humbert Humbert (James Mason), and Lolita's mother Charlotte (Shelley Winters) watching a monster movie in Stanley Kubrick's *Lolita*.

you might look at the persons next to you for emotional cues or other kinds of information to calibrate your own cognitions, emotions, evaluations, or interpretations. Here the psychological term "social appraisal," used for cases where people evaluate a situation through other people's emotional expressions, might be helpful. Surely one does not glean information from each and everyone. The cues must derive from reliable – that is, trustworthy and competent – persons: a group of Uzbeks, some Bavarians in the audience, or the admired film critic next to you.[8]

II. HOW DO I EXPERIENCE MYSELF IN RELATION TO THE OTHER VIEWERS? THE EXPERIENTIAL MODE

But strong emotions and affects as well as concomitant expressions not only have a bearing on the degree of awareness – they also affect the *experiential mode* of audience interrelations. They can push social relations toward individuation or collectivity, detachment or closeness. In fact, the two extremes of audience relation comprise a phenomenologically distanced, antagonistic I–you relationship at one end of the spectrum and a phenomenologically close, mutual we-connection at the other.

Now, it is not unlikely that despite the *equalizing* tendencies of the cinema, which I have argued for in Chapter 3, and possibly in stubborn resistance to them, some viewers might enter the auditorium with a strong will to be *different*, distinguishing themselves by whatever means from the rest of the audience, and thus establish a phenomenological I–you (or we–you) antagonism from the start. In an article on Indian multiplex cinemas, Adrian Mabbott Athique has shown how the middle-class audiences of the multiplex look down on and try to distance themselves from non-multiplex audiences in regular cinemas.[9] If such a middle-class multiplex patron was forced to attend a screening in a *non*-middle-class cinema, he or she may initially be averse to any we-connection with the rest of the audience. In turn, other viewers might, from the beginning, feel *alike* to their co-viewers, because they share markers of identity they deem crucial. As we have seen in Chapter 3, fans of *Star Wars* or Apichatpong Weerasethakul might at the beginning feel *closer* than usual to their co-viewers, because they have a medium or strong we-intention to watch the movie with other *Star Wars* or Apichatpong fans. However, and this is important, the concrete aesthetic experience in the cinema may still transform the initial attitude. A specific cinematic experience can easily pit one fan against another in anger (see Chapter 9) and unite in laughter even the most elitist snob with his previously sneered-at co-viewers (see Chapter 7). It is therefore important to shed further light on the types of experiential modes during the cinematic experience.

Let us begin at the antagonistic end. Some of the most extreme cases of audience antagonism come in moments when the joint action of movie-watching suddenly falls apart: either because of the *perception* of someone else's audible expression or due to an *imaginary* distancing characteristic of emotions like shame or guilt. Just think of a moment when you are deeply involved in a moving melodrama like Max Ophüls's *Letter From an Unknown Woman* (1948) – and suddenly someone in the audience laughs condescendingly about the film. The contempt and derision expressed by the other spectator – who *devalues the film* and, implicitly albeit not necessarily intentionally, *ridicules your own evaluation and emotion* – destroys your highly emotional engagement.

At the same time, the derisive laughter also reminds you that this other viewer experiences and evaluates the film quite differently, thus contradicting your background assumption of the collective constellation: Tacitly presupposing that the others were experiencing the film in a very similar way (see Chapter 3), the nasty laughter disrupts your presumed state of shared reality. As a consequence, you might feel an upsurge of irritation or anger.

What is more, in the cinema we often feel particularly *moved* by laudable prosocial acts, as when a mother sacrifices her own well-being for the social advancements of her daughter (*Imitation of Life*, 1959) or a father conceals his terminal illness from his family to spare them emotional hardships (*After the Wedding/Efter Brylluppet*, 2006). Precisely because these acts are so admirably social, they become quasi-sacred for us. Along these lines, Florian Cova and Julien A. Deonna argue that we feel moved when a positive core value that possesses some kind of "transcendental significance" for us, as a moral community, becomes salient.[10] If we agree with Nietzsche that the sacred is whatever one cannot laugh at in a given culture, the laughter at these quasi-sacred, deeply moving moments must have a particularly disruptive effect.[11] The person whose laughter *spoils* the film (in both senses of the word) cannot be part of one's community of feeling and values, because he or she does not share what is "sacred" in that moment.[12] The situation has changed into a paradigmatic state of distanced I–you social antagonism.

The antagonism in this example depends on the perception of an active and evaluative expression of emotion, insofar as the other viewer utters his or her derision and contempt non-verbally through laughter. Here we deal with an objectively observable antagonism, particularly when you shush the disturber or even insult him. This is not the case when shame or guilt comes into play. Here the antagonism is more passive and hidden, dependent as it is on what may well be an *imagined* standpoint. It is therefore experienced primarily by the person who is ashamed or feels guilty, but rarely by the others who are present. In fact, the other spectators may be entirely unaware of your feelings of shame or guilt. When I felt membership guilt as a Bavarian during the screening of *One Day in September*, my girlfriend might not have noticed it at all. Hence I–you antagonisms do not always entail a symmetrical distance: The phenomenological distance of person A to person B is not necessarily that of person B to person A.[13]

While in antagonistic forms of I–you relationship emotions strongly posit the fellow viewer as an opposed 'other', there are also neutral forms of affective audience interrelations that occur in moments of strong *individuating* immersion. When we are deeply involved in a moment of sadness, the emotional experience can reduce our awareness of others, keeping us at bay in a non-antagonistic way. The same goes for suspense and its fearful subtypes that elsewhere I have called "dread" and "terror" and that strongly focus us on the film.[14] As Christine Tappolet points out: "there is reason to think that different types of emotions have a different impact on attention – positive emotions are thought to widen and not to narrow our attentional focus – it is certainly plausible to claim that fear narrows the focus of attention."[15] Thus fearful immersion keeps us emotionally individuated in a non-antagonistic way – until the moment we actively seek the closeness of others, by holding hands or otherwise.

At first sight this may sound inconsistent with what I have claimed about the pleasure in functioning and social flow. In Chapter 3 I have argued that when we lose ourselves collectively in immersed viewing, pleasure can derive from the fact that we are dedicated to and lost in a quiet activity together. Yet I don't see this as a contradiction, because the pre-reflective pleasure in being collectively lost in immersed viewing has to be conceptually kept apart from the feeling of closeness due to a shared emotion. While the former *can* connect us when focused upon, it should not be confused with feeling individuated emotionally (due to sadness) or feeling close (due to shared joy).

Finally, at the other end of the continuum, we find the phenomenologically close, mutual we-connections. These affective collective experiences are the opposite of social antagonism: the viewers experience something together, not individually and parallel to each other. Phenomenologically close we-connections can come in different degrees of awareness, from a background phenomenon to a foregrounded experience with a high degree of consciousness: The "sense of us" is often a plural *pre-reflective* self-awareness, but it can also become self-reflective and thus can have the collective experience as its intentional object.[16] In moments of strong affective we-connection the viewers not only share the basic joint commitment and we-intention to watching the film together as part of an anonymous group; nor do they merely act jointly when they watch the movie together. They emphatically share an emotion, are infected by emotional contagion, or feel together. In the following chapter I will define these three types of affective we-experience in more detail. At this point another personal example might suffice to illuminate what I have in mind.

In Fall 2006 the documentary *Germany – A Summer's Tale / Deutschland – Ein Sommermärchen* reached the German movie-theaters. It retold the fortunes (and misfortunes) of the German football team during the World Cup that had taken place in Germany during the preceding summer, which was perceived by many Germans as 'magical' (hence the reference to the fairy tale in the film's title). Once the film arrived at the moment when the German player Oliver Neuville scored the long-awaited 1-0 goal against Poland, something unusual happened in the Berlin movie-theater. Watching again what, from the German perspective, was arguably the single most intense moment of the World Cup, we, the anonymous viewers in the multiplex auditorium, exploded into a loud round of cheers and applause.[17] Here the situation cannot be characterized by saying that I was happy and my neighbor was happy and all the others were also happy. Rather than being individually happy, we were happy *together*. It was a moment of cinematic shared happiness. Our joyful collective outburst created a brief feeling of phenomenological closeness and, at the same time, expressed this feeling of proximity in an audible way: like a giant magnet, the situation centripetally drew the individual viewers together, evoking a fleeting feeling of mutual we-connection among anonymous strangers. But to repeat, during such moments of phenomenological 'fusion', viewers who share feelings do not somehow forget that they are individuals and mistakenly take their own experience for the experience of the others.[18]

III. HOW FLUCTUATING IS THE EXPERIENTIAL MODE? THE DEGREE OF CHANGEABILITY

Since the distanced I–you antagonisms and mutually close we-connections only emerge *during* and *because of* the collective cinematic experience, they are undeniably fleeting. What is more, as a particularly time-bound experience, watching a film means following a sequential process whose constant metamorphosis also affects the phenomenology of viewer relations. Hence not only the degree of awareness can change swiftly (as argued in section I), but also the phenomenological distance between viewers is subject to permanent transformations. Like the bellows of an accordion, the audience members might feel pushed from antagonistically distant to mutually close in one scene and pulled from we-connected to individuated in another.

Moreover, it would be blatantly wrong to conceive of the audience as a monolithic block where *everyone* feels either connected or distanced. Instead, the auditorium can be one big collective now, and then disintegrate quicksilver-like into various subgroups and even individuated spectators in the next instance. Here it might be helpful to draw a distinction between *habitual* communities based on diachronic relations and *episodic* or *short-term* collectivities that emerge in the here and now (in section VI we will further refine these rough distinctions).[19] Obviously both types of social connection exist in the movie-theater: The former *pre-exist* the cinema, the latter come about only *in* and *through* the cinema. On the one hand, we find couples, families, and groups of friends, subgroups of the audience who have a history in common. On the other hand, we have the fleeting, short-term collectivity of the audience (or parts of it), based on we-intentions, joint attention, joint action and, especially, affective we-experiences. The former can easily turn into *fractions* of the audience and thus *decouple* themselves momentarily from the larger episodic community, for instance when they discover something only they have in common due to a shared history. At the same time, habitual communities can easily *dissolve* into an episodic community or even *divide* the habitual community into those who become part of an episodic community and those who don't. The case of laughter will turn out particularly instructive in Chapter 7.

This raises the question of *how stable* the mode of audience interrelation is and *how often* and *how quickly* the collective experience changes. Sometimes there may be hardly any change, while at other times the collective experience is constantly metamorphosing in a protean-like fashion. Here we can expect considerable differences between films and genres. But depending on various other factors – for instance, how intimate and significant one's co-viewers are – we can also expect significant differences between two screenings of the same film. Very broadly speaking, we might expect the affective audience interrelations of the quiet-attentive viewing to be more stable and static, while the viewer relationships of the expressive-diverted type will be more fluid and changing. The reason is that in the latter the thoughts, evaluations, or feelings of individual viewers are publicly available through verbal and non-verbal expressions. Thus differences become more easily accessible than in quiet-attentive viewing.

IV. HOW MUCH CONTROL DO I HAVE OVER THE COLLECTIVE EXPERIENCE? THE DEGREE OF VOLITION AND INFLUENCE

Sometimes we can willfully 'steer' our emotions in the direction of I–you antagonism or mutually close we-connection, but sometimes the emotional response simply overcomes us and settles the mode of our relation to other viewers for us. We can therefore distinguish *degrees of volition*.

In his book *How Emotions Work* Jack Katz usefully distinguishes between *doing* an emotion and *being done* by an emotion. This is obviously not to say that we are completely free to choose to be angered or disgusted or moved. Yet Katz convincingly shows that sometimes there is a leeway that grants us a degree of volition when it comes to our emotions. Emotion psychologists deal with similar phenomena when they talk about *emotion regulation* and *emotional contagion* – two concepts that will prove useful for my phenomenological aims below. In this respect it will also prove illuminating to look at the *range of influence* I have over the collective experience in the cinema: Am I passively influenced by the other viewers or do I actively try to influence them? Just as the emotional expressions of others may evoke emotional reactions in me, I know that other viewers may infer information about my feelings, attitudes, and behavioral intentions from *my* emotional expressions. The audience effect is not a one-way street: "doing an emotion" can also have effects on my co-viewers.

Consider the following examples. On any given Saturday evening you might find yourself in a position in which you willfully react *against* the response of other viewers and thus put yourself deliberately in an I–you relationship. Having decided to watch a comedy like *Bridesmaids* (2011) or *The Hangover* (2009) in your local multiplex theater, you are surrounded by violently giggling teenage girls or outrageously laughing adolescent guys. While on another occasion you might have found these films hilarious, the social context – its situational framing – has put you in a position where you don't want to be part of their community of laughter, and thus you willfully distance yourself, resulting in a feeling of annoyance *both* about their laughter and the film. In other words, you find the film annoying *because of* the emotional reactions of the audience. Paraphrasing Rimbaud's famous formulation, you might think: *We is an other*.[20] Now, another viewer in the exact same cinema may choose a diametrically opposed strategy. Take a professor of English dragged along by her daughter and her friends. Under different circumstances she might have found these comedies below her wonderfully refined taste. However, due to the girls' passionate laughter she gives herself over to their enthusiasm and deliberately decides to enjoy the film by laughing with them. No matter what she tells her colleagues at the English department the next day, *during* the film she has thoroughly enjoyed it.[21] In both cases the viewers to a certain degree do their affective responses more than they are done by them. They have exercised some *control* over their affective life.

But the question of control is also at stake when we consider the degree of *influence* we can wield over our co-viewers. As we have seen in Chapter 4, when you stubbornly stay silent during the screening of *Bridesmaids* or *The Hangover*, you *nolens volens* communicate aversion against the humor embraced by the film and/or the joyful conviviality of the audience, expressing something like "Come on, this is not worthy of laughter!" However, it may well be that your communicative silence remains rather inconsequential, if your co-viewers don't realize that you do not want go along. If it is indeed your intention to convince your co-viewers that this is not something to laugh about, you may resort to motor, vocal, or verbal expressions such as looking at your watch demonstratively, sighing angrily, or even commenting acerbically. The thoroughly amused English professor, in turn, might laugh all the more loudly in an act of affective impression management.[22] She tries to forcefully animate her rather quiet husband to laugh with her and the girls so that they might enjoy the film *together*: "Come on, this is indeed worthy of laughter!"

In light of these examples I want to briefly elucidate the concepts of emotion regulation and emotion work for our discussion of the audience effect. Here I loosely follow Christian von Scheve's helpful integrative model that combines ideas from the psychological theory of emotion *regulation* (mostly associated with the work of James Gross) and the sociological theory of emotion *work* (predominantly connected to studies by Arlie Hochschild).[23]

A first strategy of emotion regulation – *situation selection* (1) – refers to the choice of preferable affective circumstances and hence takes place prior to the actual collective experience in the cinema.[24] Broadly speaking, we have three options. First, we can choose the appropriate *type of film*: if I want to go to the movies with a specific person or group of people, I may choose a film that does not cause embarrassment, but results in a positive experience. Second, we can decide on the *type of co-viewers* we take to the cinema, knowing that there is company that fits a specific type of movie better than others. A teenage boy is unlikely to take his grandmother to a dress-up screening of *Star Wars* just as his grandmother might shun the embarrassment that may come if she takes him to a matinee of her favorite 1950s melodrama. Third, choosing the right *type of cinema* may also be important as it allows us to include preferred types of co-viewers and exclude others. Think of adolescents who prefer to watch a comedy in a megaplex on a Saturday evening, because they have *grosso modo* more freedom to talk and express themselves than in a more bourgeois arthouse theater where they might face disciplining repercussions.[25]

However, even if we have tried to do everything to select the right situation, once we are settled on a specific cinema we have no influence over what co-viewers crowd the auditorium. We might end up sitting amid rebellious rabble-rousing teenage boys or a group of senior citizens who do not find a specific raunchy comedy funny at all. Another way to regulate our affective experience may therefore be the strategy of *situation modification* (2), that is, the change of the physical environment. If looking for a different seat is not an option in the crowded theater, shushing the teenage boys could be an alternative strategy. Inversely, just as the English professor stimulated her quiet husband, we may try to inspire the bored elderly people by initiating what we hope could be contagious laughter: if they catch it, the experience will become more enjoyable for them *and* ourselves. Again, emotion regulation can work both on oneself and the others, intrinsically and extrinsically, on my amusement and theirs.

However, not all situations can easily be modified – after all, it might be dangerous to oppose rabble-rousers. This is why it can help to make a kind of *internal* situation selection by refocusing one's attention. James Gross calls this strategy *attentional deployment* (3).[26] *Ignoring* the noise of the teenage boys or the silence of the elderly co-viewers, while simultaneously *concentrating* on the film or the laughter of other viewers may help to positively change the affective audience relation.

By initiating a *cognitive change* (4) – a modification of how to appraise or reappraise a situation – the viewer has yet another possibility to alter the emotional response: switching the *evaluation* of a situation can change the situation for oneself. Think of downward social comparison: by comparing oneself favorably to less fortunate others, one can decrease the negative impact of a situation.[27] Hence the angry viewer might appraise the conduct of the loud teenage boys as "typical lower-class behavior," and the ostentatious silence of the elderly people may be reappraised as "age-related ignorance" (see Chapter 9).[28]

The final emotion regulation strategy – *response modulation* (5) – refers to physiological change, experiential transformation, and alteration of expressive behavior. It implies a change of the ongoing emotion *itself*, which is to say neither the situation surrounding it nor the cognitive processes preceding it. By trying to breathe steadily in order to control our anger at the noisy kids, we can decrease our physiological arousal and thus we *down*-regulate the emotion. Or we laugh all the more forcefully to make the film more amusing for ourselves: increasing our expressive behavior, we *up*-regulate the affective experience. Note that in the latter case we *internally* change our own emotion, which is not the same as the communicative laughter meant to *externally* change the behavior of the elderly viewers.

So far my description may sound as if the collective affective experiences in the cinema were largely 'in our own hands.' But harking back to the shameful primal-scene scenario or the episode of membership guilt, we realize that viewers are often *done by* their emotion and thus lack volition. In their book *All Things Shining* Hubert Dreyfus and Sean Dorrance Kelly describe the loss of agency in moments of collective cheering and rising with a crowd of sports fans, a highly eloquent description that might remind us of collective laughter in the cinema which can equally 'carry us away.' I will therefore quote the passage at length: "It is *my* muscles, of course, that generate the motor actions – straightening the legs, raising the arms, emitting the inarticulate utterance that means 'Hooray!' But there is a strong sense in which I perform these movements without ever having decided to do so. The activity is out of my control in the sense that I do not perform it voluntarily. It's not as if I was forced to jump up and cheer either, of course. It was always an option for me to adopt a kind of ironic distance from the situation, or even [. . .] to walk away. But so long as I find myself taken over by the situation, there is an important sense in which I am no longer the source of my own activity."[29] I vividly remember how in a Berlin multiplex cinema a considerable share of the audience – both female and male – exploded into loud cheering when toward the end of *Salt* (2010) Angelina Jolie chokes the male villain (Liev Schreiber) to death in a dexterous and extremely clever move. The audience clearly felt as if *overcome* by an urge to cheer.

This is neither to say that a lack of control over one's emotions depends on the emotions to be collective; nor is emotional contagion the sole source of an emotion that seems out of one's control. Above we have also encountered a number of cases in which viewers were overcome by an emotion that did not converge with the emotions of others but rather stood in *opposition* to them – from the shame in the primal-scene scenario to my feeling of membership guilt vis-à-vis my Jewish-American girlfriend. What unites *all* of these examples, however, is the fact that they stand at the far end of those volitional cases described at the beginning of the section: While in those earlier examples we could intentionally influence our emotions toward divergence or convergence, in the later cases the mode of our social relation with other viewers is settled for us by an emotional response that has overwhelmed us.

V. WHAT'S THE IMPACT OF THE SITUATIONAL FRAME? THE STRAIN OF EMOTION WORK

In previous chapters we have heard about the obligations and responsibilities that come with being part of an audience. Specific audiences demand specific display rules and feeling rules: what expressions we are expected to show and what emotions are appropriate to be felt. The *situational framing* is a particularly important facet of the audience effect which can easily change the viewers' cognitive schemata: Depending on their knowledge of how the audience is put together, viewers watch the film with a different set of expectations about implicit display and feeling rules and thus respond with different emotions.[30]

The situational framing can be important both on an *abstract-institutional level* and on an *intimate-personal* one. With regard to institutions we only have to think of the difference it makes if students have to watch a film in a seminar room as part of a course for which they get credit or whether they organize a screening on their own with their student organization. In the first case the students will likely be cautious that their teacher does not catch signs of boredom or frustration, whereas in the latter case they might feel completely at ease. Or take the case of the press screening in which I watch the film with a group of other critics: Here I am supposed to take notes and show a restrained professional attitude. I have to avoid vocal expressions and refrain from overt breakouts of emotions, which could be sanctioned through future disrespect by fellow-critics. In his semio-pragmatic theory, which I have discussed in Chapter 2, Roger Odin has captured these differences on the institutional level quite adequately.

But very divergent display rules and feeling rules may also apply in more intimate-personal circumstances. Let us suppose a man takes two dates to the same tear-jerking melodrama, say a film like *The Notebook* (2004). The first time he goes to the cinema with a 'traditional' woman who expects him to show a certain kind of machismo, whereas the second time he visits the movie-theater with a 'progressive' companion who is not at all averse to a man expressing tender feelings. In the first case he is not supposed to shed tears, while in the second this might be welcome or even expected.

In his cinema memoir *Moving Places* Jonathan Rosenbaum gives us a vivid illustration of the situational framing and shows how different audiences can change the viewer's cognitive schemata, the horizon of expectations, the display and feeling rules, as well as the emotions of the very same film. Rosenbaum recalls how he, as young *Jonny*, watched the Doris Day movie *On Moonlight Bay* (1951) in one of the theaters in Florence, Alabama, owned by his grandfather. Describing his experience in the present tense and from a third-person perspective, Rosenbaum notes how during a romantic nocturnal kissing scene between the male and the female protagonist Jonny "feels the magic of the mood. The audience around him is somber, spelled by the smooching and the blue moonlight."[31] Rosenbaum, just like the rest of the audience, seemed genuinely moved; the term "spelled" implies, moreover, that they watched the film in motionless, respectful silence. The response of the mixed, rather anonymous audience of the Florence theater thus suggests an implicit feeling rule along the following lines: "Oh my god, how can one *not* be moved by a romantic kissing scene in moonlight?"

Two years later the situation is very different. Rosenbaum watches the same film in a boys' summer camp in Maine. Unsurprisingly, "there is hooting boys' laughter all around you, maybe just to show that they really don't care, that they know this is only a sappy movie."[32] Rosenbaum's description does not tell us if the derisive laughter and devaluating attitude of the other boys *contradicted* his response at that moment – after all, he may have been equally enthralled as in the mixed Florence audience, albeit secretly. But it seems more likely to me that they *confirmed* his response, suggested by the frame of mind the exclusive boyish audience put him into all along. The all-male audience would not 'allow' him to be engrossed by such a movie. In this case the implicit feeling rule might sound like: "Ugh, how *can* one be moved by a kissing couple in moonlight?"[33]

Different situational framings can lead to strong divergences not only *between* two viewings, but also *within* a single one, for instance along gender lines. This comes across particularly vibrantly in Rosenbaum's account of a screening of the Elvis Presley film *Love Me Tender* (1956) which he attended as a thirteen-year-old boy. When Elvis first appeared on the screen "the girls went wild, screaming in ecstasy, while the boys, Jonny among them, hissed and booed with equal fury, each faction trying to drown out the other. [. . .] virtually the same sexual warfare was waged across the river at the Colbert a few days later. In both theaters it was too noisy to follow more than a few fragments of the dialogue, and much of it had to be lip-read. *How utterly ridiculous*, Jonny thought with a scowl, scoffing still more when a dead Elvis appeared at the end in double exposure, to sing the title tune, and some of the teenage girls nearby began to sob inconsolably."[34] The reaction of the boys – and "Jonny" Rosenbaum as part of them – shows that they cannot accept the tears and ecstatic screaming of the girls. Judging the girls' response as ridiculous, they work themselves into a fury expected from them as young boys in the US in the 1950s. Importantly, both groups might feel a close mutual we-connection due to and against the others, their experience exemplifying a we–you antagonism.

However, it would be an exaggeration to claim that the situational framing can fully determine one's emotions and affective interrelations to other viewers, as if being part of a certain audience implied the push of an emotion button. I have already hinted at the possibility that young Rosenbaum might not have been completely in accordance with his condescendingly laughing friends in the boys' camp. He may have acted *against* his own feelings, simply to conform in an act of affective impression management that was expected from him. He might have even been aware of this discrepancy. A similar diagnosis may apply to the example of the man who organizes two dates with two women: since it is likely that with one of them he will have to 'manage' his emotions and 'work' on them more strongly and consciously than with the other, he may experience a certain tension – a disagreement between what is expected from him and what he would personally prefer to feel.

Here we are dealing with another interesting facet of the phenomenology of the audience effect: As a viewer I sometimes have the *conscious* feeling that – even though I don't want to – I have to go along with the others or have to act according to the call made by their presence, due to an institutional frame or the intimate presence of a specific co-viewer. I may either have the feeling that I must *actively force myself into* a specific behavior or feel *passively pulled by* a demanding call to act according to social demands (see also the sections on laughing along with others and forced tears in Chapters 7 and 8). In both cases I experience the 'social pressure' as a strain or estranging tension that I would not experience otherwise. One could describe it as an experience of being forced or pulled *outside of myself*, an impression that I am not completely *at home*. I will call this experience the *strain of emotion work*. It can be experienced as a mild tension, but it can also reach strong levels.

The situations in which the strain of emotion work makes itself felt are manifold. Think of watching *Twelve Years a Slave* (2013) with an African American friend. Or think of a viewer who has to follow a film quietly and attentively in an arthouse theater, even though she feels like engaging in a relieving conversation with her partner about the strong effect it has on her. In Chapter 4 I have referred to Goffman's distinction between *tight* and *loose* regulations in social gatherings.[35] Importantly, what might look like a loose social regulation from a third-person perspective ("Come on, the young boy Jonny only has to *laugh* at a romantic scene with his friends") might in fact be experienced as a rather tight rule ("Oh no, why do I *have to* laugh at this wonderful scene with these boorish boys?!"). In other words, for a viewer who feels the strain of emotion work the situation comes across as tight on *the level of experience* – no matter how it may look from outside.

What I am describing is a feeling that refers to *behavioral demands* and *feeling rules*. But note that this call to act according to the rules of an institutional frame or the (presumed) expectancies of specific individuals is different from the *direct* influence of other co-viewers. Just picture the difference of (a) becoming aware of an *annoying co-viewer* who you are angry at and (b) becoming aware of the *tension* you feel because you are not allowed to shush or even insult him due to some co-viewers in the audience who would not appreciate this behavior at all. In the first case you could still shush him if you wanted to; in the second case you have to refrain from doing so because your boss sits one row behind you. Hence the intentional object of the experience that I am describing is not a specific co-viewer or group of co-viewers, but precisely the tension or discrepancy you feel *because* you have to behave and feel in a certain way. It is thus a meta-affective response: You feel a tension because you have to behave and feel in a certain way.

VI. HOW IMPORTANT IS THE TYPE OF RELATIONSHIP TO THE OTHER VIEWERS? THE DEGREE OF FAMILIARITY, CLOSENESS, AND SIGNIFICANCE

My sixth suggestion toward a phenomenology of the audience effect concerns the type of relationship to other viewers. As Rosenbaum once put it: "it mattered *whom* I saw movies with – which was always part of the place where I saw them."[36] The strength of the audience effect can depend on the familiarity and physical closeness of other viewers, but especially also on the significance, or *phenomenological weight*, they have for us.

No doubt, how *familiar* I am with my co-viewers can strongly influence my emotional reaction in a positive or negative way. Because a person is very familiar to me I can be particularly annoyed or embarrassed, but I can also feel more secure, attached, or amused. Inversely, the anonymity of the audience may influence the emotional valence of my experience as well.[37] Think of a viewer who, sitting next to his Asian friend, feels angry about a film because it contains racist jokes.[38] The very same viewer might, unfortunately, care much less about the racist jokes when seeing the film with her white friends or alone. Oftentimes we appreciate a familiar scene, an allusion, or an image of a city precisely when we are with persons to whom we are connected in an intimacy that emerges over long stretches of time. In the next chapter we will see that these shared experiences from the past can be an important enabling condition for shared emotions.

Somewhat schematically we can distinguish between the following degrees of familiarity: *very familiar* collectives (for example, a family or old friends), *familiar* collectives (for example, a couple newly in love), *medium familiar* collectives (for example, a group of co-workers or a couple on a first date), *medium unfamiliar* collectives (for example, fans surrounded by other fans), *unfamiliar* collectives (for example, Germans among Germans), and *very unfamiliar* collectives (for example, completely unknown co-viewers in a foreign country). Often, of course, we do not only have one type of relationship to other viewers. Instead, it is quite likely that we entertain various relationships at the same time, placed within each other rather like Chinese boxes – for instance, when a German *Star Wars* fan goes to a German cinema with his family, including the spouses of his children and some of their friends, to watch the midnight opening of a new *Star Wars* film among other fans.

Physical closeness – over and above familiarity – can also play a role in the strength of one's relationship to other viewers. One only has to think of a boy who happens to sit directly next to a girl he has been secretly in love with for a long time: excited by the smell of her perfume, he is now unable to concentrate on the movie. Had he seen the girl at the entrance, but lost her in the crowd flocking into the multiplex auditorium, the effect of her presence would be infinitely lower.

Ultimately, most important for the audience effect is the *significance* (or phenomenological weight) other co-viewers have for me. With the notion of *significance* I want to raise attention to the fact that not every physically close familiar person has an equal effect on my film experience, nor is every unknown person equally unimportant to me. Even if the teenage boy is equally familiar with his siblings, it will certainly be his parents who cause the embarrassment when watching a sex scene. On the other hand, a very attractive neighbor may develop a high degree of significance even if – or precisely because – the person is completely unknown. (Barthes' little essay "Leaving the Movie-theater," discussed in Chapter 2, is a prime document of the eroticism of the cinema.) Let me add a more ethically charged example: Imagine a Turkish viewer who watches Atom Egoyan's *Ararat* (2004), a film thematizing in complex ways the Turkish genocide against the Armenians, with members of the Armenian-Turkish community. Even if the rest of the audience may be completely unknown to him, the knowledge about the Armenian identity of his co-viewers may evoke a feeling of membership *guilt*. Had he watched the film with non-Armenian compatriots he might have experienced *anger* or *shame* about the Turkish past. Again, the co-viewers are significant, even if they are unfamiliar. Along these lines we can imagine numerous examples in which categories like ethnicity, gender, class, age, or religion have an audience effect despite the co-viewer's anonymity.

VII. WHERE DOES THE AFFECTIVE AUDIENCE INTERRELATION ORIGINATE? THE SOURCE OF THE AUDIENCE EFFECT

A final useful suggestion toward a phenomenology of the audience effect may be the *source* of the emotions and affects involved: do they derive primarily from the aesthetic experience of the film or exclusively from the social experience of the auditorium? Again, I will propose a continuum.

At one end of the spectrum we find those states of audience interrelation *directly* related to the movie: they derive from emotions and affects that the film intends to evoke (or, at any rate, we *believe* it intends to elicit). Take fear in horror films. Since the viewers share the frightening film as their collective intentional object and appraise the film as threatening, they *collectively* experience the shared emotion of fear while watching the film. The mutually close we-connection coming from the collective cheering and applauding in *Germany – A Summer's Tale* or *Salt*, mentioned above, can serve as another example, and so can the collective screaming that may accompany the extremely shocking conclusion of *Friday the 13th* (1980).

Somewhere in the middle of the spectrum are affective audience interrelations *indirectly* related to the movie: They are based on emotions evoked by the film, but are *not* meant to be elicited by the filmmakers. Under most viewing conditions the film clearly lacks this effect. In specific social circumstances, however, the film can have either the positively uniting effect of a close we-connection or the negatively distancing effect of a detached I–you antagonism.

In terms of we-connections we can think of the in-group feelings – and hence feelings of belonging together – that cinephiles might have experienced during screenings of rarely available films in the pre-digital age. Remember that for a long time in the history of film it was difficult to see certain films, especially for people living in remote, rural areas. Watching a film by, say, Murnau, Ozu, or Rocha may have involved a "pleasure of being part of the lucky few who could watch this rare film," as Laurent Jullier and Jean-Marc Leveratto put it.[39] The cineastes, cinephiles, or cinemaniacs watching these films might not only have experienced a feeling of social distinction toward those unable to see the film, but also of gratefulness for and pleasure in being part of this community able to watch this film at this point in time. Occasionally, one can still get similar feelings of belonging to a special collective, for instance at film premieres in which the stars or the filmmakers are present, at film festivals during a rare screening that is sold out immediately, at midnight blockbuster premieres, or in other restricted events one has to know about in advance (as in the case of Secret Cinema screenings).[40] Closely related are audience effects based on film screenings during which the viewers go through some extraordinarily bodily experience that may even involve physical strain (and hence affective responses in a wider sense of the term): "The element of physical endurance of some cult celebrations, like full-length screenings of *Empire* (1964), marathons of the *Heimat* series (1984), the timing of the original 'midnight movies' (literally at midnight), festivals' all-nighters, or intimate 'sleepover' viewings, enhances films' status to the level of cult, as a rite involving debutantes, survivors and veterans," Mathijs and Mendik note.[41] And finally we may think of audiences who do something illicit, like teenagers who sneak into a porn cinema or audiences who attend the illegitimate screening of a censored horror film.[42]

Turning to negative audience effects, we may once again think of the primal scene of collective viewing. The shame a teenage boy feels while watching a sex scene in, say, Catherine Breillat's *Romance* (1999) relies on the erotic arousal caused by the explicit moment of the film. But only because his parents are sitting next to him, the film can become the source of the shameful experience. A slightly different case is the anger a viewer might feel at a fellow viewer's derisive laughter. Again, his or her emotion does not relate directly to the film, but this time is caused by another person's expression of emotion. I do not *imagine* someone else's perspective (as in shame), but I *perceive* and react to another person's actual response. Similarly, a viewer might respond with condescending laughter when someone reacts to an apparently unspectacular scene with a cry of shock (see Chapter 7).

Last but not least, a different social or cultural background can 'rip the audience apart,' making some viewers feel deeply detached from and even antagonized to the rest – a fact anecdotally captured by poet Selima Hill when recounting her first cinema viewing experience. Since the film was apparently very boring for her, she fell asleep. Upon waking up she sensed a strange difference in experience between herself and the rest of the audience. Her friend Elizabeth was crying and other viewers felt uplifted by what they had seen: "Everybody sitting around me in the dark knew something that I didn't know, because they were real Catholics and I was only pretending. The film was called *Never Take No for an Answer* [1951] but in my ignorance I didn't even know what the question was. All my friends had been transformed, their faces shone, they couldn't move, while I just rolled my tie up and down and counted the bars on the radiator."[43] In all of these cases the audience's joint action disintegrates into parallel actions of individuals or individuated subgroups.

Finally, at the other end of the continuum we can locate affective audience interrelations entirely *unrelated* to the film. These originate in emotions beyond the aesthetic experience of the movie and are anchored exclusively in the here and now of the cinema. There are, for example, *antagonistic* states like *disgust* at an unkempt, malodorous neighbor, *envy* that a young boy feels for another kid who enters the cinema with precisely the huge box of popcorn that his mother has just denied him, or *jealousy* in the face of a happy couple openly embracing and fondling each other. The antagonism might reach from single viewers resenting one another to whole subgroups within the audience pitched against each other for various extra-aesthetic reasons. A participant of Annette Kuhn's study on memories of moviegoing in 1940s Britain, for instance, remembers how a neighborhood cinema could become a battleground due to an unintended act of trespassing: "Whole families used to take over and monopolize 'their' cinema at the top of the street, and woe betide any stranger that inadvertently sat in their rows of seats."[44]

Here we might also think of how divisions along race, class, and gender lines can (quite literally) separate subgroups within the audience and create a (however mild) feeling of detachment and opposition. In one of her ethnographic studies on moviegoing in India, Lakshmi Srinivas observes: "Cinema theaters reflect and reinforce stratification in the larger society. Seating is variously priced and distinguished into 'Balcony', middle level, and 'Gandhi Class', – which are the seats at the lower level close to the screen and which are typically priced at a fraction of the seats in the Balcony. Physically too seating may differ with the Balcony offering upholstered seats for its middle-class viewers while cheaper seats are of molded plastic or wood."[45] Giuseppe Tornatore's *Cinema Paradiso* (1988) illustrates this type of class distinction with recurring moments in which a snobbish man sitting in the balcony literally spits down on the lower-class people in the auditorium. He reacts to, and openly displays, his aversion to some of their responses, which he deems inappropriate.[46]

But the affective audience interrelations brought forth by extra-aesthetic reasons – and hence reasons unrelated to the film – do not only come in antagonistic form. They can also comprise positively *integrating* states, such as

Figure 5.2: A snobbish viewer on the balcony spitting down on the lower-class spectators in Giuseppe Tornatore's *Cinema Paradiso*.

the pleasure and mutual arousal of the couple that openly embraces each other in the public privacy of the cinema's darkness. More generally, the cinema can function as an *amalgamating meeting ground* for various social groups that creates feelings of attachment, social cohesion, and belonging together. This goes for the oft-described immigrant and female audiences of the Nickelodeon era. But it also goes for members of youth subcultures. Gina Marchetti, for one, has pointed out that "[a]s a dark, but public, place outside the realm of parental and social authority operating in the home and at the workplace, the cinema is a place to gather and meet like-minded fellows during leisure time. [. . .] In one sense, no matter what may or may not be on the screen, the movie-theater has consistently been an important aspect of the lives of many subcultural members."[47] Similarly, the above-quoted participant of Annette Kuhn's study on moviegoing memories points out the cinema's function as an integrating neighborhood site that could even figure as an extension of home: "'[W]herever the cinema was situated the population from the surrounding streets 'adopted' this cinema as their own, if ever you wanted to find someone quickly you just went to the cinema they frequented!.'"[48]

No doubt these extra-aesthetic audience interrelations can have a strong affective effect. They will mark the end of my line of inquiry, though, since the emotions they originate in are simply too contingent and too unspecific for the cinema. There is one exception: the emotion of anger. Toward the end of this book I will devote a whole chapter to it, not only because it is such a pervasive, primitive, and powerful example of the audience effect, but also because the very structure of the cinematic dispositive turns the movie-theater into a place highly conducive to anger.

Needless to say that all the painstaking distinctions I have introduced in this chapter hardly play a role once we watch a film alone – the various types of affective viewer interrelation are possible only in the collective situation of the cinema. To put it bluntly, when we watch a movie alone we simply cannot have these experiences. For better or worse.

NOTES

1. Quoted from O'Leary/O'Rawe (2013), pp. 353–4.
2. Barker (2005), p. 357.
3. Social self-categorization – the tendency to perceive oneself as a member of a social collective – can have profound effects and lead to group-based emotions that are felt by individuals on behalf of a social collective. Von Scheve/Ismer (2013), pp. 408–9.
    Margaret Gilbert defines "membership guilt" as the feeling of guilt over what a group of which one is a member has done: "This is not, of course, to feel guilt over what one did oneself. One may have been entirely guiltless, personally, in the matter" (Gilbert, 2002, p. 136).

4. Group-based emotions can also be elicited in solitude, but in this case the physical co-presence of my girlfriend strongly amplified my feeling of membership guilt.
5. Schachter (1959), p. 13ff.
6. Coan/Schaefer/Davidson (2006).
7. Of course, there is at the same time also a game of flirting, approaching, and rejecting at stake in this scene.
8. Bruder/Fischer/Manstead (2014), p. 147.
9. "The [regular] cinema halls are thus closely associated with raucous acts of mass participation, such as screaming, applauding, whistling and singing. However, for much of the multiplex clientele, this 'active' mode of spectatorship (where audiences boo the arrival on screen of the villain, sing and dance during the film songs, and throw coins at the screen) was actually seen to devalue their own experience of going to the cinema. A large component of the eagerness of multiplex viewers not to mix with the 'cheap crowd' in traditional cinema halls appeared to stem from a rejection of the latter's emotionally demonstrative and 'undisciplined' watching of films" (Athique, 2013, pp. 382–3).
10. Cova/Deonna (2013), p. 454.
11. See Dreyfus/Kelly (2011), p. 194.
12. Note, however, that not every kind of laughter during a film dealing with a "sacred" subject matter needs to be derisive and hence devaluing. My introductory example of viewers who laughed during the screening of Claude Lanzmann's *Sobibor* would be a case in point: They did not spoil the memory of the Holocaust and its millions of victims, but laughed *at* the German perpetrators. Yet as my discussion also made clear, it would not have been appropriate for everybody to laugh: There was a sense that the *German* viewers must not laugh, no matter how positive their intention, while for non-Germans and especially Jewish viewers this was a valid possibility.
13. Goffman (1961), p. 129.
14. On dread and terror, see chapters 6 and 7 of Hanich (2010). See also Hanich (2014).
15. Tappolet (2009), p. 336.
16. Schmid (2014b), p. 7.
17. As we have heard in Chapter 4, applause is not as common by far as in the opera or the theater, but it occurs in the cinema as well. In India, applauding seems to be quite regularly part of the cinematic experience. In her ethnography of "active viewing" in Indian cinemas, Srinivas has observed: "Viewers may applaud when the lights go off and again when they are turned on at the end of the film, like theater crowds clapping when the curtain rises and falls. Viewers talk of stars entering the narrative as '. . . coming on' or 'coming out' as if onto a stage. Star-characters, introduced dramatically into the narrative, are greeted with thunderous applause and whistles, as are scenes of comedy and dances" (Srinivas, 1998, p. 336). See also the examples in Breakwell/Hammond (1990), p. 26; Paech/Paech (2000), pp. 54–5; Athique (2013), pp. 382–3.
18. Compare also how Stephane Dunn describes the audience experience of African American viewers during the 1970s blaxploitation era: "Part of the exhilaration experienced by various black viewers stemmed from the shared energy and pleasure invested in the fantasy unfolding onscreen and from the expectation of black triumph." According to Dunn, the audience must have experienced its affective we-connection as joyfully empowering: "The black cultural identification enabled via the soul music, vernacular language, black ghetto setting, and visibility of black characters positioned as anti-white power or 'the Man' most certainly enhanced the collective experience of viewing pleasure" (Dunn, 2008, pp. 21–2).
19. See also Walther (1923), p. 48.

20. Stawarska (2009), p. 74.
21. Richard Abel has observed that many early French film critics before the First World War were obsessed with socially distinguishing themselves from the mass audience: "Some like [René] Doumic and [Louis] Haugmard generally took a position of social and moral superiority, with its attendant tone of condescension masking fear. Others like [Rémy de] Gourmont and [Adolphe] Brisson were somewhat ambivalent about finding themselves wrapped up in the experience of an 'alien' milieu" (Abel, 1988, p. 15).
22. "[A]ffective impression management involves actively trying to convey [to others] that one is experiencing an affective state that is appropriate for the given context" (Kelly/Iannone/McCarty, 2014, pp. 177–8.
23. Von Scheve (2012); Gross/Thompson (2007); Hochschild (1979).
24. In media and communication theory the widely used terms "mood management" and "selective exposure" could also fall into this category, but to my knowledge they have only been used for media content and not for the co-present audience.
25. In a Belgian study, Philippe Meers and his colleagues found that neighborhood cinemas were only visited "by people actually living near these cinemas. A key issue here was the importance of a community spirit, which was still very much alive in the different city districts, resulting in a feeling among our respondents of neighborhood cinemas as 'their' theaters" (Meers/Biltereyst/van de Vijve, 2008, p. 210).
26. Gross/Thompson (2007), p. 13.
27. Gross/Thompson (2007), p. 14.
28. Hence there are two forms of *choosing a situation* in the cinema: the external one of situation selection (1) and the internal one of attention deployment (3). Similarly, there are two ways of *changing a situation* at the movies: the external one of situation modification (2) and the internal one of cognitive change (4).
29. Dreyfus/Kelly (2011), pp. 202–3.
30. There is plenty of evidence for this "framing effect" in media psychology and empirical aesthetics. For instance, in a laboratory study my colleagues and I have shown how watching disgusting images *as art* rather than documentary photographs for instructional purposes changes the emotional response to disgusting images: the positivity rating was higher when our participants watched the image with a cognitive "art schema" activated (Wagner et al., 2014).
31. Rosenbaum (1995), p. 41.
32. Rosenbaum (1995), p. 41.
33. Gerda Walther has drawn attention to similar cases of what she calls experiencing "in the name" or "in the spirit" of a group or community. She gives the example of a policeman who, *as a policeman*, arrests a poor man for stealing, even though he, *as himself*, would rather let the person run. The policeman can fully accept his role as policeman and not feel a distance to his private person at all; but he might also feel removed or estranged from his role, being fully aware of his "split personality" (Walther, 1923, pp. 104–5).
34. Rosenbaum (1995), p. 130.
35. Goffman (1963), p. 198ff.
36. Rosenbaum (1995), pp. 174–5. See also Abercrombie/Longhurst (1998), p. 34.
37. Fischer/Manstead/Zaalberg, p. 175.
38. See, for instance, Breakwell/Hammond (1990), p. 75. For an empirical study dealing with similar effects, see Banjo et al. (2015).
39. Jullier/Leveratto (2012), p. 147. Today the situation is often quite different for cinephiles. As the two authors note: "the problem is no longer to be unable to access it, but to have enough time to watch [. . .] everything."

40. On the Secret Cinema, see Klein (2013). See also www.secretcinema.org/ and www.guardian.co.uk/film/2012/jul/05/secret-cinema-new-way-pull-audiences?intcmp=239 (last accessed 14 February 2017). Ernest Mathijs and Xavier Mendik have referred to the viewers' "sense of belonging to a group" that spectators described *after* having seen – but possibly also *during* – the avant-premiere of *The Lord of the Rings* (2001–3) or a rare screening of *One Second in Montreal* (1969) (Mathijs/Mendik, 2008b, p. 4). Carter Moulton similarly argues that midnight blockbusters provide fans with social prestige and self-esteem, partly because attending the screenings shows commitment and expertise within the fan community. Moulton also refers to the late screening hours when most people are already asleep, which also bestows a sense of exclusivity on the audience (Moulton, 2014, pp. 363, 365 and 368).
41. Mathijs/Mendik (2008b), p. 4.
42. See also what Mathijs and Mendik write about fans of cult films: "audiences of cult movies stress their rebellious attitude, and they frequently consider themselves outsiders, renegades roaming the borders of what is morally acceptable" (Mathijs/Mendik, 2008b, p. 5).
43. Quoted from Breakwell/Hammond (1990), p. 12.
44. Kuhn (2002), p. 42.
45. Srinivas (1998), p. 330. Along similar lines, Athique writes in his article on Indian multiplex cinemas: "The crowd at the multiplex was 'decent' or 'good', while the crowd at the normal cinema was 'dirty', 'cheap' or 'bad'." As one participant of his study sample put it: "No clean and hygienic. Too crowded. Crowd not good" (Athique, 2013, pp. 380 and 377).
46. See also Meers/Biltereyst/Van de Vijver (2008), p. 211; Altenloh (2001 [1914]), p. 278.
47. Marchetti (2008), p. 412.
48. Kuhn (2002), p. 42.

CHAPTER 6

Feeling Close: Conceptualizing the Cinema's Affective We-experiences

[O]ur response to film is in some measure a function of our being a member of an audience, since some of our feelings are doubtless collective and due to contagion.

Arthur C. Danto[1]

You leave the cinema with the feeling that you have shared an experience, that you went through an adventure together. And even if you leave the auditorium with your eyes lowered, you feel connected to the crowd – at least to this community into which the film has turned its viewers.

Michael Althen[2]

In the previous chapter on affective audience interrelations we briefly heard that the cinema allows viewers to occasionally experience phenomenologically close, mutual we-connections with others in the cinema hall. In this chapter I will take a more detailed look at this specific audience effect. Three types of affective we-experience will be distinguished: shared emotion, emotional contagion, and feeling together. I consider it important to keep these affective we-experiences apart, not only to arrive at the well-made scholarly language Etienne Souriau advocates (quoted in Chapter 1), but also because the phenomenologies of these types of we-connection are sufficiently different.

I. SHARED EMOTION

To avoid confusion about the term "shared emotion" from the outset, let me address two possible points of contention. First, *shared* emotions should not be confused with *collective* emotions. In their article "Towards a Theory of Collective Emotions," Christian von Scheve and Sven Ismer define collective emotions as "the *synchronous convergence in affective responding* across individuals towards a specific event or object."[3] This is a rather broad definition, but its advantage is that it allows the gathering of a number of related phenomena under the same umbrella term. Von Scheve and Ismer discuss, for instance, "collective emotional orientations" such as the *tendency* of a particular society to experience certain emotions.[4] They also look at "group-based emotions" like collective guilt which individuals can undergo *in solitude*, for example when a member of a particular in-group performs unfavorably or someone else ascribes certain qualities to that person.[5] The authors make, moreover, room for both micro- and macro-sociological perspectives. Not least, they allow for aggregate and non-aggregate accounts: Collective emotions can be seen as the *sum of* their individual parts or as *something more or other* than that. "This view does not necessarily presuppose that collective emotions are qualitatively different from individual emotions and that convergence is established exclusively in face-to-face encounters. In its most basic form, this definition does not even presuppose or require mutual awareness of others' emotions," von Scheve and Ismer write.[6] Precisely because their definition is so broad, however, it calls for conceptual distinctions. An important distinction for our purposes is that shared emotions are a *subcategory* of collective emotions.

As a second preliminary note I need to draw attention to the ambiguous nature of the adjective "shared." Gerald Echterhoff and colleagues helpfully distinguish four meanings of "sharing." The first meaning is *communicating or disclosing*. Here individuals make their personal responses – say to a film – known to others: "the audience becomes aware of what another individual believes or feels, but it does not require that the audience has something in common with the speaker or that the audience agrees with what the speaker communicates."[7] Hence this meaning does not emphasize commonality in experience, but it underlines the important role of communication of emotions – and, as we have seen, the expressive-diverted audience is particularly conducive to it.

The second meaning of sharing refers to *dividing up*, as when a task is shared by a group of people and the participants distribute specific parts among them. A shared activity, from this perspective, is not a joint action; sharing rather highlights the differences between the individuals concerned with the task. The third meaning discussed by Echterhoff and colleagues implies *partaking in a consensus*, for instance when individuals share an opinion. Here the meaning refers to an objective condition of "sharedness" that an outside observer can identify. The fourth and final meaning is the one I am interested in: *experiencing in common*. Here individuals experience an agreement and commonality in terms of attention, emotion, thought, judgment, belief, and so on.

But what is a shared emotion then? In the following I try to synthesize a definition by drawing on the growing philosophical and sociological literature on what sometimes also goes by the name of "emotional sharing" (Dan Zahavi), "shared feeling" (Hans Bernhard Schmid), or "feeling-in-common" (Max Scheler). My definition rests on four requirements that have to be met for an affective phenomenon to qualify as a "shared emotion:" (1) same kind of emotion; (2) shared intentional object; (3) mutual awareness; and (4) phenomenological closeness.

1. Same kind of emotion

For two or more viewers to share an emotion in the cinema they need to experience the *same kind* of emotion, not just a similar one, and not at all a dissimilar one. In case a cinema audience shares the emotion of joy or fear or anger, the viewers involved need to go either through a joyful or a fearful or an angry emotion episode at the same time. This might sound trivial, but not every affective we-experience is based on the same kind of emotion. Later we will encounter an affective phenomenon called *feeling together* that is not based on the *same* kind of emotion, but comprises different, albeit *matching* emotions. Demanding that the kind of emotion has to be the same does not imply, however, that the *intensity* of the emotion must be identical for every person sharing the emotion.[8] Provided the other three criteria are met, you and me share the emotion of fear even if you are only mildly afraid, while I am extremely scared. (But here we can already sense the importance of requirement (4): it's certainly also possible that we feel phenomenologically apart and hence do not share the emotion, because in your mild form of fear you tend to consider my strong fear as strange or eccentric or ridiculous.)

2. Shared intentional object

Going through the same kind of emotion at the same time is not sufficient, however, for an affective phenomenon to count as a shared emotion. We must also rule out that we have the same kind of emotion by accident. Sharing an emotion therefore means that we are directed toward the same object – our emotion must have the same aboutness.[9] For example, we wouldn't call it sharing an emotion if viewer A is joyful about the positive outcome of the film, whereas viewer B is joyful because he has just received a text message saying that his sister has given birth to her first son. Nor would we speak of a shared emotion when I feel anger, hatred, or disgust *toward* my co-viewers and they are equally and simultaneously angry with me, hate me, or are disgusted by me. In all of these cases the viewers experience the same kind of emotion, but they don't share the same intentional object.

Closely connected is the claim that a shared emotion has to derive from an *immediate* response that is not "mediated" by the person with whom I share the emotion.¹⁰ If two viewers share an emotion about something, they both immediately respond to the shared *intentional object*, but they don't respond to each other's *responding*. This distinguishes shared emotions from emotional contagion, where the emotion causally depends on someone else's emotion, as we will see below. And it also distinguishes shared emotions from affective forms of empathy and sympathy where togetherness is likewise mediated: When I feel *with* you (in empathy) or *for* you (in sympathy) I do it, in a sense, *because of* you. In affective empathy and sympathy the individual is directed to the emotion of another individual – the other individual's emotion is the object. The expression "feeling *with*" someone in empathy might, of course, tempt us into thinking that one shares the emotion. However, according to the definition suggested here, this is not the case.

A number of contemporary phenomenologists have emphasized this point. Following Husserl, Dan Zahavi characterizes *empathy* as "a form of other-directed intentionality, which allows foreign experiences to disclose themselves as foreign rather than as one's own."¹¹ Similarly, Hans Bernhard Schmid writes about *sympathizing* with someone else: "Here, the object of person A's feeling is different from the object of person B's feeling (the latter being person A, or person A's feeling)."¹² Among early phenomenologists Gerda Walther has stressed this difference as well. She writes that an experience of community (*Gemeinschaftserleben*) should not be confused with a cognitive form of empathizing (*einfühlen*). When I grasp or infer another person's experiences via this type of empathy I am well aware that this is still the other person's experience and I don't confuse it with my own. Even when I coincidentally have the same experience as the other person, I still know that the two experiences are closed off, separated, and thus stand next to each other: *this* is how I feel – and *that* is how the other person experiences. We recognize that there is a kind of wall between the two of us – a phenomenological distance.¹³

A second distinction Walther offers refers to a more contagious form of empathy (*mitfühlen*).¹⁴ Here one might 'catch' the experience of the other person and experience it *with* him or her. For instance, I realize and empathize with the joy of another person, say, about a good grade. The *object* of joy might be neutral to me, but I feel with the other person and therefore experience joy, so to speak, with him or her. In this case we have a greater "inner unity," but we don't undergo an experience of community, because we don't respond to the same object: While the other person is happy about the good grade, I am happy because she is happy, but we are not happy about the same thing.¹⁵ Hence in episodes of shared emotions the persons sharing are not directed toward each other. The English translation of Max Scheler's *Miteinanderfühlen* renders it consequently as an "*immediate* community of feeling."¹⁶

Of course, this does not rule out that a group of people might indeed share an emotion that derives from their empathizing or sympathizing response to a shared object: Viewers in the cinema regularly share an emotion that, at least partly, derives from their joint empathy with a character. Think of a moment of an audience's shared fear that is based, among other things, on the empathetic response to a deeply frightened character. The phenomenon of empathy with characters shows us, by the way, that empathy does not depend on reciprocity: When I empathize with someone else, this other person does not necessarily have to empathize with me. Characters on the screen, due to their fictional status, obviously cannot reciprocate anything. Shared emotions, on the other hand, do require some kind of mutual awareness.

3. Mutual awareness

For an emotion to be shared we cannot presume a coincidental parallel of qualitative identical emotions: for the same emotion to be shared, some form of intersubjectivity or mutual awareness is necessary. Zahavi puts it unmistakably: "To claim that we are sharing an experience while claiming that this is something you remain unaware of doesn't seem to make that much sense."[17] Similarly, Mikko Salmela suggests "that we restrict shared emotions proper to those emotions that people experience together in contexts in which individuals can be mutually aware of sharing the same emotion."[18] Hence when we share an emotion I have to have some idea that you undergo the same emotion as I do and that you know that I know it. Just think of two viewers sitting in closed-off viewing cabins next to each other and watching the same film: They would be in closer physical proximity than two viewers in a cinema sitting five rows apart, but they wouldn't be able to share the emotion due to a lack of mutual awareness.

Mutual awareness does not imply a strong truth claim, however, as I can be wrong about your emotion just as you can be wrong about mine. We cannot be certain, because whatever we might feel when we share a feeling cannot itself be a guarantee for the truth of the sharedness.[19] We are dealing, then, with a similar situation as in the case of joint action in quiet-attentive viewing: Under specific conditions we *presume* the sharedness until proven otherwise.

This does not imply, however, that mutual awareness is something we have to actively focus upon when sharing an emotion: We need not be reflectively aware of the emotional sharing; it can remain at the fringe of consciousness. Obviously, we can focus on the fact that we are sharing an emotion, but then the sharing itself becomes the intentional object of the experience. Nor does a shared emotion necessarily require a close physical proximity. As Salmela points out, traditionally mutual awareness in shared emotions has required "the actual physical co-presence of individuals, but technological advances have created new forms of co-presence."[20] Today smartphones or video chat applications allow for co-presence while not in each other's physical proximity. Co-presence therefore implies that the viewers are *present to each other*. Of course, in the cinema auditorium the *immediate* physical co-presence is a given, but this does not mean that mutual awareness cannot also occur in what in Chapter 10, my conclusion, I will call *medial* co-presence.

4. Phenomenological closeness

An "affective bond" or "unification," as Zahavi calls it, is a final important requirement for an emotion to be shared. As we have seen above, for Walther, too, the experience of community implies a phenomenological closeness. Schmid even talks of a "fusion" between those who share an emotion. This also implies a certain amount of de-individuation. Freud speaks of losing "the sense of the limits of one's individuality" and giving up one's "distinctiveness in a group."[21] For Zahavi, too, the difference between self and other must not be overly salient, otherwise it will prevent an experience of togetherness: "What you need is a certain amount of self-alienation – to decrease your distance from, and make you more like, the others."[22]

While a certain loss of distance and individuality seems to be a requirement for most phenomenologists, there is a controversy of how far the affective closeness can go. Szanto and Zahavi underline that there is a *plurality* requirement: A certain self-other differentiation needs to remain, which is why they reject Schmid's notion of fusion. "Sharing has nothing to do with fusion, nor with a merged unity. Sharing involves a plurality of subjects, but it also involves more than mere summation or aggregation," Zahavi writes.[23] Schmid defends his position by claiming that sharing an emotion does not imply that the participants somehow forget that they are individuals and mistakenly take their own experience for the experience of others: "There is ample room for awareness of interpersonal difference in phenomenal fusion, only that the differences in question are not of the kind of an unbridgeable abyss between monads, but rather of the kind of difference at play between different parts to a unified whole."[24]

We should therefore posit different *degrees* of felt closeness and distance, and hence different degrees of sharedness of an emotion.[25] These degrees of closeness and distance may have to do with the *intensity* of the emotion, but they can also depend on the *kind* of emotion. In this respect Dan Zahavi raises the interesting question of whether (or not) all emotions can be shared in the same way.[26] Arguably, this is not the case, as not all emotions equally allow for an affective closeness to others.[27]

Given that the umbrella category of collective emotions does not presuppose an emotional closeness, I would like to suggest a conceptual distinction between *spread* and *shared* collective emotions here. Experiencing a *spread* collective emotion implies that we all have the same immediate emotional response to a shared object or event (like a film) and are mutually aware of it, but nevertheless feel individuated and hence (somewhat) detached from each other. An example could be certain moments of being sadly moved to tears. As we shall see in Chapter 8, even if the entire cinema feels sadly moved to tears and thus experiences a *collective* emotion, the viewers need not necessarily experience a *shared* emotion. Although in this moment the emotion of *being moved* may be spread (even wide-spread) in the cinema, the viewers don't experience it in a we-mode. Instead, they tend to undergo the emotion in an I-mode. Or think of collective embarrassment: Even if I presume that other viewers may also feel embarrassed about the explicit sex scenes that we are all confronted with while watching Abdellatif Kechiche's *Blue Is the Warmest Color/La vie d'Adèle* (2013) or Gaspar Noë's *Love* (2015), I don't feel connected to them, let alone fused with them. Something similar may arguably also account for shame and guilt – emotions that can certainly come in a collective form – but we hardly experience them as evoking a felt closeness to others.

This is different when we experience a *shared* emotion proper. Here we all have the same emotional response *and* we feel a certain affective closeness to each other. A good example would be the shared joyfulness expressed through collective laughter, which we experience in a we-mode.[28] Consequently, we can look at the phenomenon of shared audience emotions *ex negativo*: Viewers don't share an emotion if the emotion *distances* them from each other or even pits them in an *oppositional stance*. But we can look at the phenomenon also from a positive side: Shared emotions derive from emotions that open us to others and even connect us to them. Think of joy and hilarity. Or consider fear, whose isolating tendency can create a wish to share the fearfulness or even to flee into the arms of someone else. As Hans Bernhard Schmid notes, "some structure of mutual openness is an integral part of sharing."[29]

Schmid warns us, however, not to jump to any metaphysical conclusions. He argues against the idea of a metaphysical collective 'we' beyond the individual 'I' and the 'thou' as the proper subject of the shared emotion.[30] To count the 'we' as a third subject is as futile for him as waiting for the team to show up in the stadium after all the players have entered the field: "The shared feeling is nothing *in addition* to what the participating individuals feel. Rather, it is that feeling, and it is that feeling *in a certain respect*."[31] But stating that there is no *ontological* supra-entity involved is not to say that *phenomenologically* we cannot experience a shared emotion as a 'we.'

Note that among the most important enabling conditions for shared emotions, Anita Konzelmann Ziv also lists "diachronical relations" based on, for instance, situations jointly experienced in the past.[32] Joel Krueger also emphasizes the importance that a "diachronic narrative intimacy," the intimacy that emerges over long stretches of time, can have for those sharing the emotion.[33] And Salmela, too, points to the weight of "shared attitudes" that derive from a history of common experiences. No doubt, intimate relations resulting from a shared past can have a strong effect on emotional sharing. But in contrast to the four requirements discussed above, they are not necessary.[34]

Hence we can formulate the following working definition: Two or more people can be said to share an emotion when their experience of the same kind of emotion is based on a shared intentional object to which they have an immediate response with mutual awareness and some form of phenomenological closeness.

II. EMOTIONAL CONTAGION

What is emotional contagion, then? Currently, there seems to be no agreement among philosophers and social psychologists on how to exactly define this phenomenon. Still, many authors, from Edith Stein and Max Scheler to Dan Zahavi and others, reserve a special category for it, not as a mere *precursor* to collective emotions, but as a collective affective phenomenon in its own right.[35] In his "classification of the phenomena of fellow-feeling," Scheler, for instance, puts "emotional infection" next to "community of feeling," "fellow-feeling," and "emotional identification."

At the beginning it may help to approach emotional contagion by separating it from the related concept of *mimicry*. Following social psychologist Ursula Hess and her colleagues, we can distinguish between *emotional* and *behavioral* mimicry: Emotional mimicry refers to the imitation of *emotion expressions* of others, whereas behavioral mimicry describes the imitation of *non-emotional behaviors* (for example, foot-tapping). Mimicry implies the matching of non-verbal *displays*, but it doesn't necessarily lead to emotional contagion and hence a convergence in emotions.[36] Coming back to our sing-along example from Chapter 4: When the initially inattentive and disengaged Hans takes the hint from his rebuking friends and feels the weight of their normative expectations, he decides to sing along, applaud, and smile with the others. He mimics them in a truly expressive way to fulfill his obligations. Yet he does not feel the joy the others are feeling when watching the film. He engages in behavioral and emotional mimicry, which leads to what I have called synchronically acting together, but it is at least possible that he is not affected emotionally. Just because he has equal expressions of emotions, and engages in similar motor movements, does not mean that he has the same kind of emotion, let alone that he shares the emotion.[37]

But let's assume the not so unlikely scenario that after a while Hans indeed starts feeling enjoyment after he has been singing and clapping with the others. Here it is the *feedback* from the mimicking of his friends' facial and vocal expressions, as well as their postures, that leads Hans to 'catch' their emotions.[38] Hans certainly hasn't become a fan of *The Sound of Music* all of a sudden – a film he may still consider kitschy and cliché-ridden. Instead, he enjoys being part of the singing cinema audience with its unusual form of liveliness and expressivity, and he also enjoys the collective enjoyment of his friends. Mimicry and feedback have made him 'catch' their emotion – their emotion was contagious.

We should note, however, that there are different opinions among leading social psychologists working on emotional contagion. Hatfield and her colleagues describe the process of emotional contagion as consisting of three stages: mimicry, feedback, and contagion proper: "People tend: (1) to automatically mimic the facial expressions, vocal expressions, postures, and instrumental behaviors of those around them, and thereby (2) to feel a pale reflection of others' emotions as a consequence of such feedback. The result is that (3) people tend to catch one another's emotions."[39] Here mimicry is an integral part of and causally related to contagion, which it elicits. Ursula Hess and her colleagues, on the other hand, prefer to separate mimicry and emotional contagion.[40] For Hess et al., emotional mimicry implies the conscious or automatic *imitation* of a non-verbal emotional display of another person. The result is a *matching* of non-verbal expressions that is observable. Emotional contagion, on the other hand, refers to the outcome of *any* interactional process in which individuals come to 'catch' another's emotion, and it implies a matching of subjective *emotional experiences* between these individuals. Emotional mimicry can be one of the processes leading to emotional contagion, but it is not its only cause, nor does it necessarily lead to it: "Even though many studies on emotional mimicry also find evidence for a matching subjective experience in the same experiment, these two do not necessarily co-occur."[41]

For Hess and colleagues, both *conscious* and *automatic* imitation seem to be possible starting points for emotional contagion. This means that viewers can also initiate it to some degree. By *voluntarily* allowing himself to become affected by the collective enjoyment – by not 'fighting back' emotional contagion – our fictitious Hans has 'worked' himself *into* the feeling. Max Scheler adds a slightly different point: He concedes that contagion can be used instrumentally when we deliberately expose ourselves to or avoid emotional gatherings that influence us in one way or another (in this case psychologists would speak of "mood management"). Although the contagion process itself remains (largely) involuntary, its outcome would be intended.

On the other hand, emotional contagion is often *involuntary*, something viewers undergo.[42] There are instances in which viewers are affected – and 'infected' – by someone else's emotion and have no control over this process anymore once it is underway. Neither do they choose to become affected, nor are they immediately able to reflect on the process. Suddenly being overcome by a contagious urge to laugh with others might be a case in point. But not all instances occur suddenly. Just think of a situation in which you follow a suspenseful film with focused attention. Gradually, however, you might be taken over by a collective lack of interest and conspicuous signs of boredom, as when viewers move in their seats, yawn, and start to whisper. Boredom was contagious. This is not to say that there are no ways to block contagion. Just as we can decide to allow ourselves to become emotionally infected, we may brace ourselves with a number of avoidance strategies, ranging from paying little attention to the others to taking a decidedly oppositional stance, as we have heard in the previous chapter.

Coming back again to our fictitious Hans: Once he has 'caught' the joy of his friends, he feels joy *like* them. But does he feel the *same* kind of joy? Here we discover a crucial difference between shared emotions and emotional contagion, because the intentional object of Hans's emotion differs from that of the others. His friends share an emotion: They collectively enjoy the *film*, and their joint singing and the applauding response *to it*. Via contagion Hans also experiences joy, but he does not share their joy about the film: In his emotional-contagion joy he predominantly enjoys being part of a singing and clapping audience.[43] Summarizing Max Scheler's position, Anita Konzelmann Ziv writes: "S can get infected with the joy of S' by taking up some mimics or sounds expressing the joyful state of S' without taking up the content of the joy of S'. The feeling S is infected with is 'empty', a mere shell lacking its proper object and content, or being filled with a different content."[44] This is a point we need to emphasize: What overtly looks like the same kind of emotion and may by and large feel similar, has a different intentional object and thus cannot be a shared emotion.

But if the emotions are not the same, can we still speak of an affective we-experience? Some philosophers claim that emotional contagion is merely *self*-centered and therefore cannot be considered as an affective *we*-experience. Scheler admits that we often encounter "a common making of expressive gestures" which have the "effect of producing similar emotions, efforts and purposes" among the people involved.[45] But there is no understanding of others or mutual awareness: "the participant takes the experience arising in him owing to his participation to be his *own* original experience, so that he is quite unconscious of the contagion to which he succumbs."[46] For Scheler there is no *directing* of feeling toward the others: "it is characteristic of emotional infection that it occurs only as a transference of the *state* of feeling, and does *not* presuppose any sort of *knowledge* of the joy which others feel. Thus one may only notice afterwards that a mournful feeling, encountered in oneself, is traceable to infection from a group one has visited some hours before."[47] Following Scheler, Dan Zahavi equally maintains that emotional contagion should not be conflated with emotional sharing and hence doesn't constitute a we-experience.[48] Harking back to von Scheve and Ismer's definition, we could simply conclude that emotional contagion amounts to another type of *collective emotion* since we are clearly dealing with a synchronous convergence in affective responding here.

However, in comparison to other examples of collective emotions given above – for instance, an individual experiencing collective guilt or a nation being prone to collective emotional orientations – there is a direct *nexus* between the physically co-present viewers via a *mutual contagious influence*. And maybe we can still save some room for a we-connection by asking ourselves if Scheler and Zahavi's conclusions really strike us as phenomenologically convincing in *all* instances?

No doubt, in some cases of emotional contagion we don't experience any 'we-ness.' A viewer who catches the boredom of his co-viewers may not feel bored *with* them – he may simply feel bored. But at other times Scheler and Zahavi's conclusion strikes me as too harsh: When I am infected by the cheerfulness expressed in the sudden outburst of laughter of others, can I not very well feel cheerfully connected to them, even if I don't share their intentional object? Take the case of contagious laughter about a scene that you wouldn't find funny if you had watched the film alone, but which overwhelms you in the cinema right now. With regard to the content of the film, your laughter may remain 'empty' and after the film the whole experience might feel shallow. Even in the midst of collective laughter you might experience a slight distance to the others in terms of the content of laughter, just like Hans is not completely attached to his friends, the devoted *Sound of Music* fans. Hence this kind of collective laughter is clearly not the same as when you all find the film funny and you *share* the cheerfulness in laughing together about it. Still, this doesn't rule out that you experience a we-connection to those who laugh. However, strictly speaking, only those cases qualify as affective we-experiences in which viewers experience a mutual closeness.

Hence we can formulate the following working definition: Two or more viewers can be said to undergo an episode of emotional contagion, *as an affective we-experience*, when they have come to 'catch' other viewers' emotion, their subjective emotional experiences match, and they feel some form of phenomenological closeness.

III. FEELING TOGETHER

There is yet a third type of affective collective experience in the cinema that we have to distinguish. Following H. Andrés Sánchez Guerrero, we do not necessarily have to conceive of collective affective intentionality as a matter of sharing emotions or emotional contagion.[49] Focusing on a lesser-known affective phenomenon, Sánchez Guerrero suggests the category *feeling together*. He claims that we can be focused on the same object and feel something together about it *without* having the same kind of emotion. In this case the emotions we feel together are not *variants* of the same kind – they are *different* emotions. But these different emotions match so well that we nonetheless experience a we-connection. Astonishingly, then, different emotions can result in feeling together.

What is crucial for the affective we-experience of feeling together is a joint caring or *caring with one another* about the same object due to a number of common existential background orientations.[50] Our emotions are expressions of this caring: by responding emotionally I show you and you show me that we both care about the situation, even if our emotions differ in kind. Hence what we share is the significance – we could also say the phenomenological weight – a given situation has *for us* (Sánchez Guerrero also speaks of a shared evaluative perspective). Importantly, we care about the situation *as a group* rather than individually. Using Matthew Ratcliffe's term, Sánchez Guerrero subsumes feeling together as an "existential feeling."[51] It is a background feeling that we do not focus on reflectively, but which becomes part of our overall experience. The concrete phenomenological mix of a given situation will thus differ in comparison to a solitary viewing constellation.

Here is an example: Assume, again, you watch a film like *Twelve Years a Slave* (2013) with your African American friend. You respond with various mini-expressions of moral outrage: you shake your head, sigh angrily, or even mumble "Damn racists!" These expressions show your friend that you are affected and that you value what is shown as something to be concerned about. Simultaneously your friend expresses the same care to you through his dead silence and by wiping away a tear. It is obvious that in this situation you don't share the same *emotion*, but your individual emotions match and you feel connected via your shared *caring*. In fact, you might even feel a certain obligation to let your friend know how much you care about the film, lest he consider you as cold or insensitive. You may be concerned that he might not have realized your expressions, which is why you increase the conspicuousness of your response, from head movement to non-verbal expression to verbal exclamation (see also Chapter 8 on "forced tears"). Both of you show each other that you care about caring with one another – your emotional expressions communicate that you share an evaluative perspective. With Goffman we could also say that you demonstrate to each other your "committed 'presence' in the situation." But the example of *Twelve Years a Slave* also shows that sometimes emotions need to be expressed with a certain obviousness and unambiguousness to avoid misunderstandings. Not in every situation is it clear that we indeed care with one another.

But the caring with one another does not always have to be morally deep. It can also involve situations that might look banal or even reprehensible from the outside, but which still resonate strongly with the persons involved. Take the empirical study by Dolf Zillmann and colleagues mentioned in the introduction: In what has come to be known as the "snuggle theory of horror," the media psychologists clearly dealt with different emotion expressions, separated along gender lines in their undergraduate student population, emotions that nevertheless matched – and thus may have initiated an experience of feeling together.[52]

If we focus only on the situations while watching *Friday the 13th, Part III* that yielded most pleasure, we can find the following constellations: In the company of the *male participants* the female confederates of the psychologists pretended much distress by exclaiming "Oh my God!" or "Yech . . . Oh, how gross!" during gory scenes. They sat in a rigid, upright position, displayed restlessness by fidgeting with their hands, or startled heavily in moments of cinematic shock. In the company of *female participants* the play-acting male confederates, in turn, encouraged the main protagonist of the film by uttering "That's the idea . . . use the knife!" or cheered a female character on, exclaiming "All right . . . you got him good this time!" after she had struck the killer with an ax. In both cases male and female participants felt that matching emotions were displayed: They enjoyed the film more than when the (fake) companions displayed the opposite emotional behavior. As we have heard, male participants enjoyed the horror film most in the company of a distressed woman (and least in the company of a woman showing fear mastery), whereas female participants enjoyed the movie most in the company of a calm man (and least when sitting next to a man who seemed worried or even frightened).

One possible interpretation of these findings is that they enjoyed these constellations most because their partners showed, via emotion expressions, that they cared for the horror film in what was considered a gender-appropriate way. Now, in and of itself this does not necessarily reveal a we-connection of feeling together. But the study contains a further finding: Male students of low appeal gained markedly in sex appeal and positive character traits when they displayed fearlessness and a somewhat macho behavior. This modification in perspective on the companion certainly hints at a possible we-connection, because otherwise the evaluation of the companion would not change in a positive way. Consequently, we may speculate that a *feeling together* existed based on matching emotions: Both female and male participants valued and cared about the film in their own way, but their emotional expressions showed that they cared about it *with* one another.

Provided the emotions match, it is not how *precisely* we care about the film, but rather that we care about it so strongly. Feeling together implies, then, that we discover that we all care with one another for the significance the cinematic experience has for us, even though our emotions veer in different directions. We could even go a step further and claim that our background default assumption in a collective aesthetic experience like the cinema is that we all care about the film *as such* with one another. After all, we all came here from various places to watch this specific film and hence we (seem to) share an evaluative perspective. This is a more emphatic way of saying what in Chapter 3 I have called the *we-intention* that we share when we watch a film together, in its various degrees from weak to strong we-intention. The stronger we care about the film and presume that we care *with* one another, the more problematic an emotion expression will become that does *not* match. This allows us to pinpoint some of the decisive differences between *feeling together* and *emotional contagion*: In feeling together there is a shared intentional object, but the emotions diverge; in emotional contagion there is no shared intentional object, but the emotions converge.

Thus we arrive at the following working definition: When two or more viewers focus on the same intentional object and jointly care about this object due to a number of common existential background orientations, they can feel something together in a mutually close we-connection despite undergoing different emotions. Here the differing emotions match well because they are expressions of precisely the joint caring.

IV. THE PLEASURE IN AFFECTIVE COLLECTIVE EXPERIENCES

Enabled by the specific spatial, social, and technological characteristics of the movie-theater, the three types of affective we-experience are responsible for the emergence of something that does not exist before the beginning of the movie: a however brief mutual we-connection among anonymous strangers. Of course, not all viewers are anonymous to each other. Here we might think back to the distinction between habitual communities based on diachronic relations, on the one hand, and episodic or short-term collectivities that emerge in the here and now, on the other hand.[53] Generally, the habitual communities of couples, families, or friends are *embedded* in the larger short-term collectivity of the audience, which is itself hardly a stable entity, but constantly changes, as we have seen in Chapter 5.[54] At the same time, habitual communities can easily *dissolve* into an episodic community, *transcending* the group boundaries of families, partners, and friends. In the darkness of the movie-theater affective we-connections can even *overcome*, momentarily, such pre-existing sociological categories as race, class, gender, ethnicity, sexual orientation, and religion.[55]

It is undeniable that collective experiences of the affective kind can be a source of pleasure.[56] (1) There can be pleasure in realizing a mere correspondence and convergence in our emotional response. (2) There can also be pleasure in realizing an absence of distance and difference, experiencing a sense of affective closeness and connectedness instead.[57] (3) There can even be pleasure in losing the sense of the limits of our individuality or group belongingness and merging in an affective collectivity.[58]

Yet Walther points out that the feeling of unification (*Gefühl der Einigung*) does not necessarily have to have a positive tone. She therefore contrasts a *mere* unification with a *positive* unification.[59] What this tells us is that the affective collective experiences of shared emotion, emotional contagion, and feeling together are not necessarily pleasurable, but can be a foundation for pleasure. The various forms of pleasure mentioned above can arise together with the affective collective experiences and are causally dependent on them. For instance, the pleasurable feeling of emotional sharing is not the same as the collectively shared emotion, but derives from it. It is a sort of second-order state – a state of shared pleasure about the shared emotion.

Finally, we should not presume that the pleasure of the collective cinema experience in general derives exclusively from other *affective* collective experiences. As we have seen in Chapter 3, pleasure can simply be based on the joint action of watching a film together. Here we take pleasure not in an affective experience we undergo together, but in the mere fact that we *do* something together. Additionally, pleasure can also come from an experience of social flow. In this case we take pleasure in the fact that we are lost in a shared activity that functions smoothly. And following section V in Chapter 4, we can assume that sometimes individual pleasure can be based on an emotion that *I* want to have for myself *in contrast* to the other viewers. It flourishes on an urge to distinguish myself: I have these strong emotions vis-à-vis the film – and *you don't*.

Hence we should keep in mind that (a) affective collective experiences are strongly connected to pleasure, but they can also have a neutral hedonic tone, (b) they are often the source of pleasure but are not necessarily tied to it, and (c) the cinema also provides pleasures based on collective experiences other than affective ones.

From the "medium shot" in the third part, we will now zoom in even further and point three "close-ups" on very specific emotions and affective expressions: The case studies in Chapters 7, 8, and 9 will phenomenologically investigate breaking out in laughter, being moved to tears, and feeling angry about other viewers. These experiences are not only sufficiently widespread in the cinema but also come with a strong audience effect, and are thus particularly suitable to further demonstrate what is at stake in this book.

NOTES

1. Danto (2005 [1979]), p. 100.
2. Althen (2002), pp. 79–80 (my translation). Althen, who died prematurely in 2011 at the age of forty-eight, was arguably the pre-eminent German film critic of the last two decades.
3. Scheve/Ismer (2013), p. 406 (original emphasis).
4. Von Scheve/Ismer (2013), p. 408.
5. Von Scheve/Ismer (2013), p. 409.
6. Von Scheve/Ismer (2013), p. 411.
7. Echterhoff/Higgins/Levine (2009), p. 497.
8. Walther (1923), pp. 25–6.
9. See, for instance, Szanto (2015).
10. Konzelmann Ziv (2009), p. 99.
11. Zahavi (2015), p. 88.
12. Schmid (2008), p. 66.
13. Walther (1923), pp. 73–4.
14. Contemporary psychologists distinguish along similar lines between *cognitive* and *affective* empathy. While cognitive empathy emphasizes the ability to accurately infer another person's feelings, affective empathy refers to a process during which the perception of another's emotional state generates a matching state in the one who perceives. See Hess/Houde/Fischer (2014), p. 97.
15. Walther is not blind to the fact that *einfühlen* and *mitfühlen* can be the basis for and lead to an experience of community, but they are neither a necessary precondition nor should they be confused with experiences of community.
16. Scheler (2008 [1923]), p. 12.
17. Zahavi (2015), p. 89.
18. Salmela (2012), p. 42.
19. Schmid (2008), p. 81.
20. Salmela (2012), p. 42.
21. Freud (1949 [1921]), pp. 27 and 40.
22. Zahavi (2015), p. 94.
23. Zahavi (2015), p. 90. Zeynep Okur Güney challenges the importance of a self-other distinction by citing phenomena "where the distinction between I and you is totally dissolved, such as moments of orgasm, collective religious and spiritual rituals, or an infant's melting into the holding mother's arms after breastfeeding in a sleepy but not asleep state" (Güney, 2015, p. 103).
24. Schmid (2014a) p. 10.
25. Although not arguing from a phenomenological perspective, Salmela (2012) makes a similar claim about degrees of collectivity in shared emotions. For Salmela, shared concerns are necessary conditions for an emotion to be shared. Following Raimo Tuomela, he distinguishes between plain I-mode concerns, pro-group I-mode concerns, and we-mode concerns. Consequently, he connects the strength of the participants' concerns to weakly, moderately, and strongly shared emotions. See also Salmela (2014).
26. Zahavi (2015), p. 98.
27. As Güney puts it: "when experiencing emotions such as hate, envy, jealousy, shame, or anger, the distinction between self and other is strongly manifest, whereas in compassion, love, or sympathy it diminishes" (Güney, 2015, p. 105).
28. Note, however, that just because we show the same communicative displays and signals

– facial, vocal, and postural expressions – this does not mean that we *share* an emotion. As Chapter 7 will show, this also goes for laughter: Not every kind of laughter is felt as shared.
29. Schmid (2008), p. 84.
30. Schmid (2008), p. 82.
31. Schmid (2008), p. 82. The example is quite similar to those introduced by Gilbert Ryle to illustrate the notion of "category mistake." See Ryle (2009 [1949]), pp. 6–7.
32. Konzelmann Ziv (2009), p. 104.
33. Krueger (2016), p. 270.
34. Konzelmann Ziv concedes that strong forms of sharedness are possible also with only very weak forms of diachronic relations, as long as another dimension (for instance, a strong synchronic physical closeness) is very prominent (Konzelmann Ziv, 2009, p. 104).
35. See Stein 1970 [1922/5]; Scheler (2008 [1923]); Zahavi (2015).
36. Hess/Houde/Fischer (2014), p. 95.
37. In the phenomenological tradition, Gerda Walther has made a similar point when she distinguishes experiences of community from mimicking (*nachahmen*) (Walther, 1923, p. 76).
38. Social psychologists Hatfield, Carpenter, and Rapson, for one, claim that "people tend to feel emotions consistent with the facial, vocal, and postural expressions they adopt" (Hatfield/Carpenter/Rapson, 2014, p. 113). However, it is important to note that the facial-feedback hypothesis – the assumption that facial expressions can influence one's emotional experience – has been put into doubt recently: see Wagenmakers et al. (2016). The research of Hatfield and her colleagues is not crucial for our purposes, however, because they are interested in the *process* of emotional contagion and not in its *experience*.
39. Hatfield et al. (2014), p. 113.
40. Scheler also makes this distinction between emotional contagion and mimicry and rejects the idea that the latter is a necessary condition for the former: "the process of infection does *not* lie in the imitation of others' expressed experiences, even though these may actually bring it about" (Scheler, 2008 [1923], p. 15, original emphasis).
41. Hess/Houde/Fischer (2014), p. 96. In both approaches we find a strong focus on one-on-one interactions or small groups at the expense of emotional contagion among crowds. For the latter we would have to go back to early crowd and mass psychology (Le Bon, McDougall, Freud). Hatfield and her colleagues provide historical and anthropological evidence for the phenomenon, even though they do not claim that their model can appropriately explain it (Hatfield et al., 2014, pp. 114–19). In light of their evidence for strong contagion examples such as mass hysteria, fear, or panic, it is all the more astonishing that Hatfield et al. maintain that those who are infected by someone else's emotion merely feel a "pale" or "dim" reflection of it (Hatfield et al., 2014, p. 113).
42. Scheler (2008 [1923]), pp. 16–17. See also Schaub/Suthor (2005).
43. This does not rule out the possibility that at some point Hans starts liking the film, which would allow him to fully *share* the emotions with his friends. For an example, see the fictitious professor of English in my previous chapter.
44. Konzelmann Ziv (2009), p. 104.
45. Scheler (2008 [1923]), p. 12.
46. Scheler (2008 [1923]), p. 12 (original emphasis).
47. Scheler (2008 [1923]), p. 15 (original emphasis).
48. Zahavi (2015), p. 87.
49. Sánchez Guerrero (2011).
50. Note that the term "caring" (*Sorge*), which he borrows from Heidegger, is not the same as

the shared "concerns" that play a crucial rule in Salmela's account of shared emotions; and it is certainly not the same as a cognitive "appraisal." Sharing an appraisal would imply the same emotion, as when we both appraise the horror movie as threatening and therefore both feel scared.
51. On existential feelings, see Ratcliffe (2008). On existential feelings in films, see Eder (2016).
52. Zillmann et al. (1986).
53. See also Walther (1923), p. 48.
54. Again, what Richard McCulloch has to say about *The Room* seems valid on a more general level: "Each time the film is screened in a cinema, individual attendees (almost always in small groups) effectively become part of a temporary community, one that exists only in that place and until the cinema has emptied" (McCulloch, 2011, p. 203).
55. Here we should remind ourselves of the difference between an *objective membership of a group or community* (like a family, race, class, or nation) and *being part of a subjective we*. One might be classified among the former by someone else, regardless of one's own will, whereas the latter is something I can only experience from within. To put it differently, just because I belong to a certain group objectively does not imply that I experience the group as a *we* subjectively (Zahavi, 2015, pp. 94–5).
56. See also chapter 9 of Hanich (2010).
57. Salmela, for instance, calls collective emotions "intrinsically rewarding," because they "involve feelings of closeness and solidarity" (Salmela, 2014, p. 160). For Echterhoff et al., shared realities allow people "to obtain or maintain a sense of connectedness and belonging" (Echterhoff/Higgins/Levine, 2009, p. 500).
58. Freud (1949 [1921]), p. 27.
59. Walther (1923), pp. 45–6.

PART IV

Close-up:
Case Studies of Affective
Audience Effects

CHAPTER 7

Chuckle, Chortle, Cackle: A Phenomenology of Cinematic Laughter

It is false that crying is always a sign of misfortune in this life and just as false that laughter is always a sign of good fortune.
>   Moses Mendelssohn[1]

[T]he shortest distance between any two supposedly unrelated individuals within the same public space is comedy.
>   Jonathan Rosenbaum[2]

I. THE AUDIENCE EFFECT OF LAUGHTER

When director Joe Dante was asked by an interviewer about the change of the film experience ushered in by private streaming and video-on-demand at home, his answer was quite explicit: "the thing about comedies is they need an audience. [. . .] You want to be in a theater and see a picture with an audience and get that collective audience reaction. Comedies are just not as funny when you're staring into your computer by yourself."[3] Dante's comments echo what many empirical studies have shown: There is a strong connection between being with others and the likelihood of that important "collective audience reaction" called laughter.[4] In fact, of all the phenomena described in this book, the audience effect of laughter seems the most widely scrutinized empirically.

Take, for instance, a study by Robin Dunbar and his colleagues. Trying to find out whether the pain threshold of humans increases with collective laughter, they asked participants to watch scenes from *Mr Bean*, *The Simpsons*, or *South Park* in two conditions: alone or in a group.[5] It turned out that the laughter rates of the participants were significantly higher in the group condition: "experiencing comedy in a group ramps up the laughter response."[6] Similarly, Paul Deveraux and Gerald Ginsburg tested and videotaped participants in three conditions: alone, with a stranger, and with a friend.[7] The participants watched a 3 minute 45 second clip consisting of a scene from *Ghostbusters* (1984), a baby playing in a bathtub, and a clip from *The Pink Panther Strikes Again* (1976). Again, it turned out that in the two social settings the participants laughed more often. (Unexpectedly, however, the laughter was longer in the stranger condition.) A recent study by Jennifer Hofmann and colleagues showed that even watching a film with a *virtual* companion, who expresses amusement on the screen, can lead to more laughter.[8] Thus we are dealing with robust empirical evidence here: People are much more likely to laugh about a comedy with others than alone.

However, the sheer *amount* of laughter should be identified neither with an *increase of enjoyment* nor with a *higher evaluation* of the film as funny. In a brief overview of previous studies, Michael J. Platow and colleagues demonstrated that there is in fact contradictory evidence: some studies find that the humor ratings increase, others don't.[9] In their study, Devereux and Ginsburg likewise conclude: "Respondents who laughed more did not report being happier or more amused and they did not find the video clip funnier than respondents who laughed less."[10] At this point we have to come back to Joe Dante's claim that comedies are "just not as funny" when one watches them alone, as well as a similar assertion by Henri Bergson, who postulated that "You would hardly appreciate the comic if you felt yourself isolated from others. Laughter appears to stand in need of an echo."[11] Although I intuitively agree with Dante and Bergson, from a strictly empirical point of view we don't have conclusive evidence for this audience effect yet. While it seems plausible that the presence of others often allows us to *enjoy* a comedy more and also makes us *evaluate* it as more amusing, the only unquestionable fact so far seems that the co-presence of others in the cinema yields more reasons for laughing – and this also goes for laughter *disconnected* from the comic.

One crucial goal of this chapter is to widen the discussion concerning laughter in film studies, a discussion that seems to me too restricted to our response to gags, jokes, puns – in short, to the aesthetic categories of the comic and the ridiculous. However, when we laugh in the movie-theater – but also in company at home – we often respond to aspects that have little to do with aesthetic categories but rather derive from the collective viewing constellation. In the darkness of the movie-theater one can hear aggressive, nervous, degrading, evaluating, embarrassed, shocked, disgusted, irritated, or contagious laughter. One can even go so far as to claim that there is hardly a piece of furniture connected to so many forms and functions of laughter as the cinema seat. That laughter is not a grey monolithic block but a gem that shimmers and sparkles in many colors will become clear, I hope, when I lay out my phenomenological typology of laughter below.

Describing the rich variety of laughter in the cinema should also make us immune to a virus that has infected even the most prominent theorists of laughter from Henri Bergson to Helmuth Plessner: unnecessarily reductive generalizations that ascribe a single totalizing function to laughter. Bergson reduces the phenomenon to sadistic laughter about the comic (or, maybe better, the ridiculous). For the French philosopher laughter is a cruel and cold social punishment that chastises inflexibility.[12] However, in the cinema we often laugh both *with* others and *against* others. We can become an integrated part of a group, but we can also *actively* distance ourselves from others and be *passively* distanced by them. Thus laughter allows for a dissolution of hierarchies and social stratifications, but it also allows us to distinguish ourselves from others. Laughter is a great unifier, but it can also be a great individualizer. It is therefore inaccurate when Bergson notes, "Our laughter is always the laughter of a group."[13] Moreover, laughter can imply that we are passively overwhelmed, but it can also be an active act of communication. On the one hand, it resembles largely involuntary bodily responses like startled screaming. On the other hand, it becomes speech-like and achieves the complexity of a verbal exclamation that can categorize as well as communicate aesthetic judgments. Following the terms of Michael Tomasello introduced in Chapter 4, it can be a "communicative *display*," an indicator without intention, but it can also be a "communicative *signal*," intended and strategically selected for a social motive.[14]

In the next section we will see that cinematic laughter not only knows many *objects* (over and above the comic and ridiculous), but also has many *functions* (apart from being a pleasurable affective response to something we consider funny). What's more, laughter also comes in many *forms*. Thus, please keep in mind that the manifestations of laughter I am going to describe have a broad range in terms of their 'physiognomy': they can reach from very brief outbursts to continuous laughing and from sharp, superficial snaps to deep belly laughter. The sociologist Norbert Elias has tried to capture this variety with the richness the English language allows: "One may chuckle, chortle, giggle, cackle, burble, snigger and titter or crow, smirk, simper, guffaw and cachinnate."[15]

II. A PHENOMENOLOGICAL TYPOLOGY OF CINEMATIC LAUGHTER

Apart from my own penchant for categorizations that drive this entire explorative study, the impressive variety of laughter makes it a prime candidate for typologizing attempts to come to terms with its diversity.[16] In 2010 I suggested a first typology of *cinematic* laughter in a German essay, which I present here in a translated and thoroughly revised form. My revisions are mostly motivated by the publication of Lenz Prütting's monumental and impressive three-volume study on laughter that came out in 2013. It does not seem as if Prütting had known my small essay. But interestingly, and hardly surprisingly given our common roots in the lived-body phenomenology of Hermann Schmitz, we have come to some similar conclusions (despite the infinitely more fine-grained discussions Prütting offers in his roughly 2,000 pages, from which my revisions have profited).[17]

In the following I will try to stake out a few conceptual claims without erecting barbed-wire fences. All in all I have unearthed ten types of cinematic laughter – a list that, I am sure, could be extended or refined. As we have seen in previous classifications above, drawing distinct categorical borders will not be possible at all times.[18] There is an unavoidable subjectivity in the choice and naming of the ten types of laughter. Nevertheless, I find it helpful to introduce these categories so we can cultivate the field of cinematic laughter more fruitfully. As Susan Sontag once wrote: "Many things in the world have not been named; and many things, even if they have been named, have never been described."[19] This is what I am trying to do in this section for cinematic laughter.

I will gradually move from *film laughter* (laughter about the movie) to *cinema laughter* (laughter in response to other viewers) in order to indicate laughter's increasing intertwinement with the co-presence of other spectators. However, we should be aware that laughter in the cinema always and necessarily implies expressive-diverted viewing. In Chapter 4 I have paved the way to conceptually distinguish laughter along these lines. First of all, laughter can be a form of *re-acting to the film*: if a viewer is overcome by an urge to laugh out loud, this re-action is not addressed to anyone, but in the social context of the cinema nevertheless communicates something to others. Laughter can also be a type of *play-acting for other viewers* when a viewer lightheartedly responds to the film by laughing about it, but in fact addresses the other viewers, for instance by laughing down on the film in a tongue-in-cheek fashion or to show off connoisseurship. Laughter can further be a form of *inter-acting with other viewers* when it takes on the form of a film-related and intended communication between viewers who respond – via laughter – to another's response. Finally, laughing can be a form of *jointly re-acting to the film* when a number of viewers laugh out loud collectively and this response is more than a mere aggregation of re-acting individuals. As an expressive response, jointly re-acting via laughter is addressed to the other viewers and hence includes the double communicative signal that I *and* we find this scene worthy of laughter. (Thus the only form of expression identified in Chapter 4 not included here is *synchronically acting together*: collective laughter seems too little synchronized and coordinated in order to fall into this category.)

1. Amusement laughter: laughing about the comic and ridiculous

The most widespread laughter type in the cinema is most likely laughter about the comic and the ridiculous. Certainly it is the one considered most prototypical. What we perceive as comic or ridiculous in a film – what *strikes us* with amusing force – are surprising and unthreatening non-fulfillments of expected norms.[20] When we are confronted with amusing ambivalences and contradictions, we experience them as corresponding tensions of our lived-body; in turn, these lived-body tensions are the felt equivalents of the unthreatening ambivalences and contradictions of the film. Laughter is a bursting and often quasi-automatic response that tries to *balance* these contradictions-cum-tensions via its typical eruptive, outward-directed exhalation.[21]

Our responses to the comic and the ridiculous are not the same, though. When we perceive something as *comic* we judge it, via our lived-bodies, as the Other of a valid norm, which through our *benign* laughter (*Belachen*) we still accept despite its break with the norm. The *ridiculous* is also an Other of a valid norm, but its more far-reaching break with the norm is answered with an *aggressive*, sometimes sadistic form of laughter (*Verlachen*) that implicitly demands an adjustment to the norm. If we were in a pleonastic mood, we could say that we find the comic *funny*, whereas we consider the ridiculous *ludicrous*. Just think of the following variations of *the* stock example in various theories of the comic: When watching a scene with an absent-minded, warmhearted professor with huge glasses who reads a book while walking down the street and then slips on a banana peel, one might express the fact that one finds it funny with benign laughter; when watching a similar scene with an extremely arrogant macho type who falls on the ground the same way and lands in a heap of dog pooh, one might find it ludicrous and respond with aggressive laughter. In both cases the viewers perceive a break with the expected norm of the dynamic gestalt of walking, but in the latter case they answer with sadistic *schadenfreude*.

Laughter about the comic and ridiculous always implies a mini-crisis of personality. Confronted with the unthreatening and amusing ambivalences and contradictions of the filmic object or event, we feel overwhelmed and momentarily lose the sovereign control over our physical existence. We *fall into* laughter – we are *overwhelmed* by it – because we cannot deal with this mini-crisis via words or controlled facial expressions, bodily gestures, and movements.[22] Thus despite the overwhelming mini-crisis of personality that it implies, laughter makes sense and has meaning and therefore cannot be compared to unavoidable eruptions like sneezing, coughing, or the knee-jerk reflex. However, we are not in reasoned control of the situation anymore; we do not respond at the height of our autonomy as a person, but relinquish to the body, which emancipates itself, as it were, and takes over.

In laughter we therefore have to temporarily give up what Hermann Schmitz calls our unfolded "personal emancipation." This implies that we lose our controlled goal-oriented and fluid movements; our controlled relaxed face; our controlled goal-oriented gaze; our controlled upright posture; our controlled respiration characterized by a balance between inhalation and exhalation; and our controlled capacity to articulate ourselves, which is characterized, among other things, by speaking full sentences.[23] Instead, the body shakes, the face looks distorted, the upright position bends in convex and concave forms, respiration is characterized by a stuttered asymmetry between inhalation and exhalation, and articulation is down to a stuttering and stammering bare minimum, as if to express "I can't speak anymore, therefore I cannot but laugh."[24]

We find ourselves, in other words, in what Schmitz dubs "personal regression." This fall into the abyss of personal regression can be a deep one, where the control over the body is small, but it can also be a flat one, where the degree of self-assertion is high. In any case, it is never more than a *mini*-crisis, because we know that laughter always comes with a return ticket. Our ecstatic and exhaling bursting into laughter always 'dies' after a while; it 'eats itself up.' Unless it takes on a pathological form, laughter never remains out of control for long. According to Prütting, this "uruboric impulse" of laughter, which eventually takes us back to the height of personal emancipation, is a "protection function immanent to the lived-body."[25] It allows us to let ourselves faithfully fall into the regressive experience of laughter, despite our knowledge that it implies a temporary loss of full sovereignty over our bodies and hence a form of self-distancing.

Laughter about a comedy thus comes with a double safety net: there are not only the various forms of safe distance characteristic of the cinematic experience (fictional, temporal, spatial), but there is also the security that all laughter implies a kind of resurrection after the fall without long-term effects.[26] On top of that, we know from the beginning that laughter depends on a certain attitude on our part: If we assume an attitude of *willing submission*, this propels the uncontrollability of laughter; if we take on an attitude of *defiant self-assertion*, laughter will be limited. If we don't want to laugh about the comic or the ridiculous, we can try to assume an aloof attitude and resist defiantly.

On the other hand, herein lies precisely one of its enjoyable aspects: The personal regression of laughter comes with the pleasure of not having to remain, for once, in full sovereignty over one's body. We can safely let go and have a bodily quasi-automatism take over. In its most intensive and, presumably, most pleasurable form, laughter about the comic and ridiculous is sudden and explosive and implies an almost compulsive response. As a form of *reacting*, this eruptive laughter about the comic and ridiculous is the epitome of laughter that can also occur in non-social environments, for instance when we watch a film alone at home. Most *social* theories of laughter – from Bergson onwards – neglect this kind of eruptive laughter because it has no communicative function when it occurs in solitude. After all, with whom would I communicate in my empty living room? However, in the context of the *cinema* this kind of overwhelmed, bursting laughter communicates a positive value judgment, since we simultaneously evaluate as amusing what we laugh at. Our laughing-out-loud involves the involuntary but clear and audible praise: "Oh my god, this is hilarious!" It is an expressive acclamation that the other viewers might share – *or* reject.

In terms of *intensity*, the humorous response to the comic and ridiculous naturally does not always need to be fully eruptive and quasi-automatic. In some instances we respond in far more controlled and active ways. Laughter can take the abrupt form of a bursting explosion, but also the gradual form of a melting erosion.[27] Prütting therefore suggests a polar continuum. At one end of the spectrum we find the bursting, overwhelming, quasi-automatic laughter with a maximum loss of autonomy and a minimum of self-assertion. In between are forms of joyful laughter of low intensity in which the viewer's loss of autonomy and his or her self-assertion are equally balanced. At the other end of the spectrum we can locate fully controlled forms of laughter which imply only a minimum loss of self-control. In this case we cognitively *understand* that something is meant to be funny and appreciate this intention – sometimes slightly patronizingly – with restrained laughter. The active control is high and we might just as well inhibit the laughing response and remain silent. Insofar as our laughter is meant to appreciate the comic *intention*, our laughter contains a grain of solidarity and communicativeness: implicitly I show solidarity with the director and the comedians who are responsible for the film; explicitly I show solidarity *with* – and communicate this solidarity *to* – those other viewers in the auditorium who find the film truly funny and who would be irritated by someone remaining silent.

In terms of *form*, we can equally discover differences in laughter, depending on how the comic and ridiculous reveal themselves to us: Are they offered immediately, gradually, or in an ongoing way? We have heard that for Prütting the form of laughter mimics, so to speak, what we laugh about: The lived-bodily tensions typical of laughter are the felt *equivalents* of the unthreatening ambivalences and contradictions of the film. Prütting therefore distinguishes between the comic that teleologically builds up toward a revelation of a punchline or *Pointe* (think of a joke or a prank), the comic that relies on an episodic recurrence of gags, and the comic without punchline whose temporal-dynamic gestalt is funny (think of the eccentric walk of a penguin). Correspondingly, our laughing response – the mimetic correlate – takes on the form of an explosive laughter, recurrent outbursts, or an ongoing commentary-like laughter.

Of course, not all viewers laugh all the time. Philosophers of aesthetics – and many phenomenological aestheticians among them – have underlined the fact that we have to assume an aesthetic attitude in order to make an aesthetic experience. An equivalent argument goes for the comic and the ridiculous: We actively have to admit their affordances in order to be able to laugh about them; a *humoristic* attitude is necessary for us to laugh about something funny. Or to put it differently: in order to make an aesthetic experience of the comic and the ridiculous we have to assume an aesthetic attitude, and the proper aesthetic attitude of the comedy is a humoristic one. Thus I have to actively opt for – open up for – the comic and the ridiculous.

But apart from this *situational attitude* toward laughter, there is also a more general *personal disposition*. Whether one is inclined to laugh or not can have various reasons, among other things cultural ones. It surely makes a difference if someone has suffered a personal loss very recently and therefore cannot laugh about morbid humor; if he has to 'keep face' because he is surrounded by his cool buddies whose macho subculture does not allow them to laugh about feminine humor; or if he was raised by parents who have told him – for instance, for religious reasons – that laughing is devil's work.

2. Relief laughter: laughing away as alleviation

The second type of laughter literally implies laughing *out* loud. It is not at all a response to something funny, but rather serves to laugh something *away*. Think of an intensely startling moment of cinematic shock that presses in on the viewer in a thriller; think of the horrific violence or monstrosity that the viewer is all of a sudden confronted with in a horror film; or think of the unexpectedly close depiction of disgusting objects or events with which the viewer cannot cope properly in a gross-out comedy: These are moments in which the spectator is suddenly overcome by an overly obtrusive aspect of the – phenomenologically speaking – *under*-distanced film. In these instances the viewer feels overwhelmed, 'cornered,' and constricted, and as an answer suddenly and wholly intuitively reacts with laughter. Here, again, Plessner's definition of laughter as a response to a crisis of the person seems apposite. As an eruptive, expressive, outward-directed response to an otherwise unanswerable mini-crisis, laughter relieves and liberates the viewer's constricted, beleaguered body by distancing the shocking, horrific, or disgusting film. Note that I am not talking metaphorically here: the film is *experienced* as overly close, just as the lived-body is *experienced* as constricted. By laughing – after all, an expansive outward movement of the body that goes along with exhalation – we try to get rid of what seems to be *too close*. When the film is felt as too shocking, horrific, or disgusting, laughter can work as a relief response to emotions like fear or disgust in the sense of a *reduction of tension*.

Yet it can also be a relief response in the sense of a feeling that *something distressing is over*. When after a plot twist or a change of perspective the scary or disgusting nearness suddenly turns out to be less harmless – for instance, the source of shock emerges as a friend of the protagonist who has played a prank – the viewer may respond with this distancing type of laughter by *further* laughing away the beleaguering source of constriction. We can therefore consider it as a type of triumphant laughter: the triumph of having overcome the distress. The closeness of the frequently sharp and brief outbursts of this type of laughter to the scream seems obvious. To be sure, it is not the same if people scream out loud or laugh about something, but both reactions have in common that they are explosive, expansive, eruptive responses. This is also one of the reasons why horror and humor in the splatter film, as well as disgust and humor in the gross-out comedy, go together so well.[28]

3. Conversion laughter: laughing as evaluative transformation

In Chapter 4 we have seen that a consequence of expressive behavior can be the modification of a film's intended emotions and meanings. Laughter is a forceful ally in such transformative attempts, because it often implies a performative value judgment which does not depend on an intellectual act, but is expressed with one's entire body. It can imply a positive *approach* or a negative *distancing*; it can be a negative laughing down that devalues and *degrades* the object, and it can be a positive laughter that appreciates and *upgrades* the object of laughter. Laughter can thus have a vertical (or longitudinal) tendency to evaluate along an up–down axis: (1) laughter as a smug sign of superiority; (2) laughter as a sign of equality where one recognizes a film or its maker as on an equal level as oneself; (3) laughter as a subversive act that wants to turn an inferiority position upside down.[29] (Even if it is not always clear for an outsider if the laughter is meant in a positive or a negative way, we cannot deny the fact that it often carries a value judgment in it.)

The transformative act of laughter can go in a benign-humorous or a contemptuous-aggressive direction. The former humorously and ironically transforms a serious film with a lighthearted, tongue-in-cheek change of perspective into something worthy of laughter.[30] Think of the humorous cult surrounding trash films or horror films, with *Ed Wood* (1994), *The Room*, or *The Evil Dead* (1981) as cases in point.[31] These films were originally conceived as scary, dramatic, or shocking, but through a humorous change of perspective viewers have started considering them as hilarious. Here it can also help to create what we could call *humor atmospheres* that increase the readiness to accept something as funny. Think of private DVD evenings in which alcohol, marihuana, or sweet food can contribute to humorous evaluations of a deadly serious film. Or think of ritualistic trash film viewings like the ones once organized by the "Friends of the Strange Film" (*Freunde des schrägen Films*) in Berlin's Babylon-Mitte cinema. Such laughter contexts make it less likely that other viewers might be offended.

But evaluative transformations via laughter can also have a contemptuous and ridiculing air. As a kind of acoustic, non-verbal speech-act they imply a negative judgment of taste that evaluates the film as kitschy or boring or overly pretentious. Since one can hardly imagine this kind of laughter in the private sphere of the home, I consider it an aggressive signal to *other viewers* – a signal that communicates an evaluation close to a grammatical utterance like "What nonsense!" or "How lame!" In contrast to the very personal characteristics of voice, intonation, dialect, and semantic content – which could identify an individual viewer and thus might create an embarrassing situation – the rather anonymous laughter allows staying, somewhat cowardly, in the enveloping darkness.

In 1918 the famous French critic and proponent of the photogénie concept, Louis Delluc, gave an example of such contemptuous laughter. In a text entitled "The Crowd" he observed that "refined creatures" in the audience like to "parade their superiority in public" by laughing *down* at "so-called popular films": "few weeks have gone by without a distinguished audience having spent an hour in joking, chuckling, and engaging in other ferocious convulsions." In comparison to a Charlie Chaplin film, where this wouldn't be possible, the audience enjoys their "devastating mockery."[32] These viewers obviously took pleasure in exposing their supposed cultural superiority via laughter. Their ridiculing laughter may have been implicitly directed at those *absent* individuals involved in the making of the film, but it could also have been more explicitly addressed to the *present* individuals in the auditorium who did not express their contempt but rather followed the film in silent, even rapt attention and thus seemed to have liked the film.[33] For those high-minded viewers who considered the film worthy of ridicule, a contemplative or emotional response must have been inadequate and quite literally ridiculous. Hence ridiculing the film and its makers by way of laughing could simultaneously imply a degradation of other immersed viewers.

More recently, Adrienne MacLean has used her own scornful laughing response to Darren Aronofsky's *Black Swan* (2010) as a starting point to illuminate a further reason why people might contemptuously laugh about a film.[34] Here the laughing *at* rather than *with* the film derives less from *her* self-ascribed superiority of taste, but rather from a feeling that the film and its makers flaunt *their* unearned superiority. This feeling of unjustified authority – a strong form of pretentiousness – can be discovered on the filmic level, but it is also informed by promotional and publicity materials, including interviews with the director: "one reason *Black Swan* is funny is its pomposity about its own aesthetic status and uniqueness," MacLean notes.[35] Laughter is thus an attempt to transform the status of the film and degrade it. In their high seriousness the film and Aronofsky as its director have put themselves on a high cultural pedestal, assuming a superior position. But the high status assigned to the film also derived from the critics and the laypeople's discourse surrounding it. Now, aesthetic experiences by no means have to be an egalitarian affair: there is nothing wrong with looking 'up' to a work of art in admiration, in awe, in puzzlement, and even anxiety about its complexity and superior knowingness. But some viewers have a fine sensorium that the position of superiority has to be rightfully earned.[36] If this is not the case, the punishing effect that laughter can have, according to Bergson, assumes a corrective function for the audience: "my friend and I were reacting to the film's ignorance, as it were – its ignorance sometimes of the subject matter (it just didn't care that much about being correct about ballet) but also its ignorance of us and the fact that we might know things that would render the film's self-importance and reliance on stereotypes and cheap sentiment ludicrous," McLean writes.[37] Her laughing 'up' at the film is also a question of power: Do I want to feel dominated by the film or do I try to dominate it?

What made McLean laugh were the film's incongruities, exaggerations, clichés, and kitsch. Of course, these incongruities, clichés, exaggerations, and kitsch have to be recognized in the first place. Since not everyone will have the same knowledge about films, we can expect divergences within the audience. What might come across to some as the laughing audience's blaséness – and hence a self-ascribed superiority – is very different for those who laugh 'up' at the film's self-ascribed superiority.[38] This brings us back to the vertical aspect of laughter: While the arrogant viewers described by Delluc laugh 'down' at the film to demonstrate their superiority, McLean's laughter 'up' at the film disputes the film's superiority and hence does not accept her own inferiority.

The philosopher Alfred Stern insisted most outspokenly on the evaluative function of laughter and on the pleasurable freedom that comes with 'speaking out' negative judgments by laughing about values oppressing us: "Laughter [...] becomes a kind of symbolic liberation from social pressure for those individuals who suffer from it."[39] Early film theorist Ricciotto Canudo commented quite similarly: "Since the comic is essentially irreverent, it gives a deep sense of relief to individuals oppressed in every moment of their real lives by social discriminations, so emphatically present. This sense of relief is one of the factors of that nervous motion of contraction and expansion called laughter."[40]

This shows us the subversion potential that can inhere in laughter: An individual or a group of people may reject norms it finds oppressive or wrongheaded, thus assuming a temporary position of sovereignty, even in instances of political and social oppression. However, it's not only laughter as a speechlike act of evaluation that is important here, but also the potentially subversive form of *how* we laugh. As Samuel Weber has noted, certain types of laughter can break down the barriers of propriety: Articulate and reasonable discourse may be progressively drowned out by a body out of control.[41] In contrast to a negative comment uttered verbally, the subversive potential of laughter can thus also reside in its simultaneous rejection of decent behavior when someone laughs particularly wildly about a film.

4. Comprehension laughter: laughing as signal of understanding

As we have seen with other forms of expression, in the social situation of the cinema the expressive response of laughter is invariably an act of communication. But sometimes viewers use laughter also as a more or less deliberate communicative tool to signal understanding to others. This also implies comprehending the comic. Unlike the almost involuntary response to the physical moments of slapstick, many forms of the comic need to be understood as funny first. The more complex and demanding this act of understanding seems – because the joke is difficult to get or because the comic depends on prior knowledge – the more necessary we might find it to signal our understanding. Take Mae West's oft-quoted question "Is that a pistol in your pocket or are you just glad to see me?" Its naughty playfulness demands a mental leap not everyone might make. This is the moment for narcissistically or altruistically signaling understanding, especially if one expects the other viewers not to have understood the point.

The *vain* viewer, proud to have spotted the comic core, joyfully and rather narcissistically honors his or her own insight and communicates it to the other viewers. He or she – of *all* people! – has discerned something important at this very moment: "Wow, look how clever I am!"[42] The *selfless* viewer, on the other hand, altruistically communicates that there is something peculiar to understand: "Hey, people, think again: this was indeed funny and worthy of laughter!" In an early psychological study on laughter in response to funny film clips, psychologists Raymond G. C. Fuller and Alan Sheehy Skefffington have shown that this type of laughter can indeed be beneficial to viewers: "The laughter of others may [. . .] act as a situational cue which conditions the listener to search for a humorous interpretation of the material, directing the perceiver to 'see the funny side' of things."[43] (In Chapter 5 we have heard of the notion of "social appraisal," which we can also employ for viewers who appraise a situation via the laughter of others.)

To be sure, there are also occasions when laughter signals understanding of something neither intended to be funny nor experienced as such: *intratextual* hints to earlier moments in the story (when watching a sequel) or to later ones (in a prequel); *intertextual* references to arthouse movies, to genre films, to underground classics; *intermedial* allusions to other media or art forms as well as to highbrow cultural capital and pop-cultural knowledge of all kinds. Highly allusive postmodern films like Quentin Tarantino's *Kill Bill* (2003) or Wes Craven's *Scream* (1996) could initiate this ambiguous signal-laughter just as much as parodies of the *Scary Movie* (2000) type.[44] The same goes for films bursting with references to the history of art and literature – think of works by Peter Greenaway or Jean-Luc Godard. In these cases Prütting would use the term "triumphant eureka laughter."[45] But we could also speak of *deictic laughter*, as the viewer directs the other's attention by laughing pointedly, so to speak.[46] Deictic laughter functions a bit like the pointing gesture that is so important to developmental psychologist Michael Tomasello's notions of joint attention and shared intentionality. But since it is *me* who points out something to *you*, this deictic form of laughter also individualizes me.

The temporality of comprehension laughter is mostly backward-directed: it points at something that has just occurred in the film. However, there are also forward-directed forms of comprehension laughter that indicate one should follow the scene with heightened awareness. In a comedy, signal laughter can express that a viewer has already understood that an annoying character is going to undergo a painful, disgusting, or embarrassing situation any time soon and wants to signal this insight laughingly. Another example eliciting understanding signal laughter could be a historical film in which a vainglorious character predicts something with full conviction that we know will never happen. Here laughter signals our understanding and our superiority over the character whose vanity we punish.

Due to the ambiguity of its signal – either narcissistic or altruistic or a bit of both – the deictic laughter might lead to various effects: social *distinction* (*from* other unknowing viewers), *instruction* (*to* other unknowing viewers), and *inclusion* (*of* other knowing viewers). On the one hand, this kind of laughter can be regarded as a gesture of power based on personal wittiness or wealth of cultural capital. On the other hand, it also creates a bond among those who are in the know, ranging from genre aficionados to well-educated highbrows. Last but not least, the laughter can also derive from the imaginary tacit agreement that exists between the alluding filmmaker and the discerning viewer – a pleasurable moment of *recognition*, both in the straightforward sense of grasping something and the more philosophical dialogic sense of recognizing an Other.

5. Recognition laughter: laughing as expression of detection

The cinematic experience also knows peculiar moments in which we suddenly recognize specific locations, objects, persons, or actions on the screen that are very familiar to us and in one way or another *are* – or at one point *were* – important to our identity. We recognize the street we live in; we recognize a song that we often listened to as a kid; we recognize an object popular twenty years ago (a particular technology, toy or type of clothing); we recognize a dialect very typical for the region we come from; we recognize an actor that we used to like and haven't seen in years; we recognize a dance, a sport, or a manner of gesticulating from our home country. Following Jean-Pierre

Meunier and Vivian Sobchack, what happens here is a switch in our subjective relation to the screen and a change in mode of filmic consciousness: from a *fiction* (or *documentary*) consciousness to a *home movie* consciousness. It is a particular form of home movie consciousness because the film reminds us of who we are or once were (as Sobchack points out, the more appropriate French term for home movie is *film-souvenir*).[47] We look 'through' the film as a fiction or document and recognize something from home, sometimes literally so. Even though this sudden recognition is not always accompanied by laughter, it certainly can be.

But what type of laughter is it? We undoubtedly do not laugh about something comic. Depending on how the recognition touches our identity the response might have very different affective tinges: nostalgia, pride, embarrassment, or even aggression about one's former self. Think of the delightful feeling of pride, however mild it may be, when we recognize something important to our own identity. We feel acknowledged by the film, even honored: "Something that defines my identity is worthy enough of becoming public in a movie." It is the recognition of a recognition (again in the philosophical sense of the term).[48] And this delightful feeling we might laughingly communicate to others: "*This* location, object, person, or event on the screen is connected to *me*." East Germans from the former GDR come to mind who – against the abrupt Westernization of their part of the country – delightedly laughed at the sight of original GDR props in such comedies as *Sonnenallee* (1999) or *Good Bye, Lenin!* Their recognition laughter was infused by a kind of happy nostalgia (or *Ostalgie*, as it was called in Germany). In turn, a viewer might also react negatively, for instance with embarrassed laughter, when he hears the 'backwoods' dialect of his village he has just escaped from. Here it becomes once again important where one watches the film and who the co-viewers are. The embarrassed viewer might laugh all the more forcefully when in the company of his big city hipster friends to signal a distancing act from his past. The East Germans, on the other hand, might laugh particularly strongly when knowing that other East Germans are in the audience, to create a bond among them.

Against the background of the following anecdote, reported by Lakshmi Srinivas, we can see that the relative inconspicuousness of laughter can be 'safer' and more adequate for these acts of recognition than verbal commenting. During a screening of *Thelma und Louise* (1991) in a Boston cinema, a male viewer suddenly jumped up when the two heroines drive through Oklahoma and shouted "Oklahoma! Hey guys, it's Oklahoma!" The viewers in front of him turned around and shushed him. The man, who had been a graduate student in Oklahoma, was apparently so delightfully excited that he needed to communicate this verbally. Had he merely *laughed* about his delightful and nostalgic recognition, he might have avoided his punishment.

6. Laughter-laughter: laughing about another's laughter

In Chapter 4 I have pointed out that other viewers' expressive re-acting can become a source of pleasure in its own right. This not only goes for funny shrieks or exaggerated screams, but also for laughter. It is not at all uncommon that for a fleeting moment the gestalt of a remarkably funny laughter of one or more viewers dominates the dark anonymity of the cinema. Think of an unusually sharp roar, a machine-gun-like chattering, a hysterical cackling, or a droning laughter coming up from the deepest recesses of the body's insides. During such moments this ear-catching laughter all of a sudden stands out as an audible figure on the acoustic ground of the auditorium; it momentarily displaces the film as the dominating focus of attention and assumes the role of the intentional object of some viewers' amusement. These viewers consequently *feel entitled* to respond to the amusing laughter – or *cannot help* but react to it – by laughing themselves. The amused laughing-about-laughter thus comments on and evaluates the amusing laughed-about-laughter: "I laugh about your laughter because how you laugh makes me laugh." Importantly, by implicitly evaluating this laughter as amusing, the other's laughter becomes the object of laughter and it therefore must not be confused with contagious laughter. Just as in other cases of amused laughter about the comic, the reason is the sudden realization of a harmless incongruity between an idealized expectation of a gestalt and the actual instantiation that contradicts it. Note, however, that not every laughter-laughter is amused and benevolent. It can also assume an aggressive nature, as when the respondent evaluates the laughter as annoying and distracting in its remarkable conspicuousness. This aggressive response already belongs to our seventh type.

7. Disdain laughter: laughing depreciatively about another's response

Sometimes viewers comment on other viewers' expressive behavior or reaction to the film by laughing (down) *at* them. In contrast to the positive evaluation of the amused laughter-laughter, this type of laughter implies a negative judgment: It devalues the other spectators' response – more or less aggressively – as inappropriate, unworthy, ridiculous, or embarrassing. The conspicuous laughter of the previous category that other viewers might find positively funny can become an object of this negative depreciative laughter, but in principle this goes for all forms of expression discussed in Chapter 4: an overly loud startled scream (re-acting), a misfired joke (play-acting), a stupid part of a conversation (inter-acting), and so on. The devaluation can happen in various degrees, from a mildly unappreciative giggle to aggressively hacking, scornful laughter. But in every case the laughter comes across as a lofty, sometimes even arrogant, signal that attempts to degrade those viewers laughed at. Here we have to come back to the spatial verticality of laughter: By laughing depreciatively I can *further* 'degrade' someone who I already consider lowly due to his or her inappropriate or ridiculous behavior, or I can 'pull down' and 'put in the right place' below me someone who I think has put himself in an unduly elevated position. Consider a viewer who wants to gain social recognition by cracking a poor joke or cash in cultural capital by making a superfluous comment. This is another occasion when Bergson's definition of laughter as punishment is accurate: "Laughter is, above all, a corrective. Being intended to humiliate, it must make a painful impression on the person against whom it is directed. By laughter, society avenges itself for the liberties taken with it."[49] Prütting correctly describes what he calls "resentful laughing at" (*missgünstiges Verlachen*) as a "wrestling for dominance."[50]

8. Embarrassment laughter: laughing about oneself

Yet laughter can also come in the form of an embarrassed, nervous laughter about one's own foregoing response in order to cover it up or make it disappear. Think of an overly loud, shrieking scream after a moment of startle in a horror film, or a misplaced exclamation disrupting a suspenseful silence. When the viewer him- or herself considers this as an *unwanted* breach of the tacit norm of inconspicuousness (and not a *willful* provocation), a feeling of embarrassment or even shame might result. All of a sudden the viewer feels exposed in front of the others, standing out 'nakedly' and unpleasantly, isolated from the collectivity of viewers who seem to fix their eyes on the embarrassed one. The embarrassment or shame about this exposed position has a consequence: The viewer does not only feel isolated and surrounded by imagined or real gazes, but also experiences his or her surrounded lived-body as constricted.[51] Hollow and somewhat desperate laughter is a perfect way to magically and quickly re-transform what is experienced as a shameful world. The explosive exhalation of laughter breaks through the wall of the lived-body constriction and simultaneously expresses a humble plea for re-entry into the imaginary collectivity of the auditorium. The magical open-sesame of laughter expresses something like: "Sorry, forget about it, I immediately take it back!" And: "Please let me re-enter into your collectivity and let me disappear from your penetrating views into the dark anonymity!"

Is it because this embarrassed laughter about oneself is a sign of humbleness that makes it often sound somewhat childish? In comparison to the disdainful laughter discussed above, laughing about oneself does not 'vertically' degrade someone else but oneself. Jens Roselt has pointed out that despite the darkness of the auditorium only those who do not show perceptible, bodily reactions can escape the danger of exposing themselves.[52] A remarkable aspect of this type of laughter is that it tries to re-transform an experience of being exposed by further exposing oneself. Astonishingly, laughter can do the trick and relativize the prior exposition.

9. Mimicry laughter: laughing actively along with others

There are also instances when we *actively* initiate a mode of laughing along with others, either because we don't want to stand out negatively *ourselves* or because we don't want *others* to laugh on their own and hence feel isolated. Feeling more or less emotionally detached, we go along with the laughing crowd. One motivation could be the wish to avoid appearing as the one who hasn't got the joke. Another motivation is voiced by a participant in Annette Hill's empirical audience study on violent entertainment: "A guy falls to his death and everybody laughed at that and I felt as if maybe I should laugh with them, and I did. I can't understand why I did that. I suppose you try to fit in with everybody else so you're not left out."[53] This form of laughter can be seen as a form of *conformity*.

But it can also imply *solidarity* when we actively laugh because we do not want to devalue the laughing response of the others by remaining ostentatiously silent. As we have seen variously throughout this study, laughter can be an acoustic offer to join an emotional community of laughter. Rejecting this offer can come across as impolite, exposing, and even degrading, because silence evaluates the behavior of the others as inappropriate: "In comparison to you, who laugh at this poor joke, I don't find it worthy of laughter." Or: "Unlike you, I don't belong to those who laugh about violence because I find it morally reprehensible." Moreover, it can imply that I don't care whether they are left isolated and 'out in the open.' Carl Plantinga once suggested the term "cooperative viewer" to designate a spectator who allows the film to achieve its intended emotional effect.[54] However, the viewer may not only act cooperatively vis-à-vis the film, but even more so with regard to the other viewers. As with embarrassed cover-up laughter (type 8), we are dealing with a form of laughter that acknowledges the apprehension – of ourselves or others – to leave the comfortable 'invisibility' that comes with being embedded in a group.

Although outwardly it might seem as if this type of laughter was laughter about the film, it is in fact an immediate response to the laughter of the other viewers: a laughing *along with* them *because of* them. Harking back to the distinction made in Chapter 6, we could call it a form of behavioral and emotional *mimicry*, because the laughing viewer imitates the emotional expression and behavior of the other spectators, but there is no emotional convergence typical of emotional contagion.

10. Contagion laughter: laughing together with others

Laughter is notoriously contagious. When we let ourselves be *passively* pulled into laughing together with others, this implies an almost involuntary response to the infectious laughter of other viewers. Similar to the *emotional* contagion we encountered in Chapter 6, in contagious laughter we do not share the same intentional object – we simply laugh together with the other viewers, not really knowing why we laugh nor controlling what we laugh about. And in contrast to the amused laughter-laughter (type 6), we do not laugh *about* their laughter, but *with* their laughter.

The collective contagious laughter has a specific lived-body dynamic to which every single participant delegates a part of his "personal emancipation" (Hermann Schmitz). This means that one has to give oneself up to a certain degree. Note, however, that when viewers are affected – and infected – by the laughter of others, they have already allowed this to happen by having taken an attitude of willing abandonment to the situation. An attitude of strict defiance can also block and avert the contagiousness of laughter (which is not to say that *after* one has abandoned oneself to the situation one would be easily able to control the force of contagious laughter).[55] And note also that not every kind of laughter in the cinema is contagious; embarrassed or even desperate laughter usually does not evoke a resonance response from us.

How often we are infected by collective laughter can be deduced from a simple fact: in the movie-theater we often laugh about things that we would otherwise not even ignore (as Woody Allen might have put it) and that we consider unfunny in retrospect. Some things are laughed about simply because other people laugh about them and we are infected by their laughter.[56] As we have seen above, there seems to be no agreement in empirical studies as to whether laughing with others implies an increase in enjoyment and appreciation of a film. But let's assume both are plausible: This would imply that when watching a film with others, spectators can laugh more and enjoy the *film* more; or they can laugh more and enjoy the *cinematic situation* more. Or both.

If we recapitulate these ten types, we can see how laughter moves on a continuum from *film*-laughter to *theater*-laughter: The list starts with types of laughter that are almost exclusively related to the film – think of the comic laughter or the relieving laughing-away response. It moves on to types that respond to the film but are in fact directed at the audience – remember the connoisseur laughter. And it ends with types of laughter responding almost exclusively to the audience – laughter-about-laughter or infected laughing-with, for instance. Once again this should alert us to the fact that many varieties of laughter make sense – and, in fact, are possible – only in the social context of collective viewing. After all, I can only be affected by the laughter of others if there *are* others. And in terms of the laughter-about-laughter it would be very strange indeed if – sitting alone at home – I found my own laughter so funny that I laughed about myself.

III. COLLECTIVITY AND INDIVIDUALITY IN CINEMATIC LAUGHTER

As we have heard from Bazin, "laughter allows the audience to become aware of itself."[57] Although laughter does not make highly demanding calls on consciousness and therefore easily allows us to follow the film simultaneously, it always has a tendency to draw our attention – however slightly – away from the screen. In fact, the more eruptive the laughter, the more difficult it is to sustain one's immersion. On the one hand, laughter is, as we have seen, a bodily response: it is eruptive and outward-moving, it puts the body in motion and distorts it, leading to a postural concavity or convexity. Even if only mildly, our attention is therefore literally torn away from the film by our own bodily reaction. On the other hand, there are the audible responses of the other spectators. The louder the other viewers laugh, the more easily they enter one's field of consciousness. Thus our own laughter and the reactions from the rest of the audience are constant reminders of the cinematic here – and it is in this here-and-now of the auditorium that laughter can play out the strong social effects so crucial for a study on the audience effect. Accordingly, we may distinguish the ten types of laughter along the lines of individuality and collectivity, exclusion and inclusion.

On the one hand, *excluding* laughter favors social distinction and the creation of distance: Laughter can become a great individualizer and divider – a kind of Warsaw Pact of social interaction, erecting an iron curtain within the audience. Here we can think of the vain form of connoisseur laughter (type 4) or the depreciative laughter about another viewer's response (type 7). On the other hand, *including* laughter can tear down barriers and social hierarchies: It can be the great equalizer – a kind of Schengen Agreement that abolishes all boundary posts. Just consider contagious laughter (type 10) or collective laughter about something funny (type 1). Obviously, both tendencies can occur at the same time: Including laughter can also have an excluding effect and thus imply hostility toward those who do not laugh.[58]

Especially during films that combine various types of gags and jokes, simple puns and sophisticated wordplay, rough slapstick and gross-out humor, satire and parody, allusion and intertextuality, we can expect constant changes and reshufflings of laughing collectives. In films which inevitably spark various types of laughter, the alliances will be fluent, causing ever-new in- and out-groups, diversions and gaps, but also inclusions and new emergent temporal laughing collectives. While some viewers feel excluded by one type of joke (say, sexual innuendo), they might feel included by another (slapstick, for example), siding with one group of audience members at one moment, becoming part of a new subgroup at another. Like a wheat field suddenly caught in a strong gust of wind, the audience is moved around here and there; like the crystals in a kaleidoscope, the viewers find themselves next to one part of the audience one moment and united with a different part in the next.

Important causes for this constant flux are the explosiveness and temporality of laughter, which is usually short-lived and bound to the present moment: It comes – and then it's already gone. Lawrence Kimmel calls it a "simple affirmation of the moment": "In the instant and instances of laughter, past and future vanishes, and nothing leads up to or away from this moment."[59] The sudden outbursts and accentuations of the present moment in laughter are extremely difficult to convey in language, yet in Chapter 2 we have encountered a felicitous attempt to capture the dynamic changes of laughing collectives in a passage from Bazin worthy of being quoted again: "You laugh and your neighbor laughs too. At first it is all the same laughter. But I have 'listened in' to this gag twenty times in different theaters. When the audience, or at least part of it, was made up of intellectuals, students for example, there was a second wave of laughter of a different kind. At that moment the hall was no longer filled with the original laughter but with a series of echoes, a second wave of laughter, reflected off the minds of the spectators as if from the invisible walls of an abyss."[60] Due to different levels of education, the audience, united in laughter at first, can easily be splintered into two subgroups of laughing intellectuals and silent non-intellectuals an instance later.

Laughing collectives are open, fleeting, and have a transient membership. Their emergence remains random, incalculable, and spontaneous.[61] Viewers may swiftly move from experiencing what in Chapter 5 I have called a close mutual *we*-connection, to feeling thrust into an antagonistic *I–you* relationship in the next instance, only to find themselves all of a sudden in an affective *we–you* interrelation that includes both a feeling of closeness to some viewers and a feeling of antagonism to others. In fact, laughter allows us to refine the distinction of affective audience interrelations in the cinema even further.

(1) My laughter can be embedded in an affectively close *we*, where I laugh with you and all the others, and we all feel emphatically part of this 'we.' Maybe the most famous filmic illustration of such a laughing collective can be found at the aforementioned ending of King Vidor's silent film classic *The Crowd* (1928). In the very last scene we see the reactions of a theater audience watching a clown. The laughing crowd – a stand-in for the cinematic audience – responds by moving their bodies back and forth.[62] The affectively close 'we' does not know an Other in the auditorium; there is no experienced outside to this 'we,' except for the clown on stage.[63]

Figure 7.1: Laughing spectators in King Vidor's silent film classic *The Crowd*.

(2) However, laughter can also result in a more oppositional affective audience interrelation of *we–thou* (second-person singular). For instance, we might experience someone else, who laughs very annoyingly, as standing isolated outside of our laughing collective, because his or her excess of laughter marks a conspicuous difference in behavior. As Prütting has shown, laughter has a "situational appropriateness" (*situative Stimmigkeit*) that matches the situation or not.[64] When laughter is not appropriate to us we consider it as inauthentic or forced, which shows that we always intuitively appraise the other's laughter and match it with a certain norm. Sometimes someone stands out with the individuality of his or her laughter to a degree that expresses a situational *in*-appropriateness.

(3) The Bazin example illustrates that laughter may also evoke an antagonistic experience of *we–ye* (second-person plural) when it pits fractions of the audience against each other: Those who have understood the sophisticated second joke in the Chaplin film may have felt elevated as a 'we' and looked down on those who remained silent. Or think of viewers from the region of Nord-Pas-de-Calais who may have felt united as a 'we' against those other Frenchmen in the audience who laughed about their stereotypical representation while watching *Bienvenue chez les Ch'tis* (2008).

(4) Laughter may, moreover, create a less specific *we–they* experience,

in which this 'they' is rather undefined, a vague outside of the group that remains indeterminate and is not reflected upon. The experience of cult film fans or genre aficionados could be an example. By signaling, via inside-group laughter, their communion with other fans they simultaneously close themselves off to others outside this group without reflecting on these others, let alone considering them as objects of their laughter. Their laughing collective is based on what Goffman calls "inside secrets" whose possession marks an individual as a member of a group and "helps the group feel separate and different from those who are not 'in the know.' Inside secrets give objective intellectual content to subjectively felt social distance."[65] Sharing humor thus allows both the creation of a feeling of togetherness and the marking of the boundaries of the group without necessarily making the outside of the group a defining factor.[66]

(5) Individual viewers may also be removed from any kind of 'we' experience. They may feel positively individualized or negatively isolated; in any case they experience social distance and thus stand, in one way or another, against other viewers. Sometimes it may be directed merely against *one* viewer – an experience we could call the *I–thou* mode (second-person singular). If a viewer laughs amusedly about another's laughter this would be the benign version; if a spectator laughs depreciatively about another's response this could count as the aggressive version of the I–thou mode.

(6) At other times a single viewer may feel distanced from or opposed to a bigger group or even the entire audience. We could call this the *I–ye* mode (second-person plural). A case in point may be the vain understanding laughter of a single viewer who tries to cash in his cultural capital. As we have heard from Richard McCulloch, knowledge can be a form of power also in the cinema, and an individual connoisseur laughter displays a distinctive surplus of knowledge. Here we are dealing with an *active-intended* attempt to stand out via individualizing laughter.

But I can also feel *passively* and *unintentionally* individualized, for instance by those who laugh about something I do not find worthy of laughter. Surely this can have negative effects, including the feeling of isolation and exclusion so vividly captured by Wolfgang Koeppen in his great post-war novel *The Hothouse* (1953), where he describes his protagonist Keetenheuve's experience during a visit to the cinema: "People were laughing next to Keetenheuve, people were laughing in front of him and behind him. Why were they laughing? He did not understand. It appalled him. He was expelled. He was excluded from their laughter. He hasn't seen anything funny. [. . .] These were rather sad than funny incidents! But they were laughing around Keetenheuve. They were laughing out loud. Was Keetenheuve a foreigner? Had he travelled among people who cried differently, laughed differently, people who were different from him? Maybe he was a foreigner of feeling, and the laughter from the dark surrounding him flooded him painfully like an overly strong wave and threatened to suffocate him."[67]

Of course, one does not always have to feel a strong antagonism; the opposition of the I–ye mode can also be experienced as a mere difference. Jonathan Rosenbaum, for instance, remembers from his youth in the segregated state of Alabama how, one day, he realized that the African-American viewers in "the colored section" on the balcony responded to the film with "dark laughter," and thus in a way quite different from the way he did.[68]

(7) Finally, we can think of an *I–they* experience in which the rest of the audience remains a vague backdrop that isn't reflected upon, comparable to the we–they mode. An example would be a viewer whose laughter expresses a very personal recognition (type 5), for instance because she has spotted a place or an object that is very dear to her. This viewer may feel *individually* affected and recognized. The rest of the audience does not play a role for her in this instance, even though on a pre-reflective level she might be aware that this moment of recognition relates to her personally, but not to the other viewers in the audience.

IV. COLLECTIVITY IN CINEMATIC LAUGHTER ABOUT THE COMIC

With the distinctions of the previous section in mind, I will for the remainder of this chapter return once more to laughter about the comic or ridiculous in order to refine my description of the collective aspect. When we laugh collectively about something funny or ludicrous, this entails a physical outburst that expressively exhales both an I- and a we-statement, as we have seen in Chapter 5. We simultaneously exclaim to the others "*I* find this worthy of laughter individually" and to each other "*We* find this worthy of laughter collectively." We not only show that we share the same humor, assume the same situational attitude and have the same personal disposition. We also express both a shared evaluation (this is funny or ludicrous for us collectively!) and a shared emotion (we are feeling amused together!). If we follow Alfred Stern, this must have a strong effect: "Nothing unifies humans more than the discovery that they evaluate similarly and that they are connected through a common world of values."[69]

In comparison to full-blown sentences, laughter makes possible an easier and more effective form of confluence of individual responses in the dark (even if it doesn't allow for the neat synchronization and coordination of synchronically acting together). As Norbert Elias has pointed out, due to the audible component of laughter we don't have to look at each other to feel as one.[70] (As we will see in Chapter 9, anger in the cinema is often fueled by a lack of possible eye-contact that would allow balancing out the felt asymmetries typical of anger.) Moreover, the darkness 'equalizes' and 'democratizes' laughter: laughter in the dark cannot easily be mapped onto concrete persons, as identity markers such as gender, race, class, and age are often more difficult to distinguish than in speech. Thus the resulting laughing collectives can momentarily dissolve social hierarchies and categories such as man/woman, old/young, or white/non-white. Again, early film theorist Ricciotto Canudo captured this effect nicely: "The comic can suppress hierarchies, it can join together the most different beings, give an extraordinary impression of the mixture of the most separate universes, which in real life are irreducibly distinct from one another."[71]

The inclusive type of laughter opens up to the world. It has a centrifugal spatiality outward and implies a transcendence of the self in the sense that one *ex-plodes*, *ex-hales*, and thus *ex-presses* from inside out and forward into a space shared with others.[72] When laughing together about something funny one can feel subjective social distances decrease or even disappear. We feel, as it were, centripetally pulled together. Moreover, there might be an action tendency to communicate: Brief eye contacts with one's unknown neighbor may become a possibility; one may even dare to talk to him or her briefly and exchange a comment. To appreciate this change of social relations, just consider how much more difficult this would be during a deeply moving moment of a melodrama. Approaching the weeping neighbor can easily come across as an intrusion into someone else's intimate experience (more on this in Chapter 8).

If we consider certain kinds of benign laughter as a joyful regression, as I indicated above, we can conclude that *collective* benign laughter is a pleasurable and harmless form of collective regression. For a brief moment those who join in the laughing collective give up their self-control and allow a temporary diffusion of the rigid boundaries of individuality characteristic of personal emancipation. For once I agree with those who describe the cinema in Freudian terms as a regression-enabling dispositive. However, we do not regress problematically to a child-like sense of triumphant ego-position. The regression of collective laughter is not dangerous, because the uroboric impulse of laughter takes us immediately and without any conscious thought back from the personal regression to personal emancipation.

Obviously laughing collectives are not always benign. According to Prütting, laughter can imply a positive, benevolent devotion to something pleasant and a negative, aggressive attention to something unpleasant.[73] We only have to think of ethnic, nationalist, or misogynist humor and the aggressive collective laughter it might entail. This tendency is vividly, if one-sidedly, captured in Max Horkheimer and Theodor W. Adorno's characterization of what Prütting calls "laughing mobs": "Laughter about something is always laughter at it, and the vital force which, according to Bergson, bursts through rigidity in laughter is, in truth, the irruption of barbarity, the self-assertion which, in convivial settings, dares to celebrate its liberation from scruple. The collective of those who laugh parodies humanity. They are monads, each abandoning himself to the pleasure – at the expense of all others and with the majority in support – of being ready to shrink from nothing. Their harmony presents a caricature of solidarity."[74]

Why not distinguish therefore between *cold* and *warm* laughing collectives? Arguably, an audience breaking out in cold, aggressive, sadistic, degrading laughter will imply a different collective experience than a warm, elevating, embracing, open laughter. Following Stern, the collective laughter of the laughing mob does not elicit a lasting consolidation effect, but merely a superficial union, since collective refusal and exclusion depend only on the lowest common denominator, whereas collective inclusion presupposes a much higher denominator.[75] Hubert Dreyfus and Sean Dorrance Kelly therefore remind us of the *ethical* implications of being carried away in laughter: "To recognize when it's appropriate to let oneself be swept up and when it's appropriate to walk away is a higher-order skill that is crucial for us in the contemporary world."[76] We therefore have to make "meaningful distinctions between dangerous and benign ways of being swept away."[77] In other words, it can be morally wrong to join collective laughter in its cold and cruel variant, just as it is sometimes called for to show one's commitment to a warm laughing collective. Just think of the stubborn refusal to be carried away by collective laughter that we have encountered in Chapter 5: It might not only destroy the pleasure of one's companions, but also place oneself in a position outside of the community.

NOTES

1. Mendelssohn (1997 [1761]), p. 148.
2. Rosenbaum (1995), p. 150.
3. R. Mele (2016). Available at https://www.pastemagazine.com/articles/2016/05/joe-dante-on-hollywoods-broken-system.html (last accessed 3 June 2016).
4. An oft-cited statistic by Robert Provine and Kenneth Fischer claims that people are approximately thirty times more likely to laugh in the presence of another person than in a solitary situation, when no media are involved. When media-use is included, social laughter is still *over five times* as likely than laughter that occurs alone (Provine/Fischer, 1989, p. 300).
5. Dunbar et al. (2012).
6. Dunbar et al. (2012), p. 1163.
7. Devereux/Ginsburg (2001).
8. Hofmann et al. (2015).
9. Platow et al. (2005), p. 543.
10. Devereux/Ginsburg (2001), p. 236.

11. Bergson (1914 [1900]), p. 5.
12. Bergson (1914 [1900]), p. 198. In his comment, Lenz Prütting is particularly acerbic: He calls Bergson's *Le Rire* "a botch of startling moral and intellectual meagerness" and "an excess of reductionism" with "alarmingly inhumane tendencies" (Prütting, 2013, pp. 1261 and 1269, my translation).
13. Bergson (1914 [1900]), p. 6.
14. Similarly, Lenz Prütting underscores the difference between a laughter that responds without addressing anyone (*Bekundungslachen*) and a laughter that interacts with others (*Interaktionslachen*). The latter he calls "performative acts of a non-linguistic type" (Prütting, 2013, p. 1497, my translation).
15. Quoted from Schröter (2002), p. 861.
16. See also the brief typology in Huron (2006), pp. 28–9. A recent film studies attempt to come to terms with different types of laughter can be found in Pomerance (2013). Focusing on cinematic laughter implies that we can ignore some types of laughter that occur only outside of the cinema. Think of laughter caused by tickling, laughing gas, alcohol, or sleep deprivation, but also the uncanny kind of laughter Prütting calls "phobos laughter," that is, the involuntary response to having barely survived one's own annihilation (Prütting, 2013, pp. 1817–18). Even among the kinds of laughter that can occur in the cinema I will restrict myself to those types that are directed at the *movie* or other *viewers* as members of the audience proper (and thus not to inattentive *mere present others*, as I defined them in Chapter 4). Laughing in *schadenfreude* about someone who stumbles in the dark and spills his 5-liter cup of popcorn does not interest me here; neither does the derisive laughter at a cinema-owner who introduces a famous Thai or French director and variously mispronounces the name in a funny way.
17. This is not the place to criticize Prütting's impressive achievement. Suffice it to say that for a scholar who has been working in the theater for many years he has a very strong tendency to tie interaction laughter tightly to eye contact, as if laughing in the dark cannot work as a form of interaction.
18. On the problem of drawing clear-cut boundaries between types of laughter, see also Seel (2002), p. 749.
19. Sontag (2009 [1964]), p. 275 (emphasis added).
20. The following section owes a great deal to Prütting's discussion of "geloiastic laughter" about the comic and ridiculous. Prütting himself builds on and modifies the theories of Laurent Joubert, Helmuth Plessner and Hermann Schmitz. See Prütting (2013), p. 1821ff.
21. Prütting (2013), p. 1560.
22. Plessner (1970 [1941]).
23. Prütting (2013), pp. 1506–7.
24. Prütting (2013), pp. 1507 and 1687.
25. Prütting (2013), p. 1491 (my translation).
26. This distinguishes laughter from cinematic fear, as fearful experiences do not always imply this safety from long-term effects. See Hanich (2014).
27. Prütting (2013), p. 1554.
28. See, for instance, Paul (1994) and Carroll (1999).
29. See also Prütting (2013), pp. 1865–6.
30. Following Nicolai Hartmann, Peter L. Berger and others, one can distinguish between the *sense of humor* on the subjective side and the *comic* on the objective side: the viewer's ability to find something funny and comic vs. the comic as a perceived quality of the object. See, for instance, Berger (2014).

31. Apart from the variously mentioned article by McCulloch on the reception of *The Room*, see also Cornea (2013).
32. Delluc (1988b [1918]), p. 160.
33. This laughter can also be read as an implicit laughing down on other people absent from the cinema but not involved in its making – and even a laughter about one's own self in the past. This is at least an interpretation suggested by Noël Burch. Discussing a number of early cinema comedies such as *Uncle Josh at the Moving Picture* (1902) and *How They Do Things on the Bowery* (1902), which show country bumpkins coming to the big city and making grave, sometimes fatal mistakes and thus making the more respectable (lower-) middle-class vaudeville audiences laugh about the warnings these films issue to people who have newly arrived in the city, Burch notes: "The cleverness of these warnings lies in the fact that they make vaudeville customers laugh at the expense of those they might once have been but no longer want to be, their cousins newly arrived from the country. By laughing at them the new citizens could feel that, by contrast, they were well integrated into urban life" (Burch, 1990, p. 117).
34. McLean (2013).
35. McLean (2013), p. 152.
36. For a joyful submission to complexity, see the late Gilberto Perez's response to his first viewing of Jean-Marie Straub/Danièlle Huillet's *History Lessons/Geschichtsunterricht* (1972): "People around me were walking out [. . .], and I certainly didn't understand everything, but I understood enough to be gripped. No one would dispute that Straub and Huillet's films are difficult, but it seems to me that what people find most difficult is giving up the notion that they have to understand everything" (Perez, 2016, p. 63).
37. McLean (2013), p. 145. Her laughter would have been a less aggressive, more warmhearted one if Aronofsky had winked at the more informed viewers that he is aware that they might consider his film as kitsch. It might have even created a bond. But this is not the case. *Black Swan* is not self-aware kitsch. McLean (2013), p. 144.
38. Chuck Kleinhans points out that for people with "high-culture tastes or backgrounds, [such films] can be received as total parodies. It is especially easy for media people (who can spot the formal clichés that underline the content conventions) to do so. But these films function in a different way with the general mass audience: spectators are engrossed by the situation and the exaggeration simultaneously" (Kleinhans, 1994), p. 184).
39. Stern (1974), p. 493 (my translation).
40. Canudo (1988 [1911]), pp. 63–4.
41. Weber (2004), p. 39.
42. In a slightly different context, Laura Mulvey also wrote about this understanding laughter: "This reaction marks the gap between the unselfconscious 'I see' and the self-consciousness of '*I see!*' The audience reacts as it might to gags or jokes, for which decoding is not essential to the very process of understanding but also involves a similar moment of detachment, a moment, that is, of self-conscious deciphering" (Mulvey, 2006, p. 149).
43. Fuller/Skefffington (1974), p. 534.
44. Matt Hills discusses several forms of intertextuality and types of pleasure connected to them (Hills, 2005, pp. 182–97).
45. Prütting (2013), p. 1710.
46. Note that the notion of deixis should not be understood as a purely linguistic category here. Instead, I follow Beata Stawarska's more extended use of deixis: "it denotes a social and corporeal expertise, which harnesses and mobilizes our abilities to orient in a shared spatial environment using the repertoire of available perceptual skills" (Stawarska, 2009, p. 57).

47. Sobchack (1999), p. 242.
48. On recognition, see the famous Hegel-inspired study by Honneth (1995).
49. Bergson (1914 [1900]), p. 197.
50. Prütting (2013), p. 1866.
51. See also Prütting (2013), pp. 1537–9 and 1645–7.
52. Roselt (2005), p. 227.
53. Hill (1997), p. 29.
54. Plantinga (2009), p. 97.
55. Prütting (2013), p. 1888. See also Plessner: "Only by self-control can we continue to be disinterested spectators in the presence of genuine laughing" (Plessner, 1970 [1941], p. 56).
56. Here, I think, we are not far from explaining the function of the laughter track in TV sitcoms, but this is another problem I cannot address here.
57. Bazin (1967b [1951]), p. 121.
58. Zijderveld (1982), p. 75.
59. Kimmel (1998), pp. 178 and 181.
60. Bazin (1967a [1948]), pp. 146–7.
61. Röcke/Velten (2005), p. xv.
62. Vidor obviously overstates the identicalness of the viewers' responses somewhat for rhetorical reasons. He tries to make a point about the loss of individuality in the lonely crowd of the modern big city.
63. I interpret the *theater* audience in *The Crowd* as a stand-in for a laughing *cinema* audience. However, bearing in mind the distinction I offered between the collective experience of the theater and the cinema, we cannot take this analogy too far. As mentioned in Chapter 3, the live presence of the clown on stage introduces a crucial difference.
64. Prütting (2013), p. 1706.
65. Goffman (1959), p. 142.
66. Goffman (1959), p. 142.
67. Koeppen (2004 [1953]), p. 115 (my translation).
68. Rosenbaum (1995), p. 24.
69. Stern (1974), p. 497 (my translation).
70. Schröter (2002), p. 870.
71. Canudo (1988 [1911]), p. 63.
72. As Plessner puts it: "The laughing person is open to the world. The consciousness of elevation and standing out from the crowd [. . .] signifies at one and the same time detachment from the given situation and openness or flexibility. Disengaged in this way, man tries to engage others. And it is not a matter of chance that the outbreak of laughter begins immediately, more or less 'apoplectically,' and, as if to express the openness of the laugher, rings out into the world as he exhales" (Plessner, 1970 [1941], p. 115, translations slightly modified, J.H.).
73. Prütting (2013), p. 1440.
74. Horkheimer/Adorno (2002 [1944]), p. 112.
75. Cf. Prütting (2013), p. 1438.
76. Dreyfus/Kelly (2011), p. 212.
77. Dreyfus/Kelly (2011), p. 211.

CHAPTER 8

When Viewers Silently Weep: A Phenomenology of Cinematic Tears

A tear tickles in the dark. In dignified secrecy I rub it off my cheekbone with the tip of my finger.

Thomas Mann[1]

I. INTRODUCTION

In her book *Having a Good Cry*, Robyn Warhol describes the response of an almost forty-year-old lawyer watching Steven Spielberg's *Saving Private Ryan* (1998). The man is overwhelmed by a wave of patriotic nostalgia about a national past when "for the last time we all were together, behind one thing, fighting evil." At some point the lawyer feels that he is beginning to cry, something he almost never does outside the cinema: "A wave of sensation wells up from behind his breastbone to someplace in his head; his eyes begin to water, and if anyone were to speak to him, his voice would crack in answering, because of the tightness in his throat." Sitting among anonymous strangers the lawyer is thankful for what's so characteristic about the cinema: "He takes no pains to conceal his tears, because the signs of his crying are so faint, no one would see them. Especially in this darkened theater, he runs no risk of appearing effeminate."[2]

This passage is revealing for a number of reasons. For one thing, it lends evidence to Walter Benjamin's remark that in the cinema people, who are no longer moved or touched by anything in everyday life, learn to cry again.[3] In fact, the cinema is one of the foremost places for shedding tears in our culture, and movies, whether watched in the cinema or elsewhere, are regularly listed among the strongest triggers of tears. A psychological survey conducted in the UK, for instance, showed that British men and women ranked sad movie moments as the second-most frequent situation that made them cry.[4] What is more, Warhol's passage underlines the strong bodily effect of weeping: Although they usually develop more gradually and hardly ever hit you as suddenly as affective responses like shocks or laughter, tears force attention to specific regions of the body. Not least, we can sense from the passage that the lawyer is aware of his surroundings as a potential source of embarrassment or shame: The other viewers are taken as a, however vague, threat to his masculinity. At the same time, weeping in the cinema rarely strikes a communicative note but remains mostly silent; often it creates a 'cocoon' or 'bubble' around the tearful viewer. And still: The other viewers remain present in their own way, and this is only one of the reasons why weeping is so interesting for a study of the audience effect.[5]

In this chapter I am not detailing a causal theory of crying that explains *why* we cry in the cinema.[6] Nor will I be able to predict *when* a specific viewer weeps about a movie. There are substantial individual differences in crying proneness and frequency. These differences can depend on age, gender, genetic factors, personality, attitudes toward crying, socialization, and culture as well as the social setting. Physical reasons like hormone level, sleep deprivation, and neurological diseases can play a role just as much as psychological states like depression, anxiety, burnout, being in love, or homesickness. Stressful life events like suffering from a loss or a life-threatening disease can be factors just as much as substance abuse (alcohol, coffee, cocaine) and medication (antidepressants, oral contraceptives).[7] I will simply presume that in cases when viewers cry, we can identify common characteristics of their experience. In other words, I am interested in the phenomenology of crying and, particularly, how we feel our relationship to other viewers change when we realize that tears are welling up.

I begin by discussing a number of crucial features that characterize most cinematic weeping. But this chapter will also demonstrate that – comparable to the types of laughter discussed in Chapter 7 – it is useful to distinguish different kinds of weeping that come with sufficiently different experiences to set them apart. I call them *axiological* tears, *sentimental* tears, *personal-relevance* tears, *forced* tears, and *shared* tears. Furthermore, I will focus on the experience *during* the film and thus won't pay attention to cases when people start crying only afterwards: when walking toward the subway, in their cars, at home . . . It is a well-known fact that crying can be severed in time from its causing event and postponed to a later point, which may well have to do with the embarrassment of tears. This important topic deserves further research, but I cannot pursue it here.

More than in previous chapters, the phenomenological method could be vulnerable to charges of incompleteness. Just think of variations in gender, which current scientific studies take as universal: "Nearly 20 studies, which applied very different research methods, have all yielded evidence that women cry more frequently and more intensely than men," psychologist Ad Vingerhoets informs us.[8] Then again, differences in frequency and intensity do not necessarily compromise what my phenomenology reveals about the structural characteristics of cinematic weeping. Until we have convincing evidence that women *experience* their cinematic tears differently (not just more frequently and more intensely), I remain hopeful that my phenomenological descriptions will resonate with female readers as well.

II. SILENTLY TEARING UP: WEEPING VS. CRYING

Let us begin with an observation that is as commonplace as it is remarkable, and that years of observations in the field confirm just as much as anecdotal evidence from various sources: In Western cinemas viewers usually shed tears *silently*. One hardly ever encounters the strong communicative signals of conspicuous body movements, sighing, whining, wailing, or even spasmodic sobbing.[9] Viewers tend to hide their tearful response, a tendency particularly prevalent among male viewers. The screenwriter and literary critic Willy Haas once commented on the tears of his friend Franz Kafka: "I can still see Kafka in front of me like that: his face averted, lest one of us observe him, wiping the tears from his eyes with the back of his hand."[10] Female filmmaker Lynne Tillman equally maintains: "I have learned to cry silently during movies."[11] Even though viewers can be strongly moved to tears, tears in the public space of the cinema are mostly an intimate matter. Even people with low crying thresholds do not openly cry out loud.

Outside the cinema, tears place a serious demand upon the environment because they seem to beg for a reaction.[12] Tears are so obviously there, they are so conspicuously communicating a significant emotional turmoil that those who see someone else cry are expected to act. This implies, in turn, whenever we have tears in our eyes, special attention is paid to us. Jack Katz has described in minute detail how crying works as an effective social interaction strategy used to elicit desired responses from others.[13] In the cinema, viewers renounce this communicative potential of tears. But just because acoustic crying, sighing, spasmodic sobbing, wailing, or whining rarely occur does not mean that weeping remains entirely inconspicuous: Viewers may have to swallow, tremble their lips, move down in their seat, lower their head, and shield parts of their face. They sniffle quietly, pull out their handkerchiefs inconspicuously, hide the moistness of their eyes by blinking back their tears, and wipe their cheeks with the tip of their finger, like Thomas Mann in the epigraph. In Katz's description we can sense the balancing act this can imply: if one does *not* wipe away one's tears, they may become too prominent and draw attention to oneself, but "if one *does* wipe the tears away, or clear the throat as a prophylaxis against breaking out into a more audible sob, one's attempt to stay in the background itself risks being seen."[14]

Yet doesn't the fact that people attempt this balancing act precisely indicate their lack of communicative intention?[15] Following Arthur Koestler, I therefore suggest a semantic distinction between weeping and crying, terms I have used interchangeably thus far: "*Weeping* has two basic reflex-characteristics which are found in all its varieties: the overflow of the tear-glands and a specific form of breathing. [. . .] *Crying*, on the other hand, is the emitting of sounds signaling distress, protest, or some other emotions. It may be combined with, or alternate with, weeping."[16] Although this distinction might not accurately map onto ordinary language use, it will serve us as a helpful heuristic: By definition, weeping does not emit conspicuous sounds, and we therefore rarely cry when we have a 'good cry' at the movies.[17] Note, however, that it is not always clear whether the silence of our tears depends on an active act of *inhibiting* the more acoustic forms of crying or whether they are simply our *adequate response* to an event that needs no communicative signal to others.

This leads us to the important question of intersubjectivity and the audience effect of weeping: Why do viewers usually shy away from exposing their tears? Why do we shed tears silently even when we are *joyfully* moved to tears? What is it about the weeping experience that makes it so different from laughter, even though these two expressive responses have often been studied together (think of Alfred Stern, Helmuth Plessner, or Jack Katz)?

The reason why viewers do not engage in strong crying responses may simply be that extended instances of convulsive sobbing and whining are distracting: One's attention would be dragged away from the film and toward the act of crying itself. Silent *weeping*, instead, allows for a deeper and more ongoing emotional involvement with the film. Yet harking back to Warhol's lawyer, we also have to consider the emotions of embarrassment and shame, which many viewers experience when tears well up too conspicuously, as another crucial motive to avoid crying. (In the following I won't make a conceptual distinction between the two emotion terms embarrassment and shame: In my account they merely designate different intensities, comparable to anger and rage in the chapter hereafter.)

III. A DETACHING-INDIVIDUALIZING EFFECT (I): EMBARRASSMENT AND SHAME

In Western culture adult crying is predominantly a private phenomenon and rarely occurs in face-to-face social interactions. As Vingerhoets points out, "in the majority of cases (75%), people cry at home, with either no one (37%) or just one person (29%) present" (in the remaining 9 per cent of the cases there are two or more persons around).[18] The public display of tears is limited to a few occasions like funerals, award ceremonies, or sport events. Apart from these instances, public crying results in – or is at least threatened by – embarrassment or even shame. Shedding tears in the anonymous, alien crowd of the cinema is no exception. Even if some people talk about it quite frankly in retrospect, during the film cinematic tears remain a secretive secretion.

In Herbert Blumer's famous Payne Fund studies we find colorful evidence for this claim. A nineteen-year-old, female college sophomore, for example, admits: "As soon as an event occurs which is the least bit sad my throat chokes up and very often I shed tears; I have never sobbed or made boisterous noises, thank goodness, for crying is a chief source of embarrassment with me; if I can get by with silent sorrow I feel all right." For a fourteen-year-old female high school sophomore, tears even spoil the pleasure of the film: "I don't like to cry because when you do and other people are not crying you appear conspicuous and this is not a pleasant feeling."[19] Some viewers therefore try to fight the embarrassment of weeping by pre-emptively striking a sarcastic pose. Lakshmi Srinivas, as we have seen, describes how male Indian viewers make derogative responses about viewers who cry.[20] Irony, joking, sarcasm – these are coping responses that try to keep tears at bay.[21]

But where do embarrassment and shame come from? Part of the answer has to do with the fact that tearing up implies a visible sign of losing control: It distorts our composed posture and literally defaces us. Moreover, weeping often does not only imply tears, but also the excretion of mucus, a bodily fluid considered repugnant. Even more importantly, tears are considered a physical indication of weakness and vulnerability. Film scholar Johnson Cheu notes: "For me, the act of crying, at least publicly, is not so much the fear of appearing feminine, as it is the fear of appearing vulnerable."[22] For people who think they have to appear strong and in control, the shedding of 'warm' tears is far from 'cool.' This feeling of vulnerability might well be connected to the fact that we literally soften up and *nolens volens* shed our hard-body shells – the expression "to dissolve in tears" underlines that a solid form makes way for a liquid one. Dreading the appearance of vulnerability goes for many male viewers, and male teenagers specifically, but women are not exempt either. Deborah Jermyn, for instance, has drawn attention to the reluctance of scholars to admit to their own weeping: "This reticence is arguably all the more keenly felt by female scholars, whose intellectual authority is even more likely to be undermined by such a 'feminine' display."[23]

Feeling embarrassed or ashamed has a pronounced intersubjective effect. Jack Katz has shown that the phenomenology of shame comes with the sense that one no longer belongs to a community but is – in fact or in imagination – negatively exposed in front of this group. Shame is defined by an experience of *individually standing out* and *being distanced or detached* from a group that seems to judge negatively.[24] When we feel embarrassed or ashamed, the other viewers are no longer considered as people we share an activity with, but they become an evaluating audience. Weeping discreetly, viewers therefore try to avoid the attention that would make them stand out.

However, even in covert weeping the sheer *threat* of embarrassment and shame is dangling over the viewer's head like the sword of Damocles because of the aforementioned body movements and sounds that come with it. Co-viewers are therefore to varying degrees present in consciousness, even if often only marginally. Embarrassment and shame can carry on even after the film has ended. Deeply moved viewers therefore tend to leave the auditorium quietly and discreetly, talking little, acting reclusively. Still wrapped in their own emotionality, they shun the potentially embarrassing gaze of others.

IV. A DETACHING-INDIVIDUALIZING EFFECT (II): THE SELF-CENTEREDNESS OF WEEPING

Yet the detaching-individualizing effect of weeping is not only connected to embarrassment and shame, but is deeply intertwined with emotions like *sadness* and *being moved* that precede or accompany weeping.[25] When viewers experience these emotions and break out in tears, they rarely open up to the world: They do not experience an action tendency to approach others, but instead are thrown back onto themselves, strongly focusing on the saddening or moving object and thus feel as if encapsulated in a bubble surrounding them (in adult weeping the communicative function is muted and this is especially so in the case of the cinema).

This description is in line with the account of a number of other scholars. Christoph Demmerling and Hilge Landweer, for instance, describe the phenomenology of sadness as constricting and enclosing: "The sad person 'locks him- or herself up,' 'seals him- or herself off' from the world, 'drowns' in sorrow. Strong forms of sadness lead to paralysis and a loss of drive."[26] This stands in marked contrast to the high activation and levitation tendency of happiness. Moving on to crying we find a similar position in Plessner, who has described the phenomenology of shedding tears as isolating, separating, secluding – a characterization certainly less accurate for communicative crying than for cinematic weeping.[27] And Jack Katz, not least, equally discovers a boundary between self and world during tearful moments: "Tears at times are part of *a self-embracing, self-protecting, self-isolating, and self-enclosing act* that withdraws one from pain or indignity. And at other times tears emerge in a kind of self-humbling act that creates *a respectful distance* from something sacred, exquisitely precious, overwhelmingly inspiring, or awesomely beautiful [. . .]."[28]

In this regard Bert O. States' observations about the experience of stage tragedies seem worthy of quoting as well: "Tragedy creates what could be called a magnificent *loneliness*, felt most deeply in the absolute stillness of the auditorium [. . .]. What the audience shares in such moments, and in the play at large, is less important than what *isolates* each spectator vicariously in the experience."[29] For States the laughter of the comedy is the dialectical opposite of the silence in tragedy: "the genre that produces laughter for its living is the most social of all the dramatic forms [. . .], just as tragedy is the most nonsocial, at least from the standpoint of emotional logic."[30] Hence what Sue Harper and Vincent Porter discovered in *male* cinema viewers in Britain after the Second World War sounds valid for most instances of weeping: "Men who found themselves on the verge of tears reported a sense of isolation from others in the audience."[31]

In Abbas Kiarostami's film *Shirin* (2008) we can find a visual equivalent of this phenomenological isolation from others: In a series of long takes the director shows us Iranian women (plus Juliette Binoche as the single non-Iranian actress) watching a melodrama in offscreen space that we never get to see. Kiarostami films these women almost exclusively alone in close-up, with the other viewers hidden in the dark.

We can find indications for the detaching-individualizing tendency even in the specific breathing patterns, body postures, and corporeal motions that come with adult silent weeping, especially when we look closer at the striking contrast between the inward-directed, individualizing characteristics of weeping with the outward-directed, communalizing features of laughing. While the breathing pattern of weeping consists in a series of gasping *in*-spirations, the breathing pattern of laughing is characterized by the exact opposite:

Figure 8.1: Juliette Binoche as an individualized, silently weeping viewer in Abbas Kiarostami's *Shirin*.

bursts of *ex*-piratory puffs. While in weeping the muscles go flabby and the bodily posture reflects a bodily escape from the outer into the inner world, laughter contracts the muscles and throws the body into violent motion, thus communicating an opening up to the exterior world.[32]

In weeping there is not only a felt *increase in distance* to the other viewers, but we can also observe a *breach of distance* to the object or act we weep about: in weeping we are deeply intertwined with an object or act that seems to press in on us.[33] When a film moves us to tears, we often feel hit with a special force deep down in our own identity.[34] In fact, we are moved at a level so intimate that it becomes hard to share it with others, even if they potentially undergo the same experience. In most cases of weeping, the film therefore seems to address me individually. Precisely because weeping is often a personal and intimate phenomenon, viewers rarely feel left alone when their co-viewers do not weep *with them*. Weeping solitarily is thus clearly different from laughing alone (for an exception, see the section on "forced tears" below; see also the part on "shared tears"). In fact, because we presume that this moment is personal and intimate for each viewer individually, we refrain from disturbing them and keep a respectful distance. Knowing about the communicative effect crying can have, we resort to silent weeping to avoid *dis*-tracting them.

But we also avoid *at*-tracting them. Silent tears quietly signal to others that there is *no need* to act on our weeping; we do not cry out for attention or even beg for help. And this may also be the case because we know that confronting other viewers with our tears can have an awkward or intimidating effect on them.[35] Personally, I always hesitate approaching people who shed tears in public: I feel strangely pushed and pulled at the same time, because I am unsure what these tears express.[36] While I want to respect the intimacy of their tearful experience, I simultaneously feel obliged to lend support.[37] As a consequence, in the cinema I am torn between realizing that the weeping stranger next to me may deserve my compassion as well as a respectful distance.[38]

No doubt the weeping of others can also spur more negative audience effects like being *angry* about the anti-immersive distraction coming from viewers who sniffle, rummage around in their bags in search of a tissue, or even blatantly cry. In an online forum on tears at the movies a spectator called Libby remembers watching *The Joy Luck Club* (1993): "The violins were coming up big time, and I was fighting with myself not to start really crying when, suddenly, I was distracted by the sound of the person behind me just sobbing; really, I was listening, deep into the film's story, and then I just hear this jagged intake of breath behind me and I'm out."[39] One can even feel *ashamed* of the tears of those one is closely connected to: A colleague once told me that her teenage son does not go to the movies with her anymore, not because he is ashamed to weep in front of his mother, but because of her tears, which he finds utterly embarrassing.

V. FIGHTING WITH TEARS: WEEPING AS EFFORTFUL DOING OR BEING DONE BY

The passages above should have indicated that I don't consider weeping as a simple bodily reflex that signals an emotion, but as a complex expressive behavior that makes the weeping person sensitive to the social surroundings (even if feeling simultaneously distanced as if in a personal bubble): "Crying provides rich evidence that it is an *effortful doing* that a person knowingly alters (which is not to say 'freely' alters) in response to variations in his or her context," Jack Katz points out.[40] For one, just like laughter, weeping in the cinema depends on my personal attitude towards tearing up: Do I resist with all my inner force the power of the movie by erecting a mental bulwark? Or do I allow myself to be overwhelmed easily by lowering, from the beginning, all thresholds of crying? I can decide to watch a film with a distanced, ironic, even cynical attitude; or I can approach it with a close, sentimental stance. Here, as elsewhere when it comes to weeping, metaphors of hardness and softness seem appropriate: If I *harden* up, tears won't easily break through my inner barrier; if I *soften*, I can more readily dissolve in weeping. Depending on one's viewpoint, one will call the former person stiff and cold-hearted or the latter a weakling and a softy.

In comparison to rather neutral affective states, the emotionally charged moments that lead up to an episode of weeping come with a growing inner bodily pressure: a gradual increase of lived-body tension.[41] In the cinema the build-up of this lived-body tension in most cases occurs gradually as the film follows an emotional trajectory of tension and relief. Particularly in contrast to laughing and screaming, most weeping is not characterized by a sudden onset; in the majority of cases it develops comparatively slowly with a longer duration: Laughter comes and goes – weeping comes and goes on; laughter resembles a *bursting explosion* – weeping equals a *melting erosion*.

In the cinema, tears only in very rare cases imply powerlessness over the body. As we have seen, even when viewers are deeply involved and strongly overwhelmed by their tears, they rarely undergo sudden crying attacks that convulsively shake their entire cramped and tense bodies. Hardly ever are they flooded by tears, break out in loud sobbing, and 'cry rivers.' Cinematic weeping predominantly comes in a much milder, softer, quieter, and more gradually developing form. A good indication is that viewers can often resist their tears (or at least try to do so), engaging in what Balduin Schwarz calls an "inner fight."[42] The *New York Times* describes the case of a sixty-two-year-old architect who considers himself a frequent crier but doesn't like other viewers to realize that he is shedding tears: "If he knows the movie is almost over and feels a sad scene coming on, he will take protective measures. 'I fight it back just so it won't happen,' he said. 'You force yourself to think about other things. You bite your tongue. It's painful, but it works.'"[43] Similarly, in an online forum a female viewer called Sonja admits that she has to "fight" her tears very strongly when she watches *Johnny Got His Gun* (1971): "I do not permit myself to cry – but once the camera shows Johnny lying in bed and we, the viewers, can hear him think, the emotional pressure starts. In fact, it does not stop throughout the whole film."[44]

Of course, not everyone is successful in winning this fight, nor would all viewers even want to resist the interior pressure of tearing up, as we will see below. When viewers watch a sad, pitiful, depressing, joyful, exhilarating, or beautiful scene and are emotionally captivated, tears seem to besiege them from within. Yet emotions can take possession of viewers forcefully without resulting in tears. When they watch a film they can usually fight back the surge of tears before they eventually give in and break down. Often, viewers have to release the hold of themselves in order to release a load of tears. Schwarz calls this an "inner act of letting go," and Plessner speaks of an "act of inner capitulation."[45] I therefore posit that there is often a certain willingness, a voluntary element, a readiness to surrender. (However, in some instances weeping can also take place more suddenly, overwhelming the viewer with an unexpected force, as when a viewer might be reminded of a personal incident and the sad or nostalgic memory is foregrounded vividly and all of a sudden; see the section on personal-relevance tears.)

Western cultures mostly take a strong self-composed masculine individual as the ideal – an individual who controls his or her behavior. The crying person contradicts this ideal, seemingly losing control, giving in to tears that distort the bodily and facial composure and (allegedly) 'cloud' rational thoughts. While it is obvious that we are dealing with an ideology of masculine self-control here (Schwarz decries it as "the ethos of the masculinity cramp"), this bias has real consequences.[46] The more one has interiorized this norm, the stronger one will fight back tears; the more one watches the film in a masculine context, the less likely one can enjoy what in section VII I call "the pleasure of tears."

VI. THE FOREGROUNDED BODY: VIEWERS' SELF-AWARENESS IN WEEPING

In weeping, viewers don't respond *through* a transparent, backgrounded body, as in affectively more neutral, unobtrusive moments of everyday conduct, but very much *with* a body that makes itself felt. Even more than in laughter, weeping spectators live through a remarkable corporeal transformation of a self-experience in which an otherwise "absent" body enters awareness.[47] Upon watching a sad or moving scene, viewers will be affected more or less with the entire lived-body, feeling 'enwrapped' in the emotional state, with an emphasis on the upper body. But once they are overwhelmed by – or give in to – tears the bodily experience becomes concentrated on very concrete areas: The eyes are overflowing with a bodily secretion; tears may be running down one's cheeks, wetting and warming the face. Oftentimes the nose becomes fluid as well, resulting in an urge to sniffle or to blow one's nose. People sometimes start breathing with a slightly open mouth in order to avoid rendering their unusual breathing patterns too obvious. The lips may start to tremble, and the throat can equally draw attention when swallowing all of a sudden becomes problematic (viewers say they "got very choked up").

Still, it would be entirely wrong to claim that in weeping we pay no more attention to the movie. The advantage of tears lies in their proximity to the central perceptual engagement of the movies: the act of viewing. Even if tears put a liquid film between us and the film, they are transparent enough, both in the metaphoric and the literal sense, to allow for a continuous engagement with what is happening onscreen. At the same time, it would be a mistake not to concede that weeping consumes parts of our attention, especially when the 'overflow' of tears and mucus is strong and the social context in the cinema puts a high intersubjective pressure on the spectators to hide their tears. Precisely because of this strong bodily awareness, weeping implies that viewers, to some degree, become aware of their response to the movie – that they are confronted with and give in to something powerfully emotional.[48] Tears thus put the exclamation mark of an external outpouring behind the internal turmoil of an emotional experience.

It is important to note that while viewers often experience their tearful affective episodes as highly *intensive*, they usually do not feel a strong *activation* of the body: When people are moved or touched, they describe their level of arousal as low and moderate at best.[49] We can best sense this decrease in action tendency when we compare it to the effects of other types of film. A film that makes us sad or moves us deeply does not make us feel light-hearted, as would be the case with a feel-good comedy à la *Sliding Doors* (1998), or tense up aggressively, like an 'adrenaline-fueled' action film of the *Fast and the Furious* (2001) kind.

VII. RELAXING, SOFTENING, EXPANDING: THE PLEASURE OF TEARS

No doubt, not everyone likes to cry. Yet for those who freely allow themselves to weep in the dark, tears can become a source of considerable pleasure, to which the proverbial expression "having a good cry" gives testimony. Crying can improve mood and bring relief, as Vingerhoets found out in a study with respondents from thirty-seven countries: "there was a high degree of consensus (over 70%) that crying generally helps us to feel better."[50] For the cinema this seems to be all the more valid: The sheer existence of melodramas or tear-jerking films – as a mainstream filmic genre that has generated high box-office incomes since the beginning of film history – seems to underline this point. As a female fan of *Titanic* (1997) put it: "It's so much better to cry because it makes the movie so much more enjoyable."[51] The author Laura Nathan-Garner likewise admits to feeling "renewed" when tearing up during a film.[52] Even an otherwise controlled writer like Thomas Mann once described how, after a movie, he stood together with a group of friends "with moist eyes in a fatuous relaxed state."[53] In a recent psychological study, which asked twenty-five viewers to provide self-selected film-clips that had moved them to tears in the past, the majority of participants immediately after the testing session reported that they felt greatly relieved and had enjoyed the experience.[54] Hence it is fair to say that, in the cinema, many viewers do not only weep 'because of' but also 'in order to': they intend to enjoy the pleasure that comes with weeping.[55]

But where exactly does this pleasure reside? For Balduin Schwarz the feeling of pleasantness has to be located in the *relief* from inner pressure that comes with painful forms of crying.[56] If we followed Edmund Burke's distinction between pleasure and delight, crying would have to be called a form of delight: it would not be pleasurable in and of itself – enjoyable would be the release from an unpleasant state.[57] This seems to hold true for strong types of crying with a forceful perturbation of the body. But in episodes of the more common quiet and soft type of cinematic weeping the pleasure of tears lies elsewhere: in the lived-body's tendency to dissolve, soften, grow warm, and expand.[58] When a person dissolves into tears, the lived-body gives up its cool, tense, hardened state required by daily life in general and masculinity specifically and acquires a momentary state of softness and warmth.[59] Gisela Berkenbusch has aptly described tear-jerkers as "fictional softeners" (*fiktionale Weichmacher*).[60] In order to appreciate the softening effect of weeping, we do not have to believe the problematic talk of the "healing powers" of tears. The softening and warming of the lived-body simply provides a pleasurable feeling that is not unlike the softening feeling one experiences when getting a relaxing facial massage (which, again, distinguishes the softer, milder cinematic weeping from the more convulsive crying, which can be very exhausting). Moreover, as tears flow, the viewer seems to be freed from a pressing constriction (or tension) and starts to experience a feeling of lived-body expansion. Hermann Schmitz even talks about a "flight from constriction into expansion."[61] It is this transformation of the lived-body from a tight, cool, and tense state into a soft, warm, and expanded one that makes weeping at the movies so pleasurable.[62]

Yet don't these softening, warming, and expansive tendencies accompany at least some kinds of everyday weeping as well? Sure. But in most cases we cannot experience them as fully and enjoyably as the tears of aesthetic experiences. First, in non-cinematic weeping our personal existence is often too intricately interwoven with the cause and the emotions that we give in to. Crying over the death of my grandfather is not enjoyable because I suffer from an actual great loss, whereas the death of Bambi's mother remains comparatively harmless due to her fictional status. Second, aesthetic experiences are free from responsibilities to act.[63] When Jack Dawson (Leonardo DiCaprio) drowns onscreen in *Titanic*, we can enjoy our weeping because there is no chance for us to intervene. Third, we can enjoy even the ambivalent tears caused by movies running counter to our moral convictions because aesthetic distance grants us a certain leeway in terms of moral evaluation: We do not have to be morally outraged as much as in real life because we know that the depiction is merely fictional. And, not least, unlike everyday weeping, tears in the cinema are finite and pre-packaged: they are not only available 'on demand,' but the length and the intensity of our involvement can be more or less foreseen.

But, importantly, weeping in the cinema is not all the same. In the remainder of this chapter I will therefore distinguish five predominant types of cinematic tears according to how viewers experience them.

VIII. A PHENOMENOLOGICAL TYPOLOGY OF CINEMATIC WEEPING

1. Axiological tears: weeping as value response

The general characteristics of cinematic weeping I have discussed thus far inform and define the first specific type. I reserve the term *axiological tears* for it as they refer to moral and aesthetic values. Since axiological tears are arguably the most widespread type in the cinema, I posit them as the standard from which all other types of cinematic weeping deviate in one way or another.

Axiological tears are an intuitive value response of my body to the aesthetic object: the film. When I feel deeply saddened, touched, or moved by a film and shed axiological tears, my weeping body responds to positive moral and aesthetic *values* I find expressed in and by the film, values that seem highly positive yet at the same time precarious, rare, ephemeral to me. To be more precise, I, through my body, react to precarious positive values that I *personally* perceive as expressed via the *form-content qualities* of the film. Whether other viewers also perceive these values and find them worthy of tears is not crucial here – it is *in me* that they intimately resonate. When I shed axiological tears I discover positive values such as compassion, care, generosity, goodwill, beauty; I respond to something I find awe-inspiring, elevating, wonderful, grandiose, cute, beautiful, rare, etc. In short, I weep about something I intuitively judge, in one way or another, as significant and meaningful. This corresponds to what Milena Kuehnast and her colleagues found out about the emotion of being moved, both in its sad and joyful variants.[64] As mentioned in Chapter 5, Cova and Deonna also consider being moved as a response to positive values central to us, made salient often against a negative background.[65] When weeping we do not simply respond emotionally to these positive values, but our body gives a specific weight to our emotional response. Weeping, as a rare act in adult life, is a particularly valuable value response: It honors what we find worthy *of* tears *with* tears.

Importantly, how we judge the degree these positive values have been *realized* in the filmic world influences the valence of our axiological tears: Upon appraising the positive values as threatened, unrealizable, or lost, I feel *sadly* moved to tears; when I feel *joyfully* moved to tears I judge the positive values unexpectedly confirmed, often against all the odds. Although joyfully being moved to tears is often overlooked in discussions of cinematic weeping, it is no less important.[66] Viewers shed axiological tears over the death of the beautiful heroine (in *Love Story*, 1970) and the unlikely rise of the working-class hero (in *Rocky*, 1976), over two lovers parting at the airport (in *Casablanca*, 1942) and families reunited after a long separation at an air base (in *Armageddon*, 1998).

What is more, in axiological tears my response is an answer to these positive values *as such*. Balduin Schwarz also speaks of a "pure value response" (*reine Wertantwort*).[67] When I shed tears over the deeply moving beauty of Terrence Malick's *Days of Heaven* (1978) and *The New World* (2005) or the remarkable prosocial acts of communal homage and parental love in films like *Imitation of Life* or *After the Wedding*, I respond to these values as such: they do not have a specific personal relevance *for me*, even if they simultaneously resonate very deeply *in me*. In its *pure* form, axiological weeping means being directed to form-content qualities that let shine forth values of an ethical and/or aesthetic nature for me in a very concentrated and pregnant way.[68] It is therefore useful to make a distinction between an *intimate resonance* and a *personal relevance*: The beautiful prosocial act of a character in the film *intimately resonates* in me, because it touches me deeply to see how these characters care for each other, but its *personal relevance* is not strong enough to propel me simultaneously into remembering or imagining something vividly, as it is characteristic of personal-relevance tears, discussed later. Of course, this distinction cannot always be a neat one. Still, as we shall see further below, personal-relevance tears have a distinct phenomenology, because other mental acts like remembering and imagining are foregrounded, and we become aware of them, at least to some degree.

For some it might sound overly commonsensical, but it seems important to remind ourselves that we do not simply weep about what Alfred Stern calls the "precarious character of our highest values" (the content).[69] Our weeping also depends on *how* the precariousness of these values is presented to us (the form). Content and form are intertwined in such extremely intricate ways in a film that it would be preposterous to deal with them in mere passing here. Suffice it to say that we can glean the significance of form from the simple fact that the various manifestations of a standard scene – think of a character delivering the sad news to another character that a loved one has died – can move viewers to astonishingly different degrees.[70] This is why I use the formulation that our weeping responds to the values expressed via the *form-content qualities* of the film.

But if axiological weeping is indeed a value response, why don't we want to make our evaluating act more public? Alfred Stern has argued that humans like to impose their personal hierarchies of values, and the preceding chapter has shown that this can certainly be the case for the evaluating response of laughter. Given that we pay homage to positive values, why don't we display these tears more prominently through audible forms of sobbing and crying in order to give it the proper recognition? And given that weeping can imply a display of our sensitivity to the plight of others or to morally beautiful acts, why do we hesitate to make them more proudly available, comparable to the connoisseur laughter we have discovered in Chapter 7? Stern answers that we are ashamed of weeping in public because it sometimes reveals what is most *intimate* about our personality.[71] This can clearly be the case when films touch upon private memories or imaginations, as we shall see in the section on personal-relevance weeping. But what is so intimate about one's value judgment of, say, a prosocial act of moral beauty in a social melodrama like Ken Loach's *I, Daniel Blake* (2016)?

I claim that *silent* weeping is an adequate response also because it does not corrupt the integrity of the moment; we show proper respect to values we honor with tears by leaving the situation intact for everyone. Here we also find a further reason for the embarrassment and shame that can come with crying. As we have heard, many scholars, including me, easily admit *in writing* and *after the fact* that they have wept in the cinema. This raises the question of why they do not feel embarrassed to admit publicly to their readers – with a certain detachment and even pride – what during the film is threatened by embarrassment and shame. My answer is that in the cinema viewers fear the shame of diverting the audience's attention away from the scene and toward themselves. Honoring the moment also implies *not* drawing too much attention egotistically to oneself, especially because the honored values are often prosocial ones like compassion or care.[72]

Now, this all seems very much the case also for the often-ignored moments when we are *joyfully* moved to tears. When people shed joyful axiological tears they are not flat-out happy. "Something negative is appreciated in joyful crying," Katz notes.[73] While they seem outright positive at first sight, in joyful moving instances a negativity flashes up in the midst of positivity, and this negativity derives precisely from the fleetingness, ephemerality, fragility, or scarcity of the moment. Katz accordingly emphasizes "singularity as a subtheme in joyful forms of crying."[74] It is not the mundane, widespread, and normal, but the *singularly* beautiful, moving, sublime, awe-inspiring, or elevating that moves us to joyful tears. What is moving, for instance, about the heroic self-sacrifice of a character in a disaster movie is not only its prosocial valuation of the community over individual interests, but also its exceptional character – were it a routine act, it wouldn't move us.

In addition, in many cases of joyful weeping viewers experience a relief from hardships, a liberation from strife overcome, a disappearance of anxiety. Just think of the lovers that are finally united at the happy ending. The relief viewers experience is paralleled – as it were, mimetically – in the relaxation of the body that comes with tears: We honor the relief with a relieving response of the body.

Developing an argument by Alfred Stern, we could claim that joyful axiological tears express a *positive* value judgment about the unexpected realization of a value particularly significant to us, and at the same time a *negative* value judgment about the precariousness and ephemerality of this positive value.[75] This stands in contrast to explosive joy, where we live entirely in the moment and the fragility of the value does not affect our emotion: "it is perfectly appropriate to feel joy at rather shallow events, like finding money in the street, the rain ceasing, or victory in a video-game. Joy can be [. . .] light or superficial. By contrast, there is no such thing as being 'lightly' moved," Cova and Deonna note.[76] The values we respond to with our joyful tears have a gravity and depth – they cannot be unimportant and superficial. Consider also the difference in phenomenology: In joy we feel light and unburdened and have an action tendency to open up and embrace the world.[77] In contrast, we usually remain enwrapped in joyful weeping, insisting on the intimacy of the experience, even if viewers might feel a greater openness to intimate others and start holding hands or even embracing each other. Joyful axiological tears in the cinema therefore do not correspond to the conspicuous collective outbursts of laughing together.

2. Sentimental tears: the guilty pleasure of weeping

Phenomenologically, there is a felt difference between the deeply moving experiences of the previous type and what I want to call *sentimental tears*.[78] We find this difference well articulated in a quote by Robyn Warhol in which she describes how warm tears sometimes overcome her *even though* she knows the film is based entirely on tried-and-tested clichés and *even though* she considers herself a critical viewer doing research precisely on such "manipulative" formulas: "I ought to be immune to the kind of manipulations the film depicts, if a critical awareness of formulaic effects is any defense against their power over audiences. [. . .] And yet tears roll out from under my glasses and down my cheeks, requiring me to wipe my eyes surreptitiously so that my husband sitting next to me, will not see how easily, indeed how ludicrously, I can be made to cry." She recognizes that her tears do not derive from a genuine feeling, but are based on a familiar narrative formula – and this happens even despite her efforts to defuse the power of this formula by analyzing and even ridiculing it. "And yet for me – and I assume for other viewers who habitually cry at the movies – something about the physical appeal of having a good cry transcends the film's cynicism and even my own."[79]

This passage contains four crucial characteristics of sentimental tears. (1) In moments of sentimental weeping viewers are – to varying degrees – aware that they are shedding tears over something they personally evaluate as sentimental or even kitschy (I use the term *kitsch* to designate more intensive forms of *sentimentality*). (2) Viewers experience a self-reflective conflict between their personal evaluation and the tears they shed all the same, because the act of weeping seems to valorize something that does not 'deserve' one's precious tears. (3) Hand in hand with this conflict between ego and superego (in Freudian terms) goes a however mild feeling of shame or guilt. (4) Nevertheless, viewers let themselves be overwhelmed by – or give in to – tears because they appreciate the bodily pleasure of a 'good cry.' The familiar term *guilty pleasure* nicely captures this experience: Somehow it does not feel right to dignify the film with our tears – and still . . .

Following Ludwig Giesz, I do not consider sentimentality or kitsch as qualities of the filmic *object*, but as a subjective act of consciousness: a spectator's experience that *can*, but does not have to be, accompanied by sentimental tears. And this experience can certainly also occur in relation to what others widely hail as art: While many viewers consider Terrence Malick's *To the Wonder* (2012) or Jean-Pierre Jeunet's *Amélie/Le fabuleux destin d'Amélie Poulain* (2001) as great art, others debunk it as sentimental; and while some critics would denounce Isabel Coixet's *My Life Without Me* (2003) or Derek Cianfrance's *The Light Between Oceans* (2016) as pure tear-jerking kitsch, others experience it as deeply moving and worthy of axiological tears. However, when viewers go through an episode of sentimental weeping they do sense a conspicuous contradiction between an ideal how-it-should-be and the actual sentimental or kitschy how-it-is: There is a tendency toward an overload, a too-much, a synaesthetic oversaturation. The aesthetic object seems obtrusive and importunate. Numerous scholars have therefore characterized the experience as sweet, sticky, or saccharine.[80] At the same time there is an awareness of a highly unambiguous, unsubtle form and style. According to Clement Greenberg, "Kitsch is mechanical and operates by formulas."[81] And in the words of Leslie Jamison: "the tropes are too easy, the narrative too predictably mannered, [. . .] the language cloying rather than fresh."[82]

Let me emphasize again that in sentimental weeping the viewers *themselves* experience the movie as sentimental or kitschy.[83] We therefore have to distinguish it from a different phenomenon. Think of instances when viewers are genuinely moved, but simultaneously sense that their co-viewers in the cinema (or other absent but imagined spectators) may evaluate the film as sentimental or kitschy. Here, too, the viewers fight out a self-reflective conflict, but this time between the viewer's judgment and the judgment of others which seems to stand for the cultural norm. In this case the opposition does not take place, so to speak, between *self and self*, but plays out between *self and other*. The viewer may also experience shame or guilt here, but he or she may also insist proudly on his or her aesthetic judgment against the cultural norm.

Just think of differences in cultural prestige between media and art forms, a point raised by Deborah Jermyn. While playing a scene from *Sex in the City* (1998–2004) during a class on American quality television, Jermyn feels that it's somehow wrong to out herself "as someone who cries at TV": "Perhaps it's permissible for theater lecturers to wipe a few tears away at Cordelia's death in *King Lear*, or for a music professor to need a moment after sharing Mozart's Requiem with a group. After all, these are fine artistic accomplishments which must be analyzed in terms of their power to move their audiences. But crying during a TV Studies class?"[84] We may also think of the discrepancies in cultural capital between genres and filmic modes. Not a few male viewers resent tear-jerkers and women's weepies.[85] But there are other genres and filmic modes – recent scholarship describes them as "male weepies" – which allow them to shed a tear or two: sports films like *Invictus* (2010), but also certain war films (*Saving Private Ryan*) and disaster movies (*Deep Impact*, 1998) come to mind.[86] Moreover, the respectability of the director and the filmic mode might grant a certain leeway as well. It is certainly easier for male viewers to cry in response to the melodramatic art cinema of Lars von Trier (*Breaking the Waves*, 1996), Pedro Almodóvar (*All About My Mother/Todo sobre mi madre*, 1999), or Wong Kar-wai (*In the Mood for Love*, 2000) than to a classical women's weepie like King Vidor's *Stella Dallas* (1937).

So far I have indiscriminately talked about embarrassment and shame, on the one hand, and guilt, on the other hand. But maybe we should introduce a rough heuristic here. Above, I have claimed that we shed axiological tears over the positive values we perceive expressed in the film via its form-content qualities. In sentimental tears we feel *embarrassed* because we weep despite the *form*; or we feel *guilty* because we weep regardless of the *content*. On the one hand, in sentimental weeping we may feel embarrassed or ashamed about being overwhelmed and even manipulated by the stereotypical scenes and clichéd formulas – in short, the *deplorable aesthetics* – that Robyn Warhol talks about. We consider these scenes as 'cheap' because they do not demand a high artistic 'investment' from the filmmakers, and our own psychological and cognitive 'costs' are inadequately low. On the other hand, we may experience guilt because we are weeping sentimental tears despite the fact that the scene plays with female stereotypes or racist clichés and thus disseminates a *questionable ideology*.[87]

We therefore look down on our own sentimental weeping: Our tears devalue – as it were, inflationarily – genuinely axiological tears and the positive values they pay tribute to. Moreover, while our aesthetic and moral disagreement remains concealed, our tears seem to signal agreement. However, in comparison to *laughing* indecently with a guilty conscience about a racist or misogynist joke, an expression that equally makes a wrong value judgment, sentimental tears are less directly available to others.

This is why tear scholars like Schwarz have recommended a "repressive calm" that counters a "feeblish devotion" to objects that cannot legitimately ask for our tearful dedication.[88] But this might not always be easily achieved. In Robyn Warhol's quote above we sense a power that overcomes her forcefully despite her critical weaponry: Unable to resist the movie's manipulative tactics, she feels defenseless, abandoning herself to pleasurable tears. And even those who would be able to resist, in moments of sentimental weeping freely give in to their tears or even force them to flow. Why? They do so because guilty pleasure is a form of pleasure after all – even though these tears do not feel quite right, they feel so right at the same time. At least for some viewers sentimental weeping comes down to a pleasurable lived-body experience with its tension-and-relief structure and the relaxing quality inherent to it: Bathing in sentimental pathos is also, in some ways, like or receiving a relaxing facial massage.

Is the philosopher Konrad Paul Liessmann correct, then, when he claims that the kitsch experience must be Immanuel Kant's nightmare because everything resembles the "charm and emotion" Kant rejects, effectively invalidating an aesthetic judgment?[89] When it comes to the sentimental tears at stake here, this seems wrong to me: In sentimental weeping, viewers *know* precisely that their tears are not appropriate, but they engage in it anyway because of the bodily pleasure that comes with it.

As indicated, shedding sentimental tears can come with strong audience effects. While tears are often described as the only bodily fluid that does not evoke disgust, in their sentimental form they can elicit a considerable amount of *distaste* among entirely cool and calm viewers who are able to somehow perceive the warm, sentimental tear flow of others next to them. Following Robert Solomon, we can locate one reason for the ensuing distanced I–you antagonism in a general distaste for emotions, especially of the 'sweet' and 'softer' kind: "feeling 'cuddly' just isn't 'cool'."[90] But the resentment might also be directed more concretely at the value judgments expressed by these tears: "Tears, even if they are common, are still precious, and their production appears to be inevitably linked to claims about what is precious in life or in one's own nature," Jack Katz notes.[91] This is the reason why some viewers sneer at the 'false' or 'cheap' tears of others.

But isn't this entirely elitist? Not necessarily. It is one thing to question someone else's first-person experience: If viewers feel indeed deeply moved to tears by *Gone with the Wind* (1939), *Titanic*, or *The Notebook*, one cannot deny that at that moment they shed axiological tears.[92] Since they don't wage the self-reflective conflict between their personal evaluation of something as sentimental and the tears they shed, these viewers experience their tears as genuine axiological ones and not as sentimental tears. It is something else, however, to disagree, from a critical perspective, with what these viewers consider worthy of tears: If someone sheds seemingly genuine axiological tears over fake values, this can become a matter of legitimate dispute. The other person's axiological tears may therefore very well be called sentimental from a third-person perspective.

Following the heuristic distinction between shame and guilt I proposed above, one could consider the sentimental tears of one's neighbor as either embarrassing or blameworthy. In the former case, one's negative response relates to the embarrassing shedding of tears over *cheap aesthetics*; in the latter case, one's critical stance refers to weeping despite a *false ideology*. The former derives from a difference in aesthetic evaluation manifesting itself in the absence and presence of tears, and here connoisseur snobbery can play a major role. In his defense of sentimentality Solomon therefore points out that one "should be suspicious about the depth of class prejudices underlying even the most abstract aesthetic argument and the extent to which the charge of 'sentimentality' is in fact an attack on unsophisticated taste."[93] Solomon is sensitive to the ambiguity of the word "cheap," which connotes both low aesthetic quality and low socioeconomic status.[94] Similarly, Leslie Jamison points to a fear of commonality, a fear that our feelings could resemble those of everyone else (especially those, one may add, that we consider 'lower' than ourselves): "This is why we want to dismiss sentimentality, to assert instead that our emotional responses are more sophisticated than other people's [. . .]."[95]

However, one's neighbor's tears can also be interpreted as a blameworthy sign of falling for (or being unaware of) problematic ideologies. Viewers who weep about *Gone with the Wind*, *Titanic*, or *The Notebook* can be charged with blinding themselves to the problematic race, class, and gender representations of these films in favor of a pleasurable upsurge of tears. Ludwig Giesz therefore points out the one-sided "genius of the kitschy eye": discovering only the moving aspects while simultaneously veiling everything negative, thus de-demonizing life.[96]

And while it is hard to imagine that someone would respond with the angry, even aggressive reactions we will hear about in the following chapter when realizing that another person is silently weeping, ironic or even sarcastic comments about sentimental tears as an inappropriate response may well take place.

3. Personal-relevance tears: weeping over memories and imaginations

When viewers shed what I call *personal-relevance tears* they not only *perceive* the film audiovisually, but simultaneously engage in another act of consciousness: They also *remember* or *imagine*. Their relation to the film is therefore of a different kind, as the viewers' perceptions of the film are complemented and suffused with mental visualizations of past or future events, whose vividness and concreteness varies and thus may dominate the film experience to various degrees. The values expressed via the form-content qualities of the filmic object do not merely resonate intimately (as in axiological tears), but have a strong personal relevance for the viewer. In a recent article Winfried Menninghaus and I spoke of a *reality* and a *possibility* mode respectively. In the first case, the viewer is reminded of what *was*; in the second case, the spectator imagines or daydreams about what *could* or *will happen*.[97] In both cases the film is not the only intentional object, and the tears flow as a result of the intricate interplay between perception and memories/imaginations that have a strong personal relevance.[98]

Consider these two drastic examples that I will use to make my point particularly obvious. A first viewer may be reminded of a personal loss *in the concrete past*, because in the previous month his mother has died and now he is confronted with a very similar scenario when watching *Terms of Endearment* (1983). While he sees Emma Greenway-Horton (Debra Winger) talking to her sad children in the hospital, he 'sees,' through his teary eyes, scenes with his own mother pass in front of his 'mental eye.' A second viewer imagines a scenario *in the potential future*, because, just like the character in *My Sister's Keeper* (2009), he knows that his sister has been diagnosed with cancer and will die soon. He is either passively drawn to these thoughts or actively initiates them. In either case, they are mentally 'superimposed' on the moving images on the screen.

There is ample evidence that we are dealing with a widespread phenomenon here. For instance, in Blumer's early study on movie effects the sociologist found out that sometimes a film is "intimately linked" to an individual's "personal career" and thereby evokes tears. Blumer quotes a twenty-year-old college sophomore whose parents divorced when she was young: "It is almost impossible for me to feel no desire to cry, when I see a movie in which the break-up of a home is featured or where the results of such a break are the subject of the play."⁹⁹ In an experimental study, the psychologist Thalia Goldstein similarly showed that participants whose own parents had divorced reacted with a greater degree of sadness to *Kramer vs. Kramer* (1979), a film about divorce.¹⁰⁰ Last but not least, the influence of strong *imaginations* can be gleaned from a letter of a San Quentin inmate who admits, after a prison screening of the sentimental Frank Capra movie *It's a Wonderful Life* (1946), that the film has sparked a "silent reflection" of his loved ones at home.¹⁰¹

It goes beyond the scope of my investigation to decide whether personal experiences *always and necessarily* are causally connected to our tears. It is possible that *unconscious* memory processes often or even always influence our response. For my phenomenological typology of weeping, taking a standpoint on this question is not crucial, because there is an obvious experiential difference between moments when we weep and *consciously* remember or imagine, and instances when *unconscious* memories may have influenced our tears. What would merit a more in-depth empirical investigation, though, is my hunch that particularly vivid memories and imaginations can lead to a more intense and abrupt welling up of tears: the higher the personal relevance and the less purely axiological the tears, the more likely it is that weeping turns into crying.¹⁰² Feeling strongly reminded of a recent loss can even push the aesthetic experience completely to the margins and an episode of personal sorrow takes over. Finally, we should not overlook that apart from the *negative* memories and imaginations in most examples above, *positive* thoughts can equally lead to tears. Joyful personal-relevance tears can flow, for instance, when viewers imagine the imminent birth of their first child upon seeing the beautiful (if sometimes painful) images of Stan Brakhage's *Window Water Baby Moving* (1959) or remember a glorious real-life sports victory in such patriotic films as *Das Wunder von Bern/The Miracle of Bern* (2003) or *The Miracle* (2004).

4. Forced tears: the imperative to expose one's weeping

In Chapter 7 I mentioned moments when viewers actively *laugh along with others*. Analogously, in the cinema viewers may feel that they have to produce tears, that they should show the strong emotional response of weeping to their immediate neighbors (I say "immediate neighbors" because the signal usually seems to remain one of oblique weeping rather than conspicuous crying). Here it is not the film that asserts a 'pressure' to weep, but the viewer's immediate social surroundings that 'push' him or her to weep. While prima facie this type of weeping might seem to be a response to the film, it actually depends on an audience effect. And again, as in laughing, when one feels an imperative to weep, this can be a sign of *conformity* as well as *solidarity*.

Let us look at the *compliant* act of weeping along with others first. As Jack Katz points out: "Quite often, when people cry they have reason to anticipate that if they *don't* cry, their perspectives will be misconstrued, or at least construed to their disadvantage."[103] Lest you want to be accused of being cold-hearted or unimpressionable, you may have to shed tears with the other weeping viewers around you. In order not to stand out awkwardly you, too, want to express care, compassion, or deep appreciation of something overwhelmingly moving – with your tears.

What could, in turn, be incentives to force one's tears not in conformity but in *solidarity*? First, you might think that your companion strongly expects you to *share an emotion*. Since you know that this film is your best friend's favorite melodrama you may want to give her the pleasure of a shared emotional evaluation by forcing yourself to shed a (somewhat conspicuous) tear or two, even though you don't find the film as moving as she does. Likewise, one may also feel compelled to weep in order to create what in Chapter 6 I have called an instance of *feeling together*. Consider a female viewer who assumes that her male companion, who seems truly enraged by a sad and harrowing scene of political injustice, wants her to *care* about this scene as well and therefore thinks that he expects a gender-appropriate act of weeping to validate the scene appropriately.

Ad Vingerhoets notes that the special power of crying derives from the fact that "more than any other kind of emotional expression, it is regarded as an *honest* display of very intense emotion."[104] This is, again, why we respond so disappointedly to 'crocodile tears' and 'sentimental tears' – tears that are perceived as insincere. Paradoxically, the imperative to show genuine tears can be felt so powerfully that some people go as far as *faking* them. The author Laura Nathan-Garner admits that she hardly ever cries when watching films, but when watching movies with her friend Lisa she senses a need to show her involvement by pretending to weep, as in the case of the Ian McEwan adaptation *Atonement* (2007): "Sure enough, when my eyes wandered left, I spied Lisa swabbing her eyes. 'Quick!' I told myself. 'Dab your tear ducts!' As I had done countless times before, I lifted my pointer finger to my face – left eye, then right – and wiped down and over."[105] Nathan-Garner hates "not being able to show – to prove – the sadness or pain" she feels during movies: "After 30 years of relatively tear-free movie viewing experiences, I see my shortage of tears as a character flaw."[106] To her chagrin, others cannot perceive the goosebumps and the hollow stomach she does indeed experience when watching sad or moving scenes as an adequate proof. Needless to say, this strong focus on her companions distracts her from her engagement with the film.

It's likely that the pressure to weep conformingly or in solidarity increases with visibility: the more exposed the viewer feels, the more forceful the pressure to shed tears. Here we can locate an advantage of the cinema over private viewings: the movie-theater not only hides one's *overabundance* of tears more effectively, it also more thoroughly discloses the *lack* of moist eyes.

5. Shared tears: the pleasure of weeping collectively

The previous discussion of forced tears has indicated that the cinema also knows cases of weeping *with* others. While I would claim that viewers break out in axiological, sentimental, and personal-relevance tears predominantly *despite* their co-viewers, there are instances in which cinemagoers enjoy weeping *because* of the collective environment. I reserve a special category for this type of weeping because viewers experience it differently. Even though collective weeping feeds on and is based on axiological, sentimental, or personal-relevance tears, it changes the 'flavor' of these types of weeping in three crucial respects.

First, under specific circumstances viewers do not feel embarrassed when weeping with others: the threat of shame is markedly reduced or disappears altogether. Second, when viewers share tears they have a conscious experience of emotional closeness, however strong it may be. In Chapter 6 I have distinguished between experiencing a *spread* and a *shared* collective emotion. The former implies that we have the same immediate emotional response to the shared object of the film and are mutually aware of it, but nevertheless feel individuated and hence somewhat detached from each other. This is what occurs, I claim, in most cases of axiological, sentimental, and personal-relevance tears: Even if the entire cinema feels sadly moved to tears, the viewers do not experience it in the we-mode of a *shared* collective emotion. However, when viewers do indeed share their tears, they give up the I-mode and experience together with others. Is it too far-fetched to claim that Terence Davies was able to capture this we-mode in a movie-theater scene in *Distant Voices, Still Lives* (1988)? Davies does not isolate a single weeping character in a close-up (as Kiarostami in *Shirin*), but groups two women together as a kind of weeping mini-community, deeply moved by Henry King's *Love Is a Many-Splendored Thing* (1955). Looking ahead at the screen, the two weeping sisters Maisie (Lorraine Ashbourne) and Eileen (Angela Walsh) are illuminated from below and above, as if the lighting was supposed to indicate their we-experience. Such emotional closeness can also find an expression in behavior: Viewers may share their supply of tissues or grab the hand of their partner, thus creating a physical as well as a phenomenological bond that bridges the individualizing gap otherwise characteristic of axiological, sentimental, and personal-relevance tears. Third, a noticeable shift in pleasure emphasis occurs, from the individualized pleasure of tears to the pleasure of shared weeping with others. Collective weeping, just like collective laughter, can be enjoyable because it implies knowing that one shares an affective value response.

To what degree weeping can become a shared rather than an individual experience depends, at least in part, on the degree to which viewers can eliminate the threat of shame. Viewers will experience embarrassment only if they feel

Figure 8.2: The two sisters Maisie (Lorraine Ashbourne) and Eileen (Angela Walsh) weep together in Terence Davies's *Distant Voices, Still Lives*.

exposed, due to their tears, in front of an imagined or real cinematic community. Depending on specific *situational framings*, the threat of shame can either be held at bay or it does not come to exist in the first place. It can be circumscribed, for instance, when the viewer feels safe and securely 'at home' in the audience as a whole (or at least a sufficiently reassuring part of it). Take the reception of James Cameron's disaster-movie-cum-melodrama *Titanic*. Its famous female teenage audiences often attended the movie in groups of friends and enjoyed weeping together. These teenage girls, for whom the threshold of public weeping is lower anyway, apparently felt interwoven enough in a community of like-minded friends. With their sheer presence as a group, the girls erected a 'bulwark' around them, thus feeling 'protected' from the shame-evoking gaze of other viewers. The intersubjective pressure remained less effective.

Or take the Japanese phenomenon of tear-seeking (*rui-katsu*). In order to release stress, viewers gather in public places like bars, clubs, or small conference rooms at a mental-health center and watch tear-jerking films, commercials, or YouTube clips. Here crying is not only allowed, but encouraged. In its May 2015 edition *The Atlantic* observes: "The audience started sniffling well before the end of the first video, a Thai life-insurance commercial titled 'Silence of Love,' which revolves around a teenage girl and her deaf father. By the ad's conclusion, the sniffling had given way to open weeping. Over the next 40 minutes, as a series of ever sadder selections played – animated shorts, movie clips, YouTube memorials for pet cats – the sobs only grew louder."[107] Weeping and even sobbing are not threatened by shame because of the situational framing: Weeping for health reasons is the prime incentive to gather as an audience.

A *common identity* can be an additional factor in transforming individualized into shared weeping. In this case the film addresses us as a 'we' and thus binds us together as a family, a group of friends, or a fan collective, but also, more abstractly, as an ethnicity, gender, religion, class, or nation. Take again the teenage girls watching *Titanic*. Their common identity consisted of their age, their gender, their shared adoration of Leonardo DiCaprio, their identification with the not-too-beautiful attractiveness of the Kate Winslet character, their devotion to the Celine Dion soundtrack, or other shared characteristics.[108] Even those who did not know each other might have formed an instant emotional community based on their common identity. Here the diachronic narrative intimacy mentioned in Chapter 6 – an intimacy based on a shared past – might play a significant role as well. Think of a family watching a home-movie that features images of a recently deceased grandfather; or consider a group of friends who go to the cinema to watch a film that was enormously important for them when they grew up together. While the family weeps together in sadness, the friends might shed tears of collective nostalgia.

Note that neither in this section nor anywhere else in this chapter have I talked about *contagious* crying, a phenomenon that scholars from Helmuth Plessner to Ad Vingerhoets have drawn attention to.[109] I am not claiming that contagious tears cannot occur in the cinema. Yet in comparison to contagious laughter, it seems a rather rare phenomenon.[110] This is the case precisely because in the cinema crying usually takes on the form of silent weeping: We hardly *hear* others crying, and in the darkness of the movie-theater we cannot *see* them shedding tears clearly enough to be fully infected by their weeping either.

NOTES

1. Mann (1978 [1928]), p. 215 (my translation).
2. Warhol (2003), p. xv.
3. Benjamin (1996 [1928]), p. 476. Similarly, Eric Smoodin quotes an inmate who claimed after having seen Frank Capra's *It's a Wonderful Life* (1946) at a prison screening that the movie made him "realize I could still cry" (Smoodin, 2004, p. 191). While we might read these quotes from Benjamin and Smoodin as negative comments on how modern culture or a personal life-story can de-sensitize people, we can also understand them as valid documents of the fact that we tend to weep less in later stages of life. Ad Vingerhoets points out that "increasing age is accompanied by a transition from tears of physical pain to those of emotional pain, empathy, societal pain, and finally sentimentality and perhaps even moral awareness" (Vingerhoets, 2013, p. 67).
4. Fox (2014), p. 11. Available at http://www.sirc.org/publik/crying_game.pdf (last accessed 20 December 2016). Likewise, in an international psychological study on adult crying, people had to judge how likely it was that a given situation or feeling would make them shed emotional tears: Tragic events and funerals were rated highest, but at least

among women, watching sad movies or television programs received the third-highest mean score (Vingerhoets, 2013, p. 157).
5. Psychological evidence for the audience effect of weeping is scant in comparison to studies on laughter. The most significant study I encountered is the one by Jakobs and her colleagues, mentioned in Chapter 1, on the "social context effects" of crying when watching sad film clips.
6. For a first attempt with regard to the melodrama, see Frome (2014).
7. Vingerhoets (2013), p. 166.
8. Vingerhoets (2013), p. 187. However, there is evidence that male tears have become more acceptable in recent decades. In a survey in the UK, which questioned 2,000 people, 90 per cent of the female and 77 per cent of the male participants felt "that attitudes had changed – that the taboo on male tears is now generally regarded as outdated and 'unhealthy,' and that men are allowed to be more emotionally open" (Fox, 2014, p. 2).
9. For definitions of sobbing, whining, and wailing, see Vingerhoets (2013), pp. 11, 65, and 146.
10. Quoted from Zischler (2003), p. 103.
11. Breakwell/Hammond (1990), p. 31.
12. Lutz (1999), p. 19.
13. See particularly chapters 5 ("An Episode of Whining") and 6 ("Crying in the Whirlpool") in Katz (1999), pp. 229–308.
14. Katz (1999), p. 191 (emphasis added).
15. Of course, we have to be careful with across-the-board claims. It is entirely possible that in some cultures public crying about a movie is not only accepted, but even an expected part of a expressive-diverted viewing (in the section on shared tears I mention the example of the Japanese crying bar). What is more, sometimes we might have to interpret signs of our cinema companion as precisely a communicative signal: the ever-so-slight body movements, her quiet sobbing noise, the number of times she blows her nose might make it necessary to consider her weeping as more than film-related (I will discuss some examples in the section on personal-relevance tears).
16. Koestler (1989 [1964]), pp. 271–2 (original emphasis).
17. In a similar way, Vingerhoets sets apart the visual (and potentially olfactory) side of *tears* and the acoustic aspects of *crying* (Vingerhoets, 2013, p. 27).
18. Vingerhoets (2013), p. 96.
19. Quoted from Blumer (1933), pp. 96 and 98.
20. Srinivas (1998), p. 338.
21. See also Goffman (1961), p. 114.
22. Cheu (2010), p. 72.
23. Jermyn (2010), p. 158.
24. Katz (1999), pp. 150–6.
25. On recent attempts to establish being moved as a distinct emotion, see Cova/Deonna (2013); Kuehnast et al. (2014); Menninghaus et al. (2015). Kuehnast et al. note: "although many languages provide lexicalized deverbal expressions for this feeling, such as *Rührung*, or *Ergriffenheit* (German), *ontroering* (Dutch), *commozione* (Italian), *kandoh* (Japanese), *terharu* (Indonesian), *rastrogannost', vzvolnovanost'* (Russian), *dirnutost* (Serbian), and *trognatost, umilenie* (Bulgarian), being moved is only rarely found on lists of emotion terms" (Kuehnast et al., p. 1). Moreover, the authors emphasize that English and German "converge in an idiomatic expression referring to shedding tears as a characteristic physiological expression of being moved: *to be moved to tears* and *zu Tränen gerührt sein*" (Kuehnast et al., 2014, p. 9).

26. Demmerling/Landweer (2007), p. 261 (my translation).
27. Plessner (1970 [1941]), p. 147.
28. Katz (1999), p. 221 (emphasis added).
29. States (1985), p. 171 (emphasis added).
30. States (1985), pp. 174–5.
31. Harper/Porter (1996), p. 157.
32. Koestler (1989 [1964]), p. 272. Katz similarly notes that the bodily postures in *adult* crying indicate being cut off from others: "If children open up their bodies audibly and through extensions of their limbs as they cry, adults more typically close down on themselves, enacting an embrace of themselves as they seek to hold back distress and muffle audible dimensions of their cries" (Katz, 1999, p. 187).
33. Schwarz (2014 [1928]), p. 67.
34. See also Katz (1999), p. 175.
35. Vingerhoets (2013), pp. 124 and 126.
36. But here we might be dealing with a gender difference: Women may be less hesitant to approach weeping persons.
37. As Schwarz notes, "the weeping person is surrounded by a circle of silence, one hesitates to approach and stands awestruck in the face of a process that lets the 'blood of the soul' pour out" (Schwarz, 2014 [1928], p. 83, my translation).
38. A male viewer recalls how during a screening of Spielberg's *E.T. the Extra-Terrestrial* (1982) the atmosphere changed dramatically – from the loud distracted chatter of the under-eleven kids to a more quiet-attentive viewing – and he felt compassion for his young co-viewers: "ET is homesick. He might die. I am jarred by the sound of these children weeping." Quoted from Breakwell/Hammond (1990), p. 62.
39. See "Tear Watch" (2002) (last accessed 11 July 2007; no longer available).
40. Katz (1999), p. 180 (emphasis added). See also Vingerhoets (2013), p. 2. Katz convincingly defends the claim of an active doing in crying: "It may seem odd to imply that people 'do' these little turns into their bodies, seizing on resources that they do not in any cognitive sense seem aware that they have, in order to produce the corporeal practices of crying. But if the person involved does not make a tacit turn on his or her body to find the material stuff of crying, who or what does? It is inadequate to dismiss the question with the view that the behavior of crying is somehow 'wired in' to people as an inherited response pattern. Cultural and situational variations in the practices of crying are sufficient to keep the issue vigorously alive. Biological explanations just beg the question of how they work their influence into human behavior in nonrandom, socially situated patterns" (Katz, 1999, p. 213).
41. See Schwarz (2014 [1928]), p. 46; Prütting (2013), p. 1554.
42. Schwarz (2014 [1928]), p. 74 (my translation).
43. Lee (2002). Available at http://www.nytimes.com/2002/12/29/style/noticed-another-dad-flick-and-guys-are-crying.html (last accessed 21 December 2016).
44. See "Tear Watch" (2002, my translation) (last accessed 11 July 2007; no longer available).
45. Schwarz (2014 [1928]), p. 58; Plessner (1970 [1941]), p. 126.
46. Schwarz (2014 [1928]), p. 81. See also Thomas Koebner's critique of Plessner's ideal of controlled masculinity and its implied repression, even deadening, of emotions and bodily responses. Koebner therefore suggests a more liberal concept of audience behavior that allows for tears during the film (Koebner, 2008, pp. 65 and 87).
47. See Leder (1990).
48. Vingerhoets makes a similar point when he notes that "the sensation of tears may clearly

and unambiguously signal that what is currently going on is important for the crying individual" (Vingerhoets, 2013, p. 112).
49. Kuehnast et al. (2014), p. 7
50. Vingerhoets (2013), p. 105.
51. Lutz (1999), p. 43. In the 1920s and 1930s this was no different, as this quote from a fourteen-year-old female high-school sophomore contests: "I love to cry. I always think it is a good picture if it can make me cry" (quoted from Blumer, 1933, p. 100).
52. Nathan-Garner (2010), p. 111.
53. Mann (1978 [1928]), p. 215.
54. Wassiliwizky et al. (2017).
55. See also Berkenbusch (1985), p. 40.
56. Schwarz (2014 [1928]), p. 47.
57. Burke notes about delight: "we should distinguish by some term two things so distinct in nature, as a pleasure that is such simply, and without any relation, from that pleasure which cannot exist without a relation, and that too a relation to pain. Very extraordinary it would be, if these affections, so distinguishable in their causes, so different in their effects, should be confounded with each other, because vulgar use has ranged them under the same general title. Whenever I have occasion to speak of this species of relative pleasure, I call it *Delight* [. . .]" (Burke, 1997 [1757], p. 214).
58. See Schmitz (1980), p. 126.
59. In a study with Winfried Menninghaus and other colleagues we looked at the experiential characteristics of being moved, an emotion that often goes hand in hand with tears: "Feelings of being moved were rated as wide rather than narrow, elevating rather than depressing, fine rather than coarse, warm rather than cold, open rather than closed, soft rather than hard, round rather than angular, feminine rather than masculine, and pleasant rather than unpleasant" (Menninghaus et al., 2015, p. 22).
60. Berkenbusch (1985), p. 19.
61. Schmitz (1980), p. 129 (my translation).
62. One could call this pleasurable transformation from a constricted and tense to an expansive and relaxed state cathartic. I hesitate to use this expression, however, since the word catharsis usually implies a purgation of negative emotions and hence a healing effect, which in the case of crying is highly doubtful from an empirical point of view. See Cornelius (2001).
63. Tan (1996), pp. 55 and 76.
64. Kuehnast et al. (2014), p. 8.
65. Cova/Deonna (2013), p. 454.
66. For an exception, see Warhol (2003), p. 30.
67. Schwarz (2014 [1928]), p. 61.
68. See also Schwarz (2014 [1928]), p. 70.
69. Stern (1980 [1949]), p. 206 (my translation).
70. See Hanich et al. (2014).
71. Stern (1980 [1949]), p. 28.
72. Katz (1999), pp. 183 and 191.
73. Katz (1999), p. 189. See also Cova/Deonna (2013), p. 451.
74. Katz (1999), p. 183.
75. Stern (1980 [1949]), p. 55. See also Vingerhoets (2013), p. 83 and Stern (1980 [1949]), p. 134.
76. Cova/Deonna (2013), pp. 456–7.
77. Demmerling/Landweer (2007), p. 123.

78. I use the term "sentimental tears" differently than Ad Vingerhoets, who reserves it for unexpected tears welling up in the face of positive events and which in my terminology would have to be called (joyful) axiological tears: "typical themes that evoke these sentimental tears [are] belonging, harmony, reunion, justice, self-sacrifice, empathy and compassion, altruism, and awe. These are predominantly themes connected with prosocial behaviors and morality" (Vingerhoets, 2013, p. 101).
79. Warhol (2003), pp. xvi–xvii. My distinction resembles the one by Schwarz between "sentimental emotionalism" (*sentimentale Rührseligkeit*) referring to pseudo-moving qualities and "genuine being-moved" (*echte Rührung*) referring to absolute moving qualities (Schwarz, 2014 [1928], p. 62).
80. Giesz (1994 [1971]), p. 18; Jamison (2014), p. 111; Solomon (2004), p. 235.
81. Greenberg (1939), p. 40.
82. Jamison (2014), p. 126.
83. Note that I don't make objective claims about the aesthetic value of specific films here. It is notoriously difficult, possibly even impossible, to determine the essential characteristics of sentimental or kitschy objects.
84. Jermyn (2010), p. 156.
85. Krämer (1999), p. 124.
86. See, for instance, Staiger (2011) and Woodworth (2014).
87. See also Warhol (2003), pp. 64–5.
88. Schwarz (2014 [1928]), p. 82 (my translation). Note that for Schwarz, repressing one's tears is not at all a value in itself. It is only appropriate with regard to pseudo-moving objects or events that do not deserve the valuation of our tears.
89. Liessmann (2010), p. 57.
90. Solomon (2004), pp. 236 and 242.
91. Katz (1999), p. 188.
92. See also Warhol (2003), p. 23.
93. Solomon (2004), p. 238.
94. Solomon (2004), p. 246.
95. Jamison (2014), p. 123. The entry by the viewer called "Libby" mentioned above lends evidence to Jamison's point: When he heard the person behind him weeping he realized that "everyone was just dissolving into tears and crying their hearts out, and that I just had been totally blocking out this other noise while concentrating on the film. Just as suddenly, the whole thing seemed really cheap to me . . ." See "Tear Watch" (2002) (no longer available).
96. Giesz (1994 [1971]), p. 49.
97. See Hanich/Menninghaus (2017).
98. Discussing possible solutions to the paradox of fiction, Daniel Frampton refers to this phenomenon as the *counterpart theory*: "We cry at the end of the afternoon television movie because dramatic emotions displayed on the screen are often playing out scenarios that we have been in, or might one day find ourselves in (a loved-one dying, an emotional reunion). Our emotions are real (real tears) – because it makes us think of real-world emotional events" (Frampton, 2006, p. 153).
99. Blumer (1933), pp. 98–9.
100. Goldstein (2009), p. 236.
101. Smoodin (2004), p. 191.
102. For a similar position, see Schwarz (2014 [1928]), p. 61.
103. Katz (1999), p. 192 (emphasis added).
104. Vingerhoets (2013), p. 132 (original emphasis).

105. Nathan-Garner (2010), p. 108.
106. Nathan-Garner (2010), p. 109.
107. St Michel (2015). Available at http://www.theatlantic.com/magazine/archive/2015/05/crying-it-out-in-japan/389528/ (last accessed 18 November 2016). See also Shimbun (2013). Available at http://www.japantimes.co.jp/news/2013/06/22/national/participants-ease-stress-levels-at-crying-events/#.WCBT6oWxIfo (last accessed 18 November 2016). According to Vingerhoets, alternative versions exist where viewers rent *private* rooms, thus avoiding the collective experience (Vingerhoets, 2013, p. 105).
108. Nash/Lahti (1999).
109. See, for instance, Vingerhoets (2013), p. 96.
110. There is vague evidence for this claim. In a psychological study, 168 male and female participants watched Randal Kleiser's 28-minute short film *Peege* (1973) on a TV monitor in the presence of a confederate of the psychologists who either cried, laughed, or expressed no emotion at all. In the crying condition, the confederate simulated tears and crying during the last three minutes of film: they sniffed, 'dried' their eyes with tissues and breathed in short gasps. In the laughter condition, on the other hand, the confederates chuckled at four humorous moments during the film. The authors note that their study does "not support a crying-contagion hypothesis, as increased crying by subjects did not occur when the confederates cried. However, evidence for a laughter-contagion hypothesis was obtained." The participants not only reported that they found the film more pleasant when the confederate laughed, but they laughed more themselves and also reported more positive moods (Labott et al., 1991, p. 414).

CHAPTER 9

Trouble Every Day: A Phenomenology of Cinematic Anger

[When at the premiere of *Le Retour à la raison* (1923)] the spiral and the egg-crate carton began to revolve on the screen, there was a catcall, taken up by the audience as always happens in a gathering. But [. . .] the film broke, plunging the theater into darkness. One spectator loudly vented his dissatisfaction, the man behind, evidently a sympathizer of the Dadaists, answered him; the dialogue became more personal; finally a loud slap was heard, followed by the scuffling of feet and shouting. A cry for the lights arose, the theater lit up disclosing a group locked in a struggle preventing the participants from striking any blows.

Man Ray[1]

Code of Conduct:
No eating. No slurping. No rustling. No irresponsible parenting.
No hobbies. No talking. No mobile phone usage.
No kicking of seats. No arriving late. No shoe removal.

Mark Kermode and Simon Mayo[2]

I. SCENES OF VIOLENT ANGER IN THE CINEMA

In his three-minute short film *Occupations*, a contribution to the omnibus film *Chacun son cinéma* (2007), Danish director Lars von Trier comments acerbically on the problematic sides of the audience effect.[3] Sitting among festively clad spectators in the Cannes festival palace, the tuxedo-wearing director attends the premiere of his own 2005 film *Manderlay*. Next to him, a restless man (Jacques Frantz) has taken a seat. The dark-haired neighbor, who seems rather bored, looks around, leans over to the Danish director, almost pushes him aside and informs him, with a heavy French accent, that next to his job

Figure 9.1: A French film critic (Jacques Frantz) annoys director Lars von Trier in his short film *Occupations*.

as a film critic he is also a successful businessman. Visibly irritated, von Trier tries various methods of avoidance and escape. First, he keeps staring at the screen, then he nods, before briefly glancing at the man, responding "Good." But the relentless stranger does not stop: "A very, *very* successful businessman," he underlines. Von Trier turns away, without looking at the man, trying to signal his annoyance. When the film-critic-cum-car-dealer tries to start anew, the clearly annoyed von Trier interrupts him, but the man continues his monologue: "Now, I own eight cars." Von Trier closes his eyes, tries to move the neighbor away with his hand, and at one point he puts a finger in his right ear. Very much proud and amused about his successful business practices, the stranger laughs and then asks: "And what do you do?"

Unexpectedly producing a hammer, von Trier answers smilingly: "I kill." Then he sets out to hammer eight times on the man's head, smashing the skull into pieces. Afterwards he puts the remains of the man back in his seat and sits down himself. While some of the other viewers, smeared with blood, look shocked, von Trier relaxes and finishes watching his film, now calm and content. From the screen we hear the words, "Slavery was abolished 70 years ago. If you won't obey that law of your own accord, we will compel you to do so." Considering the uncomfortable and inescapable 'chains' that sometimes tie us to our neighbors in the movie-theater, the words resonate sarcastically.

I would assume that – to varying degrees – most viewers have undergone similar experiences. Von Trier's short film illustrates – dare I say: *forcefully* but not in a *headless* way – what will be at the heart of this chapter: Other viewers can be a nuisance; their comportment can be irritating and annoying; sometimes their behavior may cause fury and rage.[4] While film studies has hardly ever paid attention to this mundane fact, a short Internet search reveals that von Trier's extravagant splatter fantasy is not at all far-fetched and even bears traces of movie-theater realism.[5]

Consider an incident that occurs in May 2008 in the German city of Münster between a sixteen-year-old adolescent and a fifty-year-old man: When the younger one asks if he can use the armrest, the older one gives a provocative answer. After an extended period of reflection, the sixteen-year-old starts beating the man up.[6] On Christmas Day 2008 a violent confrontation occurs in Philadelphia's Riverview cinema during a screening of David Fincher's *The Curious Case of Benjamin Button* (2008). A twenty-nine-year-old man tells a noisy family sitting in front of him to be quiet and then throws popcorn at the son. At one point, he pulls out his .380-caliber handgun and shoots the father in his left arm.[7] On 27 February 2010, in the Californian city of Lancaster, a viewer complains about a woman speaking on her cell phone during Martin Scorsese's *Shutter Island* (2010). The woman's boyfriend produces a meat thermometer and stabs the man in his throat. When two persons come to help, they are also injured.[8] In February 2011 a twenty-seven-year-old man shoots a man of forty-three years in the Latvian capital Riga during a screening of Darren Aronofsky's *Black Swan* after they engage in a fight over the volume at which the victim has eaten his popcorn.[9] In February 2013 a group of nine people end up fighting in a Bielefeld cinema after a forty-year-old man complains, before the movie has actually started, about the noise being made by a sixteen-year-old. Nachos and Coke fly through the air – and so do fists.[10] Last but not least, on 13 January 2014 a seventy-one-year-old man kills a forty-three-year-old man and injures his wife in a cinema close to Tampa in Florida during the previews of a screening of Peter Berg's *Lone Survivor* (2013); again an argument had broken out, this time over sending text messages.[11]

These and numerous other examples illustrate – drastically and rather strikingly – anger as an audience effect. Even if it may be an obvious and seemingly banal form of spectator influence, we must not ignore it for at least two reasons. First, anger episodes can wield an enormous power over our cinema experience and influence it in decidedly negative ways. Second, given the enormous range of other opportunities to watch films, anger's negative disruption can be a serious reason to avoid cinemagoing. Some cinema-owners have therefore responded to this problem. The Alamo Drafthouse Cinema chain, which holds screens in more than twenty US cities from Austin to San Francisco, is known for its strict behavioral policy. On their website they note: "We have zero tolerance for talking or cell phone use of any kind during movies, and we aren't afraid to kick anyone rude enough to start texting their friends during a show right out of the theater."[12] In a much-publicized announcement, the AMC cinema chain recently declared that they would allow texting in some theaters, but after an outcry on social media they immediately revoked this new policy. Texting remains prohibited in their auditoria.

This underlines that being angry with other viewers is not only a problem of snobbish cinephiles or elderly middle-class viewers. On the contrary, it will be a central implication of this chapter that there are good reasons to locate the strong anger potential of the cinema in some of its structural characteristics. Anger can affect all kinds of viewers, and it can occur in all viewing contexts, expressive-diverted viewings included. Quoting a study by Kevin L. Carter, Janet Staiger, for instance, notes that "not all African Americans appreciate call and response; one fifteen-year-old woman told [Carter], 'I think it's one of the rudest things someone can do. [. . .] It makes it very hard for a listener to hear what's going on in a movie.'"[13] Similarly, Richard McCulloch observed in his study on *The Room* that one viewer was judged as an annoying intruder who commented continuously and showed off with references to Freud and Shakespeare, thus elevating himself too conspicuously above the film and the rest of the audience. His behavior was interpreted "as self-centered and intrusive, rather than something that benefited others in the audience."[14] Hence even in the most expressive-diverted contexts there are expectations around audience behavior, and limits to what one can and should do. In this case cracking jokes, screaming and other performative expressions have to serve the group experience. Transgressions are followed by sanctions: "Individualized in a context that values the group as a whole, [he] gradually became something of a pariah, whose comments received considerably less laughter after he had been figuratively ostracized," McCulloch comments.[15]

The following notes and descriptions should by no means be seen as the final words on the phenomenology of anger in the cinema. But, as Erving Goffman wrote in the introduction to his sociological classic *Behavior in Public Places*, "I assume that a loose speculative approach to a fundamental area of conduct is better than a rigorous blindness to it."[16]

II. SOURCES OF CINEMATIC ANGER

What are the main sources of anger? No doubt, filmmakers often try to evoke indignation, anger, and outrage *intentionally*. Calculated scandals such as Buñuel's *L'Âge d'or* (1930), John Waters' *Pink Flamingos* (1972), or Herbert Achternbusch's *Das Gespenst* (1982) do not only accept audience anger as a possible response – without the outrage of (bourgeois) audiences their act of provocation would remain pointless. Stirring or rabble-rousing political films like *The Battle of Algiers/La battaglia di Algeri* (1966), *Cry Freedom* (1987), or *Mississippi Burning* (1988) try to use the emotions of enraged viewers to sharpen their perception of injustice or question the political status quo.

Engaged documentaries like *La hora de los hornos* or *Fahrenheit 9/11* (2004) follow a similar goal. Emotion psychologists are even convinced that clips from films like *My Bodyguard* (1980), *Schindler's List* (1993), *Leaving Las Vegas* (1995), or *American History X* (1998) can reliably evoke the emotion of anger among participants under laboratory conditions.[17] Last but not least, the rape/revenge genre presupposes the viewer's anger for the (questionable) cathartic pleasure when watching violent acts of revenge. Think of examples like *Straw Dogs* (1971) or *Death Wish* (1974).

Yet apart from irritation and provocation as intended aesthetic strategies, films and their makers can also upset the audience *unintentionally*. This is the case when the film remains drastically below one's expectations. Think of an extremely lengthy movie which destroys the anticipation of an entertaining night out; a particularly idiosyncratic adaptation of a beloved novel that runs counter to one's (implicit) expectation of fidelity to the work; a religious message of a film one wouldn't have expected from this particular filmmaker and that stands in conflict with one's own position. With the exception of premieres and some festival screenings, the originators of anger are not present, which means that anger has to be articulated otherwise, as Jonathan Rosenbaum's example illustrates: "I can remember one all-night midnight marathon at the Olympic [in Paris] when they first introduced the structural film to the local hippies and caused a genuine riot, everyone was so outraged – hooting, screaming, jeering, throwing things at the screen, even waving a brassiere in front of the projector."[18]

Another source of anger is the *cinema staff*, and among them first and foremost the projectionists. Especially in the pre-digital era out-of-focus images, incorrect masking, or wrongly adjusted sound could cause considerable chagrin. The same goes for air-conditioning that lowers the room temperature to that of a freezer. Popcorn leftovers from previous screenings that haven't been removed, and unpleasantly smelling seats and carpets that haven't been cleaned properly can also cause disgust-based resentment. In comparison to the filmmakers, however, the cinema staff can be reached through loud screaming or a walk to the projection booth.

Obviously, the sources of anger can also overlap, as when furious viewers direct their emotion *both* at the film and the exhibitors who project it (or at the exhibitors *because* they are present, whereas the filmmakers are not). German novelist Reinhard Jirgl remembers an incident that took place in March 1982 during a retrospective of 1920s avant-garde filmmakers, when viewers in the East Berlin cinema Babylon created havoc during films by Hans Richter, Viking Eggeling, László Moholy-Nagy, and others: a woman screamed that she came to the cinema in order to watch movies and not to see the projectionist fix a TV test pattern, to which others responded by laughing, hooting, and whistling. Yet others screamed that this was like a madhouse and demanded the ending of the projection. Since no one listened to them and the movies continued, some spectators jumped up angrily and began to tear down the screen.[19] Since the cinema staff did not follow the audience's request and the filmmakers were not available, the action tendency of anger turned toward an object: the screen had to suffer.

Finally, the most widespread object of anger – and the one most relevant for this book – are one's *co-viewers* in the cinema as well as those people in the auditorium who are inattentive and thus have become *mere present others*: whispering couples, malodorous neighbors, people who rustle with chips, nachos, or popcorn buckets, who chew their gum too loudly, who talk on their cell phones or send messages on their illuminated and widely visible devices, spectators who cry out annoying comments, who laugh in ethically questionable ways, who kick against one's seat, who come and go various times throughout the movie, who obstruct one's sightline due to height, hats or haircuts, who claim the armrest and so on.[20] For obvious reasons I will predominantly concentrate on anger based on disturbances and disruptions *during* the film. Remember, however, from Chapter 4 that by far not all noises in the cinema are considered annoying. And even unintended noise not part of expressive-diverted viewing can sometimes become a delightful distraction and relief: "A grim, angst-filled film by Ingmar Bergman became ludicrously enjoyable through the persistent hiccups of the person sitting in front of me, which provided a perfect counterpoint to the strangulated Swedish voices onscreen."[21] Remember also that not all disturbances weigh equally, as we have heard in an illuminating remark by Goffman, which is worth quoting again: "two persons in a movie-theater, quietly talking together about something entirely unconnected with the evening's entertainment, may thereby exhibit an unoccasioned mutual-involvement, and by doing so cause more resentment than those who make much more physical sound but do so in expressing their approbation or disapprobation of what is being seen."[22]

III. A MINIMAL DEFINITION OF ANGER

As the previous remarks indicate, I will not distinguish sharply between notions like being irritated, annoyed, or angry, between anger, fury, and rage. I hereby follow emotion psychologists and sociologists who question whether there is a clear-cut distinction between these terms.[23] Sometimes scholars assume a mere contrast in *intensity*: indignation and anger can be less easily controlled than fury and rage, which overcome us with mighty force. In German, some scholars make a distinction between *Ärger* and *Wut*, on the one hand, and *Zorn*, on the other hand. Unlike *Zorn*, the former are not restricted to a personal object: I can be equally angry (*verärgert*, *wütend*) about an object, an event, myself, and another person.²⁴ Three points will concern us predominantly.

First, an *obstruction of a goal*: People often undergo an anger episode when they cannot pursue a goal to its end. The well-functioning pursuit of a project is rudely interrupted when the loud music of my neighbor wakes me up at 3am, when a driver changing lanes cuts me up, when a player from the opposing team tackles me badly while I am about to shoot a crucial goal. Or let us hark back to our example from the beginning: Lars von Trier wants to attend quietly to the premiere of his film in a concentrated manner, a goal that his neighbor obstructs in a most annoying way. In short, people are flooded with anger when the expectation of finishing a project to its meaningful end is destroyed. Psychologists Elizabeth A. Lemerise and Kenneth A. Dodge therefore connect anger to a specific function: getting rid of what obstructs the goal. "From a functionalist perspective on emotion, when there is an obstacle to goal attainment, anger's function is to overcome obstacles in order to achieve goals," they write.²⁵ Similarly, Ursula Hess notes that "certain levels of anger can be conceptualized as forms of problem-solving."²⁶

Second, a *perceived breach of a norm or value*: Anger and rage often go hand in hand with a subjective appraisal that a moral norm was ignored and one's feeling of fairness was hurt (appraisal theorists of emotion would speak of "norm incompatibility" here). Psychologist James Averill, for instance, notes: "anger is a response to a perceived misdeed. [. . .] the typical instigation to anger is a value judgment. More than anything else, anger is an attribution to blame."²⁷ My irresponsible neighbor, who robs me of my good night's sleep, not only breaks the rules and regulations of our apartment building, but also shows a lack of respect for those who have to get up at 6.30am. The reckless driver, who cuts me up sharply, not only ignores the certified traffic regulations, but also risks the wellbeing of other people. The opponent who plays foul mistreats the official rules of the game as well as the important value of fair play. We will see that disturbances in the cinema – whether in *Occupations* or in real life – can also be understood as a break of a norm or as ignoring someone else's value. As Philip Fisher observes from an Aristotelian perspective: "Anger is [. . .] the most primitive and spontaneous evidence of an innate feeling for justice and injustice within human nature."²⁸

Third, a *motivation to act*: A person's action tendency – often considered a crucial element in definitions of emotions – plays a very important role in anger. An angry or furious person often has a double motivation to act. On the one hand, the function of anger is *getting rid of the obstacle*: The angry person thinks of ways to convince the neighbor that he should turn down the volume; there is an impulse to let the referee know one should be awarded with a penalty; there is a desire to make the popcorn-cruncher stop, at least during quiet moments of the movie. On the other hand, the stronger the perceived break of the norm, the stronger the wish for more than a simple elimination of the obstacle that obstructs one's goal: *the emotional imbalance has to be restored.* For moral reasons it is often not enough to achieve one's goal – the 'perpetrator' has to be punished to recreate an emotional equilibrium. One wants to make the neighbor lack sleep himself, cut the road rowdy up in return, foul the opponent oneself. Depending on how one assesses one's coping potential – the ability to deal with the situation and adjust to the change – the *motivation to act* may lead to an *action proper*. In this assessment at least two factors play a role. First: Am I entitled to act? Can I really ask the mother with the crying baby next to me to leave the cinema? Second: Am I powerful enough to act? Do I really dare tell the group of aggressive-looking men to stop their conversation during the film?

If the action tendency turns into an action proper, one can even talk of an act of *revenge*, if one defines the term loosely and does not restrict it to extreme forms of aggression. Striking back obviously does not have to imply physical acts – it can also include minimal attempts to restore the emotional equilibrium. Fisher therefore notes that "everyday acts of injustice and injury require small-scale retaliations, and these might amount to no more than a look, a moment of silence, a change of tone, or might include a warning or even an aggressive act."[29] A thick micro-sociological description à la Erving Goffman or Jack Katz would reveal numerous acts of retaliation long before the director hammers his annoyance into his neighbor's skull: Von Trier refuses to talk to the man, hardly looks at him, recedes physically, interrupts his talk, and covers his ear. These acts of revenge obviously pale in comparison to the massive breach of his neighbor; nevertheless, there is nothing wrong with understanding them as "small-scale retaliations" in Fisher's sense.

IV. ON THE PHENOMENOLOGY OF ANGER IN THE CINEMA

Let us now take a closer look at the situation in the cinema again. As a source of inspiration I will draw on the fascinating chapter "Pissed Off in L.A." from Jack Katz' *How Emotions Work* (1999), a book I have mentioned variously throughout my study and which has managed to become a classic of emotion sociology within only a few years.[30] Katz investigates in admirable detail the interactions and lived-body experiences of anger while maneuvering through traffic in Los Angeles. Although we obviously cannot adopt his analysis wholesale to the cinema, it still provides a plethora of valuable observations. In the following I will develop my phenomenology by going step-by-step through the three general characteristics of anger discussed in the previous section.

1. Goal obstructions

a. Disruption of the Subject–Object Fusion: Following phenomenologists like Maurice Merleau-Ponty, Don Ihde, and Vivian Sobchack, we can describe the standard case of a more or less immersed film experience as a successful and rather smooth, but never complete, 'in-corporation' of the filmic object *into* the lived-body experience of the viewing subject: a 'fusion' of the 'film's body' with the spectator's body.[31] The viewer follows the filmic world *by way of* the instrument of the camera and the projector. However, this man–machine symbiosis never becomes fully 'naturalized': In the cinema we are always aware to some degree that we are watching a movie. Once there is a strong disruption of whatever kind, however, this tie is cut vehemently: When a neighbor pushes me from the armrest or makes loud noises with his popcorn bucket, he pushes himself 'between' me and the film – all of a sudden my easy 'merger' with the film is disrupted. According to Katz, the logic of anger consists, among other things, of an attempt to restore this 'fusion,' which was previously presupposed as self-evident.[32]

In order to make this – potentially abstract-sounding – argument more tangible, let me refer to a second type of subject–object fusion. In the concrete here and now of the auditorium there is also a 'fusion' between the viewer and the cinema seat, which for the length of the movie more or less easily becomes 'in-corporated' as well: The more pleasant the seat, the easier the 'fusion'; the harder, edgier, narrower, and thus more resistant the chair, the more difficult the 'merger' between viewing subject and the object of the seat.[33] Once the seat's material externality to the viewer's lived-body is forgotten and its material Otherness has receded to the background of consciousness, however, one can talk of a symbiotic extension of the lived-body: The seat has become almost seamlessly 'tied' to the viewer. Once someone kicks against the back of the seat, however, its materiality all of a sudden becomes foregrounded again and thus demands attention *as a cinema seat*. The upsurge of anger about the personified pain-in-the-neck in the row behind refers to that person's ignorance: The viewer treats the cinema seat as a mere object, thus disregarding that it has momentarily been 'in-corporated' and become an extension of myself. The annoying spectator ignores my existence, as *I* am automatically kicked when he or she kicks against my chair. (Then again, the viewer might have simply recognized an *affordance* of the chair. The back of my seat is seen as an invitation to put knees against it and thus to stabilize the very sliding down into the seat "as if into a bed" that Roland Barthes talks about in his cinema essay. In cinemas where the cupholder is not attached to one's own seat but to the back of the seat in the row in front, I have often cursed the anonymous cinema architects responsible for the interior design: Every time a beer or Coke bottle is put in the cupholder, I am reminded that I cannot tell the person behind me to stop doing this, because the cupholder is an official affordance which robs me of my entitlement to complain.) What has been tacitly taken for granted now becomes foregrounded *ex negativo*: the smooth symbiosis of me and my chair.

Putting it somewhat differently, the emotion episode demands attention itself and thus withdraws attention from the film and the intended lived-body experience it would otherwise enable. During the emotional transformation my lived-body becomes foregrounded in an unpleasant way. I feel an upsurge of heat; my heartbeat accelerates; I become tense and tighten up. There is an impulse to 'break out' of the lived-body constriction – in strong cases one could even 'explode,' 'burst,' or 'blow one's top.' While my experience was dominated by my interaction with the film, it is now under the control of an upsurge of anger or rage and delegates the film to the fringe of consciousness. Precisely because of this, anger interruptions are particularly unwelcome during peak emotional moments of a film. When you feel angry with another viewer during the suspenseful climax of a thriller or a deeply moving moment during a melodrama, you are robbed of the pleasures these genres are supposed to grant. At the same time, the lived-body becomes 'hard' and closes itself off. This is very different from the soft and dissolving feeling we have encountered in moments of being moved, of which tears are a visible example. This 'hardness' of the lived-body is also anathema to a 'melting' and 'fusion' with others: There is a heightened feeling of 'I' against 'You,' because I cannot integrate with others when I am surrounded by this hard shell into which my anger puts me. As Merleau-Ponty phrased it, '[an] emotion is not a psychic, internal fact but rather a variation in our relations with others and the world which is expressed in our bodily attitude.'[34]

b. Disruption of Joint Action: We should also be aware that anger is not only a disruption of my *individual* film experience. At least as important to me are disturbances of our *joint* action, both of the quiet-attentive and the expressive-diverted kind. As we have seen, as vital parts of the cinema audience we do not watch the film individually next to each other, but focus our joint attention on the shared intentional object of the film. Like other kinds of joint action, the social flow of being collectively absorbed in watching a film can be of intrinsic pleasure. Particularly in quiet-attentive viewing, the synchronization and coordination of our joint action is comparatively easy to achieve, because we merely have to follow the film together with silent and (predominantly) motionless attention. But here we also encounter the peculiar fragility of the cinema's joint action: Whoever talks on the phone or goes in and out, can easily leave the joint action and conspicuously act for him- or herself. However weak and pre-reflective our we-connection might have been up until now, it suddenly turns into an antagonistic I–you relation: Being angry with one's co-viewers separates me and creates a phenomenological distance between the angry me and the disrupting you (either the singular *thou* or the plural *ye*).

Here we have to come back for the first time to the important point I suggested earlier: The structural characteristics of the cinema turn it into a place that makes viewers particularly vulnerable to anger and rage. When we go to the cinema, one of our prime intentions is to watch a film with others, in a quiet-attentive or expressive-diverted way, *without obstructions* (and this seems true regardless of whether we are atheists, agnostics, or believers of the cinema's social constellation). What sounds undemanding, however, depends on a number of factors that make disruptions in one form or another rather likely. The three main sources of anger – the filmmakers, the cinema staff, and our co-viewers (as well as mere present others) – can easily block our intention, whether they want to or not. A cinema experience without anger can therefore become a fragile ideal. This is especially true for one's co-viewers: In the cinema I am remarkably close to anonymous strangers (as well as persons I know) on whose ongoing will to cooperate I depend for ninety minutes or so. These other spectators are "protected" by the dark and the uni-directional seating position, which decidedly impedes mutual control and signaling via one's gaze. What is more, the cinema makes other forms of emotion regulation more complicated. On the train I can avoid a group of noisy teenagers or chatting men by moving to another compartment. But changing seats in the cinema can be difficult: All other seats might be taken; I might have to squeeze past other viewers who I have to disturb myself; I might have to pass precisely those persons that I have aggressively shushed before. And even if I find a seat elsewhere in the auditorium, I might still perceive the noise.

2. Breach of norms and values: the angry viewer as moral victim

In moments of anger an aspect that can otherwise be a source of great pleasure is unpleasantly foregrounded: the *social* element of the cinema experience. The angry viewer feels his or her existence ignored and imputes a literal *a-sociality* to the troublemakers, despite the fact that the bothered person probably knows that the bothering persons have not meant to offend him or her as a person: "Do these guys think they are alone in the cinema?!" Consider two talking viewers who put their heads together, turn their bodies to each other and thus seem to move away from the audience. They create their own social microcosm, which seems a-socially closed off, hardly taking other viewers into consideration: they erect a 'shield' that protects them and that one would have to 'break' with a sharp hissing sound or even a verbal comment if one wanted to stop them. Or consider once more the case of a spectator who kicks against your chair. Again, you might feel ignored and not recognized as a person, this time thinking, "Why is this person so unaware that this annoys me?!"

Not being recognized as a person becomes particularly blatant once you have already asked the disrupter to stop, but he or she simply goes on. Prior to that, with some good will, you might have granted him the status of "ignorant"; the assumption that he made use of the seat's affordance might count as a mitigating circumstance as well. But now you have to assume an intentional provocation. While before you felt ignored in your personal existence, now you have to assume an excessive attention to you as a person – a provocative attention you hadn't wished for.

As we have heard, anger often contains a moral component; there is a subjective understanding that the annoying act is morally wrong.[35] The angry viewer not only experiences him- or herself as a victim, but also charges the situation with a moral meaning. A person who feels personally offended by talking or seat-kicking viewers considers the norm of fairness or considerateness breached; the other person is judged as morally incompetent with regard to these norms.[36] Or think of some more specific examples. In Chapter 5 I have drawn attention to the upsurge of anger about someone whose derisive laughter devalues a film you find deeply moving and which has thus assumed a quasi-sacred value for you. The same goes for other filmic experiences that are deeply significant for you and that are crossed out and disturbed by what you judge as inappropriate behavior. Consider you are a devout Christian watching a religious epic and a couple engages in non-stop talking during Jesus's suffering on the *Via Dolorosa*. Or imagine you are a convinced feminist and someone makes a misogynist remark during a rape scene in a film like *Boys Don't Cry* (1999).

Another apposite example comes from Jonathan Freeland, who describes an incident he experienced when watching Claude Lanzmann's *Shoah* (1985): "The length of *Shoah*, the demands it imposes on the audience, make it less like seeing a movie than taking part in a ritual, a sacred rite of remembrance. I went to see it with a friend, at the Curzon cinema in London, in September 1986, just a few months after the premiere in Jerusalem. My friend made the mistake of bringing popcorn – but he did not get very far with it. He had barely begun chomping when a woman from a nearby row leaned over and slapped him, hard, on the thigh. In an accent thick with the sound and memories of prewar Europe, she said: 'Have you no respect?'"[37] As this example shows, anger goes hand in hand with a tendency to retaliate and often ends in an act of revenge proper.

3. Impulse to act: how to deal with cinematic anger

a. The Interaction Asymmetry of the Cinema: In his microanalysis of anger on the road, Katz draws attention to the emotional provocation of asymmetrical interaction.[38] A person cut up on the freeway is able to see nothing but the rear of the other car and the irresponsible driver appears only as a vague silhouette. Due to the lack of face-to-face interaction, the cut-up driver tries to make the communicative interaction more symmetrical. The challenge now becomes one of how to raise the attention of a person who oneself is overly aware of.[39] According to the motto, "You didn't pay attention to me before, but now you certainly will!"[40] As a consequence, annoyed drivers honk, they drive dangerously close, they overtake and scream, gesture, and make obscene signs.

The parallels to the cinema are obvious: in the darkness it is similarly difficult to establish a symmetrical interaction once the disrupter has *nolens volens* challenged us to interact. Mimic and gestural forms of interaction are particularly limited in the cinema: because the film as the dominating center of attention attracts the gazes of the other viewers; and because unidirectional seating makes viewers look ahead, which largely prevents accidental interactions. Cinema architecture, with stadium seating in rows that rise steeply, further prevents eye contact. And does the darkness of the auditorium not also contribute to preventing a symmetrical interaction between the bothering co-viewer and myself? If the disrupting person does not sit closely behind me or next to me, an attempt to communicate via facial expression or gestures seems hopeless. This also goes for the person sitting directly in front of me: I may have to pat him or her on the back and thus use a problematic body contact to draw attention to myself, in case I don't want to shush, hiss, or even scream. If someone sits five rows in front of me and bothers me with a strongly illuminated smartphone, the only way out would be to scream at him. Apart from the negative consequences this scream might imply for myself (a point to which I will return), in contemporary multiplex cinemas with their impressive sound systems it is particularly difficult to establish acoustic communication simply because the film is too loud. I can remember countless multiplex moments when I desperately tried to convince a viewer behind me to stop mistreating the back of my chair: Since the sound avalanche of the blockbuster basically buried all other sounds beneath it, I had no other way of drawing attention to myself than to wave.

We could go through an endless number of situations and would always end up with a similar result: The cinema considerably complicates the interaction with other viewers. Apparently aware of the resulting problems, Pathé cinemas in the Netherlands try to offer a way out: the so-called "SMS alert." Via mobile phone, viewers can send a text message to the cinema staff and inform them about possible problems.[41] But is this a viable solution? Sending a text message is not only distracting for oneself, but also a potential source of nuisance for others. Moreover, clandestinely appealing to a higher authority may make you feel like a gutless informer. On the other hand, the SMS alert might be helpful simply by offering the *possibility* to act, the thought of which can already initiate an emotion regulation process.

The interaction asymmetry can become evident also in moments of anger about the film, as object, or the filmmakers, as subjects. The indignation or anger is often directed at the latter, particularly when viewers hold a particular person, say an *auteur* with a particular signature style, responsible for the annoying effect of the movie. Hence some viewers may have canalized their anger at Michael Haneke, the director, for his schoolmasterly treatment of the audience in *Funny Games* (1997). Other viewers may have blamed Michael Bay for their fury about the patriotic bombast of *Pearl Harbor* (2001), or maybe more vaguely and less *ad hominem*, they blame "the American cinema" or "Hollywood." In contrast to one's furious hammering on the keyboard when a computer program has crashed or one's enraged response when a forehand has landed, once more, outside the tennis court baseline, viewers are often aware of concrete persons responsible for their anger and can channel their emotion at him, her, or them. While one may still be able somehow to blame the computer crash on the billionaire founder of the famous software company from Seattle, searching for the responsible person in the case of the tennis racket would be pretty much in vain. Hence in the cinema the problem resides not in naming the responsible subject, but in responding to him or her in order to remove the interaction asymmetry and to re-establish one's emotional balance.

The fact that there is indeed an impulse to strike back also against filmmakers can be observed where re-establishing an emotional balance seems possible in the auditorium itself: at premieres and festivals. Here the audience knows that the filmmaker is either present personally or could be reached via the mediation of film critics who spread strong negative audience responses. It is here that audiences start booing; and the slamming of doors and angry commenting seem much more likely than in regular screenings. Consider how film critic Doug Cummings comments on the response of angry viewers who left a screening of Albert Serra's *Honor de cavallaria* (2006) at the Palm Springs International Film Festival: "It wouldn't be so bad if they did this quietly, of course, but many of the abandoners feel the need to widely proclaim their dissatisfaction through laughter, open derision, and quips like 'I can't believe we paid for this!' and 'Oh look, something's actually happening!', thus spoiling the experience for everyone else in the theater."[42]

b. Stereotyping as Retaliation Strategy: But how do viewers react when their co-viewers are the source of disruption? One strategy is to elevate themselves – mentally *during* the film or in conversations *after* the film – above the cause of anger. Following Philip Fisher, a slight or insult comes with a feeling of diminution. As a counter-strategy the angry person tries to turn around this diminution by degrading the bothering person. Similarly, Goffman notes: "One way of correcting situational offenses is to look upon the offender as someone who is unnatural, who is not quite a human being [. . .]. We *need* to think that situational offenders are sick [. . .]."[43] Consequently, we might consider the offender *in a rather general sense* as annoying "idiots," irritating "imbeciles," or exasperating "assholes."

Often, however, the situation becomes *more specific* when the angered person, via prejudicial sociological stereotyping, ascribes the objects of anger an inferior social status.[44] What does this mean? In order to give the seemingly senseless anger episode at least some meaning, the angered person makes stereotyping assumptions about the identity of the annoying person – and this identity can only be an inadequate one that must be lower than one's own, otherwise the annoying person wouldn't behave the way he does. Since anonymous situations like street traffic or the cinema provide very limited information about the source of anger, the angered persons draw on the little hints available through the windshield or in the darkness of the auditorium. Subsequently they categorize the object of anger in everyday sociological categories like age, gender, ethnicity, and so on.

With regard to the cinema this means that the angered person – let's assume a white, middle-aged middle-class high school teacher – does not think of (or talk about) this *specific* guy who eats his popcorn in an annoyingly conspicuous manner, this *specific* pair of elderly women who talk during the film, these *specific* teenagers who keep on sending text messages, or this *specific* group of Turkish immigrants who comment loudly on the film. No, in furious thoughts *during* the film or in outraged conversations *after* the film, the angered man resorts to more degrading and generalizing categorizations like, "Why do these obese country-bumpkins have to eat junk food even in the cinema?", "Why do these old frumps always suffer from talking diarrhea?", "Why aren't these ADHD youngsters of today able to sit still for 90 minutes and constantly have to fiddle with their phones even in the cinema?", or "Why do these Turkish machos always have to make their misogynist convictions public?" Make no mistake: Should the man shush the other persons during the film or otherwise try to discipline them, he might easily become the victim of similar stereotyping. The degraded others could think of him as a "snobbish middle-class egghead who thinks he can police other people's behavior" or an "aged German Nazi who cannot get rid of his hierarchical thinking."

In a double ascription, the angered person thus holds responsible both *specific* persons and certain social groups *in general* for the apparent moral incompetence that has led to the breach of the norm: the young or the old, women or men, Turkish immigrants or German autochthones. He wants to distance himself from these general specifics (or specific generals) by assuming an elevated position. The disadvantage of this retaliation strategy is that the diminution does not really affect those who were degraded: the angered person either *thinks* of "cackling teenage brats" or "policing old farts" – the act of retaliation thus remains *imaginary*; or he complains in conversations with his friends *after* the movie about those "stupid smartphone slaves" and "typical testosterone Turks" – the revenge thus comes *belated*. To overcome one's anger, an imaginary or belated form of retaliation is often not enough.

c. The Real Act of Revenge: The avenging counter-diminution therefore often has to be *acted out* – ideally in the same moment. Katz notes: "When revenge is just a thought that is not acted upon, it is evidence of impotence, and that shows the angry person yet another way that he has been cut off from him- or herself."[45] To confront the emotional provocation of the asymmetrical interaction therefore means most of the time: to re-establish a lost emotional equilibrium; to look for emotional compensation; to retaliate a slight with a counter-slight. As indicated above, it is often not enough merely to stop the source of annoyance and thus remove the obstacle that obstructs one's goal to follow the film in an unimpeded way. Sometimes the source of anger has to be angered him- or herself by teaching him or her a lesson to remove the imbalanced emotional equilibrium.[46]

This often occurs in the name of the movie-theater collective, as the angered person considers the tacit social norms of the cinema breached. By asking the troublemaker to be quiet, the angered person appoints him- or herself as the judge of the cinema's collective norms which he or she defends. Similar to Katz's phenomenological account, Bennett W. Helm's model of collective emotions presupposes the importance of an actual or imagined larger, almost transcendental community. His starting point is *reactive emotions* like gratitude, indignation, approbation, guilt, as well as resentment (which I understand as a type of anger): "the reactive emotions play a fundamental role in constituting distinctively human communities in part because they constitute *our* respecting each other and *our* reverence for the community itself, such that I respect you and revere the community only as one of us. Thus, although the reactive emotions in general are emotions we feel as individuals, they are nonetheless emotions we feel only as members of certain communities: communities of respect," he writes.[47] According to Helm, an understanding of the community's *membership* and its *norms* is implicit in the ways we respond reactively. However, conflicts and disagreements over how to understand the community's membership and norms can obviously occur.[48] In the cinema individual viewers may have divergent views on what constitutes their community and its norms: While one group of viewers might consider themselves a group of *rowdy teenage boys*, which is supposed to display, to each other and to others, their rowdy teenage behavior, this stands in stark opposition to those who consider themselves as the community of cinemagoers caring about the film, and whose quiet-attentive viewing experience is crossed out by the norms of the other community.[49]

By now we have encountered a number of responses to the source of anger. On the one hand, there are the mild forms of retaliation: refusing a conversation, moving away in one's seat, looking in a dunning manner, tapping one's neighbor on the shoulder. On the other hand, we found drastic forms of revenge: throwing popcorn at the troublemaker, engaging in a fight or firing with a gun (not to mention misusing a meat thermometer or hammering a French car-dealing film critic to pieces). In between there are reactions such as shushing and verbal requests, which can range from a polite "Could you please be a bit quieter?" to the aggressive "Shut the fuck up!" On the one hand, shushing is a conventionalized form of ordering silence: the acoustic equivalent of the index-finger-in-front-of-the-mouth gesture. At the same time it is something more: The onomatopoeic sound of the term "Shush!" indicates that it involves a certain aggressive sharpness directed at the other person. Here we have to distinguish degrees of sharpness, however, between a mild "Ssshhhhh" and a razor-sharp hissing. The hissing sound – and even more so the aggressive voice that utters an insult – 'cuts' into the troublemaker's experience and is felt bodily.

We are dealing with an astonishing fact here that we should look at matter-of-factly: In the cinema I frequently encounter situations in which someone else tries to bar me from acting in a certain way or I attempt to prohibit another person from doing something. In our democratic and (comparatively) egalitarian Western cultures there are few social places left where a person *in public* can dare to tell another *unknown* person what and what not to do. What may be acceptable for authority persons like policemen in city traffic or teachers in class, prima facie seems strange in a place like the cinema where we deal with (more or less) equals among equals. The retaliation measures are only possible because in the social space of the cinema we not only have to follow certain conventionalized norms of behavior and thus accept certain *obligations*, but also because these obligations come with *entitlements* (as we have heard in Chapters 3 and 4 with reference to Margaret Gilbert). It belongs to these entitlements to remind others of their obligations. The fact that those who were reprimanded do usually not retort underlines that they have understood: They have breached the norms of behavior and ignored their obligations; the angered person therefore has an entitlement to reprimand.

Let us briefly return to the anger about the filmmaker and the connected problem of asymmetrical interaction and lacking possibilities to retaliate. Belated articulations *outside the cinema* such as bad journalistic reviews, devastating comments in online forums, and negative customer reviews do not help on the spot (even if they obviously count as evidence for the recipient's anger and are real acts of retaliation). As we have heard, direct acts of revenge *in the cinema* are only possible in rare cases at festivals and premieres: Viewers who boo or slam doors make an acoustically noticeable act of rejection and retaliation public. (The same goes, by the way, for gratitude and admiration – emotions expressively communicated in public via applause or in discussions after the film.)

This stands in striking contrast to the theater and the opera. Via booing or avoiding to applaud *after* the performance, and angered comments or leaving the auditorium with loud slamming of doors *during* the performance, the audience can *always* express its frustration or indignation directly to the source of anger – the actors and all those involved during the performance. In Germany, Hamburg's former mayor Klaus von Dohnanyi caused a strong media response in 2000 when he shouted during the premiere of Ferenc Molnár's *Liliom* at the Thalia Theater: "This is a decent play – it doesn't have to be performed like this!"[50]

Against this background we could add a further detail to the discussion about the so-called "screen effect." In a famous formulation the philosopher Stanley Cavell has used a pun to ascribe a double protection function to the screen: "The screen is a barrier. What does the silver screen screen? It screens me from the world it holds – that is, makes me invisible. And it screens that world from me – that is, screens its existence from me."[51] However, it is not only the filmic world that is protected from me, but also those who are artistically responsible for it – especially the actors. Yet precisely because the screen protects them from the anger of the audience, the cinema has to remain a place of asymmetrical interaction: via the film the filmmakers act on me in annoying ways, but in the cinema I have no possibility of responding to them.

In the movie-theater we therefore encounter occasional displacements of the objects of anger. When the viewers leave the cinema during regular non-festival screenings with loud verbal complaints, this act of communication cannot be directed at the filmmakers. Instead, the anger seems to have partly shifted toward the other viewers. Here, too, there may be a moral allegation involved, because those other viewers who stay seem to signal a tacit complicity with the film and its makers – and therefore, in the eyes of the angered viewer, have to be punished with a disruption of their film experience. To me, at any rate, this is the most convincing explanation for enraged comments and slamming doors.[52]

d. Complications of the Retaliation Impulse: In the cinema the emotion of anger is usually not turned on and off like a light switch. Rather, it is experienced along an increasing and decreasing excitation curve, with the curve often rising gradually. The longer my neighbor eats his chips in an annoying manner, the more often the man behind kicks against my seat, the more persistent the woman in the back wisenheimers about the film, the more my indignation grows, the more likely it will transform into anger, the more possible a further metamorphosis into fury and rage. This surely creates complications for one's retaliation impulse.

First, one has to check the adequateness of one's response. As the Lars von Trier example shows, the appropriateness of means demands sending out warning signals first and requesting adequate behavior with mild forms of retaliation. A brief gaze to the side, a mild tap on the shoulder, a gentle "Ssshh" seem apposite; a belated but all the more explosive verbal comment or even violent attack are certainly not recommendable. Second, waiting for the right moment to send out a warning signal is equally crucial. One can hardly chastise one's neighbors after a first brief comment. Additionally, one shouldn't reprimand them at the very moment when they do *not* rummage around in their 5-liter popcorn buckets. And certainly one cannot shush a person when the film's soundtrack is at its loudest and occupies everyone's aural attention. This waiting for the right moment can be nerve-racking itself and may lead to an additional anger about one's own anger.

Third, as briefly alluded to above, *demonstratively* reprimanding a troublemaker makes the victim of anger vulnerable him- or herself. Once the annoyed viewer responds conspicuously and thus exposes herself, as it were, in the protective darkness of the auditorium, others could misunderstand her intentions. Unaware of the preceding breach of the first troublemaker, other viewers might consider the annoyed viewer as a source of anger herself and could set out to call her to order ("Shut up!"). Unwittingly the angered person has exposed herself to embarrassment or further anger. This is why the more anonymous shushing, which may also be more difficult to locate exactly, can be preferable to a more personalized verbal comment. On top of that, showing conspicuously one's own anger implies drawing attention to oneself in public with an emotion that doesn't have a good reputation: "anger poses difficulties [. . .] in that it *repels* others," psychologists Lemerise and Dodge note.[53] One annoys others by one's own annoyance. Fourth, the annoyed viewer has to keep in mind that she may suffer from a counter-attack from the reprimanded co-viewer. Before, I have mentioned that co-viewers reproached for misbehavior usually don't talk back, because they understand that they have breached their obligations. However, an overly strong reproach might alter the emotional imbalance in the other direction. Responding to a very brief dialogue of one's neighbors by shouting "Stop this damn noise, you stupid assholes!" can lead to a strong retaliation (and rightfully so).

Against the background of these four complications of the retaliation impulse, merely thinking of reproaching someone else bears considerable stress potential. Most angry viewers therefore do not retaliate. Often there is an intuitive process of weighing pros and cons, calculating the risks and measuring the costs. As a consequence, viewers who want to correctly adjust the force of their retaliation, who keep an eye on the opening and closing of the window of opportunity, and who think of the possible counter-effects invest great attention efforts. This obviously affects one's attention to the movie negatively.

Anger can therefore be accompanied by a wish that someone else might ride to the rescue by reprimanding the troublemaker *before* one has to act oneself.

Or else one might hope to join a veritable choir of shushing co-viewers in order to enforce the general anti-noise momentum with one's own contribution. The relief when others show their anger as well can go as far as feeling gratitude toward them. Inversely, it can be disappointing or annoying to realize that no one else seems to care.[54] Again, this has to do with one's commitment to how one imagines the ideal community of cinemagoers. If others do not react with anger, they fail to show commitment to this community – it is as if they only cared for themselves.[55]

e. *Anger Ebbing Away*: However, once an angered viewer has indeed dared to reprimand an annoying co-viewer and the act of retaliation turns out to be *effective*, this can imply considerable satisfaction. The moment before, he or she was a victim who had to admit the limits of his or her own will (Fisher calls anger an "'insult' to the will").[56] Now, all of a sudden, the angered person – through his or her act of retaliation – returns as an agent with a strong will. But how do we judge that our reproach was effective? The crucial yardstick is the response we receive. If we follow Bennett Helm and distinguish between forward-looking emotions (like fear or hope) and backward-looking emotions (like satisfaction or relief), we can say that anger looks in both directions: backwards because of the *ill-will* of the other person(s) we have just undergone; and forwards because of the *response* we expect from the other person(s) upon our display of anger.[57] A feeling of being completely ignored would quickly change our anger into furious rage; when feeling angry in the cinema we look for an appropriate response from the others.

What types of response can we expect? (1) Simply realizing the *end of the anger-arousing activity* – the fact one was able to silence a troublemaking co-viewer or stop him from kicking against the chair – may re-establish an emotional equilibrium. (2) Equally effective can be a sign of *corresponding anger* on the opponent's part: Upon perceiving an annoying person being annoyed, anger can gradually or even abruptly evaporate. (3) Most effective, however, might be a *sign of remorse*. The fact that anger quickly disappears once the troublemaker apologizes and thus admits his or her inconsiderateness shows us how much an anger episode is about feeling recognized by the annoying other.[58] The asymmetry of the interaction has made way for a nicely shaped symmetry; the emotional equilibrium between the two parties has been re-established; the situation is cleansed of all spoiling nuisances. A physiological arousal may still trail the emotional outbreak like a comet tail, but the emotion itself is already dissolving. Jean-Paul Sartre has famously claimed that emotional experiences imply a magical transformation of the world for the emotionally overwhelmed person.[59] In our case we would deal with a sudden transformation of anger into contentment and satisfaction.

The suddenness of the transformation of the world becomes even more obvious when you overestimate your personal entitlement to ask for silence.

Once I asked two whispering women in front of me to be quiet during a film. When one of them told me that she tries to describe the images to her blind mother, my emotional experience immediately changed from anger to embarrassment, even shame. I felt that my entitlement was too weak in comparison to the entitlement of the woman to provide her mother with a nice cinema experience. No doubt, anger is not always justified.[60] It is unlikely, by the way, that I would have felt an upsurge of anger in the first place had the woman announced the reason for her whispering. As Goffman points out: "persons present may tolerate a great deal of noise from an individual, providing he makes a general apology in advance for the necessity of making it. The apology shows that he is alive to those in the situation and hence to the gathering itself, and provides an effective substitute for the evidence of considerateness that quietness usually provides."[61]

V. POSTSCRIPT

What makes Lars von Trier's *Occupations* so amusing is first of all its strong recognition value: In his short film the Danish director stands in for countless other angry victims of cinematic disruptions. At the end of the film his revenge even offers empathizing viewers a redemptive imaginary catharsis. Yet the comic effect also derives from the grotesque exaggeration of his revenge, from the furious hyperbolic manner of how he attempts to achieve the longed-for emotional equilibrium. Hammering someone's skull into pieces more than shuts the other person up: Von Trier's (smashing) act of retaliation will have told all the other persons in the audience a lesson for the remainder of the movie. The rest is silence.

NOTES

1. Man Ray (1963), p. 262.
2. Available at http://www.bbc.co.uk/5live/films/code_of_conduct.jpg (last accessed 5 August 2016).
3. The film *Chacun son Cinéma*, produced to celebrate the sixtieth anniversary of the Cannes Film Festival, consists of thirty-three contributions each three minutes long.
4. Von Trier is not the only director with a sensibility for the exasperating side of the cinema. Among the numerous films that contain irritated viewers we find *Those Awful Hats* (D. W. Griffith, 1909), *Rosalie et Léontine vont au théâtre* (Roméo Bosetti, 1911), *Masculin Féminin* (Jean-Luc Godard, 1966), *The Blob* (Chuck Russell, 1988), *Dancer in the Dark* (Lars von Trier, 2000), *Mad Circus* (Álex de la Iglesia, 2010), and *Das merkwürdige Kätzchen* (Ramon Zürcher, 2013).
5. Anger seems to be a largely neglected field in philosophy as well. See Demmerling/Landweer (2007), p. 288.

6. Available at http://www.nwzonline.de/panorama/schlaegerei-im-kinosaal_a_3,1,80978700.html (last accessed 4 August 2016).
7. Available at http://edition.cnn.com/2008/CRIME/12/27/movie.shooting/ (last accessed 4 August 2016).
8. Available at http://articles.latimes.com/2010/mar/10/local/la-me-meat-thermometer10-2010mar10 (last accessed 4 August 2016).
9. Available at https://www.theguardian.com/film/2011/feb/21/man-shot-latvian-cinema-popcorn (last accessed 4 August 2016).
10. Available at http://www.nw.de/lokal/bielefeld/mitte/mitte/7920261_Redender_Besucher_loest_Pruegelei_in_Bielefelder_Kino_aus.html (last accessed 4 August 2016). For more examples – not all of which are related to anger during a screening – see here: http://www.thewrap.com/a-history-of-violence-at-the-movie-theater-from-1979s-the-warriors-gang-showdown-to-2015s-lafayette-tragedy/ (last accessed 4 August 2016).
11. Available at http://www.usatoday.com/story/news/nation/2014/01/13/wesley-chapel-florida-shooting-movie-theater/4457907/ (last accessed 4 August 2016).
12. Available at https://drafthouse.com/about (last accessed 4 August 2016). Similarly, under the heading "Behavior Policy," the Nickelodeon cinema in Columbia (South Carolina) notes on its website: "We have a no talking policy during films. If another member of the audience asks you to stop talking, please do so. If you are talking you will be given one warning from theater staff. If the problem persists you will be asked to leave the theater without a refund. Phone use is not permitted in the theaters, with no exceptions. The light emitted from phones is disruptive. This includes social media, texting, checking the time, and so on. You will be asked to leave without a refund." Available at http://nickelodeon.org/pricing-other-policies/ (last accessed 4 August 2016).
13. Staiger (2000), p. 48.
14. McCulloch (2011), p. 210.
15. McCulloch (2011), p. 211.
16. Goffman (1963), p. 6
17. See, for instance, Gross/Levenson (1995) and Schaefer et al. (2010).
18. Hoberman/Rosenbaum (1991), p. 315.
19. Jirgl (1996), p. 76
20. See also the comment of critic Peter Michalzik quoted in Paech (2012), p. 37.
21. Quoted from Breakwell/Hammond (1990), p. 61.
22. Goffman (1963), p. 214. Possibly, even annoying disturbances can have an expedient function and should therefore not be condemned automatically. With reference to the notion of *civil* disobedience, Jonathan A. Neufeld has introduced the term *aesthetic* disobedience, a subtype of which he also considers acts of *audience* disobedience like disruptions, protests, booing, noisemaking, and violations of other "sufficiently entrenched" and "deeply held" norms that usually govern the space of the audience (Neufeld, 2015, pp. 120 and 122). According to Neufeld, transgressing the boundaries of acceptable behavior can shed light on the weight of audience norms that otherwise go unnoticed due to habituation: "This broadly deliberative and participatory core of aesthetic disobedience draws our attention to the ways that audiences shape our aesthetic and artistic practices in much the same manner as artists do" (Neufeld, 2015, p. 122).
23. See, for instance, Schieman (2006), pp. 494–5.
24. Demmerling/Landweer (2007), p. 308.
25. Lemerise/Dodge (2008), p. 730.
26. Hess follows James Averill in this respect (Hess, 2014, p. 57).

27. Averill (2001), p. 343. Similarly, Hess notes with reference to research by Paul Rozin that "anger is conceived of as an emotion employed to condemn violations linked to notions of justice, freedom, fairness, individualism, individual choice, and liberty" (Hess, 2014, p. 58).
28. Fisher (2002), p. 178.
29. Fisher (2002), p. 176.
30. Katz (1999). Consider the entry on Katz's book in Senge/Schützeichel (2013).
31. Merleau-Ponty (2002 [1945]); Ihde (1977); Sobchack (1992). With regard to driving a car, Katz likewise speaks of a "meta-physical merger" that fuses, as it were, driver and car. They become "a humanized car or alternatively, an automobilized person" (Katz, 1999, p. 33).
32. Katz (1999), p. 47.
33. See also Hanich (2010), p. 58.
34. Merleau-Ponty (1964 [1947]), p. 53.
35. See also Schmitz (1973), p. 24.
36. Katz (1999), p. 58.
37. Available at http://www.theguardian.com/world/2015/dec/10/the-day-israel-saw-shoah (last accessed 5 August 2016).
38. Katz (1999), p. 24ff.
39. Katz (1999), p. 26.
40. Katz (1999), p. 27.
41. Available at https://klantenservice.pathe.nl/hc/nl/articles/203087788-Wat-is-een-SMS-alert- (last accessed 8 August 2016).
42. Available at http://www.filmjourney.org/?p=891 (last accessed 8 August 2016).
43. Goffman (1963), p. 235.
44. Katz (1999), p. 52ff. See also Goffman, who points out that one may rationalize an angered response to what one considers an offensive act "by reference to such things as the invidious class implications of uncouth acts (as when [one] becomes angered at someone for chewing gum too loudly, or for sniffling)" (Goffman, 1963, p. 248).
45. Katz (1999), p. 48.
46. See Schmitz (1973), pp. 44–5. In an empirical study on revenge, Mario Gollwitzer, Milena Meder, and Manfred Schmitt found that in order to derive satisfaction from an act of retaliation the avenger needs signs of understanding from the offender as to why he or she has been punished: "a central goal of revenge is to make the offender aware that he or she has caused harm and did something wrong. In other words: Revenge does not seem to be merely about paying back, it is also about delivering a message" (Gollwitzer/Meder/Schmitt, 2011, p. 372).
47. As Helm further clarifies: "Such communities can be narrower or broader, encompassing everything from the members of a particular family to the community of tennis players to the community of all persons" (Helm, 2014, p. 48).
48. Helm (2014), p. 57.
49. This point is drastically illustrated by an anecdote of the poet Ralph Hawkins in Breakwell/Hammond (1990), p. 46.
50. Available at http://www.spiegel.de/spiegel/print/d-18074406.html (last accessed 6 August 2016).
51. Cavell (1979), p. 24.
52. As Matthias Frey points out: "Walking out is a performative gesture: it is the ultimate act of spectatorial resistance. In fact, the exit is often accompanied by some verbal or otherwise physical expression of disgust" (Frey, 2012, p. 102).

53. Lemerise/Dodge (2008), p. 730 (emphasis added).
54. Christine Hammond recounts this fitting anecdote: "One Sunday night at the Wood Green Odeon a group of youths and girls were making so much more than a tolerable racket that I eventually asked them to quieten down. Some hope. Humiliated, I decided to fetch the manager. The usherette assured me that the manager would do something about it but he was busy just then with the projectionist, so she would pass on my complaint when he came down. After suffering another half-hour of mouth farts and high-pitched giggles I was stiff with indignation: at the rabble, at the management, at my 'don't' make a fuss' partner. Why does nobody else seem to care?" Quoted from Breakwell/Hammond (1990), p. 66.
55. Helm (2014), p. 54.
56. Fisher (2002), p. 171.
57. Cf. Helm (2014), pp. 49–50.
58. See also Schmitz (1973), p. 26.
59. Sartre (1993 [1939]).
60. For two fictional accounts of very similar incidents, see Lars von Trier's *Dancer in the Dark* and Albert Camus's unfinished autobiographical novel *The First Man* (1994). In *Dancer in the Dark* the two protagonists attend a screening of the Hollywood musical *42nd Street* (1933), during which Kathy (Catherine Deneuve) tells the events on the screen to her almost blind friend Selma (Björk). A man sitting a few rows in front of them complains: "Please, be quiet." When Kathy answers "Ah, give us a break. She doesn't see that well", the angry man retorts, "I paid good money to see this film." Since Kathy and Selma do not whisper but speak at a normal level, the man apparently finds his anger justified. In a memorable passage of *The First Man*, Camus describes the visits his alter ego Jacques pays to the cinema with his grandmother: "Since they were silent, the films would project a certain amount of written text intended to clarify the plot. As his grandmother was illiterate, it was Jacques's job to read these texts to her. Despite her age, his grandmother was not at all hard of hearing. But first of all he had to make himself heard over the sound of the piano and that of the audience, whose vocal responses were plentiful. Furthermore, though the texts were extremely simple, his grandmother was not very familiar with some words or others were completely unknown to her. Jacques, for his part, did not want to disturb their neighbors and was especially anxious not to tell the entire hall that his grandmother did not know how to read (sometimes she herself would be embarrassed enough to say, raising her voice, at the beginning of the show: 'You'll have to read to me, I forgot my glasses'), so he would not read the text as loudly as he might have. The result was that the grandmother only half understood, and would insist that he read it again and louder. Jacques would try to raise his voice, the shushes would plunge him into a vile shame, he stammered, the grandmother scolded him, and soon another text appeared, all the more mysterious to the poor old woman because she had not understood the preceding one" (Camus, 1995, pp. 95–6).
61. Goffman (1963), p. 214.

PART V

Fade-out: Conclusion

CHAPTER 10

The Audience Effect in the Cinema and Beyond

Without the movie house – without its architecture, its symbols, its behavioral codes, its rituals – the history of the seventh art would not be the one we know. But this means above all that, following the auditorium's decline, the style of films will change as well, and with it possibly the type of pleasure and aesthetic experience sought from moving images. Divested of the big screen, cinema of the future will inevitably be different from what we have had until now. As will its spectators.

Gabriele Pedullà[1]

I. PROSPECTS FOR THE FUTURE

In the introduction I borrowed from Susanne Langer that nothing in this study is exhaustively treated and that every subject demands further analysis, research, and invention. If I am correct in this assessment, then rich hunting grounds lie ahead of us and a lot of future hares could be chased, not least because my theoretical abstractions need concretization and the concrete descriptions call for extension and amendment. As Sarah Atkinson has warned us, "Cinema is and always has been in a perpetual state of becoming. Cinema as a concept, construct and social activity is in need of constant revision, as are its frameworks for understanding, analysis and study."[2] In order to reach a productive level of generality I had to freeze the cinema's ever-changing fluidity to an ideal type, and film historians can now begin to melt this a-historical shape. The fifteen variables listed in the introductory notes to the "Long Shot" on types of collective viewing can serve as a rough guideline to work with.

What is more, this book puts strong emphasis on the co-viewer's effect on *emotional experiences* and *affective expressions*. But it might turn out equally rewarding to penetrate in more depth that of which I only scratched the surface: the evaluative, interpretative, and ethical audience effects. As we have heard here and there throughout the preceding chapters, the co-presence of other viewers can have an impact on how we judge and interpret a film; and it can affect how we become aware of or remain oblivious to a film's racist, misogynist, or homophobic tendencies.[3] Take, for instance, this quote from Frantz Fanon's anti-colonialist classic *Black Skin, White Masks* (1952): "In the Antilles, the young Negro identifies himself *de facto* with Tarzan against the Negroes. This is much more difficult for him in a European theater, for the rest of the audience, which is white, automatically identifies him with the savages on the screen."[4] Here the sheer co-presence of a white audience changes the self-perception of black viewers, and consequently their character engagement and pleasure that come with it.

And let's not forget that the collective cinema experience is currently transformed by the intrusion of "second screens" into the auditorium. Today, illuminated mobile phone displays may not only turn into a visual source of (annoying) distraction, but the phone in my pocket is also a potential source of my own (pleasurable) diversion.[5] With my smartphone I can always slip into a state of what below I define as *medial co-presence* with other friends outside of the cinema – be it because I have received a message, be it because I do not find the film captivating enough. I have deliberately bracketed the second-screen phenomenon and the beyond-the-auditorium-connectivity that comes with it in order to fully focus on the audience effects of *physically co-present viewers*: partly because they were the dominant form for the major part of the history of cinemagoing, partly because they are extensive enough to easily fill an entire book.

And there is yet another potential point of contention I want to address with downright clarity: Just because my study has concentrated on the experience of physically co-present viewers in the *cinema* does not mean that I consider other forms of movie-watching as a-social. Jennifer Holt and Kevin Sanson note that terms like dispersion, dislocation, and disconnection are currently used to describe the downsides of platform proliferation and audience fragmentation, but they are quick to point out that this does not imply a disjointed experience.[6] How true. Many film experiences beyond the cinema are collective in their own way. A point I have mentioned in my critique of the individualization thesis seems valid here as well: We are dealing with different types of collectivity, but they are collective nonetheless. (Of course, how we *evaluate* these different types of collectivity politically or morally is an entirely different question.)[7]

Take the couple that watches a film together on their laptop while on a train ride. They share the earphones, move the screen close to their bodies and sit shoulder to shoulder. Blocking out the noises and activities of other travelers, they try to minimize distractions.[8] In Francesco Casetti's words, they create an "existential bubble" around them.⁹ The two thus have a very intimate viewing experience, both in terms of their physical closeness, but also with regard to the medium in front of them so close to their bodies. Several scholars have described this as a *personalization* and *mobile privatization* of public space, which satisfies "the contradictory impulses of moving through the world while retreating from it" (Stephen Groening).¹⁰ The outside world is momentarily held at bay, but the privacy construct is fragile: if the conductor asks for the tickets, a group of loud passengers passes through the aisle, or the train arrives at their destination, the existential bubble of our two viewers easily bursts.¹¹

Moreover, the bubble may also be fragile because the couple remain aware that other passengers could get a glimpse of what they are watching, which is why they have carefully chosen the film. With regard to the comparable case of watching a movie on an airplane, Ryan Lambie has amusingly illustrated the potential pitfalls of the wrong choice of movie: "Blissfully unaware of its content, I chose *The Disappearance Of Alice Creed* [2009] as my in-journey entertainment, only to discover that its protagonist, played by Gemma Arterton, spends much of the movie naked, handcuffed and screaming for help. I was travelling alone, and the person sitting next to me was a lady who I was convinced would look over at what I was watching at any moment and think I was some sort of sociopath. On arriving at yet another scene of nudity and screaming, my nerve left me and I put *Iron Man 2* [2010] on instead. It wasn't very good, but it was better, I thought, than sitting in fear of what the person sitting next to me might think."¹² If that's not a strong effect on one's viewing experience, what is?

As a second example, let us imagine a viewer who sits alone at home and watches the broadcast television premiere of the new James Bond installment. Via a second screen – a smartphone, a tablet, a laptop – he chats with his friends, commenting on the film via Whatsapp or Facebook. The friends crack jokes, comment on the development of the plot, evaluate the action sequences, and admire Daniel Craig's impeccable physique. For Francesco Casetti this behavior is symptomatic of the human context which many viewers expect from a film experience: "Cinema has always been associated with an audience: The new media contexts allow for the construction of *imagined audiences*, even when spectators find themselves alone in front of a computer or tablet screen."¹³ Obviously, the collective discussion among friends via second screens shares more characteristics with expressive-diverted viewing than with the quiet-attentive type: It not only implies diverted multitasking in front of the screen, but also rests on verbal communication, albeit in written form. A Conversational Theater at home? Vachel Lindsay might have approved.

Finally, with the help of virtual-reality apps, viewers can nowadays also choose to watch a film collectively in a *virtual* cinema. Outfitted with a VR headset and headphones, three friends might take a seat on their living-room

Figure 10.1: Image of a virtual-reality cinema.

sofas in, say, Amsterdam, Berlin, and Rome respectively. Via their avatars they virtually sit next to each other in the VR cinema and watch a film they have uploaded through their VR device, all the while staying aurally connected through their headsets. Should we describe their experience with the title of Wim Wenders's 1993 film *Faraway, so Close!/In weiter Ferne, so nah!* or with Sherry Turkle's book title *Alone Together*? A user called "cnnryng" left a post online from which we can glean that he tends toward the latter: "This is so depressing. Instead of getting together with your mates [you] just sit at home in your underwear and watch it with an expensive headset on. This is the future! You don't need to go outside ever!" Another commentator called "sm753", on the other hand, sounds more convinced: "This is actually a pretty damn good idea. The older you get, the further your friends move and the harder it is to 'get together' to do stuff."[14]

Of course, these examples do not exhaust the contemporary range of audience effects beyond the cinema. I know of partners living hundreds of kilometers apart who regularly turn on Skype and start a movie at the same time so that they can watch the film together. There is no physical co-presence here, but do they not share a collective experience? Or think of watching moving images on mega-screens in urban squares: some people pass by, others take a glance, yet others stop and watch jointly, before they move on and disappear somewhere in the thicket of the city streets: "these passers-by only rarely constitute an audience in the classic sense of the term; what forms instead is what I would like to call a *semi-audience*, halfway between the casual aggregate formed by passers-by and the potential community of spectators," Casetti notes.[15] And still, for a fleeting moment they might have a collective audience experience: a brief common outburst of laughter, a smile that shows a common understanding, a short exchange of opinions.

Drawing on Benjamin, Bazin, and Husserl, Christian Ferencz-Flatz has pointed out that even the experience of an isolated viewer in front of a television screen has to be described as intersubjective and collective.[16] Due to television's plural address of a mass audience, the other viewers always come as a latent background expectation: Just like the back of an object, which is always co-present to our perception even though we hardly ever reflect on it, the co-presence of other viewers in front of the screen is tacitly taken for granted. It is in exceptional moments that the background becomes foregrounded and thus makes us more fully aware of what we have taken as the norm all along. Ferencz-Flatz uses the example of a close personal acquaintance appearing on television: Suddenly we realize that millions of others must be watching our friend as well. Or think of the slippage of a TV announcer: My vicarious embarrassment is so poignant precisely because the mistake does not occur in front of me alone but countless other viewers who witness it too.

To get a better grip on these diverse audience effects beyond the cinema, it seems helpful for future discussions to offer one last round of conceptual distinctions (the very last round, I promise). In the remainder of this chapter I will therefore try to shed some light on what *forms of co-presence* we can usefully distinguish and what *types of co-present others* exist. I begin with keeping apart *physical* co-presence and *medial* co-presence.[17]

II. FORMS OF CO-PRESENCE AND TYPES OF CO-PRESENT OTHERS

1. Physical and medial co-presence

The notion of physical co-presence refers to the simultaneous presence of two or more persons in bodily proximity. Since bodily proximity knows different degrees, physical co-presence unfolds along a continuum from *immediate* physical co-presence to *mediate* physical co-presence. Viewers who are in each other's immediate proximity remain within the range of normal sense perception; in the strongest case they can even smell, touch, and taste each other.[18] A pair of lovers holding hands tightly in the back row are obviously in closer immediate physical co-presence than two viewers engaged in an angry dialogue six rows apart. The more senses involved, especially the more near senses of smell, touch, and taste, the bigger the degree of immediate physical co-presence. With the term *mediate* physical co-presence, on the other hand, I refer to the extended proximity of persons who can reach a viewer's immediate physical co-presence in an instant. Oftentimes a physical barrier separates them from each other: a door that cuts off the living room from the kitchen; a curtain that divides the black box in a museum from its white-cube surroundings; a sliding door between two train compartments.

Simply knowing that other persons are in mediate proximity can affect the film experience, both positively and negatively. Just think of the easily scared student who is relieved that his roommates are next door when he starts watching *Henry – Portrait of a Serial Killer* (1986) for a seminar on the horror film. While persons in immediate proximity can always decide to share the activity of jointly watching the film, this is not the case with persons in mediate proximity. However, the latter can turn into co-viewers after a brief temporal hiatus, for instance by entering a room. Crossing the barrier and thus switching from mediate to immediate co-presence is usually somewhat conspicuous. It announces an arrival, which can, again, have a crucial effect on the film experience. Consider the teenager watching *Fifty Shades of Grey* (2015) in her bedroom: She knows that she could quickly change the program should her parents come in. Or consider the museumgoer who is glad he does not have to watch all these disturbing Paul McCarthy videos alone anymore.

However, as many examples above have illustrated, the massive diffusion of mobile phones, portable devices, and wireless Internet connections has drastically increased the importance of another type of co-presence for the collectivity (and connectivity) of the film experience: the so-called *medial* co-presence. With Shanyang Zhao we can describe medial co-presence as a form of human co-location in which both individuals remain present at their respective sites and at the same time come into each other's electronic proximity.[19] While outside the range of naked sense perceptions, the individuals are within immediate reach of each other through a connecting medium: a telephone, a smartphone, a virtual-reality device. Does anyone seriously want to deny that there are striking differences between watching a film in other persons' physical or in their medial co-presence? To mention only one important difference: Physical co-presence grants more opportunities to show attentiveness and commitment, and at the same time allows you to detect when others are much less committed.[20] Consequently, medial co-presence comes with much looser social regulations, in the Goffmanian sense introduced in Chapter 4.

Today, the two forms of co-presence are, of course, deeply intertwined, to the point where a pure physical co-presence becomes increasingly rare. In fact, one often has to actively create it by disconnecting. But even if you personally decide to leave your phone at home, it's unlikely that your companions or even the entire audience will do so as well. For many people, being medially connected has become the norm. However, this does not devalue the arguments about physical co-presence given in this book – it simply implies that more remains to be said.

2. Mere present others, parallel viewers, co-viewers

While co-present persons *can* focus on a film in joint attention, they certainly don't have to. When I watch a film on my laptop in a crowded train compartment, the other travelers are physically very close to me (often *too* close), but they devote their attention to different objects: another film, a book, a newspaper, a computer game, their neighbor, or the landscape passing by. Hence my mode of film reception cannot be considered a joint action: I do not watch the film *with* the other travelers, but *despite* them or even against them. When watching a film at home with family or friends, in turn, physical co-presence and joint attention coincide. Here it is the breaking of the rule which contradicts the norm and which, as we have seen, can imply sanctions – for instance, when an annoyed father finally asks his daughter to stop sending messages during the film.

Among physically co-present persons it therefore makes sense to distinguish three types of co-present others: (1) mere present others, (2) parallel viewers, and (3) co-viewers. *Mere present others* are co-present others who share the same space, but do not watch a film. *Parallel viewers* are co-present others who also watch a film, but a different one. I introduce this term to highlight that we are nowadays often immersed in spaces surrounded by people who do not watch *with* us, but are still engaged with moving images on a screen. *Co-viewers* are those co-present others with whom I watch the same film. Especially in public and semi-public spaces, mere present others can immediately – and often just temporarily – turn into parallel viewers or co-viewers and vice versa. Think of the museum briefly touched upon in Chapter 3: When I visit the Tate Modern in London and stand alone in front of a monitor displaying moving images, the other museumgoers are (1) *mere present others* when they simply pass through the exhibition hall and head for the exit; or (2) they become *parallel viewers* when they step in front of another screen. Should they decide to join me in watching the same monitor, they can immediately and effortlessly turn into *co-viewers*. While our attention vectors were wildly scattered before, they are now focused on the same object. In turn, I can easily withdraw from our joint attention by moving on to the next screen without being rebuked for it.

The mere present others in the train compartment, on the airplane, or at the museum are not part of our reflective consciousness, but remain in the *background* of consciousness. With Edmund Husserl we can also say that they are part of the *horizon* of co-presented aspects. This horizon becomes explicit only when the expectation is not met, for instance when we suddenly realize that someone else is peeking over our shoulder and has switched status from mere present other to co-viewer. On the train or airplane you might be annoyed that this person dares to look at your screen, or you may be happy that he laughs with you about a funny slapstick scene. In the museum you might be startled by the unexpected presence of another person; or you might feel embarrassed about your own expressive responses because you believed you were alone in the room with your boyfriend.

Incidentally, in our screen-saturated environment – Vivian Sobchack argues that we have moved from a "screen-scape" to a "screen-sphere" – we can always be reminded to be a *mere present other* ourselves.[21] Who hasn't had the odd experience when, during a flight, someone three rows away starts laughing out loud? All of a sudden you realize, after a brief moment of puzzlement, that the person must have seen something funny in one of the films on offer – something you are currently missing.

Here we might unfold a continuum of situation-dependent background assumptions. Firstly, there are situations in which we tacitly presuppose that the other physically co-present individuals are either mere present others or parallel viewers. Would they turn into co-viewers, this would be unexpected, sometimes even unwelcome – for instance, when we watch a very private film on our smartphone in the bus. Secondly, there are situations in which we presume that the co-present persons can easily take over the role of mere present other, parallel viewer, or co-viewer. Here a fluid metamorphosis of roles is an implicit part of our horizon of experience. As mentioned, the museum would be a good case in point. Thirdly, there are situations in which we tacitly expect the co-present others first and foremost to be co-viewers. Here a change into one of the other types of physically co-present others would be unwelcome. Following what we have heard in Chapter 3, this will always be the case when we presume a strong we-intention to watch the film *together*. Think of watching a film at home with your family on a Sunday evening: When, in front of the television screen, your father starts watching a second film on his tablet (and thus oscillates between the status of co-viewer and parallel viewer), you will be bewildered. His behavior does not comply with the expectations of joint movie-watching.

Let me emphasize one last time that specific social situations come with specific obligations and entitlements, and hence with specific rules what we can expect from others. While in the museum black box I have a certain entitlement to ask my neighbor to remain quiet during an intensive scene, I would hardly dare to shush a talking neighbor on the plane. In the virtual-reality cinema I may start laughing about a clever allusion or sophisticated word-play so that my connected co-viewers can laugh *with* me; in a train compartment I wouldn't consider animating the other travelers to laugh with me, because I don't presume co-viewers in the first place. Since all these audience effects and collective experiences differ considerably, even wildly, they deserve further scrutiny, clarification, elucidation.

But this is another story and shall be told a different time.

NOTES

1. Pedullà (2012), p. 6.
2. Atkinson (2014), p. 1.
3. As Casetti points out: "An image may make itself available to a crowd or to an individual, in a public space or in private [. . .]: In each of these cases, an image acquires different valences, both experiential and political" (Casetti, 2015, p. 13).
4. Quoted from Ponzanesi/Waller (2012), p. 6 (original emphasis). Robert Stam comments on this passage: "The awareness of the possible negative projections of other spectators triggers an anxious withdrawal from the film's programmed pleasures. The conventional self-denying identification with the white hero's gaze, the vicarious acting out of a European selfhood, is short-circuited through the awareness of being 'screened' or 'allegorized' by a colonial gaze within the movie-theater itself" (Stam, 2000, pp. 98–9).
5. On the discourse surrounding the use of mobile phones in cinemas, see Hassoun (2016).
6. Holt/Sanson (2014), p. 6.
7. Despite some vague hints here and there, my own preferences were not the topic of this phenomenological study. Of course, there is no lack of critics who decry these changes of collectivity. Hardly anyone rivals Jonathan Rosenbaum – whose father and grandfather were film exhibitors in Alabama – in lamenting the loss of the communal cinematic experience: "any contemporary movie experience that relates to a community is almost by definition 'countercultural' – counter to the cultural experience of watching videos at home . . ." (Hoberman/Rosenbaum, 1991, p. 325).
8. "[O]ne can expect sound to take on – to a certain extent at least – the function traditionally assumed by darkness in a cinema-going experience: The sound received through earphones allows the individual sitting among a crowd to seclude him- or herself," Martine Beugnet writes (Beugnet, 2013, p. 201). On watching a film on a mobile phone, see also Casetti/Sampietro (2012) and Odin (2012).
9. Casetti (2015), p. 137.
10. Groening (2010), p. 1331. See also Casetti (2015), p. 137.
11. Casetti (2015), p. 48.
12. Lambie (2012). Available at http://www.denofgeek.com/movies/21761/the-weird-experience-of-watching-movies-on-planes (last accessed 19 December 2016)
13. Casetti (2015), p. 73 (original emphasis).
14. Available at https://www.engadget.com/2015/08/06/oculus-cinema-watch-movies-together/#comments (last accessed 17 December 2016).
15. Casetti (2015), p. 138.
16. Ferencz-Flatz (2016).
17. Shanyang Zhao similarly distinguishes corporeal co-presence (*face-to-face interaction*) and corporeal telecopresence (*face-to-device interaction*) (Zhao, 2003, p. 447).
18. My term "immediate proximity" overlaps with Goffman's general definition of physical co-presence: "persons must sense that they are close enough to be perceived in whatever they are doing, including their experiencing of others, and close enough to be perceived in this sensing of being perceived" (Goffman, 1963, p. 17).
19. Zhao (2003), p. 447.
20. Urry (2002), p. 259.
21. Sobchack (2014), p. 87.

Glossary

This glossary lists some of the most significant terms introduced and discussed throughout this study. For further terms, please consult the index.

Affective audience interrelations: The entire range of social relations that are based on emotions and affects as well as their concomitant expressive responses and that emerge between viewers while watching a film collectively. Affective audience interrelations are an important audience effect, since without → co-viewers they would not come about. The spectrum of how viewers experience affective audience interrelations (their experiential mode) ranges from → mutually close we-connections to → antagonistic (I–you or we–you) audience interrelations. In the former case the viewers feel phenomenologically close, while in the latter they experience themselves as socially distanced and opposed to each other. The book suggests seven phenomenological axes on which to investigate affective audience interrelations: the degree of awareness; the experiential mode; the changeability of the collective experience; the degree of volition; the strain of emotion work; the question of intimacy, closeness, and significance; and the source of the audience effect.

Affective we-experience/affective collective experience: The book distinguishes three types of affective we-experience: → shared emotion, → emotional contagion, and → feeling together. The term must not be confused with → mutually close we-connections. The latter are a result of and partly define the three types of affective we-experience.

Antagonistic audience interrelations: One end of the spectrum of how viewers experience themselves in → affective audience interrelations (opposed to → mutually close we-connections). The viewers can feel phenomenologically distanced and opposed to each other in a we–you or an I–you mode. More specifically, one can distinguish the following six constellations: (1) *we–thou* mode (second-person singular): the entire audience or a fraction of it against a concrete single viewer; (2) *we–ye* mode (second-person plural): concrete fractions of the audience against each other; (3) *we–they* mode: a concrete fraction of the audience against the rest of the audience which remains a rather vague, indeterminate backdrop and is not reflected upon; (4) *I–thou* mode (second-person singular): a concrete single viewer against another concrete single viewer; (5) *I–ye* mode (second-person plural): a concrete single viewer against the rest of the audience or a concrete fraction of it; (6) *I–they* mode: a concrete single viewer against the rest of the audience which remains a vague backdrop that isn't reflected upon.

Audience effect: The positive or negative influence other co-present viewers have on one's film experience and the influence one has on theirs. The → co-presence of other viewers can be physical (as in the cinema), but it can also be medial (as when one is connected to other viewers via a second screen). The term originates in social psychology, where it refers to the positive or negative impact observers can have on one's performance and behavior, but is slightly redefined here. This book focuses mostly on emotional and affective audience effects (→ affective audience interrelations). But it also mentions other forms like evaluative, interpretative, or moral audience effects where the co-presence of other viewers can change the value and meaning of a film as well as a viewer's ethical perspective on it. The different kinds of audience effects often influence each other, for instance when an emotional audience effect also changes the meaning or the value a film has for a given viewer.

Axiological tears: The most widespread among the five main types of → cinematic weeping. Axiological tears are an intuitive response of the viewer's body to positive moral and aesthetic values expressed via the form-content qualities of the film – values that seem highly positive yet at the same time precarious, rare, and ephemeral to the viewer. Viewers shed axiological tears about something they intuitively judge, in one way or another, as significant and meaningful.

Cinema: The minimal, a-historical definition of a prototypical cinema used for the purposes of this book presupposes a dark, public auditorium separated by a threshold from the outside world, in which viewers find themselves in the → co-presence of other viewers, follow the uninterrupted projection of a film, and are aware of site-specific behavioral rules. Historically and culturally specific movie-theaters deviate from this a-historical prototype.

Cinematic weeping: In Western cinemas prototypical cinematic weeping implies shedding tears silently; it has a detaching-individualizing effect that partly derives from the potential embarrassment of public tears; and it foregrounds a bodily experience that can be pleasurable. Since the communicative function of tears is strongly attenuated in the cinema, the book suggests using the term "weeping" rather than "crying." Altogether five main types of cinematic weeping are distinguished: → axiological tears; → sentimental tears; → personal-relevance tears; → forced tears; and → shared tears.

Collective emotions: Following Christian von Scheve and Sven Ismer, collective emotions can be defined as "the *synchronous convergence in affective responding* across individuals towards a specific event or object." Collective emotions are a broad umbrella category, a more specific subcategory of which are → shared emotions.

Collective viewing/collective spectatorship: Any constellation in which a viewer watches a film not alone but with → co-viewers. Two main types of collective spectatorship are distinguished in this book: → quiet-attentive viewing and → expressive-diverted viewing. → Audience effects can become particularly foregrounded when viewers watch films collectively, that is, with physically or medially co-present others. Collective viewing is the norm in the → cinema.

Comprehension laughter: One of the ten main types of cinematic laughter. Viewers use it as a more or less deliberate communicative tool to signal understanding to others. This can imply having understood what is comic or ridiculous in a scene, but comprehension laughter can also signal understanding of intratextual hints, intertextual references, or intermedial allusions. It has a vain side, when a viewer narcissistically honors his or her own insight and communicates it to the other viewers, and a selfless side, when he or she altruistically communicates that there is something important to understand.

Contagion laughter: One of the ten main types of cinematic laughter. A mostly involuntary laughing response to the infectious laughter of one's → co-viewers. One laughs together with the other viewers, not really knowing why and controlling what one laughs about. In contrast to amused laughter-laughter, another type of cinematic laughter, one does do not laugh *about* the laughter of others, but *with* their laughter.

Co-presence (physical and medial): The simultaneous proximity of two or more persons. Co-presence can be physical, where people are in bodily proximity, or medial, where people are in each other's electronic proximity. Since bodily proximity knows different degrees, physical co-presence unfolds along a continuum from *immediate* to *mediate* physical co-presence. People who are in each other's immediate proximity remain within the range of normal sense perception; people in mediate proximity can enter the realm of immediate physical co-presence in an instant (for instance, by opening a door).

Co-viewers: One of the three types of co-present others distinguishable in today's screen-sphere (next to → parallel viewers and → mere-present others). Co-viewers are those co-present others with whom one watches the same film, either in → quiet-attentive viewing or → expressive-diverted viewing.

Diversion (active and passive): Diversion is a specific type of attention: a *divided* attention. In → expressive-diverting viewing, spectators divide their attention between the film on the screen and the → co-viewers in the auditorium. Diversion can come in an active and a passive form: in the former case viewers willfully steer their attention to their co-viewers; in the latter case they are diverted by others, dividing their attention between film and auditorium involuntarily. The term is preferred over the more commonly used "distraction," because in film and media studies the latter is too tightly connected to the work of Walter Benjamin and Siegfried Kracauer.

Emotional contagion: One of the three types of → affective we-experience. Emotional contagion is the outcome of an interaction process in which viewers come to 'catch' other viewers' emotion. It implies a matching of subjective emotional experiences between these viewers. However, not all cases of emotional contagion imply a mutually close we-connection; in some cases the subjective emotional experiences match, but the viewers do not experience *with* their co-viewers. Strictly speaking, only those cases qualify as an affective we-experience in which viewers experience a we-ness. Emotional contagion must not be confused with the imitative behavior of emotional or behavioral *mimicry* (emotional mimicry refers to the imitation of emotion expressions of others; behavioral mimicry describes the imitation of non-emotional behaviors like foot-tapping). While mimicry can lead to emotional contagion, it does not necessarily do so.

Expressive behavior: The → collective spectatorship of the cinema knows five main forms of expressive behavior that make viewers aware of each other: → re-acting to the film, → play-acting for other viewers, → inter-acting with others, → jointly re-acting to the film, and → synchronically acting together.

Expressive-diverted viewing: One of the two main types of → collective spectatorship (next to → quiet-attentive viewing). It is expressive, because emotional responses, thoughts and judgments become explicit through → expressive behavior: facial, motor, and vocal expressions of both the verbal and non-verbal kind. It is diverted because viewers do not focus their attention primarily on the film, but in divided attention also on their → co-viewers.

Feeling together: One of the three types of → affective we-experience. When two or more viewers focus on the same intentional object and jointly care about this object due to a number of common existential background orientations, they can feel something together in a mutually close we-connection despite undergoing different emotions. Here the differing emotions match well because they are expressions of precisely the joint caring. By responding emotionally, viewer A shows viewer B that he cares about the film just as viewer B reveals to viewer A that she cares, even if their emotions differ in kind.

Forced tears: One of the five main types of → cinematic weeping. In forced weeping, viewers feel an imperative to expose their tears to their immediate neighbors for reasons of solidarity or compliance. Here it is not the film that asserts a 'pressure' to weep, but rather the viewer's immediate social surroundings 'push' him or her to shed forced tears.

Inattention: Following Erving Goffman, inattention is a form of overinvolvement in an unrelated task. Inattentive cinemagoers are those who neither pay predominant attention to the film (in → quiet-attentive viewing) nor pay divided attention to the film and their → co-viewers *as viewers* (in → expressive-diverted viewing). Examples are people who send text messages or who chatter about topics unrelated to the movie. Inattentive cinemagoers temporarily do not belong to the audience: They have, however briefly, switched status and turned into → mere present others.

Individualization thesis: An influential film historical thesis criticized in this book. It claims that the change from early cinema to classical (Hollywood) cinema came with a loss of collectivity and an individualization of the audience.

Inter-acting (with other viewers): One of the five forms of → expressive behavior in → expressive-diverted viewing. Inter-acting is a film-related and intended communication between viewers who respond to another's response. Inter-acting often depends on verbal expressions, but it can also imply pointing to something on the screen or nodding to show that one has understood. Since inter-acting implies a response to a response, it is directed at concrete others in the auditorium. Inter-acting has three subtypes: call-and-response, criticizing, and conversing.

Joint action: A term adopted from current debates about collective intentionality in analytic philosophy and phenomenology. This book claims that cinemagoers are often involved in joint actions with other viewers. → Expressive behavior, like → inter-acting (for example, conversing with one another about the film) or → synchronically acting together (for example, singing along with the songs), would be obvious cases in point. But even → quiet-attentive viewing implies a joint action based on a → we-intention and a → joint attention focused on a collective intentional object: the film. If we allow actions beyond the prototypical cases of motor movements, we can consider the attuned behavior of quietly watching and listening to a film's unfolding with others as a joint mental action based on perception, as long as the viewers take into account the normative agreement of quiet-attentive viewing (remaining silent, focusing on the film, etc.), including its social → obligations and entitlements.

Joint attention: Another term adopted from current debates about collective intentionality in analytic philosophy and phenomenology. In the cinema, paying joint attention to the film refers to the fact that individual viewers have a common understanding of what they are doing and that they are not focusing on the same intentional object by accident. They also have a minimal mutual awareness that they are perceiving the same thing: the film. However, this mutual awareness need not be reflected upon: one does not have to focus on the other viewers who are jointly attending; the mutual awareness can be relegated to the fringe of consciousness. The viewers' joint attention devoted to the film grounds the argument that → quiet-attentive viewing can be considered a form of → joint action.

Jointly re-acting (to the film): One of the five forms of → expressive behavior in → expressive-diverted viewing. Viewers who jointly re-act to a film laugh out loud together, cheer together, or applaud together. Their response is more than a mere aggregation of re-acting individuals: Jointly re-acting implies a simultaneous individual and collective response to other viewers. It thus always contains a communicative signal.

Lived-body: A technical term used by phenomenologists to distinguish the subjectively experienced body from the physical living body that can be observed and measured.

Mere present others: One of the three types of co-present others distinguishable in today's screen-sphere (next to → co-viewers and → parallel viewers). This refers to persons who simultaneously share the same space but do not watch a film on a screen. In the → cinema, mere present others are persons who are in a state of → inattention and thus pay attention neither to the film nor their → co-viewers.

Mimicry laughter: One of the ten main types of cinematic laughter. Similar to → forced tears, there are instances when viewers actively initiate a mode of laughing-along-with others, either because they do not want to stand out negatively themselves or because they do not want others to laugh on their own and hence feel isolated. While the first case is an act of conformity, the second case is an act of solidarity.

Mutually close we-connection: One end of the spectrum of how viewers experience themselves in → affective audience interrelations (opposed to → antagonistic audience interrelations). Unlike in phenomenologically distanced I–you or we–you interrelations, viewers feel phenomenologically close to each other. The three types of → affective we-experience – → shared emotion, → emotional contagion, and → feeling together – lead to or are partly defined by a mutually close we-connection.

Obligations/entitlements: Once a viewer watches a film with others, he or she has to take into account the normative agreement this entails, including its social obligations and entitlements. The two types of → collective viewing come with different obligations and entitlements. For instance, an obligation of → quiet-attentive spectatorship would be to follow the film in silence with few motor movements; an entitlement would be to shush a disturbing viewer who is not following his or her obligations.

Parallel viewers: One of the three types of co-present others distinguishable in today's screen-sphere (next to → co-viewers and → mere present others). Parallel viewers simultaneously share the same space and also watch a film, but a different one. One encounters them, for instance, when watching a film on a train or a plane, or in a museum.

Personal-relevance tears: One of the five main types of → cinematic weeping. Here viewers not only perceive the film audiovisually, but simultaneously engage in another act of consciousness: They also remember or imagine. What they perceive has a strong personal relevance and hence sparks mental visualizations of past or future events, which make them weep. This can occur in a reality mode (the viewer is reminded of what was) or a possibility mode (the spectator imagines or daydreams about what could or will happen).

Play-acting for other viewers: One of the five forms of → expressive behavior in → expressive-diverted viewing. This is a playful response to the film that is in fact addressed to one's → co-viewers. Examples are cheering, making fun of characters, or anticipating what happens next. Play-acting can occur in order to invite others to respond to the play-acting, or to make a statement to stand out as an individual viewer.

Primal scene of collective viewing: An example of a strong audience effect variously used throughout the book. The term refers to the experience of a young boy or girl who watches a filmic sex scene with his or her parents and, feeling deeply embarrassed, suddenly becomes strongly aware of the parents' presence. The term is a tongue-in-cheek reference to Sigmund Freud's concept of the *primal scene*, which refers to a child's witnessing of the parents' sex act.

Quiet-attentive viewing: One of the two main types of → collective spectatorship (next to → expressive-diverted viewing). When silently watching a film together in a → cinema, viewers are by no means always engaged in individual actions that run parallel to each other. Quietly watching a film with others often implies a → joint action based on a → we-intention in which the viewers jointly attend to a single object: the film. In comparison to the loose social regulations in expressive-diverted viewing, the behavioral codes of quiet-attentive viewing are comparatively tight.

Re-acting (to the film): One of the five forms of → expressive behavior in → expressive-diverted viewing. Re-acting is a largely involuntary and mostly non-verbal response to the film that can also occur in the private sphere when watching a film alone (for instance, a startled scream or a disgusted shriek). The re-acting viewer does not intend to convey a message, but in the collective context of the → cinema necessarily communicates his or her re-action to the others.

Sentimental tears: One of the five main types of → cinematic weeping. Here viewers are to varying degrees aware that they are shedding tears over something they personally evaluate as sentimental or even kitschy. They experience a self-reflective conflict between their personal evaluation and the tears they shed all the same, because the act of weeping seems to valorize something that does not deserve their precious tears, which results in a however mild feeling of shame or guilt. Nevertheless, viewers let themselves be overwhelmed by tears because they appreciate the bodily pleasure of a 'good cry.'

Shared emotion: One of the three types of → affective we-experience and a → subcategory of collective emotions. Two or more people can be said to share an emotion when their experience of the same kind of emotion is based on a shared intentional object to which they have an immediate response with mutual awareness and some form of phenomenological closeness.

Shared tears: One of the five main types of → cinematic weeping. Viewers who share tears have a conscious experience of emotional closeness, however strong it may be. Viewers can enjoy shedding tears only in a → collective viewing constellation. Shared weeping must not be confused with contagious crying, which is presumably a rather rare phenomenon in the cinema.

Silence: In the cinema, an important characteristic of → quiet-attentive viewing. It not only allows the film to become the predominant focus of attention, but is also positively revalued in this book as an enabling condition for the → joint attention and → joint action of quiet-attentive spectatorship. Since in the cinema we cannot *not* communicate, silence can be seen as a specific type of communication: It signals that the film and its collective reception prevail over individual reactions. Its meaning could be summarized as "We are all paying attention right now!" However, silence is fragile. Its disruption can therefore be a cause for the audience effect of anger.

Synchronically acting together: One of the five forms of → expressive behavior in → expressive-diverted viewing. A synchronized and coordinated → joint action of two or more viewers. Examples comprise speaking the dialogues together (in a cult film viewing) or singing the songs together (in a sing-along).

We-intention: Another term adopted from current debates about collective intentionality in analytic philosophy and phenomenology. The book claims that in the cinema even viewers unknown to each other have a (weak) we-intention to watch the film *jointly* rather than merely an I-intention to watch the film. For various reasons, entering a constellation of → collective viewing implies an intention (and commitment) to watching the film together. However, the degree of collective intentions that (groups of) viewers have in the cinema must be distinguished along a continuum ranging from very weak to medium to very strong we-intentions. The we-intention to watch a film together grounds the argument that → quiet-attentive viewing can be considered a form of → joint action.

Bibliography

Abel, Richard (ed.): *Encyclopedia of Early Cinema*. London: Routledge, 2005.
Abel, Richard (ed.): *French Film Theory and Criticism. A History/Anthology. 1907–1939. Vol. I: 1907–1929*. Princeton: Princeton University Press, 1988.
Abercrombie, Nicholas and Brian Longhurst: *Audiences. A Sociological Theory of Performance and Imagination*. London: Sage, 1998.
Altenloh, Emilie: "A Sociology of the Cinema: the Audience." In: *Screen*. Vol. 42, No. 3, 2001 [1914], pp. 249–93.
Altenhoh, Emilie: *Zur Soziologie des Kino. Die Kino-Unternehmung und die sozialen Schichten ihrer Besucher*. Jena: Eugen Diederichs, 1914.
Althen, Michael: *Warte, bis es dunkel ist. Eine Liebeserklärung ans Kino*. Munich: Blessing, 2002.
Anderson, Benedict: *Imagined Communities. Reflections on the Origin and Spread of Nationalism*. London: Verso, 1983.
Andrew, Dudley: *André Bazin*. Revised edition. Oxford: Oxford University Press, 2013.
Andrew, Dudley: "Film and Society. Public Rituals and Private Space." In: *East-West Film Journal*. Vol. 1, No. 1, 1986, pp. 7–22.
Andrew, Dudley: "Introduction: André Bazin Greets the New Media of the 1950s." In: *André Bazin's New Media*. Berkeley: University of California Press, 2014, pp. 1–33.
Arnheim, Rudolf: "Kino von hinten" [1927]. In: *Stimme von der Galerie. 25 kleine Aufsätze zur Kultur der Zeit*. Berlin: Philo, 2004, pp. 82–4.
Athique, Adrian Mabbott: "Imagining a 'Decent Crowd' at the Indian Multiplex." In: Karina Aveyard/Albert Moran (eds): *Watching Films. New Perspectives on Movie-Going, Exhibition and Reception*. Bristol: Intellect, 2013, pp. 371–85.
Atkinson, Sarah: *Beyond the Screen. Emerging Cinema and Engaging Audiences*. New York: Bloomsbury, 2014.
Averill, James R.: "Studies on Anger and Aggression. Implications for Theories of Emotion." In: W. Gerrod Parrott (ed.): *Emotions in Social Psychology*. New York: Psychology Press, 2001, pp. 337–52.
Aveyard, Karina and Albert Moran (eds): *Watching Films. New Perspectives on Movie-Going, Exhibition and Reception*. Bristol: Intellect, 2013.

Balsom, Erika: *Exhibiting Cinema in Contemporary Art*. Amsterdam: Amsterdam University Press, 2013.

Banjo, Omotayo O., Osei Appiah, Zheng Wang, Christopher Brown, and Whitney O. Walther: "Co-Viewing Effects of Ethnic-Oriented Programming: An Examination of In-Group Bias and Racial Comedy Exposure." In: *Journalism & Mass Communication Quarterly*. Vol. 92, No. 3, 2015, pp. 662–80.

Barker, Martin: "Crossing Out the Audience." In: Ian Christie (ed.): *Audiences. Defining and Researching Screen Entertainment Reception*. Amsterdam: Amsterdam University Press, 2012, pp. 187–205.

Barker, Martin: "*The Lord of the Rings* and 'Identification': A Critical Encounter." In: *European Journal of Communication*. Vol. 20, No. 3, 2005, pp. 353–78.

Barker, Martin: "The Pleasures of Watching an 'Off-beat' Film: the Case of *Being John Malkovich*." In: *Scope*. Vol. 11, 2008. n.p.

Barker, Martin and Kate Brooks: *Knowing Audiences:* Judge Dredd, *its Friends, Fans and Foes*. Luton: University of Luton Press, 1998.

Barnard, Timothy: "La Hora de los hornos." In: Timothy Barnard/Peter Rist (eds): *South American Cinema. A Critical Filmography, 1915–1994*. New York: Garland, 1996.

Barthes, Roland: "Leaving the Movie-theater." In: *The Rustle of Language*. Berkeley: University of California Press, 1989, pp. 345–9.

Baudry, Jean-Louis: "Ideological Effects of the Basic Cinematographic Apparatus." In: Philip Rosen (ed.): *Narrative, Apparatus, Ideology*. New York: Columbia University Press, 1986 [1970], pp. 281–98.

Baudry, Jean-Louis: "The Apparatus. Metapsychological Approaches to the Impression of Reality in the Cinema." In: Philip Rosen (ed.): *Narrative, Apparatus, Ideology*. New York: Columbia University Press, 1986 [1975], pp. 299–318.

Bazin, André: "About Television" [1958]. In: *André Bazin's New Media*. Edited and translated by Dudley Andrew. Berkeley: University of California Press, 2014, pp. 204–12.

Bazin, André: "A Contribution to an *Erotologie* of Television" [1954]. In: *André Bazin's New Media*. Edited and translated by Dudley Andrew. Berkeley: University of California Press, 2014, pp. 105–15.

Bazin, André: "Charlie Chaplin" [1948]. *What Is Cinema? Volume 1*. Berkeley: University of California Press, 1967, pp. 144–53.

Bazin, André: "Cinema and Television: An Interview with Jean Renoir and Roberto Rossellini" [1958]. In: *André Bazin's New Media*. Edited and translated by Dudley Andrew. Berkeley: University of California Press, 2014, pp. 187–203.

Bazin, André: "Limelight, or the Death of Moliere" [1952]. In: *What Is Cinema? Volume 2*. Berkeley: University of California Press, 1971, pp. 124–7.

Bazin, André: "Marginal Notes on *Eroticism in the Cinema*" [1957]. In: André Bazin: *What Is Cinema? Volume 2*. Berkeley: University of California Press, 1971, pp. 169–75.

Bazin, André: "Some Films Are Better on the Small Screen than the Large" [1954]. In: *André Bazin's New Media*. Edited and translated by Dudley Andrew. Berkeley: University of California Press, 2014, pp. 160–2.

Bazin, André: "Theater and Cinema" [1951]. In: *What Is Cinema? Volume 1*. Berkeley: University of California Press, 1967, pp. 67–124.

Bazin, André: "The Trial of CinemaScope: It Didn't Kill the Close-Up" [1954]. *André Bazin's New Media*. Edited and translated by Dudley Andrew. Berkeley: University of California Press, 2014, pp. 294–8.

Bazin, André: "To Create a Public" [1944]. In: *Cinema of the Occupation and Resistance: The Birth of a Critical Esthetic*. New York: Frederick Ungar, 1981, pp. 68–70.

Beller, Jonathan: *The Cinematic Mode of Production: Attention Economy and the Society of the Spectacle*. Lebanon, NH: Dartmouth University Press, 2006.

Bellour, Raymond: "The Cinema Spectator: A Special Memory." In: Ian Christie (ed.): *Audiences*. Amsterdam: Amsterdam University Press, 2012, pp. 206–17.
Benjamin, Walter: "Chaplin in Retrospect." [1929] In: Michael W. Jennings/Brigid Doherty/Thomas Y. Levin (eds): *The Work of Art in the Age of Its Technological Reproducibility, and Other Writings on Media*. Cambridge, MA: The Belknap Press of Harvard University Press, 2008, pp. 335–7.
Benjamin, Walter: "Das Kunstwerk im Zeitalter seiner technischen Reproduzierbarkeit" [1936]. In: *Das Kunstwerk im Zeitalter seiner technischen Reproduzierbarkeit. Drei Studien zur Kunstsoziologie*. Frankfurt/Main: Suhrkamp, 1977, pp. 7–44.
Benjamin, Walter: "[no title]" [c. 1931]. In: *Gesammelte Schriften II.3*. Edited by Rolf Tiedemann and Hermann Schwepphäuser. Frankfurt/Main: Suhrkamp, 1977.
Benjamin, Walter: "Hitler's Diminished Masculinity" [1934]. In: *Selected Writings. Volume 2. 1927–1934*. Edited by Michael W. Jennings, Howard Eiland, and Gary Smith. Cambridge, MA: The Belknap Press of Harvard University Press, 1999, pp. 792–3.
Benjamin, Walter: "One-Way Street" [1928]. In: *Selected Writings. Volume 1. 1913–1926*. Edited by Marcus Bullock and Michael W. Jennings. Cambridge, MA: The Belknap Press of Harvard University Press, 1996, pp. 444–88.
Benjamin, Walter: "The Work of Art in the Age of Mechanical Reproduction" [1936]. Translated by Harry Zohn. In: David H. Richter (ed.): *The Critical Tradition. Classic Texts and Contemporary Trends*. New York: St Martins, 1989, pp. 571–88.
Benjamin, Walter: "The Work of Art in the Age of Its Technological Reproducibility" [1936]. First version. Translated by Michael W. Jennings. In: *Grey Room*. Vol. 39, Spring 2010, pp. 11–37.
Benjamin, Walter: "The Work of Art in the Age of Its Technological Reproducibility." [1936] Second Version. Translated by Michael W. Jennings. In: Michael W. Jennings/Brigid Doherty/Thomas Y. Levin (eds): *The Work of Art in the Age of Its Technological Reproducibility, and Other Writings on Media*. Cambridge, MA: The Belknap Press of Harvard University Press, 2008, pp. 19–55.
Bergson, Henri: *Laughter. An Essay on the Meaning of the Comic*. New York: Macmillan, 1914 [1900].
Berkenbusch, Gisela: *Zum Heulen. Kulturgeschichte unserer Tränen*. Berlin: Transit, 1985.
Beugnet, Martine: "Miniature Pleasures: On Watching Films on an iPhone." In: *Cinematicity in Media History*. Edinburgh: Edinburgh University Press, 2013, pp. 196–210.
Biltereyst, Daniel, Richard Maltby, and Philippe Meers (eds): *Cinema, Audiences and Modernity. New Perspectives on European Cinema History*. Milton Park: Routledge, 2012.
Biró, Yvette: "The Fullness of Minimalism." In: *Rouge*. No. 9, 2006, n.p.
Blumer, Herbert: *Movies and Conduct. A Payne Fund Study*. New York: Macmillan, 1933.
Boillat, Alain: "The Social Imaginary of Telephony." In: François Albera and Maria Tortajada (eds): *Cine-Dispositives. Essays in Epistemology Across Media*. Amsterdam: Amsterdam University Press, 2015, pp. 217–47.
Bonitzer, Pascal: "Les deux regards." In: *Cahiers du cinema*. No. 275, April 1977, pp. 40–6.
Bordwell, David: *Figures Traced in Light. On Cinematic Staging*. Berkeley: University of California Press, 2005.
Bordwell, David: "Historical Poetics of Cinema." In: R. Barton Palmer (eds): *The Cinematic Text: Methods and Approaches*. New York: AMS Press, 1989, pp. 369–98.
Bordwell, David: *On the History of Film Style*. Cambridge, MA: Harvard University Press, 1997.
Brandl-Risi, Bettina: "Genuss und Kritik. Partizipieren im Theaterpublikum." In: Dietmar

Kammerer (ed.): *Vom Publicum. Das Öffentliche in der Kunst.* Bielefeld: Transcript, 2012, pp. 73–88.
Branston, Gill: "Why Theory?" In: Christine Gledhill and Linda Williams (eds): *Reinventing Film Studies.* London: Arnold, 2000, pp. 18–33.
Breakwell, Ian and Paul Hammond (eds): *Seeing in the Dark. A Companion of Cinemagoing.* London: Serpent's Tail, 1990.
Brennan, Teresa: *The Transmission of Affect.* Ithaca: Cornell University Press, 2004.
Briggs, Joe Bob, J. Hoberman, Damien Love, Tim Lucas, Danny Peary, Jeffrey Sconce, and Peter Stanfield: "Cult Cinema: A Critical Symposium." In: *Cineaste.* Vol. 48, No. 1, 2008. pp. 46–50.
Brown, Tom: *Breaking the Fourth Wall: Direct Address in the Cinema.* Edinburgh: Edinburgh University Press, 2012.
Bruder, Martin, Agneta Fischer, and Antony S. R. Manstead: "Social Appraisal as a Cause of Collective Emotions." In: Mikko Salmela and Christian von Scheve (eds): *Collective Emotions.* Oxford: Oxford University Press, 2014, pp. 141–51.
Burch, Noël: *Life to Those Shadows.* Berkeley: University of California Press, 1990.
Burgin, Victor: "Barthes's Discretion." In: Jean-Michel Rabaté (ed.): *Writing the Image After Roland Barthes.* Philadelphia: University of Pennsylvania Press, 1997, pp. 19–31.
Burke, Edmund: "Enquiry into the Sublime and Beautiful." In: *The Writings and Speeches of Edmund Burke.* Volume 1. Oxford: Clarendon Press, 1997 [1757].
Butsch, Richard: "Changing Images of Movie Audiences." In: Richard Maltby, Melvyn Stokes, and Robert C. Allen (eds): *Going to the Movies. Hollywood and the Social Experience of Cinema.* Exeter: University of Exeter Press, 2007, pp. 293–306.

Caminada, Emanuele: "Joining the Background: Habitual Sentiments Behind We-Intentionality." In: Anita Konzelmann Ziv and Hans Bernhard Schmid (eds): *Institutions, Emotions, and Group Agents.* Dordrecht: Springer, 2014, pp. 195–212.
Camus, Albert: *The First Man.* New York: Alfred R. Knopf, 1995.
Canudo, Ricciotto: "The Birth of a Sixth Art." [1911] In: Richard Abel (ed.): *French Film Theory and Criticism. A History/Anthology. 1907–1939. Vol. I: 1907–1929.* Princeton: Princeton University Press, 1988, pp. 58–66.
Carassa, Antonella and Marco Colombetti: "Interpersonal Responsibilities and Communicative Intentions." In: *Phenomenology and Cognitive Sciences.* Vol. 13, 2014, pp. 145–59.
Carassa, Antonella and Marco Colombetti: "On the Normativity of Interpersonal Reality." Paper presented at the 21st Annual Meeting of the European Society for Philosophy and Psychology. July 2013. https://ssl.lu.usi.ch/entityws/Allegati/pdf_pub7127.pdf
Cardwell, Mike: *Dictionary of Psychology.* London: Routledge, 2013.
Carroll, Noël: "Horror and Humor." In: *The Journal of Aesthetics and Art Criticism.* Vol. 57, No. 2, 1999, pp. 145–60.
Casetti, Francesco: "Die Explosion des Kinos: Filmische Erfahrung in der post-kinematographischen Epoche." *Montage/AV.* Vol. 19, No. 1, 2010, pp. 11–35.
Casetti, Francesco: "Filmic Experience." In: *Screen.* Vol. 50, No. 1, 2009, pp. 56–66.
Casetti, Francesco: *The Lumière Galaxy. Seven Keywords for the Cinema to Come.* New York: Columbia University Press, 2015.
Casetti, Francesco: *Theories of Cinema. 1945–1995.* Austin: University of Texas Press, 1999.
Casetti, Francesco and Sara Sampietro: "With Eyes, with Hands. The Relocation of Cinema into the iPhone." In: Pelle Snickars and Patrick Vonderau (eds): *Moving Data. The iPhone and the Future of Media.* New York: Columbia University Press, 2012, pp. 19–32.

Cavell, Stanley: "The Fact of Television." In: *Daedalus*. Vol. 111, No. 4, 1982, pp. 75–96.
Cavell, Stanley: *The World Viewed. Reflections on the Ontology of Film*. Enlarged edition. Cambridge, MA: Harvard University Press, 1979.
Châteauvert, Jean: "Regards à la caméra. Les comédiens en point de mire." In: Michel Marie and Laurent Le Forestier (eds): *La firme Pathé Frères*. Paris: AFHRC, 2004, pp. 219–36.
Châteauvert, Jean and André Gaudreault: "The Noises of Spectators, or the Spectator as Additive to the Spectacle." In: Richard Abel and Rick Altman (eds): *The Sounds of Early Cinema*. Bloomington: Indiana University Press, 2001, pp. 183–91.
Cheu, Johnson: "Let's Go Swimming: (Not) Crying at the Movies." In: Michele Byers and David Lavery (eds): *On the Verge of Tears: Why the Movies, Television, Music, Art, Popular Culture, Literature, and the Real World Make Us Cry*. Newcastle: Cambridge Scholars Publishing, 2010, pp. 67–76.
Christie, Ian: "Introduction: In Search of Audiences." In: Ian Christie (ed.): *Audiences*. Amsterdam: Amsterdam University Press, 2012, pp. 11–21.
Christie, Ian: "What Do We *Really* Know About Audiences?" In: Ian Christie (ed.): *Audiences*. Amsterdam: Amsterdam University Press, 2012, pp. 225–34.
Clover, Carol J.: *Men, Women, and Chainsaws. Gender in the Modern Horror Film*. Princeton: Princeton University Press, 1992.
Coan, James A., Hillary S. Schaefer and Richard J. Davidson: "Lending a Hand: Social Regulation of the Neural Threat Response." In: *Psychological Science*. Vol. 17, No. 12, 2006, pp. 1032–9.
Cochrane, Tom: "Joint Attention to Music." In: *British Journal of Aesthetics*. Vol. 49, No. 1, 2009, pp. 59–73.
Colombetti, Giovanna: "What Language Does to Feeling." In: *Journal of Consciousness Studies*. Vol. 16, No. 9, 2009, pp. 4–26.
Comolli, Jean-Louis: "Notes on the New Spectator" [1966]. In: Jim Hillier (ed.): *Cahiers du Cinéma. 1960–1968: New Wave, New Cinema, Reevaluating Hollywood*. Cambridge, MA: Harvard University Press, 1986, pp. 210–15.
Cornea, Christine: "'So Bad It's Good.' Critical Humor in Science Fiction Cinema." In: Murray Pomerance (ed.): *The Last Laugh: Strange Humors of Cinema*. Detroit: Wayne State University Press, 2013, pp. 75–91.
Cornelius, Randolph R.: "Crying and Catharsis." In: Ad Vingerhoets and Randolph R. Cornelius (eds): *Adult Crying: A Biopsychosocial Approach*. Philadelphia: Brunner-Routledge, 2001, pp. 199–211.
Costa, Marco, Wies Dinsbach, Anthony Manstead, and Pio Ricci Bitti: "Social Presence, Embarrassment, and Nonverbal Behavior." In: *Journal of Nonverbal Behavior*. Vol. 25, No. 4, Winter 2001, pp. 225–40.
Cova, Florian and Julien A. Deonna: "Being Moved." In: *Philosophical Studies*. Vol. 3, 2013, pp. 446–7.
Crary, Jonathan: *24/7. Late Capitalism and the Ends of Sleep*. London: Verso, 2013.
Cubitt, Sean: *The Cinema Effect*. Cambridge, MA: MIT Press, 2005.

Danto, Arthur C.: "Moving Pictures." In: Noël Carroll and Jinhee Choi (eds): *Philosophy of Film and Motion Pictures*. Malden, MA: Wiley-Blackwell, 2005, pp. 100–12.
Dayan, Daniel and Elihu Katz: *Media Events. The Live Broadcasting of History*. Cambridge, MA: Harvard University Press, 1992.
Deger, Jennifer: "Participatory Vision. Watching Movies with Yolngu." In: Virginia Nightingale (ed.): *The Handbook of Media Audiences*. Malden, MA: Blackwell, 2011, pp. 459–71.
Deleuze, Gilles: "Post-Script on the Societies of Control." In: *October*. Vol. 59, 1992. pp. 3–7.
Delluc, Louis: "From Orestes to Rio Jim" [1921]. In: Richard Abel (ed.): *French Theory and*

Criticism. A History/Anthology. 1907–1939. Vol. I: 1907–1929. Princeton: Princeton University Press, 1988, pp. 255–7.

Delluc, Louis: "The Crowd" [1918]. In: Richard Abel (ed.): *French Theory and Criticism. A History/Anthology. 1907–1939. Vol. I: 1907–1929.* Princeton: Princeton University Press, 1988, pp. 159–64.

Del Río, Elena: *Deleuze and the Cinemas of Performance. Powers of Affection.* Edinburgh: Edinburgh University Press, 2008.

De Luca, Tiago: "Slow Time, Visible Cinema. Duration, Experience, and Spectatorship." In: *Screen.* Vol. 56, No. 1, 2016, pp. 23–42.

Demmerling, Christoph and Hilge Landweer: *Philosophie der Gefühle. Von Achtung bis Zorn.* Stuttgart: Metzler, 2007.

Depraz, Natalie: *Phänomenologie in der Praxis. Eine Einführung.* Freiburg: Alber, 2012.

Devereux, Paul G. and Gerald P. Ginsburg: "Sociality Effects on the Production of Laughter." In: *The Journal of General Psychology.* Vol. 128, No. 2, 2001, pp. 227–40.

Dibbets, Karel: "The Introduction of Sound." In: Geoffrey Nowell-Smith (ed.): *The Oxford History of World Cinema.* Oxford: Oxford University Press, 1997, pp. 211–19.

Dreyfus, Hubert and Sean Dorrance Kelly: *All Things Shining. Reading the Western Classics to Find Meaning in a Secular Age.* New York: Free Press, 2011.

Dunbar, Robin I. M., Rebecca Baron, Anna Frangou, Eiluned Pearce, Edwin J. C. van Leeuwen, Julie Stow, Giselle Partridge, Ian MacDonald, Vincent Barra, and Mark van Vugt: "Social Laughter Is Correlated with an Elevated Pain Threshold." In: *Proceedings of the Royal Society B.* Vol. 279, 2012, pp. 1161–7.

Dunn, Stephane: *Baad Bitches and Sassy Supermamas. Black Power Action Films.* Urbana: University of Illinois Press, 2008.

Echterhoff, Gerald, E. Tory Higgins, and John M. Levine: "Shared Reality: Experiencing Commonality With Others' Inner States About the World." In: *Perspectives on Psychological Science.* Vol. 4, No. 5, 2009, pp. 496–521.

Eikhenbaum, Boris: "Problems of Cine-Stylistics" [1927]. In: *Russian Poetics in Translation. Volume 9: The Poetics of Cinema.* Edited by Richard Taylor. Oxford: RPT Publications/The University of Essex, 1982, n.p.

Ellis, John: *Visible Fictions. Cinema, Television, Video.* Revised edition. London: Routledge, 2002.

Elsaesser, Thomas: "Narrative Cinema and Audience-Oriented Aesthetics." In: Tony Bennett et al. (eds): *Popular Television and Film.* London: BFI, 1981, pp. 270–82.

Elsaesser, Thomas: "Pragmatik des Audiovisuellen: Rettungsboot auf der Titanic?" In: *Kinoschriften.* Vol. 4, 1996, pp. 107–20.

Elsaesser, Thomas: "The New New Hollywood: Cinema Beyond Distance and Proximity." In: Ib Bondebjerg (ed.): *Moving Images, Culture and the Mind.* Luton: University of Luton Press, 2000, pp. 187–204.

Elsaesser, Thomas: "Wie der frühe Film zum Erzählkino wurde. Vom kollektiven Publikum zum individuellen Zuschauer." In: *Filmgeschichte und frühes Kino. Archäologie eines Medienwandels.* Munich: Edition Text + Kritik, 2002, pp. 69–93.

Epstein, Jean: "On Certain Characteristics of Photogénie" [1924]. In: Sarah Keller and Jason N. Paul (eds): *Jean Epstein. Critical Essays and New Translations.* Amsterdam: Amsterdam University Press, 2012, pp. 292–6.

Esch, Amy and Christine Ehren: "Crowds Turn Out for Opening of 'Sing-a-Long Sound of Music' in NYC." http://www.playbill.com/article/crowds-turn-out-for-opening-of-sing-a-long-sound-of-music-in-nyc-com-91701.

Evans, Elizabeth and Paul McDonald: "Online Distribution of Film and Television in the UK.

Behavior, Taste, and Value." In: Jennifer Holt and Kevin Sanson (eds): *Connected Viewing. Selling, Streaming & Sharing Media in the Digital Age.* New York: Routledge, 2014, pp. 158–79.

Faure, Élie: "The Art of Cineplastics" [1920]. In: Daniel Talbot (ed.): *Film. An Anthology.* Berkeley: University of California Press, 1959, pp. 3–14.
Feldman Barrett, Lisa: "Feelings or Words? Understanding the Content in Self-Report Ratings of Experienced Emotion." In: *Journal of Personality and Social Psychology.* Vol. 87, No. 2, 2004, pp. 266–81.
Feldmann, Erich: "Considération sur la situation du spectateur au cinéma." In: *Revues internationale de filmologie.* Vol. 26, 1956. pp. 83–97.
Feldmann, Erich: "Die Situation des Zuschauers beim Filmerleben." In: *Theorie der Massenmedien. Presse, Film, Funk, Fernsehen.* Munich: Reinhardt, 1962, pp. 113–33.
Ferencz-Flatz, Christian: "Collective Awareness in TV and Cinema. A Phenomenology of Intersubjectivity in the Age of Mass-Media." Paper presented at the "Experiences, Emotions, Episodes: Contemporary Positions in Film Phenomenology" symposium at the University of Groningen, 9 December 2016.
Ferencz-Flatz, Christian and Julian Hanich: "What Is Film Phenomenology?" In: Christian Ferencz-Flatz and Julian Hanich (eds): *Film and Phenomenology.* Special Issue of *Studia Phaenomenologica.* Vol. 16, 2016.
Fiebich, Anika and Shaun Gallagher: "Joint Attention in Joint Action." In: *Philosophical Psychology.* Vol. 26, No. 4, 2013, pp. 571–87.
Fischer, Agneta, Antony Manstead, and Ruud Zaalberg: "Social Influences on the Emotion Process." In: *European Review of Social Psychology.* Vol. 14, No. 1, 2003, pp. 171–201.
Fisher, Philip: *The Vehement Passions.* Princeton: Princeton University Press, 2002.
Flanagan, Matthew: *'Slow Cinema': Temporality and Style in Contemporary Art and Experimental Film.* PhD thesis: University of Exeter, 2012.
Foucault, Michel: *Discipline and Punish. The Birth of the Prison.* New York: Vintage, 1995 [1975].
Fox, Kate: "The Kleenex For Men Crying Game Report. A Study of Men and Crying." The Social Issues Research Center, 2014.
Frampton, Daniel: *Filmosophy.* London: Wallflower, 2006.
Freeburg, Victor Oscar: *The Art of Photoplay Making.* New York: Macmillan, 1918.
Freud, Sigmund: *Civilization and Its Discontents.* The Standard Edition. New York: Norton, 2010 [1930].
Freud, Sigmund: *Group Psychology and the Analysis of the Ego.* London: Hogarth Press, 1949 [1921].
Frey, Matthias: "Tuning Out, Tuning In, and Walking Off. The Film Spectator in Pain." In: Asbjorn Gronstad and Henrik Gustafsson (eds): *Ethics and Images of Pain.* London: Routledge, 2012, pp. 93–111.
Friedberg, Anne: "Urban Mobility and Cinematic Visuality. The Screens of Los Angeles – Endless Cinema or Private Telematics." In: *Journal of Visual Culture.* Vol. 1, No. 2, 2002, pp. 183–204.
Frome, Jonathan: "Melodrama and the Psychology of Tears." In: *Projections.* Vol. 8, No. 1, 2014, pp. 23–40.
Fuller, Raymond G. C. and Alan Sheehy Skeffington: "Effects of Group Laughter on Responses to Humorous Material. A Replication." In: *Psychological Reports.* Vol. 35, 1974, pp. 531–4.

Gerrig, Richard J. and Deborah A. Prentice: "Notes on Audience Response." In: David Bordwell and Noël Carroll (eds): *Post-Theory: Reconstructing Film Studies.* Madison, WI: University of Wisconsin Press, 1996, pp. 388–403.

Giesz, Ludwig: *Phänomenologie des Kitsches*. Frankfurt/Main: Fischer, 1994 [1971].
Gilbert, Margaret: "Collective Guilt and Collective Guilt Feelings." In: *The Journal of Ethics*. Vol. 6, 2002, pp. 114–43.
Gilbert, Margaret: "How We Feel. Understanding Everyday Collective Emotion Ascription." In: Christian von Scheve and Mikko Salmela (eds): *Collective Emotions*. Oxford: Oxford University Press, 2014, pp. 17–31.
Gilbert, Margaret: "Mutual Recognition, Common Knowledge and Joint Attention." In: T. Ronnow-Rasmussen, B. Petersson, J. Josefsson, and D. Egonsson (eds): *Hommage à Wlodek. Philosophical Papers Dedicated to Wlodek Rabinowicz* (2007), http://www.fil.lu.se/hommageawlodek/site/papper/GilbertMargaret.pdf
Gilbert, Margaret: "Walking Together: a Paradigmatic Social Phenomenon." In: *Midwest Studies in Philosophy*. No. 15, 1990, pp. 1–14.
Godman, Marion: "Why We Do Things Together: The Social Motivation for Joint Action." In: *Philosophical Psychology*. Vol. 26, No. 4, 2013, pp. 588–603.
Goffman, Erving: *Behavior in Public Places. Notes on the Social Organization of Gatherings*. New York: Free Press, 1963.
Goffman, Erving: *Encounters. Two Studies in the Sociology of Interaction*. Indianapolis: Bobbs-Merrill, 1961.
Goffman, Erving: *The Presentation of Self in Everyday Life*. New York: Anchor, 1959.
Goldstein, Thalia R.: "The Pleasure of Unadulterated Sadness: Experiencing Sorrow in Fiction, Nonfiction, and 'In Person.'" In: *Psychology of Aesthetics, Creativity, and the Arts*. Vol. 3, No. 4, 2009, pp. 232–7.
Gollwitzer, Mario, Milena Meder, and Manfred Schmitt: "What Gives Victims Satisfaction When They Seek Revenge?" In: *European Journal of Social Psychology*. Vol. 41, No. 3, 2011, pp. 364–74.
Greenberg, Clement: "Avant-Garde and Kitsch." In: *Partisan Review*. Vol. 6, No. 5, 1939, pp. 34–49.
Groening, Stephen: "From 'A Box in the Theater of the World' to 'The World as Your Living Room': Cellular Phones, Television and Mobile Privatization." In: *New Media & Society*. Vol. 12, No. 8, 2010, pp. 1331–47.
Gross, James J. and Robert W. Levenson: "Emotion Elicitation Using Films." In: *Cognition and Emotion*. Vol. 9, No. 1, 1995, pp. 87–108.
Gross, James J. and Ross A. Thompson: "Emotion Regulation. Conceptual Foundations." In: James J. Gross (ed.): *Handbook of Emotion Regulation*. New York: Guilford, 2007, pp. 3–24.
Guattari, Félix: "The Poor Man's Couch." In: *Chaosophy. Texts and Interviews 1972–1977*. Los Angeles: Semiotext(e), 2009, pp. 257–67.
Guney, Zeynep Okur: "Collective Affectivity as a Flux of You, Me, and We. Comment on Zahavi's 'You, Me, and We: The Sharing of Emotional Experience'." In: *Journal of Consciousness Studies*. Vol. 22, Nos. 1–2, 2015, pp. 102–6.
Gunning, Tom: "Moving Away From the Index. Cinema and the Impression of Reality." In: Gertrud Koch, Volker Pantenburg, and Simon Rothöhler (eds): *Screen Dynamics. Mapping the Borders of Cinema*. Vienna: Synema, 2012, pp. 42–60.

Hanich, Julian and Winfried Menninghaus: "Beyond Sadness. The Multi-Emotional Trajectory of Melodrama." In: *Cinema Journal*. Vol. 56, No. 4, 2017, pp. 76–101.
Hanich, Julian: *Cinematic Emotion in Horror Films and Thrillers. The Aesthetic Paradox of Pleasurable Fear*. New York: Routledge, 2010.
Hanich, Julian: "Clips, Clicks and Climax. The Relocation and Remediation of Pornography." In: *Jump Cut. A Review of Contemporary Media*. Vol. 53, August 2011, n.p.

Hanich, Julian: "Judge Dread. What We Are Afraid of When We Are Scared at the Movies." In: *Projections*. Vol. 8, No. 2, 2014, pp. 26–49.
Hanich, Julian: "Kino als Erfahrungsraum: Die Öffentlichkeit des Kinos." In: Bernhard Groß and Thomas Morsch (eds): *Handbuch Filmtheorie*. Wiesbaden: Springer VS, 2016.
Hanich, Julian: "Kino, Theater, Fernsehen: André Bazins Publikumstheorie." In: Thomas Weber and Florian Mundhenke (eds): *Kinoerfahrungen. Theorien, Geschichte, Perspektiven*. Berlin: Avinus, 2017.
Hanich, Julian, Valentin Wagner, Mira Shah, Thomas Jacobsen, and Winfried Menninghaus: "Why We Like to Watch Sad Films. The Pleasure of Being Moved in Aesthetic Experiences." In: *Psychology of Aesthetics, Creativity, and the Arts*. Vol. 8, No. 2, 2014, pp. 130–43.
Hansen, Miriam: *Babel and Babylon: Spectatorship in American Silent Film*. Cambridge, MA: Harvard University Press, 1991.
Hansen, Miriam: *Cinema and Experience. Siegfried Kracauer, Walter Benjamin, and Theodor W. Adorno*. Berkeley: University of California Press, 2012.
Hansen, Miriam: "Early Cinema: Whose Public Sphere?" In: Thomas Elsaesser (ed.): *Early Cinema: Space, Frame, Narrative*. London: BFI Publishing, 1990, pp. 228–46.
Harper, Sue and Vincent Porter: "Moved to Tears: Weeping in the Cinema in Postwar Britain." In: *Screen*. Vol. 37, No. 2, 1996, pp. 152–73.
Hassoun, Dan: "Engaging Distractions: Regulating Second-Screen Use in the Theater." In: *Cinema Journal*. Vol. 55, No. 2, 2016.
Hatfield, Elaine, Megan Carpenter, and Richard L. Rapson: "Emotional Contagion as a Precursor to Collective Emotions." In: Christian von Scheve and Mikko Salmela (eds): *Collective Emotions*. Oxford: Oxford University Press, 2014.
Hayes, Britt: "When Is Cheering for Violence in Movies Okay?" http://badassdigest.com/2013/06/06/when-is-cheering-for-violence-in-movies-okay/
Helm, Bennett W.: "Emotional Communities of Respect." In: Christian von Scheve and Mikko Salmela (eds): *Collective Emotions*. Oxford: Oxford University Press, 2014, pp. 47–59.
Hess, Ursula: "Anger Is a Positive Emotion." In: W. Gerrod Parrott (ed.): *The Positive Side of Negative Emotions*. New York: Guilford Press, 2014, pp. 55–75.
Hess, Ursula, Stephanie Houde, and Agneta Fischer: "Do We Mimic What We See or What We Know?" In: Christian von Scheve and Mikko Salmela (eds): *Collective Emotions*. Oxford: Oxford University Press, 2014, pp. 94–104.
Hill, Annette: *Shocking Entertainment. Viewer Response to Movie Violence*. Luton: University of Luton Press, 1997.
Hills, Matt: *The Pleasures of Horror*. London: Continuum, 2005.
Hillyer, Minette: "Labours of Love. Home Movies, Paracinema, and the Modern Work of Cinema Spectatorship." In: *Continuum. Journal of Media and Cultural Studies*. Vol. 24, No. 5, 2010, pp. 763–75.
Hoberman, J. and Jonathan Rosenbaum: *Midnight Movies*. New York: Da Capo, 1991.
Hochschild, Arlie: "Emotion Work, Feeling Rules, and Social Structure." In: *American Journal of Sociology*. Vol. 85, No. 3, 1979, pp. 551–75.
Hofmann, Jennifer, Tracey Platt, Willibald Ruch, Radoslaw Niewiadomski, and Jérome Urbain: "The Influence of a Virtual Companion on Amusement When Watching Funny Films." In: *Motivation and Emotion*. Vol. 39, No. 3, 2015, pp. 434–47.
Holt, Jennifer and Kevin Sanson: "Introduction." In: Jennifer Holt and Kevin Samson (eds): *Connected Viewing. Selling, Streaming & Sharing Media in the Digital Age*. New York: Routledge, 2014, pp. 1–15.
Honneth, Axel: *The Struggle for Recognition: The Moral Grammar of Social Conflicts*. Cambridge, MA: MIT Press, 1995.

Horkheimer, Max and Theodor W. Adorno: *Dialectic of Enlightenment. Philosophical Fragments*. Stanford: Stanford University Press, 2002 [1944].

Hughes, Jessica: "The Festival Collective. Cult Audiences and Japanese Extreme Cinema." In: CarrieLynn D. Reinhard and Christopher Olson (eds): *Making Sense of Cinema. Empirical Studies into Film Spectators and Spectatorship*. New York: Bloomsbury, 2016, pp. 37–56.

Huron, David: *Sweet Anticipation. Music and the Psychology of Expectation*. Cambridge, MA: MIT Press, 2006.

Ihde, Don: *Experimental Phenomenology. An Introduction*. New York: Putnam, 1977.

Ihde, Don: *Listening and Voice. Phenomenologies of Sound*. Second edition. Albany: State University of New York Press, 2007.

Jackson Harris, Richard and Lindsay Cook: "How Content and Co-Viewers Elicit Emotional Discomfort in Moviegoing Experiences. Where Does the Discomfort Come From and How is it Handled?" In: *Applied Cognitive Psychology*. November 2010.

Jakobs, Esther, Antony S. R. Manstead, and Agneta H. Fischer: "Social Context Effects on Facial Activity in a Negative Emotional Setting." In: *Emotion*. Vol. 1, No. 1, 2001, pp. 51–69.

Jamison, Leslie: "In Defense of Saccharin(e)." In: *The Empathy Exams*. London: Granta, 2014, pp. 111–31.

Jay, Martin: *Downcast Eyes. The Denigration of Vision in Twentieth-Century French Thought*. Berkeley: University of California Press, 1993.

Jenkins, Henry: *Convergence Culture. Where Old and New Media Collide*. New York: New York University Press, 2006.

Jermyn, Deborah: "Public Tears and Private Moments – Saying Goodbye to *Sex and the City*." In: Michele Byers and David Lavery (eds): *On the Verge of Tears: Why the Movies, Television, Music, Art, Popular Culture, Literature, and the Real World Make Us Cry*. Newcastle: Cambridge Scholars Publishing, 2010, pp. 156–8.

Jirgl, Reinhard: "Kino, Wut und kleine Dialektik der Solidarität." In: Wolfram Schütte (ed.): *Bilder vom Kino. Literarische Kabinettstücke*. Frankfurt/Main: Suhrkamp, 1996, pp. 76–7.

Jullier, Laurent and Jean-Marc Leveratto: "Cinephilia in the Digital Age." In: Ian Christie (ed.) *Audiences*. Amsterdam: Amsterdam University Press, 2012, pp. 143–54.

Kaes, Anton, Nicholas Baer, and Michael Cowan (eds): *The Promise of Cinema. German Film Theory 1907–1933*. Berkeley: University of California Press, 2015.

Katz, Jack: "Emotion's Crucible." In: Dale Spencer, Kevin Walby and Alan Hunt (eds): *Emotions Matter. A Relational Approach to Emotions*. Toronto: University of Toronto Press, 2012, pp. 15–39.

Kelly, Janice R., Nicole E. Iannone, and Megan K. McCarty: "The Function of Shared Affects in Groups." In: Mikko Salmela and Christian von Scheve (eds): *Collective Emotions*. Oxford: Oxford University Press, 2014, pp. 175–85.

Kennedy, Dennis: *The Spectator and the Spectacle: Audiences in Modernity and Postmodernity*. Cambridge: Cambridge University Press, 2009.

Kennedy, Margaret: "The Mechanized Muse" [1942]. In: Daniel Talbot (ed.): *Film. An Anthology*. Berkeley: University of California Press, 1959, pp. 80–109.

Kershaw, Baz: "Oh for the Unruly Audiences! Or, Patterns of Participation in Twentieth-Century Theater." In: *Modern Drama*. Vol. 44, No. 2, 2001, pp. 133–54.

Kessler, Frank: "Historische Pragmatik." In: *Montage/AV*. Vol. 11, No. 2, 2002, pp. 104–12.

Kessler, Frank: "Notes on *dispositif*." http://www.hum.uu.nl/medewerkers/f.e.kessler/Dispositif%20Notes11-2007.pdf.

Kester, Grant H.: *Conversation Pieces. Community and Communication in Modern Art.* Berkeley: University of California Press, 2004.

Kim, Ji-hoon: "The Post-medium Condition and the Explosion of Cinema." In: *Screen.* Vol. 50, No. 1, 2009, pp. 114–23.

Kimmel, Lawrence: "Philosophy, Literature, and Laughter: Notes on an Ontology of the Moment." In: *Analecta Husserliana.* Vol. 56, 1998, pp. 175–84.

Klein, Thomas: "Das Secret Cinema als hybride Kino-Erfahrung." In: *Augenblick.* Vols. 56/57, 2013, pp. 168–86.

Kleinhans, Chuck: "Taking Out the Trash: Camp and the Politics of Parody." In: Moe Meyer (ed.): *The Politics and Poetics of Camp.* New York: Routledge, 1994, pp. 182–201.

Koch, Gertrud: *Was ich erbeute sind Bilder. Zum Diskurs der Geschlechter im Film.* Frankfurt/Main: Stroemfeld/Roter Stern, 1989.

Koebner, Thomas: "Begreifen was einen ergreift. Lernprozesse von Zuschauern." In: Margrit Fröhlich, Klaus Gronenborn, and Karsten Visarius (eds): *Das Gefühl der Gefühle. Zum Kinomelodram.* Marburg: Schüren, 2008, pp. 59–88.

Koeppen, Wolfgang: *Das Treibhaus.* Munich: Süddeutsche Zeitung Edition, 2004 [1953].

Koestler, Arthur: *The Act of Creation.* London: Penguin, 1989 [1964].

Konzelmann Ziv, Anita: "The Semantics of Shared Emotion." In: *Universitas Philosophica.* Vol. 26, No. 52, 2009, pp. 81–106.

Kracauer, Siegfried: "Cult of Distraction: On Berlin's Picture Palaces." In: *New German Critique.* No. 40, 1987 [1926], pp. 91–6.

Krämer, Peter: "Women First: *Titanic*, Action-Adventure Films, and Hollywood's Female Audience." In: Kevin S. Sandler and Gaylyn Studlar (eds): *Titanic: Anatomy of a Blockbuster.* New Brunswick, NJ: Rutgers University Press, 1999, pp. 108–31.

Krebs, Angelika: "Dialogical Love: Analyzing Joint Action." In: *Paper for the Library of Living Philosophers' Volume on Martha Nussbaum.* 5 January 2010. www.ethics-etc.com/wp-content/uploads/2010/02/krebs.pdf.

Krueger, Joel: "Doing Things with Music." In: *Phenomenology and Cognitive Science.* Vol. 10, 2011, pp. 1–22.

Krueger, Joel: "The Affective 'We': Self-Regulation and Shared Emotions." In: Thomas Szanto and Dermot Moran (eds): *The Phenomenology of Sociality. Discovering the 'We'.* London: Routledge, 2016, pp. 263–77.

Kubelka, Peter: "The Invisible Cinema." In: *Design Quarterly.* Special Issue on Film Spaces. No. 93, 1974, pp. 32–6.

Kuehnast, Milena, Valentin Wagner, Eugen Wassiliwizky, Thomas Jacobsen, and Winfried Menninghaus: "Being Moved. Linguistic Representation and Conceptual Structure." In: *Frontiers in Psychology.* Vol. 5, Article 1242, November 2014, pp. 1–11.

Kuhn, Annette: *Dreaming of Ginger and Fred. Cinema and Cultural Memory.* New York: New York University Press, 2002.

Labott, Susan M., Randall B. Martin, Patricia S. Eason, and Elayne Y. Berkey: "Social Reactions to the Expression of Emotion." In: *Cognition and Emotion.* Vol. 5, Nos. 5–6, 1991, pp. 397–417.

Lambie, Ryan: "The Weird Experience of Watching Movies on Planes." In: *Den of Geek!* 27 June 2012. http://www.denofgeek.com/movies/21761/the-weird-experience-of-watching-movies-on-planes.

Landweer, Hilge: *Scham und Macht. Phänomenologische Untersuchungen zur Sozialität eines Gefühls.* Tübingen: Mohr Siebeck, 1999.

Langer, Resi: "In the Movie Houses of Berlin West" [1919]. In: Anton Kaes, Nicholas Baer, and Michael Cowan (eds): *The Promise of Cinema. German Film Theory 1907-1933*. Berkeley: University of California Press, 2015, pp. 163-4.

Langer, Susanne K.: *Feeling and Form. A Theory of Art Developed from* Philosophy in a New Key. London: Routledge & Kegan Paul, 1953.

Leder, Drew: *The Absent Body*. Chicago: University of Chicago Press, 1990.

Lee, Linda: "Another Dad Flick, and Guys Are Crying." 29 December 2002. In: http://www.nytimes.com/2002/12/29/style/noticed-another-dad-flick-and-guys-are-crying.html.

Lemerise, Elizabeth A. and Kenneth A. Dodge: "The Development of Anger and Hostile Interactions." In: Michael Lewis, Jeanette M. Haviland-Jones and Lisa Feldman Barrett (eds): *Handbook of Emotions*. Third edition. New York: Guilford, 2008, pp. 730-41.

Levy, Sheldon G. and William F. Fenley jr: "Audience Size and Likelihood and Intensity of Response During a Humorous Movie." In: *Bulletin of the Psychonomic Society*. Vol. 13, No. 6, 1979, pp. 409-12.

Liessmann, Konrad Paul: *Das Universum der Dinge. Zur Ästhetik des Allgäglichen*. Vienna: Zsolnay, 2010.

Lindsay, Vachel: *The Art of the Moving Picture*. New York: Macmillan, 1915.

Löffler, Petra: *Verteilte Aufmerksamkeit. Eine Mediengeschichte der Zerstreuung*. Zurich: Diaphanes, 2014.

Lutz, Tom: *Crying: The Natural and Cultural History of Tears*. New York: Norton, 1999.

Maltby, Richard and Melvyn Stokes: "Introduction." In: Richard Maltby, Melvyn Stokes, and Robert C. Allen (eds): *Going to the Movies. Hollywood and the Social Experience of Cinema*. Exeter: University of Exeter Press, 2007, pp. 1-22.

Maltby, Richard, Melvyn Stokes, and Robert C. Allen (eds), *Going to the Movies. Hollywood and the Social Experience of Cinema*. Exeter: University of Exeter Press, 2007.

Mann, Thomas: "Über den Film" [1928]. In: Ludwig Greve, Margot Pehle, and Heidi Westhoff (eds): *Hätte ich das Kino! Die Schriftsteller und das Kino*. Munich: Kösel, 1978, pp. 213-15.

Man Ray: *Self Portrait*. Boston: Little, Brown & Company, 1963.

Marchetti, Gina: "Subcultural Studies and the Film Audience. Rethinking the Film Viewing Context." In: Ernest Mathijs and Xavier Mendik (eds) *The Cult Film Reader*. Maidenhead: Open University Press, 2008, pp. 403-18.

Marks, Laura: *Touch. Sensuous Theory and Multisensory Media*. Minneapolis: University of Minnesota Press, 2002.

Martin, Adrian: "What's Cult Got To Do With It?: In Defense of Cinephile Elitism." In: *Cineaste*. Vol. 34, No. 1, 2008, pp. 39-42.

Mathijs, Ernest and Xavier Mendik (eds): *The Cult Film Reader*. Maidenhead: Open University Press, 2008.

Mathijs, Ernest and Xavier Mendik: "What Is Cult Film?" In: Ernest Mathijs and Xavier Mendik (eds): *The Cult Film Reader*. Maidenhead: Open University Press, 2008, pp. 1-11.

McBride, Douglas Brent: "Romantic Phantasms: Benjamin and Adorno on the Subject of Critique." In: *Monatshefte*. Vol. 90, No. 4, 1998, pp. 465-87.

McCulloch, Richard: "'Most People Bring Their Own Spoons': *The Room*'s Participatory Audiences as Comedy Mediators." In: *Participations. Journal of Audience and Reception Studies*. Vol. 8, No. 2, 2011, pp. 189-218.

McLean, Adrienne L.: "If Only They Had Meant to Make a Comedy. Laughing at *Black Swan*." In: Murray Pomerance (ed.): *The Last Laugh: Strange Humors of Cinema*. Detroit: Wayne State University Press, 2013, pp. 143-61.

Meers, Philippe, Daniel Biltereyst, and Lies van de Vijve: "Lived Experiences of the

'Enlightened City' (1925–1975). A Large Scale Oral History Project on Cinema-going in Flanders (Belgium)." In: *Illuminace*. Vol. 20, No. 1, 2008, pp. 208–14.
Mele, Alfred: "Action." In: Frank Jackson and Michael Smith (eds): *The Oxford Handbook of Contemporary Philosophy*. Oxford: Oxford University Press, 2007, pp. 334–57.
Mele, Alfred: "Agency and Mental Action." In: *Noûs*. No. 31, 1997, pp. 231–49.
Mele, Rick: "Joe Dante on Hollywood's 'Broken' System." In: *Paste Magazine*. 25 May 2016.
Menninghaus, Winfried, Valentin Wagner, Julian Hanich, Eugen Wassiliwizky, Milena Kuehnast, and Thomas Jacobsen: "Towards a Psychological Construct of Being Moved." *PLoS ONE*. Vol. 10, No. 6, 2015, n.p.
Mendelssohn, Moses: "Rhapsody or Additions to the Letters on Sentiments" [1761]. In: *Philosophical Writings*. Cambridge: Cambridge University Press, 1997.
Merleau-Ponty, Maurice: "The Film and the New Psychology" [1947]. In: *Sense and Non-Sense*. Evanston: Northwestern University Press, 1964, pp. 48–59.
Merleau-Ponty, Maurice: *The Phenomenology of Perception*. London: Routledge, 2002 [1945].
Metz, Christian: "The Cinematic Apparatus as Social Institution – An Interview with Christian Metz". In: *Discourse*. No. 1, Fall 1979, pp. 7–37.
Metz, Christian: *The Imaginary Signifier*. Bloomington: Indiana University Press, 1982.
Mitry, Jean: *The Aesthetics and Psychology of the Cinema*. Bloomington: Indiana University Press, 2000 [1963].
Morin, Edgar: *The Cinema, or the Imaginary Man*. Minneapolis: University of Minnesota Press, 2005 [1956].
Morsch, Thomas: *Verkörperte Wahrnehmung. Körperliche Erfahrung als ästhetische Erfahrung im Kino*. PhD Dissertation. Freie Universität Berlin, 2007.
Moulton, Carter: "Midnight in Middle Earth: Blockbusters and Opening-Night Culture." In: *New Review of Film and Television Studies*. Vol. 12, No. 4, 2014, pp. 357–79.
Mulligan, Kevin and Klaus Scherer: "Toward a Working Definition of Emotion." In: *Emotion Review*. Vol. 4, No. 4, 2012, pp. 345–57.
Mulvey, Laura: *Death 24x a Second. Stillness and the Moving Image*. London: Reaktion, 2006.
Mundloch, Kate: *Screens. Viewing Media Installation Art*. Minneapolis: University of Minnesota Press, 2010.

Nash, Melanie and Martti Lahti. "'Almost Ashamed to Say I Am One of Those Girls:' *Titanic*, Leonardo DiCaprio, and the Paradoxes of Girls' Fandom." In: Kevin S. Sandler and Gaylyn Studlar (eds): *Titanic: Anatomy of a Blockbuster*. New Brunswick, NJ: Rutgers University Press, 1999, pp. 64–88.
Nathan-Garner, Laura: "Why I Don't Cry." In: Michele Byers and David Lavery (eds): *On the Verge of Tears: Why the Movies, Television, Music, Art, Popular Culture, Literature, and the Real World Make Us Cry*. Newcastle: Cambridge Scholars Publishing, 2010, pp. 108–11.
Neufeld, Jonathan A.: "Aesthetic Disobedience." In: *The Journal of Aesthetics and Art Criticism*. Vol. 73, No. 2, 2015, pp. 115–25.
Noë, Alva: *Action in Perception*. Cambridge, MA: MIT Press, 2004.

Odin, Roger: "A Semio-Pragmatic Approach to the Documentary Film." In: Warren Buckland (ed.): *The Film Spectator. From Sign to Mind*. Amsterdam: Amsterdam University Press, 1995, pp. 227–35.
Odin, Roger: "For a Semio-Pragmatics of Film." In: Warren Buckland (ed.): *The Film Spectator. From Sign to Mind*. Amsterdam: Amsterdam University Press, 1995, pp. 213–26.
Odin, Roger: "Kino 'mit klopfendem Herzen.' Anmerkungen zu den Emotionen im

Familienfilm." In: Matthias Brütsch, Vinzenz Hediger, Ursula von Keitz, Alexandra Schneider, and Margrit Tröhler (eds): *Kinogefühle. Emotionalität und Film*. Marburg: Schüren, 2005, pp. 103–17.

Odin, Roger: "Kunst und Ästhetik bei Film und Fernsehen. Elemente zu einem semiopragmatischen Ansatz." In: *Montage/AV*. Vol. 11, No. 2, 2002, pp. 42–57.

Odin, Roger: "Reflections on the Family Home Movie as Document." In: Karen L. Ishizuka and Patricia R. Zimmermann (eds): *Mining the Home Movie. Excavations in Histories and Memories*. Berkeley: University of California Press, 2007, pp. 255–71.

Odin, Roger: "Sémio-pragmatique du cinéma et de l'audiovisuel." In: Jürgen E. Müller (ed.): *Towards a Pragmatics of the Audiovisual. Theory and History*. Muenster: Nodus, 1994, pp. 33–46.

Odin, Roger: "Spectator, Film and the Mobile Phone." In: Ian Christie (ed.): *Audiences*. Amsterdam: Amsterdam University Press, 2012, pp. 155–69.

Odin, Roger: "The Home Movie and Space of Communication." In: Laura Rascaroli, Gwenda Young and Barry Monahan (eds): *Amateur Filmmaking. The Home Movie, the Archive, the Web*. New York: Bloomsbury, 2014, pp. 15–26.

O'Leary, Alan and Catherin O'Rawe: "Contemporary Italian Film-Goers and Their Critics." In: Karina Aveyard and Albert Moran (eds): *Watching Films. New Perspectives on Movie-Going, Exhibition and Reception*. Bristol: Intellect, 2013, pp. 353–67.

Olney, Ian: *Euro Horror: Classic European Horror Cinema in Contemporary American Culture*. Bloomington: Indiana University Press, 2013.

Pacherie, Elisabeth: "How Does It Feel to Act Together?" In: *Phenomenology and the Cognitive Sciences*. Vol. 13, 2014, pp. 25–46.

Paech, Anne: "Fünf Sinne im Dunkeln. Erinnerungen an die Kino-Atmosphäre." In: Philipp Brunner, Jörg Schweinitz, and Margit Tröhler (eds): *Filmische Atmosphären*. Marburg: Schüren, 2012, pp. 25–38.

Paech, Anne and Joachim Paech: *Menschen im Kino. Film und Literatur erzählen*. Stuttgart: Metzler, 2000.

Pagis, Michal: "Producing Intersubjectivity in Silence: an Ethnographic Study on Meditation Practice." In: *Ethnography*. Vol. 11, No. 2, 2010, pp. 309–28.

Pantenburg, Volker: "Attention, please: Notizen zur Aufmerksamkeitsökonomie in Kino und Museum." In: *Kolik.film*. No. 14, 2010, pp. 68–74.

Pantenburg, Volker: "1970 and Beyond: Experimental Cinema and Installation Art." In: Gertrud Koch, Volker Pantenburg, and Simon Rothöhler (eds): *Screen Dynamics: Mapping the Borders of Cinema*. Vienna: Synema, 2012, pp. 78–92.

Pasquier, Dominique: "'The Cacophony of Failure': Being an Audience in a Traditional Theater." In: *Participations*. Vol. 12, No. 1, 2015, pp. 222–33.

Paul, William: *Laughing Screaming. Modern Hollywood Horror and Comedy*. New York: Columbia University Press, 1994.

Paul, William: *When Movies Were Theater. Architecture, Exhibition, and the Evolution of American Film*. New York: Columbia University Press, 2016.

Pedullà, Gabriele: *In Broad Daylight. Movies and Spectators After the Cinema*. London: Verso, 2012.

Perez, Gilberto: "History, Then and Now." In: *Film Comment*. May/June 2016, pp. 58–65.

Plantinga, Carl: *Moving Viewers. American Film and the Spectator's Experience*. Berkeley: University of California Press, 2009.

Platow, Michael J., S. Alexander Haslam, Amanda Both, Ivanne Chew, Michelle Cuddon, Nahal Goharpey, Jacqui Maurer, Simone Rosini, Anna Tsekouras, and Diana M. Grace:

"'It's Not Funny if They're Laughing': Self-Categorization, Social Influence, and Responses to Canned Laughter." In: *Journal of Experimental Social Psychology*. Vol. 41, 2005, pp. 542–50.

Plessner, Helmuth: *Laughing and Crying. A Study on the Limits of Human Behavior.* Evanston: Northwestern University Press, 1970 [1941].

Polan, Dana: "Roland Barthes and the Moving Image." In: *October*. Vol. 18, 1981, pp. 41–6.

Pomerance, Murray (ed.): *The Last Laugh: Strange Humors of Cinema*. Detroit: Wayne State University Press, 2013.

Ponzanesi, Sandra and Marguerite Waller (eds): *Postcolonial Cinema Studies*. New York: Routledge, 2012.

Provine, Robert K. and Kenneth R. Fischer: "Laughing, Smiling, and Talking: Relation to Sleeping and Social Context in Humans." In: *Ethology*. Vol. 83, 1989, pp. 295–305.

Prütting, Lenz: *Homo Ridens. Eine phänomenologische Studie über Wesen, Formen und Funktionen des Lachens*. Freiburg: Alber, 2013.

Rancière, Jacques: "The Emancipated Spectator." In: *Artforum*. March 2007, pp. 271–80.

Rancière, Jacques: *The Politics of Aesthetics*. London: Bloomsbury, 2004.

Ratcliffe, Matthew: *Feelings of Being: Phenomenology, Psychiatry and the Sense of Reality*. Oxford: Oxford University Press, 2008.

Reason, Matthew: "*Participations* on Participation: Researching the 'Active' Theater Audience." In: *Participations*. Vol. 12, No. 1, May 2015, pp. 271–80.

Reinhard, CarrieLynn D. and Christopher Olson (eds): *Making Sense of Cinema. Empirical Studies into Film Spectators and Spectatorship*. New York: Bloomsbury, 2016.

Röcke, Werner and Hans Rudolf Velten: "Einleitung." In: Werner Röcke and Hans Werner Velten (eds): *Lachgemeinschaften. Kulturelle Inszenierungen und soziale Wirkungen von Gelächter im Mittelalter und in der frühen Neuzeit*. Berlin: De Gruyter, 2005, pp. ix–xxxi.

Roden, David: "Nature's Dark Domain: An Argument for a Naturalized Phenomenology." http://enemyindustry.net/blog/wp-content/uploads/2011/08/PhenNatFF1.pdf.

Rodowick, D. N.: *Elegy for Theory*. Cambridge, MA: Harvard University Press, 2014.

Rooney, Brendan and Eilis Hennessy: "Actually in the Cinema: A Field Study Comparing Real 3D and 2D Movie Patrons' Attention, Emotion, and Film Satisfaction." In: *Media Psychology*. Vol. 16, No. 4, 2013, pp. 441–60.

Roselt, Jens: "Chips und Schiller. Lachgemeinschaften im zeitgenössischen Theater und ihre historischen Voraussetzungen." In: Werner Röcke and Hans Werner Velten (eds): *Lachgemeinschaften. Kulturelle Inszenierungen und soziale Wirkungen von Gelächter im Mittelalter und in der frühen Neuzeit*. Berlin: De Gruyter, 2005, pp. 225–44.

Roselt, Jens: *Phänomenologie des Theaters*. Munich: Fink, 2008.

Rosenbaum, Jonathan: *Moving Places. A Life at the Movies*. Berkeley: University of California Press, 1995.

Rosenkranz, M.: "Film and Theater: The Situation of Theater Today" [1934]. In: https://www.caboosebooks.net/sites/default/files/caboose_Rozenkranz_Film%20and%20Theater_second%20version_Jan%202016.pdf

Ross, Miriam: "Interstitial Film Viewing. Community Exhibition in the Twenty-First Century." In: *Continuum: Journal of Media & Cultural Studies*. Vol. 27, No. 3, 2013.

Rosso, Stefano: "A Correspondence with Umberto Eco." In: *boundary 2*, Vol. 12, No. 1, 1983, pp. 1–13.

Ryle, Gilbert: *The Concept of Mind*. New York: Routledge, 2009 [1949].

Salmela, Mikko: "Shared Emotions." In: *Philosophical Explorations: An International Journal for the Philosophy of Mind and Action*. Vol. 15, No. 1, 2012, pp. 33–46.

Salmela, Mikko: "The Functions of Collective Emotions in Social Groups." In: Anita Konzelmann Ziv and Hans Bernhard Schmid (eds): *Institutions, Emotions, and Group Agents*. Dordrecht: Springer, 2014, pp. 159–76.

Sánchez Guerrero, H. Andrés: "Gemeinsamkeitsgefühle und Mitsorge: Anregungen zu einer alternativen Auffassung kollektiver affektiver Intentionalität." In: Jan Slaby, Achim Stephan, Henrik Walter, and Sven Walter (eds): *Affektive Intentionalität. Beiträge zur welterschließenden Funktion der menschlichen Gefühle*. Paderborn: Mentis, 2011, pp. 252–82.

Sandvoss, Cornel: "Reception." In: Virginia Nightingale (ed.): *The Handbook of Media Audiences*. Malden, MA: Wiley-Blackwell, 2011, pp. 230–250.

Sarkhosh, Keyvan and Winfried Menninghaus: "Enjoying Trash Films: Underlying Features, Viewing Stances, and Experiential Response Dimensions." In: *Poetics*. Vol. 57, 2016, pp. 40–54.

Sartre, Jean-Paul: *Being and Nothingness. A Phenomenological Essay on Ontology*. New York: Washington Square Press, 1992 [1943].

Sartre, Jean-Paul: "On Dramatic Style" [1944]. In: *Sartre on Theater*. New York: Pantheon, 1976, pp. 6–29.

Sartre, Jean-Paul: *The Emotions. Outline of a Theory*. New York: Carol Publishing, 1993 [1939].

Schachter, Stanley: *The Psychology of Affiliation*. Stanford: Stanford University Press, 1959.

Schaefer, Alexandre, Frédéric Nils, Xavier Sanchez, and Pierre Philippot: "Assessing the Effectiveness of a Large Database of Emotion-eliciting Films: A New Tool for Emotion Researchers." In: *Cognition and Emotion*. Vol. 24, No. 7, 2010, pp. 1153–72.

Schaub, Mirjam and Nicola Suthor: "Einleitung." In: Mirjam Schaub, Nicola Suthor, and Erika Fischer-Lichte (eds): *Ansteckung. Zur Körperlichkeit eines ästhetischen Prinzips*. Munich: Fink, 2005, pp. 9–21.

Scheler, Max: *The Nature of Sympathy*. New Brunswick, NJ: Transaction, 2008 [1923].

Schieman, Scott: "Anger." In: Jan E. Stets and Jonathan H. Turner (eds): *Handbook of the Sociology of Emotions*. New York: Springer, 2006, pp. 493–515.

Schlüpmann, Heide: *Öffentliche Intimität. Die Theorie im Kino*. Frankfurt/Main: Stroemfeld, 2002.

Schmid, Hans Bernhard: "Shared Feelings. Towards a Phenomenology of Collective Affective Intentionality." In: Hans Bernhard Schmid, Katinka Schulte-Ostermann, and Nikos Psarros (eds): *Concepts of Sharedness. Essays on Collective Intentionality*. Heusenstamm: Ontos, 2008, pp. 59–86.

Schmid, Hans Bernhard: "The Feeling of Being a Group. Corporate Emotions and Collective Consciousness." In: Mikko Salmela and Christian von Scheve (eds): *Collective Emotions*. Oxford: Oxford University Press, 2014, pp. 3–22.

Schmid, Hans Bernhard: "Plural Self-Awareness." In: *Phenomenology and the Cognitive Sciences*. Vol. 13, 2014, pp. 7–24.

Schmid, Hans Bernhard: "What Kind of Mode is the We-Mode? On Raimo Tuomela's Account of Collective Intentionality." Unpublished draft.

Schmid, Hans Bernhard: *Wir-Intentionalität: Kritik des ontologischen Individualismus und Rekonstruktion der Gemeinschaft*. Freiburg: Alber, 2005.

Schmid, Hans Bernhard and David P. Schweikard (eds): *Kollektive Intentionalität. Eine Debatte über die Grundlagen des Sozialen*. Frankfurt/Main: Suhrkamp, 2009.

Schmitz, Hermann: *Der Gefühlsraum*. Bonn: Bouvier, 1969.

Schmitz, Hermann: *Die Person*. Bonn: Bouvier, 1980.

Schmitz, Hermann: *Der Rechtsraum. Praktische Philosophie.* Bonn: Bouvier 1973.
Schmitz, Hermann: "Emotions Outside the Box. The New Phenomenology of Feeling and Corporeality." In: *Phenomenology and the Cognitive Sciences.* Vol. 10, No. 2, 2011, pp. 241–59.
Schröter, Michael: "Wer lacht, kann nicht beißen. Ein unveröffentlichter 'Essay on Laughter' von Norbert Elias." In: *Merkur – Deutsche Zeitschrift für europäisches Denken.* September 2002, pp. 860–73.
Schwarz, Balduin: *Untersuchungen zur Psychologie des Weinens.* Rückersdorf: Lepanto, 2014 [1928].
Searle, John R.: *The Construction of Social Reality.* New York: Free Press, 1995.
Seel, Martin: "Humor als Laster und als Tugend." In: *Merkur. Sonderheft: Lachen. Über westliche Zivilisation.* September 2002, pp. 743–51.
Seldes, Gilbert: *The Seven Lively Arts.* Mineola, NY: Dover, 2001 [1924].
Senge, Konstanze and Rainer Schützeichel (eds): *Hauptwerke der Emotionssoziologie.* Wiesbaden: Springer, 2013, pp. 187–93.
Shimamura, Arthur P. (ed.): *Psychocinematics. Exploring Cognition at the Movies.* Oxford: Oxford University Press, 2013.
Shimbun, Chunichi: "Participants Ease Stress Levels at Crying Events." In: *The Japan Times.* 22 June 2013. http://www.japantimes.co.jp/news/2013/06/22/national/participants-ease-stress-levels-at-crying-events/#.WCBT6oWxIfo.
Sitney, Sky: "In Search for the Invisible Cinema." In: *Grey Room.* Vol. 19, 2005, pp. 103–13.
Slaby, Jan: "Affective Intentionality and the Feeling Body." In: *Phenomenology and the Cognitive Sciences.* Vol. 7, No. 4, 2008, pp. 429–44.
Smith, Tim J.: "Watching You Watch Movies. Using Eye Tracking to Inform Cognitive Film Theory". In: Arthur P. Shimamura (ed.): *Psychocinematics. Exploring Cognition at the Movies.* Oxford: Oxford University Press, 2013, pp. 165–92.
Smoodin, Eric: *Regarding Frank Capra. Audience, Celebrity, and American Film Studies, 1930–1960.* Durham: Duke University Press, 2004.
Sobchack, Vivian: *Carnal Thoughts. Embodiment and Moving Image Culture.* Berkeley: University of California Press, 2004.
Sobchack, Vivian: "Comprehending Screens: A Meditation *in medias res.*" In: *Rivista di estetica.* Vol. 55, No. 1, 2014, pp. 87–101.
Sobchack, Vivian: "Fleshing Out the Image: Phenomenology, Pedagogy, and Derek Jarman's *Blue.*" In: Havi Carel and Greg Tuck (eds): *New Takes in Film-Philosophy.* Basingstoke: Palgrave-Macmillan, 2011, pp. 191–206.
Sobchack, Vivian: "From Screen-Scape to Screen-Sphere: A Meditation in Medias Res." In: Dominique Chateau and José Moure (eds): *Screens.* Amsterdam: Amsterdam University Press, 2016, pp. 157–75.
Sobchack, Vivian: *The Address of the Eye. A Phenomenology of Film Experience.* Princeton: Princeton University Press, 1992.
Sobchack, Vivian: "Toward a Phenomenology of Nonfictional Film Experience." In: Jane M. Gaines and Michael Renov (eds): *Collecting Visible Evidence.* Minneapolis: University of Minnesota Press, 1999, pp. 241–54.
Solomon, Robert: *In Defense of Sentimentality.* Oxford: Oxford University Press, 2004.
Sontag, Susan: "Notes on Camp." In: *Against Interpretation and Other Essays.* London: Penguin, 2009 [1964], pp. 275–92.
Sorensen, Roy: *Seeing Dark Things. The Philosophy of Shadows.* Oxford: Oxford University Press, 2008.
Souriau, Etienne: "The Structure of the Filmic Universe and the Vocabulary of Filmology"

[1951]. In: Kate Ince, Vinzenz Hediger, and Guido Kirsten (eds): *Discovering the Origins of Film Studies. Selected Articles from the* Revue International de Filmologie. Amsterdam: Amsterdam University Press (forthcoming).

Srinivas, Lakshmi: "Active Viewing: An Ethnography of the Indian Film Audience." In: *Visual Anthropology*. Vol. 11, 1998, pp. 323–53.

Srinivas, Lakshmi: "The Active Audience. Spectatorship, Social Relations and the Experience of Cinema in India." In: *Media, Culture and Society*. Vol. 24, No. 2, 2002, pp. 155–73.

St Michel, Patrick: "Crying It Out in Japan: Tokyo Gets into Communal Bawling." In: *The Atlantic*. May 2015. http://www.theatlantic.com/magazine/archive/2015/05/crying-it-out-in-japan/389528/

Staiger, Janet: *Perverse Spectators: The Practices of Film Reception*. New York: New York University Press, 2000.

Staiger, Janet: "'The First Bond who Bleeds, Literally and Metaphorically': Gendered Spectatorship for 'Pretty Boy' Action Movies." In: Hilary Radner and Rebecca Stringer (eds): *Feminism at the Movies. Understanding Gender in Contemporary Popular Cinema*. New York: Routledge, 2011, pp. 13–24.

Stam, Robert: *Film Theory. An Introduction*. Malden: Blackwell, 2000.

States, Bert O.: *Great Reckonings in Little Rooms. On the Phenomenology of the Theater*. Berkeley: University of California Press, 1985.

Stawarska, Beata: *Between You and I. Dialogical Phenomenology*. Athens, OH: Ohio University Press, 2009.

Stein, Edith: *Beiträge zur philosophischen Begründung der Psychologie und der Geisteswissenschaften. Eine Untersuchung über den Staat*. Second edition. Tübingen: Max Niemeyer, 1970 [1922/5].

Stern, Alfred: "Lachen, Weinen und die Welt der Werte." In: *Zeitschrift für philosophische Forschung*. Vol. 28, No. 4, 1974, pp. 485–98.

Stern, Alfred: *Philosophie des Lachens und Weinens*. Wien: Oldenbourg, 1980 [1949].

Szanto, Thomas: "Collective Emotions, Normativity, and Empathy: A Steinian Account." In: *Human Studies*. Vol. 38, No. 4, 2015, pp. 503–27.

Szanto, Thomas and Dermot Moran: "Phenomenological Discoveries Concerning the 'We': Mapping the Terrain." In: Thomas Szanto and Dermot Moran (eds): *The Phenomenology of Sociality. Discovering the 'We'*. London and New York: Routledge, 2015, pp. 1–26.

Tan, Ed S.: *Emotion and the Structure of Narrative Film: Film as an Emotion Machine*. Mahwah: Lawrence Erlbaum, 1996.

"Tear Watch." In: *Nach dem Film*. October 2002. www.nachdemfilm.de (no longer available).

Thissen, Judith: "Understanding Dutch Film Culture: A Comparative Approach." In: *Alphaville: Journal of Film and Screen Media*. Vol. 6, Winter 2013. n.p.

Thompson, Evan: *Mind in Life. Biology, Phenomenology, and the Sciences of Mind*. Cambridge, MA: Harvard University Press, 2007.

Tomasello, Michael: *Origins of Human Communication*. Cambridge, MA: MIT Press, 2008.

Tröhler, Margrit: "Orte des Spektakels bewegter Bilder: Filmische Dispositive und ihre Atmosphären." In: Philipp Brunner, Jörg Schweinitz, and Margrit Tröhler (eds): *Filmische Atmosphären*. Marburg: Schüren, 2012, pp. 53–71.

Tryon, Chuck: *Reinventing Cinema. Movies in the Age of Media Convergence*. New Brunswick, NJ: Rutgers University Press, 2009.

Urry, John: "Mobility and Proximity." In: *Sociology*. Vol. 36, No. 2, 2002, pp. 255–74.

Van Manen, Max: *Phenomenology of Practice. Meaning-Giving Methods in Phenomenological Research and Writing*. Walnut Creek: Left Coast Press, 2014.
Vernet, Marc: "The Look into the Camera." *Cinema Journal*. Vol. 28, No. 2, 1989, pp. 048–63.
Vingerhoets, Ad: *Why Only Humans Weep. Unravelling the Mysteries of Tears*. Oxford: Oxford University Press, 2013.
Von Scheve, Christian: "Emotion Regulation and Emotion Work: Two Sides of the Same Coin?" In: *Frontiers in Psychology*. November 2012, Vol. 3, Article 496, pp. 1–10.
Von Scheve, Christian and Sven Ismer: "Towards a Theory of Collective Emotions." In: *Emotion Review*. Vol. 5, No. 4, 2013, pp. 406–13.
Vorse, Mary Heaton: "Some Picture Show Audiences." In: *The Outlook*. 24 June 1911, pp. 441–7.

Wagenmakers, E.-J., Titia Beek, Laura Dijkhoff, and Quentin F. Gronau: "Registered Replication Report: Strack, Martin, & Stepper (1988)." In: *Perspectives on Psychological Science*. Vol. 11, No. 6, 2016, pp. 917–28.
Wagner, Valentin, Winfried Menninghaus, Julian Hanich and Thomas Jacobsen: "Art Schema Effects on Affective Experience: The Case of Disgusting Images." In: *Psychology of Aesthetics, Creativity and the Arts*. Vol. 8, No. 2, 2014, pp. 120–9.
Waldenfels, Bernhard: *Sinne und Künste im Wechselspiel. Modi ästhetischer Erfahrung*. Berlin: Suhrkamp, 2010.
Waller, Gregory A.: "Locating Early Non-Theatrical Audiences." In: Ian Christie (ed.): *Audiences*. Amsterdam: Amsterdam University Press, 2012, pp. 81–95.
Walther, Gerda: "Zur Ontologie der sozialen Gemeinschaft." In: *Jahrbuch für Philosophie und phänomenologische Forschung*. Halle/Saale: Max Niemeyer, 1923, pp. 1–158.
Warhol, Robyn R.: *Having a Good Cry. Effeminate Feelings and Pop-Culture Forms*. Columbus: Ohio State University Press, 2003.
Wassiliwizky, Eugen, Thomas Jacobsen, Jan Heinrich, Manuel Schneiderbauer, and Winfried Menninghaus: "Tears Falling on Goosebumps: Co-occurrence of Emotional Lacrimation and Emotional Piloerection Indicates a Psychophysiological Climax in Emotional Arousal." In: *Frontiers in Psychology*. Vol. 8, Article 41, 2017. pp. 1–15.
Weber, Samuel: *Theatricality as Medium*. New York: Fordham University Press, 2004.
Wiesing, Lambert: *Luxus*. Berlin: Suhrkamp, 2015.
Wildshut, Tim, Constantine Sedikides, Jamie Arndt, and Clay Routledge: "Nostalgia: Content, Triggers, Functions." In: *Journal of Personality and Social Psychology*. Vol. 91, No. 5, 2006, pp. 975–93.
Williams, Linda: *Hard Core. Power, Pleasure, and the 'Frenzy of the Visible'*. Berkeley: University of California Press, 1989.
Wood, Robert E.: "Don't Dream It. Performance and *The Rocky Horror Picture Show*." In: J. P. Telotte (ed.): *The Cult Film Experience. Beyond All Reason*. Austin: University of Texas Press, 1991, pp. 156–66.
Woodworth, Amy J.: *From Buddy Film to Bromance: Masculinity and Male Melodrama Since 1969*. Dissertation Temple University, 2014.

Young, Iris Marion: "Throwing Like a Girl. A Phenomenology of Feminine Body Comportment Motility and Spatiality." In: *Human Studies*. Vol. 3, 1980, pp. 137–56.

Zahavi, Dan: "You, Me and We: The Sharing of Emotional Experiences." In: *Journal of Consciousness Studies*. Vol. 22, Nos. 1/2, 2015, pp. 84–101.

Zhao, Shanyang: "Toward a Taxonomy of Co-Presence." In: *Presence.* Vol. 12, No. 5, 2003, pp. 445–55.

Zijderveld, Anton C.: *Humor und Gesellschaft. Eine Soziologie des Humors und des Lachens.* Graz: Styria, 1982.

Zillmann, Dolf, James B. Weaver, Norbert Mundorf, and Charles F. Aust: "Effects of an Opposite-Gender Companion's Affect to Horror on Distress, Delight, and Attraction." In: *Journal of Personality and Social Psychology.* Vol. 51, No. 3, 1986, pp. 586–94.

Zischler, Hanns: *Kafka Goes to the Movies.* Chicago: University of Chicago Press, 2003.

Žižek, Slavoj: "The Lesson of Rancière." In: Jacques Rancière: *The Politics of Aesthetics.* London: Bloomsbury, 2004, pp. 65–75.

WEBSITES

http://articles.latimes.com/2010/mar/10/local/la-me-meat-thermometer10-2010mar10
http://natoonline.org/data/admissions
http://nickelodeon.org/pricing-other-policies/
https://drafthouse.com/about
https://klantenservice.pathe.nl/hc/nl/articles/203087788-Wat-is-een-SMS-alert-
http://www.bbc.co.uk/5live/films/code_of_conduct.jpg
http://www.bfi.org.uk
http://edition.cnn.com/2008/CRIME/12/27/movie.shooting/
https://www.engadget.com/2015/08/06/oculus-cinema-watch-movies-together/#comments
http://www.filmjourney.org/?p=891
http://www.nw.de/lokal/bielefeld/mitte/mitte/7920261_Redender_Besucher_loest_Pruegelei_in_Bielefelder_Kino_aus.html
http://www.nwzonline.de/panorama/schlaegerei-im-kinosaal_a_3,1,80978700.html
http://www.spiegel.de/spiegel/print/d-18074406.html
https://www.theguardian.com/film/2011/feb/21/man-shot-latvian-cinema-popcorn
http://www.theguardian.com/world/2015/dec/10/the-day-israel-saw-shoah
http://www.thewrap.com/a-history-of-violence-at-the-movie-theater-from-1979s-the-warriors-gang-showdown-to-2015s-lafayette-tragedy
http://www.unic-cinemas.org/
http://www.usatoday.com/story/news/nation/2014/01/13/wesley-chapel-florida-shooting-movie-theater/4457907/
http://www.waynesthisandthat.com/moviedata.html
www.culturalpolicies.net/web/statistics-participation.php?aid=86&cid=74&lid=en
www.ffa.de
www.guardian.co.uk/film/2012/jul/05/secret-cinema-new-way-pull-audiences?intcmp=239
www.mediasalles.it
www.mpaa.org
www.secretcinema.org

Index of Names

Abel, Richard, 166n
Abercrombie, Nicholas, 19–20, 66, 114, 136n
Achternbusch, Herbert, 251
Adorno, Theodor W., 112, 212
Adventurer, The (1917), 48
After the Wedding / Efter Brylluppet (2006), 149, 230
All About My Mother / Todo sobre mi madre (1999), 234
Almodóvar, Pedro, 234
Altenloh, Emilie, 23, 32n, 114
Althen, Michael, 168, 183n
Althusser, Louis, 34
Altman, Robert, 70
Amélie / Le fabuleux destin d'Amélie Poulain (2001), 233
American History X (1998), 252
Anderson, Benedict, 139n
Andersen, Hans Christian, 49
Andrew, Dudley, 46, 60n, 69, 120
Anger, Kenneth, 19
Anrieu, Paul, 109n
Ararat (2004), 160
Armageddon (1998), 230
Arnheim, Rudolf, 62n
Aronofsky, Darren, 198, 215n, 250
Astaire, Fred, 107n
Athique, Adrian Mabbott, 130, 148, 165n, 167n
Atkinson, Sarah, 275
Atonement (2007), 239
Au revoir les enfants (1987), 52
Averill, James, 254

Bachelard, Gaston, 13
Baird, Robert, 118

Barbaro, Umberto, 78
Barker, Martin, 22, 144
Barnard, Timothy, 60n
Baron-Cohen, Sacha, 43, 54–5
Barthes, Roland, 10, 22, 34, 40–2, 43, 44, 49, 59n, 160, 256
Battle of Algiers, The / La battaglia di Algeri (1966), 251
Baudry, Jean-Louis, 8, 28n, 41
Bay, Michael, 261
Bazin, André, 8, 10, 17, 34, 42, 44–50, 60n, 61n, 69, 70, 97, 98, 207, 208, 279
Bellour, Raymond, 43, 59
Beneath the 12-Mile Reef (1953), 47
Benjamin, Walter, 10, 27n, 34, 48, 50–4, 59n, 61n, 62n, 69, 71, 104, 105n, 109n, 112, 138n, 217, 242n, 279
Berg, Peter, 250
Berger, Peter L., 214n
Bergman, Ingmar, 104, 253
Bergson, Henri, 190, 191, 194, 199, 204, 212, 214n
Berkenbusch, Gisela, 228
Berrendonner, Alain, 36
Beugnet, Martine, 283n
Bienvenue chez les Ch'tis (2008), 209
Black Swan (2010), 198, 215n, 250
Blair Witch Project, The (1999), 101
Blob, The (1988), 268n
Blue Is the Warmest Color / La vie d'Adèle (2013), 174
Blumer, Herbert, 29n, 221, 237
Bonitzer, Pascal, 101
Borat (2006), 43, 54
Bordwell, David, 32n, 34, 99
Bosetti, Roméo, 268n

Boys Don't Cry (1999), 259
Brakhage, Stan, 238
Breaking the Waves (1996), 234
Breakwell, Ian, 10
Breillat, Catherine, 162
Brennan, Teresa, 9
Bridesmaids (2011), 153
Brisson, Adolphe, 166n
Brooker, Will, 135
Brooks, Kate, 22
Brown, Tom, 100
Brüno (2009), 54
Brunetta, Gian Piero, 143
Bühler, Karl, 95, 134
Buñuel, Luis, 251
Burch, Noël, 215n
Burgin, Victor, 60n
Burke, Edmund, 228, 245n
Butsch, Richard, 29n

Cameron, James, 241
Caminada, Emanuele, 30n
Camus, Albert, 29n, 271n
Canudo, Ricciotto, 62n, 199, 212
Cape Fear (1991), 128
Capra, Frank, 238, 242n
Carassa, Antonella, 118, 127
Carpenter, Megan, 184n
Carter, Kevin L., 251
Casablanca (1942), 230
Casetti, Francesco, 4, 59n, 66, 81, 136n, 277, 283n
Cavell, Stanley, 8, 114, 265
Chacun son cinéma (2007), 248, 268n
Chaplin, Charlie, 47, 48, 51–2, 53, 54, 61n, 62n, 198
Châteauvert, Jean, 101, 102
Cheu, Johnson, 221
Christie, Ian, 32n
Christie, John, 6–7
Cianfrance, Derek, 233
Cinema Paradiso (1988), 163
Circus, The (1928), 51
City Lights (1931), 54
Coan, James A., 146
Cochrane, Tom, 83
Cocteau, Jean, 47
Coixet, Isabel, 233
Colombetti, Giovanna, 32n
Colombetti, Marco, 118, 127
Condillac, Étienne Bonnot de, 27
Cook, Lindsay, 6, 10
Cova, Florian, 149, 230, 232
Crary, Jonathan, 107n

Craven, Wes, 19, 117, 200
Crowd, The (1928), 54, 208, 216n
Cry Freedom (1987), 251
Csíkszentmihályi, Mihály, 95, 134
Cubitt, Sean, 25, 106n, 138n
Cummings, Doug, 261
Curious Case of Benjamin Button, The (2008), 250

Dancer in the Dark (2000), 268n, 271n
Daney, Serge, 83
Dante, Joe, 189, 190
Danto, Arthus C., 168
Daquin, Louis, 47
Dark Knight Rises, The (2012), 25
Das merkwürdige Kätzchen (2013), 268n
Das Wunder von Bern / The Miracle of Bern (2003), 238
Davidson, Richard S., 146
Davies, Terence, 240
Dayan, Daniel, 28
Days of Heaven (1978), 230
De la Iglesia, Alex, 268n
Death Wish (1974), 252
Debord, Guy, 105–6n
Deep Impact (1998), 234
Deger, Jennifer, 137n
Del Río, Elena, 25
Deleuze, Gilles, 53
Delluc, Louis, 62n, 71n, 92, 108n, 198–9
Demmerling, Christoph, 222
Deonna, Julien A., 149, 230, 232
Deveraux, Paul, 189, 190
Diaz, Lav, 91, 95
Dirty Dancing (1987), 123
Disappearance of Alice Creed, The (2009), 277
Distant Voices, Still Lives (1988), 240
Döblin, Alfred, 136n
Dodge, Kenneth A., 254, 266
Doumic, René, 166n
Dreyfus, Hubert, 155, 213
Dunbar, Robin, 189
Dunn, Stephane, 165n

Echterhoff, Gerald, 93, 108n, 169, 185n
Eco, Umberto, 65
Ed Wood (1994), 197
Eggeling, Viking, 252
Egoyan, Atom, 160
Eikhenbaum, Boris, 8, 136n
Eisenstein, Sergei, 54, 69
El Topo (1970), 126
Elias, Norbert, 191, 211
Ellis, John, 27n, 73, 78, 114

INDEX OF NAMES

Elsaesser, Thomas, 77, 81, 101–3, 110n, 131
Empire (1964), 162
Epstein, Jean, 97
Eraserhead (1977), 126, 130
Evil Dead, The (1981), 197
E.T. the Extra-Terrestrial (1982), 244n

Fanon, Frantz, 276
Fast and the Furious, The (2001), 227
Faure, Élie, 29n, 55, 115
Feldman Barrett, Lisa, 24
Feldmann, Erich, 56–7
Fenley, William F., 70
Ferencz-Flatz, Christian, 89, 279
Fiebich, Anika, 86
Fifty Shades of Grey (2015), 280
Fincher, David, 250
Fischer, Agneta, 58
Fischer, Kenneth, 213n
Fisher, Philip, 254, 255, 261, 267
42nd Street (1933), 271n
Foucault, Michel, 53, 113
Frampton, Daniel, 246
Frampton, Hollis, 84
Freeburg, Victor Oscar, 55–6
Freeland, Jonathan, 259
Freud, Sigmund, 6, 129, 173, 184n, 251
Frey, Mattias, 108n, 270n
Friday the 13th (1980), 161
Friday the 13th, Part III (1982), 11, 180
Friedberg, Anne, 41
From What Is Before / Mula sa kung ano ang noon (2014), 91
Fuller, Raymond G. C., 200
Funny Games (1997), 261

Gallagher, Shaun, 86
Game of Thrones (2011–), 132
Gaudreault, André, 102
Gerbi, Antonello, 106n
Germany – A Summer's Tale / Deutschland – Ein Sommermärchen (2006), 150, 161
Gerrig, Richard J., 106n
Getino, Fernando, 119
Ghostbusters (1984), 190
Giesz, Ludwig, 233, 236
Gilbert, Margaret, 77, 89–90, 108n, 125, 164n, 264
Ginsburg, Gerald, 189, 190
Godard, Jean-Luc, 99, 115, 201, 268n
Godman, Marion, 94–5, 109n, 127, 138n
Goffman, Erving, 9, 29n, 89, 115, 116, 124, 125, 137n, 158, 179, 210, 251, 253, 255, 261, 268, 270n, 283n

Goldstein, Thalia, 238
Gollwitzer, Mario, 270n
Gone with the Wind (1939), 236
Good Bye Lenin! (2003), 28n, 202
Gourmont, Rémy de, 166n
Grémillon, Jean, 47
Greenaway, Peter, 201
Greenberg, Clement, 233
Griffith, D. W., 268n
Groening, Stephen, 277
Gross, James, 154
Guattari, Félix, 111
Güney, Zeynep Okur, 183n
Gunning, Tom, 26

Haas, Willy, 219
Hammond, Christine, 271n
Hammond, Paul, 10
Haneke, Michael, 261
Hangover, The (2009), 153
Hansen, Miriam, 52, 53, 61n, 77, 101–3, 110n, 112, 131
Harper, Sue, 223
Harris, Richard Jackson, 6, 10
Harry Potter (2001–11), 126
Hartmann, Nicolai, 214n
Hatfield, Elaine, 176
Haugmard, Louis, 166n
Hawkins, Ralph, 270n
Hayes, Britt, 117
Haynes, Natalie, 126
Heidegger, Martin, 184n
Heimat (1984), 162
Helm, Bennett W., 263, 267, 270n
Hennessy, Eilis, 69, 71n
Henry – Portrait of a Serial Killer (1986), 280
Hess, Ursula, 175–6, 254, 270n
Hill, Annette, 205
Hill, Selima, 162
Hills, Matt, 215n
History Lessons / Geschichtsunterricht (1972), 215n
Hitchcock, Alfred, 46
Hitler, Adolf, 54, 145
Hobbit, The (2012–14), 126
Hochschild, Arlie, 154
Hofmann, Jennifer, 190
Holt, Jennifer, 276
Honor de cavalleria (2006), 261
Horkheimer, Max, 112, 212
Horwarth, Alexander, 105
Hour of the Furnaces, The / La Hora de los Hornos (1968)

How They Do Things on the Bowery (1902), 215n
Huillet, Danièlle, 215n
Husserl, Edmund, 17, 171, 279, 281

I, Daniel Blake (2016), 231
Ihde, Don, 92, 96, 108n, 109n, 256
Imitation of Life (1959), 149, 230
In the Mood for Love (2000), 234
Inglorious Basterds (2009), 121
Invictus (2010), 234
Iron Man 2 (2010), 277
Ismer, Sven, 168–9, 177
It's a Wonderful Life (1946), 238, 242n

Jakobs, Esther, 11, 243n
James, William, 26
Jamison, Leslie, 233, 236, 246n
Jermyn, Deborah, 221, 234
Jeunet, Jean-Pierre, 233
Jirgl, Reinhard, 252
Johnny Got His Gun (1971), 226
Joubert, Laurent, 214n
Joy Luck Club, The (1993), 224
Jullier, Laurent, 161, 166n

Kafka, Franz, 219
Kant, Immanuel, 235
Katz, Elihu, 28n
Katz, Jack, 152, 219, 220–2, 225, 231–2, 236, 238–9, 244n, 255, 256, 259, 263, 270n
Kechiche, Abdellatif, 174
Kelly, Sean Dorrance, 155, 213
Kelman, Ken, 71n
Kennedy, Dennis, 117
Kennedy, Margaret, 31n
Kermode, Mark, 248
Kershaw, Baz, 113, 121, 136n, 138n, 139n
Kessler, Frank, 36–7
Kester, Grant H., 137n
Kiarostami, Abbas, 223, 240
Kierkegaard, Sören, 97
Kiesler, Frederick, 71
Kimmel, Lawrence, 208
King, Henry, 240
Kleinhans, Chuck, 215n
Kleiser, Randal, 247n
Klemperer, Victor, 136n
Klinger, Barbara, 135
Koch, Gertrud, 24–5, 118
Koebner, Thomas, 244n
Koeppen, Wolfgang, 210
Koestler, Arthur, 220
Konzelmann Ziv, Anita, 174, 177, 184n

Kracauer, Siegfried, 58, 110n, 112
Kramer vs. Kramer (1979), 238
Krebs, Angelika, 86, 109n
Kruger, Joel, 174
Kubelka, Peter, 67, 68, 84
Kubrick, Stanley, 146
Kuehnast, Milena, 230, 243n
Kuhn, Annette, 9, 163, 164
Kuhn, Thomas, 19–20

La Petite Marchande d'allumettes (1927), 49
L'Âge d'or (1930), 251
Lacan, Jacques, 34
Lambie, Ryan, 277
Landweer, Hilge, 15, 222
Langer, Resi, 34, 62n
Langer, Susanne K., 26, 275
Lanzmann, Claude, 4–5, 165n, 259
Late Autumn / Akibiyori (1960), 101
Leaving Las Vegas (1995), 252
Le Bon, Gustave, 184n
Lemerise, Elizabeth A., 254, 266
Lerner, Yehuda, 4–5
Les Carabiniers (1963), 99
Letter From an Unknown Woman (1948), 148
Leveratto, Jean-Marc, 161, 166n
Levy, Sheldon G., 70
Lewis, Jerry, 133
Liessmann, Konrad Paul, 235
Light Between Oceans, The (2016), 233
Limelight (1952), 47, 48
Lindsay, Vachel, 67–8, 119, 120, 277
Loach, Ken, 80, 231
Löffler, Petra, 110n, 136n
Lolita (1962), 146
Lone Survivor (2013), 250
Longhurst, Brian, 19–20, 66, 114, 136n
Looking for Eric (2009), 80
Lord of the Rings, The (2001–3), 167n
Love (2015), 174
Love Is a Many-Splendored Thing (1955), 240
Love Me Tender (1956), 157
Love Story (1970), 230
Lucas, George, 8
Lucas, Tim, 130

McCarthy, Paul
McCulloch, Richard, 114, 126, 127, 129–31, 133, 138n, 185n, 210, 250
McDougall, William, 184n
McEwan, Ian, 239
MacLean, Adrienne, 198–9, 215n
Mad Circus (2010), 268n
Maes, Hans, 109

Malick, Terrence, 230, 233
Malle, Louis, 52
Maltby, Richard, 23
Man Ray, 248
Manderlay (2005), 248
Mann, Thomas, 217, 219, 228
Manstead, Antony, 58
Marchetti, Gina, 164
Marks, Laura, 14
Masculin Féminin (1966), 268n
M*A*S*H (1970), 70
Master and Commander (2003), 144
Mathijs, Ernest, 112, 123, 167n
Mayo, Simon, 248
Meder, Milena, 270n
Meers, Philippe, 166n
Mele, Alfred, 106n
Mellini, Arthur, 62n
Mendelssohn, Moses, 189
Mendik, Xavier, 112, 123, 167n
Menninghaus, Winfried, 70, 237, 245n
Merleau-Ponty, Maurice, 256–7
Metz, Christian, 8, 28n, 36, 43, 107n, 111
Meunier, Jean-Pierre, 39, 201–2
Mierendorff, Carlo, 29n
Miracle, The (2004), 238
Mission: Impossible (1996), 138n
Mississippi Burning (1988), 251
Mr Bean (1989–95), 189
Mitry, Jean, 3
Modern Times (1936), 54
Moholy-Nagy, László, 252
Moran, Dermot, 16
Moretti, Nanni, 27n
Morin, Edgar, 10, 34, 42–4, 56, 59n
Morsch, Thomas, 117
Moulin Rouge (2001), 123, 133
Moulton, Carter, 80, 133, 134–5, 167n
Mulligan, Kevin, 24
Mulvey, Laura, 41, 215n
Murnau, Friedrich Wilhelm, 161
My Bodyguard (1980), 252
My Life Without Me (2003), 233
My Sister's Keeper (2009), 237

Nathan-Garner, Laura, 228, 239
Neufeld, Jonathan A., 269
Never Take No for an Answer (1951), 162
New World, The (2005), 230
Nietzsche, Friedrich, 149
Noë, Gaspar, 174
Notebook, The (2004), 156, 236

Occupations (2007), 248–9, 254, 268
Odin, Roger, 10, 34, 35–40, 59n, 69, 156
Oliver, John, 6
On Moonlight Bay (1951), 157
One Day in September (1999), 145, 149
One Second in Montreal (1969), 167n
Ophüls, Max, 148
Ozu, Yasujiro, 101, 161

Pacherie, Elisabeth, 91, 132–3
Pagis, Michal, 92, 93, 131
Pantenburg, Volker, 83–4, 107n
Pasquier, Dominique, 72n, 109n, 113, 137n
Paul, William, 112
Pearl Harbor (2001), 261
Pedullà, Gabriele, 10, 27–8n, 31n, 62n, 71n, 79, 96, 135n, 275
Pegee (1973), 247n
Perez, Gilberto, 215n
Persona (1966), 104
Picasso, Pablo, 51, 54
Pierro le fou (1966), 115
Pink Flamingos (1972), 251
Pink Panther Strikes Again, The (1976), 189
Plantinga, Carl, 205
Plato, 8, 62n
Platow, Micheal J., 190
Plessner, Helmuth, 191, 196, 214n, 216n, 220, 226, 242, 244n
Polan, Dana, 40
Porter, Vincent, 223
Prentice, Deborah A., 106
Problem Child (1990), 128
Provine, Robert, 213n
Prütting, Lenz, 192, 194–5, 201, 209, 212, 214n
Purge, The (2013), 117

Rancière, Jacques, 62n, 105–6n
Rapson, Richard L, 184n
Ratcliffe, Matthew, 179
Ravan, Raymond, 109n
Reason, Matthew, 70
Renoir, Jean, 49
Richter, Hans, 252
Rimbaud, Arthur, 153
Rocha, Glauber, 161
Rocky (1976), 230
Rocky Horror Picture Show, The (1975), 36, 68, 107n, 112, 123, 125–6, 128
Roden, David, 16–17, 30n
Rodowick, D. N., 72n
Rogers, Ginger, 107n
Romains, Jules, 62n

Romance (1999), 162
Room, The (2003), 114, 123, 126, 127, 129, 133, 138n, 185n, 197, 251
Rooney, Brendan, 69, 71n
Rosalie et Léontine vont au théâtre (1911), 268n
Roselt, Jens, 137n, 204
Rosenbaum, Jonathan, 67–8, 71n, 83, 126, 128, 157–8, 159, 189, 211, 252, 283n
Rosenkranz, M., 45–6, 60n
Ross, Miriam, 28n
Rossellini, Roberto, 70
Rozin, Paul, 270n
Russell, Chuck, 268n
Ryle, Gilbert, 184n

Salmela, Mikko, 172, 174–5, 183n, 185n
Salt (2010), 155, 161
Sánchez Guerrero, H. Andrés, 178–9, 184n
Sandvoss, Cornel, 25
Sanson, Kevin, 276
Sarkosh, Keyvan, 70
Sartre, Jean-Paul, 84–5, 100, 108n, 267
Sátántangó (1994), 91
Saussure, Ferdinand de, 34
Saving Private Ryan (1998), 217, 234
Scary Movie (2000), 200
Schachter, Stanley, 146
Schaefer, Hillary S., 146
Scheler, Max, 18, 170, 171, 175–8, 184n
Scherer, Klaus, 24
Schindler's List (1993), 252
Schlüpmann, Heide, 78
Schmid, Hans Bernhard, 30n, 75, 77, 86, 87, 108n, 170, 171, 173, 174
Schmitt, Manfred, 270n
Schmitz, Hermann, 18, 31n, 192, 193–4, 206, 214n, 228
Schwarz, Balduin, 225–6, 228, 230, 235, 244n, 246n
Scorsese, Martin, 15, 18, 128, 250
Scream (1996), 2000
Scream 2 (1997), 117
Searle, John, 15, 77, 88, 108n
Seldes, Gilbert, 27
Serra, Albert, 261
Sex in the City (1998–2004), 234
Shakespeare, William, 251
Sheep Has Five Legs, The / Le Mouton à cinq pattes (1954), 6
Shirin (2008), 223, 240
Shoa (1985), 259
Shoham, Tamir, 121
Shusterman, Richard, 32n

Shutter Island (2010), 250
Silence of the Lambs, The (1991), 104
Simpsons, The (1989–), 189
Skeffington, Alan Sheehy, 200
Slaby, Jan, 31n
Sliding Doors (1998), 227
Smith, Tim, 74
Smithson, Robert, 84
Smoodin, Eric, 32n, 242n
Snow, Michael, 104
Sobibor (2001), 4–6, 165n
Sobchack, Vivian, 13, 28–9n, 39, 41, 202, 256, 282
Sogni d'Oro (1981), 27n
Solanas, Fernando, 119
Solomon, Robert, 235
Sonnenallee (1999), 202
Sontag, Susan, 192
Sorensen, Roy, 84–5, 108n
Sorlin, Pierre, 36
Sound of Music, The (1965), 36, 123, 125, 178
Soupault, Philippe, 54
Souriau, Étienne, 27, 168
South Park (1997–), 189
Spielberg, Steven, 15, 244n
Srinivas, Lakshmi, 112, 114, 128, 129–31, 136n, 163, 165n, 202, 221
Staiger, Janet, 116, 118, 120, 128, 131, 139n, 251
Stam, Robert, 283n
States, Bert O., 22, 97–8, 223
Star Wars (1999/2002/2005), 80, 126, 148, 154, 160
Stawarska, Beata, 28n, 121, 215–16n
Stein, Edith, 175
Stern, Alfred, 199, 211, 213, 220, 230–2
Stokes, Melvyn, 23
Strangers on a Train (1951), 46
Straub, Jean-Marie, 215n
Straw Dogs (1971), 252
Szanto, Thomas, 16, 173

Tappolet, Christine, 150
Tarantino, Quentin, 121, 200
Tarr, Béla, 91, 95
Terms of Endearment (1983), 237
Thelma and Louise (1991), 202
Thompson, Evan, 26, 32n
Thor (2011), 69
Those Awful Hats (1909), 268n
Tillman, Lynne, 219
Titanic (1997), 228, 229, 236, 241–2
To the Wonder (2012), 233

Tomasello, Michael, 117, 123, 191, 201
Tornatore, Guiseppe, 163
Tröhler, Margrit, 81, 102
Tucholsky, Kurt, 119
Tuomela, Raimo, 77, 183n
Turkle, Sherry, 278
Twelve Years a Slave (2013), 158, 179

Uncle Josh at the Moving Picture (1902), 215n

Van Manen, Max, 11–14
Vertov, Dziga, 54
Vidor, King, 54, 208, 216n, 234
Vingerhoets, Ad, 219, 220, 227, 239, 242, 243n, 244–5n, 246n, 247n
Von Dohnanyi, Klaus, 265
Von Scheve, Christian, 153, 168–9, 177
Von Trier, Lars, 234, 248–50, 254, 255, 265, 268, 271n
Vorse, Mary Heaton, 119, 131

Wakeling, Roger, 120
Waldenfels, Bernhard, 12, 84
Waller, Gregory, 32n

Walther, Gerda, 132, 134, 166n, 171, 173, 182, 183n, 184n
Warhol, Robyn, 217–18, 220, 232, 234, 235
Waters, John, 251
Wavelength (1967), 104
Weber, Samuel, 199
Weerasethakul, Apichatpong, 80, 148
Wenders, Wim, 278
What's Up, Doc? (1972), 130
Whitehead, Alfred North, 26
Williams, Linda, 8, 118
Window Water Baby Moving (1959), 238
Wiseau, Tommy, 114
Witness (1985), 120
Wollen, Peter, 41, 100
Wong, Kar-wai, 234
Wood, Robert E., 112, 123, 135–6n

Zaalberg, Ruud, 58
Zahavi, Dan, 170–3, 175, 177–8
Zhao, Shanyang, 280, 283n
Zillmann, Dolf, 11, 180
Žižek, Slavoj, 62n
Zürcher, Ramon, 268n

Index of Subjects

affective audience interrelations, 143–67, 208–11, 284
affective we-experience, 134, 150, 151, 165n, 168–85, 284; *see also* we-connection; closeness to other viewers (phenomenological)
affordances of the cinema, 69, 132–3, 196, 256–7, 259
　common, 132–3
　individual, 133
　joint, 132–3
African-American audiences, 137n, 165n, 211, 251
anger in the cinema, 13, 44, 88, 89, 90, 94, 115, 119, 121, 125, 131, 145, 148, 149, 152–3, 155, 159, 160, 162, 163, 164, 170, 183n, 203, 209, 224, 210–11, 220, 237, 248–71, 276, 279
　definition of, 253–5, 270n
　phenomenology of, 255–68
　sources of, 161, 252–3
　see also disturbance; noise; violence in the cinema
anonymity in the cinema, 8, 21, 28n, 37, 40–1, 43–4, 56, 68, 78, 80, 90–1, 117, 119, 150–1, 159–60, 181, 198, 203, 204, 217, 221, 258, 262, 266
antagonism, 127, 148–51, 162–3, 284
　I–they relation, 211, 285
　I–thou relation, 210, 285
　I–ye relation, 210, 211, 285
　I–you relation, 11, 13, 18, 44, 121, 148, 149, 151, 152, 153, 161, 208, 235, 257, 284–5
　we–they relation, 209–10, 211, 285
　we–thou relation, 209, 285
　we–ye relation, 209, 285

we–you relation, 148, 158, 208, 285
apparatus/dispositive theory, 8, 28n, 34, 41, 43, 84
applause, 47, 48, 56, 98, 102, 120–1, 124, 131, 133, 136n, 137–8n, 139n, 151, 161, 165n, 175, 177, 264–5, 289
architecture of the cinema, 3, 58, 62n, 67, 69, 260, 275
arthouse theater, 20, 104, 154, 158
attuned behavior, 86–8
audience effect
　beyond the cinema, 275–82
　definition of, 4, 285
awareness of other viewers, 5, 8–10, 11, 17, 22–4, 40–4, 46–9, 51, 61n, 69, 75–6, 78, 83, 87, 88, 90, 93, 98, 114, 116, 128, 131, 132, 133, 143, 144–7, 148–50, 151, 158, 159, 172–3, 177, 207, 218, 222, 225, 238, 240, 283n

behavioral rules/norms, 3, 56, 66, 78–9, 81–2, 86, 88, 89, 90, 92, 101–3, 108n, 113, 124, 125–7, 135n, 138n, 156–7, 158–9, 199, 204, 248, 254–5, 258–9, 262–4, 269n, 275, 281–2
being-moved, 53, 149, 157, 174, 217, 219, 222, 224, 227, 228, 229, 232, 234, 236, 240, 243n, 245n, 246n, 257
　joyfully, 220, 230, 231
boredom, 36, 41, 51, 91, 97, 108n, 109n, 116, 154, 156, 177–8; *see also* sleep
box-office numbers *see* cinema admissions

call-and-response, 92, 119, 120, 128, 137n
changeability, degree of, 151–2
cheering/booing, 37, 66, 97, 102, 117, 119, 120, 121, 123, 124, 128, 135, 151,

155, 161, 165n, 180, 261, 264, 265, 269n
cinema, minimal definition of, 3, 27n, 275, 285
cinema admissions, 21–2
cinephiles, 120, 130, 161, 166n
class, 29n, 79, 103, 112, 131, 148, 155, 160, 163, 181, 199, 212, 215n, 236, 242, 251, 262, 264, 270n; *see also* ethnicity; gender; race; sexual orientation
closeness to other viewers (phenomenological), 18, 37, 42, 55, 69, 112, 148, 150–2, 158, 161, 164, 173–5, 178, 181, 182, 208, 240, 290; *see also* community; distance to other viewers (phenomenological); we-connection
closeness to other viewers (physical), 7, 23, 42, 69, 119, 159–60, 172, 184n, 258, 260, 277, 279–81, 282
cognitive film theory, 58, 74
collective emotion, 18, 47, 94, 109n, 168–9, 173–4, 175, 178, 185n, 240, 263, 286, 291
  shared *see* shared emotion
  spread, 173–4, 240
collective viewing types *see* quiet-attentive viewing; expressive-diverted viewing
comedy, 5, 10, 18, 28n, 42, 48, 51, 54, 61n, 62n, 69, 70, 91, 95, 100, 112, 117, 122, 125, 129, 130, 133, 137n, 144, 153–4, 189–90, 194–7, 201, 202, 215n, 223, 227
community
  co-present, 132
  episodic/short-term, 151–2, 181
  fictitious, 132
  habitual, 151–2, 181
  imagined, 77, 132, 139n
computer/laptop, watching a film on a, 8, 19, 20, 22, 26, 27–8n, 30–3n, 81, 91, 104, 132, 133, 189, 276–7, 281
conformity, 158, 205, 238–9
control, social, 9, 35–6, 51–4, 61n, 87, 111, 126, 156, 251, 258, 281
Conversational Theater, 67–8, 119, 277
co-presence, 4, 6, 7, 9, 11, 20–1, 24, 28n, 36, 39–40, 42–4, 47, 50, 51, 55, 57, 58, 75, 78, 81–2, 85, 91, 98, 132–3, 165n, 166n, 172–3, 178, 190, 192, 276, 278, 279, 283n
  forms of, 279–80, 286–7
  types of co-present others, 281–2
couples, 9, 11, 26, 29n, 57, 72n, 76, 79, 82, 90, 106n, 123, 132, 144, 145, 146, 149, 151, 153–4, 156, 158, 160, 162, 164, 165n, 180, 181, 233, 240, 253, 259, 271n, 276–7, 278
co-viewer, definition of, 281, 287
crying, 131, 162, 189, 255; *see also* tears; weeping
cult film/trash film, 10, 70, 112, 114, 123, 124, 125–7, 130, 133, 135–6n, 162, 167n, 197, 210, 292
cultural capital *see* distinction

darkness, 3, 8, 9, 32n, 37, 40–2, 43, 45, 49, 50, 53, 62n, 69, 78–9, 81, 83, 86, 90, 106n, 113, 145, 164, 181, 190, 198, 203, 204, 211–12, 214n, 217, 223, 242, 248, 258, 260, 262, 266, 283n
dating, 6, 9, 29n, 32n, 95, 145, 156–8, 160; *see also* couples
deixis, 118, 201, 215–16n
devaluation *see* evaluation
dialogue, lip-synching of, 87, 96, 123, 134
disgust, 5, 10, 44, 60n, 116–18, 119, 144, 162, 166n, 170, 190, 196–7, 201, 221, 252, 270n, 291
dispositive, 8, 27n, 28n, 29n, 34, 42–3, 51, 78, 81, 83, 101, 107n, 130, 164, 212; *see also* apparatus/dispositive theory
distance to other viewers (phenomenological), 18, 38–9, 44, 56, 58, 69, 78, 92, 121, 122, 128, 131, 146, 148–9, 151, 153, 155, 161–3, 171, 173–4, 178, 182, 189, 191, 205, 207, 210, 212, 221–3, 224, 225, 235, 240, 258, 262; *see also* antagonism
distance to the film (phenomenological) 41, 46, 48, 100, 144, 194, 196–7, 215, 224, 225, 229
distinction, 103, 122, 128–31, 161, 163, 166n, 191, 198, 200–1, 204, 207, 210, 234; *see also* hierarchy in the auditorium
distraction, 32n, 42, 53, 69–70, 71n, 78, 90, 104, 110n, 112, 136n, 145, 203, 220, 224, 239, 244n, 253, 260, 276–7; *see also* diversion
disturbance, 67, 71n, 73, 96, 109n, 115, 149, 224, 253, 254, 257, 258, 259, 269n, 271n; *see also* anger; noise; retaliation/revenge
diversion, 44, 91, 112–14, 116, 128, 131, 135, 146, 276, 287; *see also* distraction; expressive-diverted viewing
divided attention, 112, 113, 114, 135, 287, 288; *see also* inattention; diversion
documentary film, 4–6, 35–6, 37, 39, 59n, 119, 145, 150, 202, 252
drive-in theater, 36, 83, 120, 146
DVD/Blu-Ray, 20, 66, 79, 91, 137, 197

dyadic viewer–film relation, 7, 21, 36; *see also* triadic viewer–film–audience relation

early film/cinema, 10, 53, 61n, 77, 101, 102–3, 110n, 112, 215n; *see also* individualization thesis
embarrassment, 6–7, 10, 18, 38, 44, 49, 53, 78–9, 91, 100, 119, 122, 127, 137n, 145, 148–9, 154–5, 156, 159, 160, 162, 174, 183n, 190, 198, 202, 203, 204–5, 218, 220–2, 224, 231, 233, 234, 236, 240–1, 266, 268, 271n, 279, 282, 286, 291; *see also* primal scene of collective viewing; laughter, embarrassment
emotion regulation, 38, 152, 153–5, 258, 260
emotion work, 153–4, 156, 158–9
emotional contagion, 55, 56, 58, 72n, 76, 91, 110n, 134, 150, 152, 155, 168, 171, 175–8, 181, 182, 184n, 205, 206, 287; *see also* laughter, contagion
empathy, 97, 99, 171–2, 183n, 242n, 246n, 268
entitlement, 79, 88, 89–91, 108n, 124, 124–5, 203, 257, 264, 267–8, 282, 289, 290; *see also* obligation
equalizing effect, 45, 78–9, 128, 148, 207, 212
erotics (of the cinema), 6–7, 9, 40, 42, 49, 117, 118, 160, 162
ethics, 5, 41, 54, 84, 90, 104, 107n, 119–20, 149, 160, 167n, 179, 205, 213, 214n, 229, 230, 231, 235, 246n, 253, 254–5, 258–9, 265, 276, 285
ethnicity, 94, 137n; 160; 181, 212, 242, 262–3; *see also* class; gender; race; sexual orientation
evaluation, 38, 147, 148–9, 152, 165, 179, 180, 254, 276, 277
  through laughter, 124, 157, 165, 190, 195, 197–9, 203, 205, 211, 259
  through tears, 229–37, 238, 239, 240, 246n
exclusion, 38–9, 93–4, 122, 154, 207–8, 210, 213; *see also* inclusion
experiential mode, 148–52
expressive behavior *see* re-acting; play-acting, inter-acting, jointly re-acting; synchronically acting together
expressive-diverted viewing, 23, 65, 67, 89, 107n, 111–39, 152, 169, 192, 243n, 251, 257, 258, 277, 287–8

facial feedback, 175–6, 184n
family viewing, 6–7, 18, 20, 31n, 37–40, 49, 70, 79, 83, 137n, 153, 154, 160, 224, 242, 271n, 281, 282

fans, 80, 125–6, 133, 134–5, 148, 155, 160, 167n, 178, 210, 242
fear, 11, 18, 118, 133, 146, 149–50, 161, 166n, 170, 172, 174, 180, 184n, 185n, 196, 197, 214n, 221, 231, 236, 267, 277, 280; *see also* screaming; shock
feeling together, 76, 170, 178–81, 182, 239, 288

gender, 11, 14, 88, 131, 157, 160, 163, 180, 181, 196, 212, 218, 219, 221, 226, 228, 234, 235, 236, 239, 242, 244n, 259, 262, 276; *see also* class; ethnicity; race; sexual orientation
guilt, 5, 145, 148–9, 155–6, 160, 164n, 165n, 169, 174, 178, 233–6, 263
guilty pleasure *see* tears, sentimental

handholding, 146, 150, 232, 240, 279
happiness *see* joy
hiding effect, 9, 53, 239
hierarchy in the auditorium, 78–9, 109n, 122, 127–8, 130–1, 166n, 191, 197–9, 204, 207, 212, 251, 262–2; *see also* class
home movie, 35, 37–9, 101, 202, 242
horror, 11, 112, 116, 117, 125, 133, 144, 146, 161, 162, 180, 196, 197, 204, 280; *see also* fear; screaming; shock
humor, 48, 130, 144, 153, 190, 195–7, 200, 207, 210–11, 212, 214n

IMAX cinema, 20, 25, 36, 69
immersion 7, 9, 24, 26, 40, 42, 45, 46, 48, 61n, 62n, 69, 95, 102, 104, 134, 135, 144, 149–50, 198, 207, 224, 256, 257
inattention, 71, 76, 89, 114–16, 288; *see also* divided attention
inclusion, 93, 131, 201, 207, 212, 213; *see also* exclusion
Indian audiences, 112, 128, 129, 130–1, 137n, 148, 165n, 167n, 221
individualization thesis, 77, 101–3, 104, 110n, 131, 276, 288
influence, degree of, 153–6
inter-acting with others, 116, 118–20, 124, 125, 127, 128, 129, 131, 134, 145, 192, 203, 288
intertextuality, 200, 207, 215n
intimacy of social connections *see* co-viewers, familiarity of
invisibility in the cinema, 8–9, 102, 205, 239, 265; *see also* darkness; awareness of other viewers

INDEX OF SUBJECTS 323

Invisible Cinema, 67–8, 71n
isolation, feeling of *see* distance to other viewers

joint action, 6, 73–9, 86–7, 89–96, 103, 104–5, 106n, 108n, 113, 123–5, 127, 133–4, 138n, 148, 151, 162, 169, 172, 182, 257, 281, 289; *see also* synchronically acting together
joint attention, 73, 75–7, 82–4, 86, 87–8, 89, 92, 103, 108n, 116, 151, 201, 257, 281, 289
jointly re-acting to the film, 116, 120–2, 124, 128, 129, 133–5, 145, 192, 289
joy, 16, 18, 31n, 48, 98, 144, 150, 151, 170, 171, 174, 175, 177, 222, 232

kitsch, 176, 198, 199, 215n, 233–6, 246n, 291; *see also* sentimentality

laptop *see* computer/laptop, watching a film on a
laughter, 4–6, 7, 12, 18, 22, 25, 35, 43, 48–9, 51–5, 62n, 70, 72n, 96, 109n, 115, 119, 120–2, 126, 128, 129, 130, 131, 133, 135, 137n, 138n, 139n, 144, 146, 149, 153, 155, 157, 158, 165n, 184n, 189–216, 220, 223–4, 225, 226, 231, 232, 235, 238, 243n, 247n, 251, 253, 271n, 279, 281–2
   amusement (about the comic and ridiculous), 12, 48, 51, 54, 94, 193–6
   comprehension, 48, 94, 124, 200–1, 286
   contagion, 121, 154, 176, 178, 206, 242, 286
   contemptuous, 93, 148–9, 157–8, 162, 198, 259, 261
   conversion (evaluative transformation), 124, 197, 197–200
   disdain (depreciation of another response), 203–4
   embarrassment, 122, 204–5
   laughing collectives, 48–9, 148, 153, 155, 174, 178, 240
   laughter-laughter, 203
   mimicry, 205, 290
   recognition (expression of detection), 201–2
   relief, 126–7, 196–7
   typology of, 191–207, 214n
   vertical aspect of, 192, 197–9, 203, 204, 209, 215n
lived-body 18, 192, 193, 194, 196, 204, 206, 225, 227, 228, 235, 255, 256–7, 289

constriction 16, 196–7, 204, 222, 228, 245n, 257
expansion 18, 196–7, 199, 228, 245n
look into the camera, 9, 100–1

media competency, 25–6
melodrama/tear-jerker, 18, 69, 116, 129–30, 132, 148, 156, 212, 223, 228, 231, 233, 234, 239, 241, 257
mere present others, 115, 128, 214n, 253, 258, 281–2, 287, 288, 289–90
midnight blockbusters, 80, 126, 133–5, 160, 161, 167n
mimicry, 175–6, 184n, 287
   behavioral, 175–6
   emotional, 175–6
   see also laughter, mimicry
motor activity, 6, 54, 83, 86, 87, 88, 89, 92, 98, 102, 107n, 111, 121, 123, 153, 155, 175, 179, 193–4, 196, 215n, 219, 22, 243n, 252, 270
multiplex/megaplex cinema, 9, 20, 36, 69, 99, 148, 150, 153, 154–5, 160, 165n, 167n, 260
museum, watching a film in a, 20, 27n, 50–1, 53, 61n, 90, 104, 108n, 81, 83, 90, 105, 280, 281–2, 290; *see also* mere present others; parallel viewers

negative audience effects, 3, 4, 9, 17, 38, 43, 44, 72n, 125, 126, 155, 159, 161, 162, 210, 221, 224, 280, 283n; *see also* anger; antagonism; disgust; disturbance; embarrassment; guilt; noise; nostalgia; primal scene of collective viewing
neighborhood cinema, 41, 102, 163, 164, 166n
noise, 7, 9, 23, 36, 69, 85, 96, 108n, 109n, 115, 125, 135, 154, 155, 157, 221, 243n, 246n, 250, 253, 256, 258, 266, 267, 268, 269n, 276; *see also* cheering/booing; screaming; talking
non-theatrical collective film experience *see* computer/laptop, watching a film on a; Virtual Reality cinema; train, watching a film on a; plane, watching a film on a; television, watching; *see also* watching a film alone
nostalgia, 38, 39, 202, 217, 226, 242

obligation, 79, 88–91, 108n, 115, 124–7, 156, 175, 179, 264, 266, 282, 290; *see also* entitlement

parallel viewers, 281–2, 290
passivity (of the viewer), 8, 45, 46, 47, 66, 71n, 74, 96, 105–6n, 112, 113, 130, 152, 158, 191, 206, 210, 237
Payne Fund Studies, 29n, 221, 237
personal emancipation, 194, 206, 212
personal regression, 194, 212
phenomenology, as method
  criteria for success of, 14–15, 96
  limits of, 16–17, 218–19
  misconceptions about, 15–16
  reasons for using, 11–14, 24, 26–7
plane, watching a film on a, 7, 20, 277, 281, 282
play-acting for other viewers, 116, 117–18, 119, 123, 124, 125, 128–9, 131, 134, 136n, 145, 180, 192, 203, 290–1
pleasure in functioning, 95–6, 134, 150
pornography, 101, 117–18, 133, 162
primal scene of collective viewing, 6–7, 18, 145, 155–6, 160, 162, 280, 291; *see also* embarrassment; shame
private film viewing, 7, 37, 38–9, 41–2, 49, 66, 120, 137n, 197–8, 239; *see also* family viewing; television, watching
public sphere, cinema as, 10, 67, 102, 131

quiet-attentive viewing, 67, 73–110, 111–12, 113, 125, 127, 128, 130, 132, 134–5, 152, 172, 244n, 257, 258, 263, 277, 291

race, 4–6; 79, 131, 145; 156; 158, 159, 163, 165, 179, 181, 185n, 212, 235, 236, 276, 283n; *see also* class; gender; ethnicity; sexual orientation
re-acting to the film, 116–18, 119, 124, 131, 145, 192, 203, 291
recognition, 201–2, 204, 211, 216n, 231
retaliation/revenge, 130, 255, 259, 261–7, 268, 270n; *see also* anger; disturbance

sadness, 11, 38, 132, 217, 221, 222, 226–7, 230, 239, 243n
sanction, mutual *see* control, social
screaming, 7, 25, 37, 51, 76, 84, 87, 96, 105, 116, 118, 119, 124, 131, 144, 157–8, 161, 165n, 191, 197, 203, 204, 225, 251, 252, 260
seat, 6, 29n, 40, 53, 67, 69, 102, 109n, 116, 154, 163, 163, 248, 252, 253, 256–8, 259, 260, 263, 265, 267
second screen, 19, 21, 30–1n, 276, 277, 285
Secret Cinema, 161, 167n
semio-pragmatism, 35–40, 59n, 156

sentimentality, 56, 199, 232–7, 238, 239, 240, 242n, 246n, 291; *see also* kitsch
sexual orientation, 14, 30n, 181, 276; *see also* class; ethnicity; gender; race
shame *see* embarrassment
shared emotion, 76, 77, 81, 134, 150, 159, 161, 168–75, 177, 182, 183n, 185n, 211, 239, 291–2
shock, 69, 105, 118, 144–5, 161, 162, 180, 190, 196–7, 218
shushing, 36, 125, 130, 149, 154, 159, 202, 250, 258, 260, 262, 263, 264, 266–7, 268, 271n, 282
silence in the cinema, 66, 69, 73, 76, 77, 84–5, 87–8, 90, 92–3, 96, 102–4, 106–9n, 111–13, 116, 122, 130, 131, 134–5, 136n, 153–5, 157, 179, 195, 204, 205, 264, 267; *see also* quiet-attentive viewing
Silent Cinema, 7, 28n
sing-along, 36, 123, 125, 133, 175, 292
situational framing, 153, 156–9, 241
sleep, 32n, 76, 85, 86–7, 90, 108n, 136n, 162; *see also* boredom
smartphone/iPhone, 20, 22, 26, 27–8n, 66, 70, 76, 82, 86, 87, 89, 104, 107n, 116, 125, 128, 172, 248, 250, 253, 257, 260, 262, 269n, 276, 277, 280, 282, 283n
smell, 9, 29n, 69, 160, 162, 243n, 252, 253, 279
social appraisal, 58, 147, 200
social facilitation, 4, 56, 70
social flow, 95–6, 134, 150, 182, 257
social inhibition, 4, 43, 44, 56, 133, 220
solidarity, 109, 185, 213
  in laughter, 195, 205
  in weeping, 238–9
stage theater, 8, 17, 23, 27n, 30n, 40, 45–7, 50, 56, 57, 61n, 66, 71n, 72n, 74, 78, 96–101, 105–6n, 109n, 112, 113, 120, 136n, 137n, 138n, 139n, 208, 223
stillness/immobility, 8, 84, 87, 92, 107n, 113, 128, 130
synchronically acting together, 116, 123–4, 125, 127, 128, 133, 134, 145, 175, 192, 211, 292
synchronization of response, 51, 53, 54, 87, 93, 95–6, 117, 133, 135n, 211, 257; *see also* synchronically acting together

talking, 7, 36, 53, 67–8, 70, 71n, 76, 82, 84, 85, 86, 89, 90, 92, 93, 94, 96, 102, 109n, 113, 116, 118–20, 125, 127, 128–31, 136n, 137n, 139n, 153, 154, 165n, 177, 202, 212, 248, 250, 251, 253, 257, 258,

259, 261, 262, 265–6, 268, 269n, 271n, 277, 282; *see also* call-and-response; cheering/booing; dialogue, lip-synching of; inter-acting with others; noise; screaming; shushing
tears, 13, 48, 49, 144, 157–8, 174, 179, 217–47, 257
   axiological, 218, 229–32, 233, 234, 235, 236, 237, 238, 240, 246n, 285
   contagious, 218, 242
   forced, 158, 179, 218, 224, 238–9, 240, 288
   personal-relevance, 218, 226, 230, 231, 237–8, 240, 243n, 290
   sentimental, 218, 232–7, 239, 240, 246n, 286, 291
   shared, 47, 48–9, 218, 224, 240–2, 243n, 292
   see also being-moved; crying; sadness; weeping
television, watching 8, 17, 20–2, 25, 27–8n, 30n, 41–2, 44, 49–50, 66, 90–1, 104, 106n, 122, 132, 216n, 234, 243n, 246n, 277, 279, 282; *see also*, computer/laptop, watching a film on
text message, 30–1n, 76, 85, 89, 96, 107n, 108n, 115, 125, 128, 135, 170, 250–1, 260, 262, 269n, 277; *see also* inattention; disturbance
3D film, 66, 69–70, 71n
train, watching a film on a, 19, 20, 276–7, 280, 281, 282

triadic viewer–film–audience relation, 7, 21; *see also* dyadic viewer–film relation

value judgment *see* evaluation
violence in the cinema, 248–50, 264, 266, 268
Virtual Reality cinema, 19, 277–8, 280, 282
volition, degree of, 152–6

watching a film alone, 4, 6, 7, 9–10, 11, 20, 22, 27–8n, 30–1n, 49, 50–2, 55–6, 70, 85, 88, 91, 95, 101,104, 116, 121,122, 127, 132, 133, 136n, 145, 159, 164, 178, 189–90, 194, 207, 277–9, 281, 282; *see also* computer/laptop; plane, watching a film on a; private film viewing; television; train, watching a film on a
we-connection, 18, 122, 148, 150–2, 158, 161, 165n, 168, 178–81, 208, 257; *see also* affective we-experience; closeness to other viewers (phenomenological)
we-intention, 55, 73, 74, 75, 79–82, 86, 87–90, 103, 132, 148, 150, 151, 181, 282, 292
weeping, 13, 47–9, 144, 212, 217–47
   as opposed to crying, 219–20
   bodily effect of, 218, 221, 223–4, 225–7, 233, 235, 244n
   detaching-individualizing effect of, 220–4
   pleasure of, 221, 226, 227–9, 232–6, 239, 240, 245n
   see also being-moved; crying; sadness; tears

EU representative:
Easy Access System Europe
Mustamäe tee 50, 10621 Tallinn, Estonia
Gpsr.requests@easproject.com

www.ingramcontent.com/pod-product-compliance
Lightning Source LLC
Chambersburg PA
CBHW050837230426
43667CB00012B/2036